D1525695

The concept and definition of personhood is central to current debates in ethics. Should 'personhood', for example, determine the allocation of scarce medical resources, and its perceived absence allow the termination of life?

In a wide-ranging discussion notable for its clarity, Stanley Rudman traces the development of modern ideas about personhood. He argues that concepts of person are socially constructed, and that the relational understanding of persons in a number of theological discussions can act as an important corrective to the individualistic notions of person which have been popular in secular philosophy since the Enlightenment. Early Christian views of divine speech, communication and relations between the persons of the Trinity can help to define an ethic which understands personhood in relation to other people, to the environment, and to God.

# CONCEPTS OF PERSON AND CHRISTIAN ETHICS

# NEW STUDIES IN CHRISTIAN ETHICS

*General editor:* Robin Gill

*Editorial board:* Stephen R. L. Clark, Anthony O. Dyson,
Stanley Hauerwas and Robin W. Lovin

Christian ethics has increasingly assumed a central place within academic theology. At the same time the growing power and ambiguity of modern science and the rising dissatisfaction within the social sciences about claims to value-neutrality have prompted renewed interest in ethics within the secular academic world. There is, therefore, a need for studies in Christian ethics which, as well as being concerned with the relevance of Christian ethics to the present day secular debate, are well informed about parallel discussions in recent philosophy, science or social science. *New Studies in Christian Ethics* aims to provide books that do this at the highest intellectual level and demonstrate that Christian ethics can make a distinctive contribution to this debate – either in moral substance or in terms of underlying moral justifications.

# CONCEPTS OF PERSON AND CHRISTIAN ETHICS

## STANLEY RUDMAN

*Head of Religious Studies,*
*Cheltenham & Gloucester College of Higher Education*

PUBLISHED BY THE PRESS SYNDICATE OF THE UNIVERSITY OF CAMBRIDGE
The Pitt Building, Trumpington Street, Cambridge CB2 1RP, United Kingdom

CAMBRIDGE UNIVERSITY PRESS
The Edinburgh Building, Cambridge CB2 2RU, United Kingdom
40 West 20th Street, New York, NY 10011–4211, USA
10 Stamford Road, Oakleigh, Melbourne 3166, Australia

© Stanley Rudman 1997

First published 1997

Printed in the United Kingdom at the University Press, Cambridge

Typeset in Baskerville 11/12½pt    CE

*A catalogue record for this book is available from the British Library*

ISBN 0 521 58171 0 hardback

# Contents

# General editor's preface

This book is the eleventh in the series New Studies in Christian Ethics. In many respects it returns to the pattern set in the very first book in the series, Kieran Cronin's well received *Rights and Christian Ethics*. Both books offer an important service for Christian ethics, providing reliable guides for the discipline through a complex area of philosophical discussions. It is the great merit of Cronin and Rudman that both authors show a knowledge of these discussions which is still rare amongst theologians and yet both also offer a position of their own which is distinctively theological.

Stanley Rudman sets out and contests the division being made by a number of secular philosophers (such as Peter Singer) between 'persons' and 'human beings'. He regards such divisions as both internally inconsistent and as having dubious ethical consequences (in Singer's case involving a justification of infanticide). For Rudman, human personhood 'is importantly related to relationships and communication between people as well as individual rationality and purpose. All of these features are best understood in a context of moral agency which includes human biology and environment, rational purpose and social belonging'. He argues at length that relational understandings of 'persons' – present within a number of theological understandings of 'persons' – are important correctives to the individualistic understandings, centring upon consciousness, that have been popular in secular philosophy since the Enlightenment. He then reviews the way this relational understanding was developed within the early Trinitarian and Christological debates, and argues that, appropriately qualified, a specifically theological understanding does still have ethical relevance today. He concludes with an understanding of persons in relation to other persons, to the environment and, finally, to God as Trinity.

This is emphatically not a piece of theological imperialism. Stanley Rudman is sympathetic to Charles Taylor's position in *Sources of the Self* which opposes reductionist accounts of personhood and argues for an implicit notion of order based ultimately upon theism. Yet neither author wishes to claim that it is *only* theism which can support an adequate understanding of persons 'as human beings who are normally and essentially communicative'. Rather they believe that theism offers the most consonant account. For Rudman, adequate understandings of persons today 'chime well with the use of "persona" and "prosopon" in some of the theological thought of the early church, and can be linked with a view of God as person, which is characteristic of biblical tradition and still relevant to Christian ethics today.'

All of this fits well the two key aims of this series – namely to engage centrally with the secular moral debate at the highest possible intellectual level and, secondly, to demonstrate that Christian ethics can make a distinctive contribution to this debate, either in moral substance or in terms of underlying moral justifications. It is hoped that Stephen Clark's *Biology and Christian Ethics*, planned for a later stage in the series, will add further to the debate which Stanley Rudman initiates here. These are important issues for Christians and non-Christians alike.

ROBIN GILL

# Acknowledgements

Many debts have been incurred in the writing of this book over several years, none more so than to my wife, Sylvia, and our now grown-up family. Without their patience and co-operation it would not have been possible. I should also like to thank Professor Basil Mitchell for his timely support and encouragement, Professor Adrian Thatcher for his perceptive comments, and several colleagues, Peter Scott, Melissa Raphael and Craig Batholomew who read drafts and made useful suggestions. The series editor, Professor Robin Gill, and the officers of the Press have been unfailingly courteous and helpful.

# Abbreviations

| | |
|---|---|
| *APQ* | *American Philosophical Quarterly* |
| *ChQR* | *Church Quarterly Review* |
| *CJP* | *Canadian Journal of Philosophy* |
| *ERE* | *Encyclopaedia of Religion and Ethics* (1908–26) |
| *IJPR* | *International Journal for Philosophy of Religion* |
| *JP* | *Journal of Philosophy* |
| *JR* | *Journal of Religion* |
| *JRE* | *Journal of Religious Ethics* |
| *JTS* | *Journal of Theological Studies* |
| *NTS* | *New Testament Studies* |
| *PAS* | *Proceedings of the Aristotelian Society* |
| *PPA* | *Journal of Philosophy and Public Affairs* |
| *PQ* | *Philosophical Quarterly* |
| *RGG* | *Religion in Geschichte und Gegenwart* |
| *RS* | *Religious Studies* |
| *SJT* | *Scottish Journal of Theology* |
| *St Patr* | *Studia Patristica* |
| *TG* | *Theologie und Glaube* |
| *TP* | *Theologie und Philosophie* |
| *TS* | *Theological Studies* |
| *ZNW* | *Zeitschrift für die neutestamentliche Wissenschaft* |

# Introduction

There is an ancient story which runs as follows. A man was walking along the road when he saw in the distance what he thought was an animal. When he got closer he saw that it was another human being. And when he got closer still he saw that it was his brother. How do we view others? Are the distinctions of 'animal, human being, brother' ethically relevant? The theme of this book is an exploration of the concept of personhood in relation to a Christian ethic. Not just, 'who am I?', but 'who are *we*?', where 'we' might include all living creatures. What the concept means, and whether it is as important as it has been claimed to be, are just two of the questions we shall try to answer.

Personhood has occupied a position of importance in ethics since Locke and particularly since Kant. Among contemporary moral philosophers the questions and issues have been refined, but a strongly positive attitude to ethical personhood has been endorsed by writers such as P. Singer, M. Tooley and D. Parfit, although there are equally strong voices of dissent (e.g. R. M. Hare; B. Williams), which regard personhood as too ambiguous to bear such weight. The emphasis in either case has been on rational, moral criteria linked with personhood.

In Christian ethics the position is rather different. There has been a long tradition of relating ethical demand to the nature of God who is understood in personal terms as holy and loving, but emphasis on personhood in an ethical context has come to the fore in recent discussions about the Trinitarian nature of God and the comparison between human and divine personhood in terms of relationality.

I

Whether personhood should have the importance that is currently attributed to it is the subject of this investigation. Not all the claims can be accepted. Some are incompatible. There is a need to listen to the arguments and sift them carefully. There is also a need to understand at least the main outlines of a long and complex historical development.

Concepts of person are socially constructed. They embody social and religious values about the nature of human personality and individuality in relation to society, and are usually associated with other significant ideas about the nature of the self, such as mind, body or soul; or freedom, responsibility and accountability; personal identity and survival; relation to others, including non-human animals and the environment; belief in God.

Mauss' essay (1938) on the concept of person forms the starting point for an examination of how and why 'person' has become such an important but 'fragile' and vexed concept.[1] Mauss regarded the concept of person as having reached its clearest expression in Fichte. His thinking was strongly influenced by Durkheim, whose high estimate of the individual was combined with a strong belief in the importance of society. The relation of individual and community remains a significant issue today. Personhood cannot be understood in terms of the isolated individual. Mauss also draws attention to the need for a supporting metaphysic, which he discerned in the Christian faith, firstly in its Christological debates and later and more clearly in the emphasis on personal experience found in revivalist groups of the eighteenth century.

Various criteria have been proposed for distinguishing 'persons' from entities that are not persons. It has become widely accepted in recent ethical discussion that 'person' is a moral concept and that the criteria for distinguishing 'persons' from other entities must be moral criteria. There are dissentient voices, however, and some philosophers are sceptical about the value of such a concept as 'personhood' because it is elusive, vague and ambiguous. This, combined with its normative status, makes the dissenters wary.

'Personhood' has also played a prominent role in contemporary debates about the identity of 'persons', both in the sense of what criteria are relevant to establishing personal identity (should one rely on material or mental criteria, body or mind ? Does body in this case simply stand for the brain?) and the criteria that are relevant to establishing what constitutes identity over time (is X at time 1 the same as X at time 2?). What is the relationship of persons and human beings? Are they identical? What are the criteria of personhood? Are all or only some human beings persons? Who or what else, apart from human beings, qualify as persons?

'Persons' have been variously defined in terms of material criteria such as body or brain, mental criteria such as self consciousness, rationality or intentionality, moral criteria such as rights or respect, and religious criteria such as soul or relationship to God. Since the nineteenth century, but particularly in recent years, 'persons' have come to occupy a position of unparalleled regard in the competing value-systems of pluralist societies. What Kant said of rational persons is now claimed by or for all persons. 'Rational beings are called persons because their nature already marks them out as ends in themselves . . . unless this is so, nothing at all of absolute value would be found anywhere.'[2] So highly are persons regarded across a wide spectrum of popular opinion (e.g. groups campaigning for a better status for their constituents – civil rights, women's rights, animal rights, to name but a few), that some philosophers have wondered whether 'person' has become a term of pure evaluation, devoid of clear descriptive content.

'Person' has become a boundary concept over which there is debate because it is so highly prized, on the one hand, yet at the same time its application is contested. Some traditional social and religious values, particularly with regard to non-human animals and the environment, have come to be regarded as inadequate and even grossly defective, and the application of personhood has become part of this re-evaluation and re-positioning of personhood and value. Feminists and others have put a fundamental question-mark against what they see as the unjustified assumptions of Enlightenment thought, which has tended to exalt rationality and human rights as marks of personhood. Personhood is understood by feminists primarily in terms of embodiment and relationality. One of the purposes of our analysis will be to disentangle the different lines of thought which contribute to the meaning of personhood in contemporary ethical debate and to assess their significance.

Although 'persons' are often thought of as essentially rational human beings, capable of moral agency, and valuable for that reason, there is another view which thinks of persons as essentially human beings, normally rational, but including also those who are not yet fully rational, such as infants, and potential human beings such as foetuses, and all those, such as the senile, who have lost their rational faculties. It is sometimes assumed that 'human being' is a purely biological category, unlike 'person' which is a social or moral category, and that the two views represent conflicting models which may not even be strictly comparable. 'Persons, not humans, are special', according to one writer.[3] In fact, both 'person' and 'human being' may represent something of value and what we are dealing with is a clash of values, in that each is prizing something different or representing a different way of catching the value of personhood.

The meaning of 'person' is certainly more complex than the straightforward contrast of 'person' and 'human being' allows. In its long history, 'person' has meant a number of things. As the mask worn by the actor in ancient drama, 'persona' may refer to the face or outward appearance, which may disguise as well as reveal who I really am. Similarly, psychologists may refer to the 'persona' as a social front or shadow self which conceals or hides the real self. On the other hand, it may also refer to an ideal or inner self, which contains the secret of who I really am. Ideal, real, fictitious, unconscious selves – who is to decide? For the sociologist, the person may refer to a role in society, and who I am may be understood in terms of my occupation and other roles I occupy. Not surprisingly, in view of their search for the true self, religions may find the person in the self which survives death or in communion with God.

In contemporary ethics it is the contrast of 'person' and

'human being' which has dominated discussion. This contrast, even opposition of person and human being, will be examined in Part 1 through some of the writings of contemporary moral philosophers, particularly P. Singer, M. Tooley and D. Parfit, all of whom have given personhood a significant place in their thinking. Important differences in their positions will be pointed out, but it will be argued that all three have been too ready to develop the distinction of person/human being found in Locke's account of personal identity, and to couple it with Kant's emphasis on personhood as the embodiment of value *par excellence* in the modern world.

Although 'personhood' has continued to be associated with 'human being', both in popular thought and philosophy, recognition of the logical distinction of person and human being has led to increasingly frequent attempts to specify the essential criteria of personhood without reference to accidental properties of being human, until eventually they have been not only 'separated out' but 'contrasted' and even 'set in opposition'. One of the reasons for this has been the neglect of the overall context in which discussion about personhood and being human are set. So, for example, neglect of the idea that human being is not simply a biological category, but may represent a term of value within a religious/theological context, has contributed to the polarisation of the concepts of 'person' and 'human being' and to the failure to understand a theological ethic, which supports an ethic of personhood without devaluing human being or setting personhood and human being in opposition.

Part 1 as a whole, therefore, is marked by the attempt to reposition personhood and being human, and to indicate their closeness and the links which connect them. It also illustrates how ideas once applied pre-eminently to God have been diffused and attributed almost exclusively to others, especially human beings, in order to support their perceived worth. The quasi-sacred character of 'persons' is at the heart of many dilemmas of modernity, and discussions in Feuerbach about personhood are examined to illustrate these developments. This historical background, which helps to explain why personhood often holds the position it does in modern thought, also confirms the need for caution about proposals that construe 'person' as a purely moral term.

Part 2 is concerned to explore a different set of contrasts and relationships involved when a religious/theological context is taken into account and God is thought of as person (or Trinity of persons). This view adds another dimension to the idea of person, and makes it necessary to reconsider what is involved in being both person and human. Moreover, if God is a person, who or what else might be regarded as a person?

The idea of divine personhood is complex, and it requires both analysis and historical investigation. Although the picture is still incomplete in some respects, it is becoming clear that the introduction of 'person' terminology into the theological debates of the early church was drawing on 'prosopological' exegesis which attempted to relate divine speech in the Bible to the different persons of Father, Son and Holy Spirit. In the doctrinal debates surrounding the credal formulations, however, terminological correctness and the translation of terms in East (Greek) and West (Latin) created considerable problems, which were to reverberate for many centuries. The Greek *hypostasis* (subsistent reality) would normally have translated the Latin *substantia* (substance), but the Alexandrian use of *mia ousia, treis hypostaseis* (one being or substance, three subsistent realities) was adopted and developed by the Cappadocians into a Trinitarian exposition which capitalized on the flexibility of hypostasis to represent divine reality in distinction and relation. This has encouraged some recent commentators (e.g. Lossky; Zizioulas; LaCugna) to argue that the Cappadocians were responsible for the introduction of an ontology of relational personhood. 'The concept of the person with its absolute and ontological content was born historically from the endeavour of the Church to give ontological expression to its faith in the triune God . . . If God does not exist, the person does not exist . . . The person, both as a concept and as a living reality, is purely the product of patristic thought.'[4] Against this must be set uncertainties of interpretation in the terminological disputes of the fourth century. Philosophically and theologically divine personhood remains an issue of lively debate, involving questions of divine impassibility, embodiment and temporality. For some commentators, however, it has to be said that divine personhood is a red herring in relation to human personhood, because, whatever terms are used, personhood cannot be predicated of God's triune being in the modern sense of individual agent. For a variety of reasons modern philosophers have been more willing than theologians to examine what might be meant in saying that 'God is a person'. On the other hand, they have not always appreciated what is involved in the Trinitarian discussions. Theologians, while recognising the importance of God's personal agency and purpose and God's personal character of holy love and loyalty, have preferred to speak of God's triune being, since God is not strictly speaking a being at all, but Being itself.

In Christian tradition, however, there is another way, more securely attested, of referring to divine personhood. This is based on the analogy of divine and human personhood and God's creation of humanity in the divine image (*imago dei*, cf. Genesis i 27). How this image is to be construed (e.g. in terms of physical likeness; rationality; spirit; responsibility; relationship) raises further questions. Theological anthropologies are constructed out of human experience with the help of revelation. It is not possible to bypass this process in favour of a single revealed theological anthropology. The attempt to model human relationships on intra-divine Trinitarian relationships seems to be in danger of overstepping this limit and positing a knowledge which we do not have. To suggest that interpersonal relationships are impossible without Trinitarian foundations is unnecessarily to disinherit those whose personalism is humanistic but not Christian. What the Christian rightly affirms is that participation in the mystery of God's Trinitarian life is mediated for Christians through faith in Christ and participation in the body of Christ in worship and service.

It is important for Christian theology to be able to indicate the nature of divine personhood and to be able to relate this to (the relational nature of) human personhood. But they remain different. It is mistaken, we contend, to argue that without

Trinitarian presuppositions the resultant human person must become a self-enclosed individual, isolated from effective relationships with others. Even if Trinitarian relations are the ontological presupposition of all relations, this does not give Christians the right to assert this as if it were an empirical truth about all relationships. It is only because of the judgement that relations are essential for the understanding of human persons (which may have empirical support) that we are led to recognise the important way in which the relationality of divine persons may be significant for human personhood. W. Pannenberg has made a good case for thinking that from the point of both human self-understanding and a Christian understanding of God as Father, Son and Holy Spirit, divine personhood embodies ecstatic relationality (the way in which personhood is manifested in relation to another) more fully than human personhood, which necessarily retains elements of self and autonomy.

Divine and human personhood are analogous, but not identical. The importance of the analogy is that it lends support to a view of human personhood (which has support in human experience also) which allows for a transcendental dimension to existence. It is impossible to capture fully what a person is; there is always more to be said, more to be discovered, not simply in the sense that the human story continues into the future, but that being human involves qualities of character and community which point to the realisation of perfections rarely or never found in any human character or community, yet fundamental to human existence and valuing. Personhood is a way of distinguishing what is of ultimate value from the rest of nature. The *imago dei* motif in Christian theology draws attention to the relationship of divine and human personhood. If humanity is made in the image of God, then creation provides a substantial basis for understanding human values.

What was begun and undertaken gloriously in creation, however, was immediately threatened and distorted by the exercise of human freedom against God. The story of human creation is overshadowed in scripture by humanity's refusal to abide by the conditions of the original covenant between God and humanity. The Old Testament narrates successive attempts to restore the covenant on the part of God, but in the last resort humanity always refuses to identify with what God wills. A variety of mediatorial instruments (law, sacrifice, obedience of heart and will) are tried, but in the end all fail. The New Testament narrates the coming of the One who fulfils the ancient promises. Reflection on his death and resurrection leads to the view that as an instrument of salvation the law is ineffective and can be done away with, although its ethical stipulations (e.g. do not kill) remain valid and are to be kept. New and more demanding stipulations (e.g. do not be angry; refuse lustful desire) become part of the new covenant. The sacrificial system is replaced by the one eternal sacrifice of Christ whose life and death was offered to God without reserve in a way that was felt to fulfil all prophetic expectation. This fulfilment, which the early Christians found in the life and teaching, death and resurrection of Jesus, is the beginning of a new and final era of salvation, in which the transformation of human personhood is the first fruits of a transformation of the whole of creation. It is not surprising that the intra-divine life should be the source of this transformation. Caution is needed, however, in applying this to concrete, practical ethical problems and situations. The transformation associated with personhood is of crucial importance, but human personhood cannot be assimilated to divine personhood without the lifelong process of what in an earlier generation was called 'sanctification'.

What is involved in a Christian ethic is explored by asking what a Christian perspective requires, and developing a view which allows faith commitments full expression but without denying the role of critical reason. The effect of regarding humanity as in need of, and capable of, divine renewal and transformation is examined in order to develop a narrative Christian ethic which is not incompatible with a natural law ethic, but able to do more justice to the richness of insights stemming from the Christian faith, particularly in terms of relationality.

The problematic of a Christian ethic which is both universal and contextual in reference can be overcome, it is argued in Part 3, by closer attention to the Christian story of God's covenant with humanity which culminates in the coming of Christ, and to a contextual emphasis in the consideration of contemporary ethical situations and issues. The new covenant issues in an ethic of love modelled on Christ's teaching and example. One of the central features of this is 'love of neighbour', which does not exclude anyone, even the enemy. Some recent discussions of Christian ethics (e.g. Hauerwas) have argued that this requires a 'qualified' rather than a universal ethic, and a recognition that a Christian ethic as practised by Christians should not be distorted by harnessing it to secular premises and secular goals. The ideal of a rational ethic common to all persons is regarded by Hauerwas as mistaken and unworkable. The view taken in this study is that such a view ignores valuable features of both a Christian and a common ethic. For that reason we outline a modified form of Habermas' rational discourse ethic, not in order to devalue the insights of communitarians, but in order to bring communitarian and liberal ethical standpoints closer together. The significance of both forgiveness and human rights in a Christian ethic is considered in order to indicate two structural features of such an ethic. The study concludes with a discussion of other concerns which have featured in Christian thinking about personhood, including the eschatological transformation of all creation.

# PART I

## 'Person' in contemporary ethics

# CHAPTER I

# 'Une catégorie de l'esprit humain: la notion de personne'

The concept of person was still 'fragile' when, in 1938, Mauss gave the lecture which now forms the title of this chapter. Since then, the cult of personhood has grown to such an extent that we can ask whether it is not in danger of obscuring the truths it originally stood for, because too much attention has been focussed on the individual and the significance of self-consciousness.[1] The dangers attending the cult of the individual, whether in economic, social or ethical terms, have been frequently noted. If the modern fascination with 'personhood' were no more than an expression of liberal individualism, however, it would not be necessary to try to disentangle the theological roots involved in contemporary ethical debate, or to analyse the growth of ideas about intersubjectivity in modern personalism. In fact, the story of 'personhood' is rich and complex and contains a number of unresolved challenges for philosophers and theologians, not least in the field of ethics.[2] The present study is offered as a modest contribution to understanding some of these, and particularly in the interface between philosophical and theological ethics.

Changes in society and changes in concepts of person interact; changing concepts reflect, confirm or challenge social practices. Because of its strategic significance in Western society, the concept of person has been intimately related to other important concepts. For example, personhood was once closely connected with language about the 'soul', although today it is more likely to be connected with the language of 'bodies, rights and freedoms'. The link with 'soul' is retained chiefly through ideas of rationality, purpose and self-consciousness. The present study argues that 'person' is an important value term, rightly associated, though not identical, with 'being human'. It also had a long history of theological use to denote 'divine reality'. Its later links with questions of self-identity, self-consciousness and moral responsibility, as in Locke, represent a transition to modern usage in which it now serves as a focus for modern crises of self-identity and moral responsibility. Its lofty Kantian moral use still inspires many to campaign for the extension of moral worth to entities not universally accepted as persons, such as non-human animals or even trees and plants, rivers and mountains. One of the significant but lesser noticed features of certain modern ideologies of personhood, it is argued, is the transfer of attributes associated with divine personhood to human persons, a transfer which becomes explicit in Feuerbach's reduction of theology to anthropology.

Discussion about what it means to be a 'person' is found in both moral philosophy and the philosophy of mind. Both of these contexts are important, and we shall keep returning to them in the course of our study. There are also other important contexts, in social anthropology and theology, which need to be taken into account if we are to arrive at a balanced conclusion. We shall look first at the use made of the concept by the social anthropologist Marcel Mauss, because his Huxley Memorial Lecture (1938) with the title, 'Une Catégorie de l'Esprit Humain: La Notion de Personne, Celle de "Moi"', encapsulates many of these issues in a brief compass, and his answers, although sometimes misleading, point to relevant questions which need to be addressed.[3] It is brief but rich in detail. It raises a number of problems of interpretation, but the overall thesis is fairly clear. What is commonly understood by the term 'person' in the modern Western world developed over many centuries. By tracing some of the main elements of that development it is possible, Mauss believes, to illuminate contemporary beliefs and shed light on how this important human concept is still changing. It is still (in 1938) 'imprecise, delicate and fragile' and 'requiring further elaboration',[4] but it exercises a strong influence on the way people think and especially on the understanding of morality.

In his introduction, Mauss alludes briefly to the Aristotelian categories, including substance, cause, time and space, and suggests that the researches of Hubert, Durkheim, Lévi-Bruhl and himself are really concerned with examining some of the sociological implications of these categories. He then turns to the 'self', which he calls a 'category of the human mind', ignoring the fact that it is 'substance', not 'self', which is a category in Aristotle and that his own explanation of what he means by category (something 'innate') has been at best impressionistic, at worst unclear. He recognises, however, that what he is presenting is only tentative and sketchy, a 'summary catalogue of the forms that the notion of "person" has assumed at various times and in various places',[5] rather like an unfinished portrait or piece of sculpture.

Further limitations are noted. His examination is not linguistic or psychological. It relates to law and morality, to social history. He is concerned not with the 'self', but with human notions of the self. Much of our vocabulary for discussing this is quite recent in origin, but there is a recognisable concept of the self both in pre-historical civilisations and in historical times from ancient Greece onwards which is not unrelated to modern developments.

In the earlier part of the lecture, Mauss brings together anthropological material about the Pueblo Indians of Zuni, the tribes of the American North-West (the Kwakiutl) and the primitive tribesmen of Australia, because the 'name' represents a way of thinking about the self in terms of the individual's role and position in the tribe, whether in sacred drama or family life. He alludes to the relationship of such roles and relationships ('personnages') to family history and belief in re-incarnation, but does not develop this theme. He is concerned mainly to contrast the defined but submerged role played by the individual in the above societies, compared with the more self-conscious individuality of the modern period. Section III, entitled 'The Latin "persona"', picks up the idea of 'mask' or role, but is more concerned to trace the emergence of 'self'. He suggests that, although ancient Indian and Chinese civilisations had a concept of 'person' as 'self', in the metaphysics of

Vedanta, Taoism and Buddhism these concepts took on a fairly rigid form which did not allow the concept of the human person to break free from its dependence on tribe and religion to become a complete entity, 'independent of all others save God'.[6] The decisive epoch or culture in this development was Rome.

This idea is developed in the following section, in which he argues that the decisive factor was the transformation of tribal rituals, at one stage associated with masks and legends linking the fraternity with the foundation of Rome, into legal rights for all clan members, so that 'all had a civil "persona"' and became Roman citizens. The development of the institution of forenames, surnames, and pseudonyms points in the same direction, says Mauss: 'the personal nature of the law had been established, and "persona" had also become synonymous with the true nature of the individual'.[7] Only the slave was excluded; he did not even own his own body, although Christianity conferred on him an eternal soul. Section V attributes this advance to the efforts of the Stoics, particularly the Schools of Athens and Rhodes, as evidenced by Cicero and Polybius, and later by Seneca and Marcus Aurelius. There was interchange between Greek and Roman terms, *prosopon* and *persona*, to the enrichment of both. 'Persona' came to include both role and innermost character, moral as well as judicial person, 'a sense of being conscious, independent, autonomous, free and responsible'.[8] Even so, the concept 'lacked any sure metaphysical foundation',[9] until Christianity remedied this.

In the next section (VI) Mauss follows Schlossmann[10] in underlining the importance of the transition from role-player to human being. So important was the idea of moral person that it could be applied to any legal entity such as a corporate body.[11] The Christological and Trinitarian debates of the early church finally gave the term 'person' a new dimension and complexity. How this related to the understanding of the human person is not discussed by Mauss. He simply asserts that Cassiodorus' definition of person as 'rational individual substance' (*substantia rationalis individua*) summarises this development. 'It remained to make of this rational, individual substance what it is today, a consciousness and a category'.[12]

There then follows a rapid survey of developments which found their focus in the post-Enlightenment period of the last 150 years when the notion of person became the category of the self, in which self-knowledge and psychological consciousness predominate. Philosophical discussions about human nature up to the seventeenth century are plagued by Christian presuppositions about the soul. Even Spinoza, who believes only in the survival of the noetic soul, remains enmeshed in traditional thought forms. According to Mauss it was Christian sects like the Moravians, Puritans, Wesleyans and Pietists, who established the identity of 'person' and 'self' and 'consciousness' as a result of their stress on individual experience. Hume and Berkeley assisted this development by their speculations, but even Kant, who states the idea of self clearly, hesitated when confronted with the question whether the self is a category. The concluding paragraph of section VII is worth reproducing in full, because, despite its sustained ambiguity, it represents the conclusion to which Mauss has been heading:

The one who finally gave the answer that every act of consciousness was an act of the 'self' (moi), the one who founded all science and all action on the 'self' (moi) was Fichte. Kant had already made of the individual consciousness, the sacred character of the human person, the condition for Practical Reason. It was Fichte who made of it as well the category of the 'self' (moi), the condition of consciousness and of science, of Pure Reason. From that time onwards the revolution in mentalities was accomplished. Each of us has our 'self' (moi), an echo of the Declaration of the Rights of Man, which had predated both Kant and Fichte.[13]

The conclusion (in Fichte) is remarkable, and the historical development (from American Indian to Moravian pietist) uneven, but the thesis he develops is full of challenge and vitality. In 1938, on the eve of World War II, there is a certain prescience about Mauss' reference to personhood as a 'fragile' concept. His conviction about its moral significance appears more than justified by developments since then. Yet his lecture does not appear to have had a major impact at the time or since. It remained a footnote in learned journals. With hindsight, however, it is significant that unlike many commentators before or since he was able to recognise clearly that concepts of personhood reflected human attitudes and values. It is for this reason that Mauss' lecture is given a programmatic position in our examination. As we shall see, Mauss may have been unaware of some of the values and attitudes he was himself imparting into his historical survey, but he was not unaware that his anthropological survey was part of a narrative related to contemporary concerns of his own generation, concerns which he believed were also relevant to the future of civilisation. The comparative absence of reference in later writers to Mauss' view of 'person' as a social construct of great significance but uncertain future is all the more surprising in view of the large and growing literature on different aspects of personhood in the twentieth century.[14] One reason for this may have been the very fact to which Mauss drew attention. 'The sacred character of the human person' had become one of the unquestioned assumptions of modern liberal thought. The impact of Mauss' essay may also have been muted by its brevity and broad generalisations. Moreover, as Mauss himself noted, even fundamental forms of life and thought are subject to change and decay, and he held out no certainty that the concept of 'person' would continue to occupy the significance it had attained in Western social thought. There is plenty of evidence that, at the end of the twentieth century, the concept of person has become more contested and fragmented than ever before,[15] but the ideal of becoming 'one's own person' or a person in one's own right is strongly embedded in every spectrum of discourse among all levels of society, religious and secular alike. Along with high ideals and the acknowledged significance of the 'person', however, the human person is subject to constant abuse and disfigurement in private and public life.

Mauss' fears for the future of the concept (the way in which future generations would think of 'persons' and the effect of this on public and private morality) are not without justification, but there is no sign of any abatement of interest in

issues relating to personhood. The appearance of a volume of
essays specifically devoted to an anthropological cum philosophical examination of Mauss' thesis may have been
prompted by the continuing attention given to personhood in a
variety of contexts, particularly in the philosophy of mind and
ethical theory.[16]

Mauss' overall conceptual scheme and some of his assumptions are challenged by several contributors to this volume. The
theme and central ideas of Mauss' lecture are located in earlier
writings by Durkheim and in a neo-Kantian view of the self
derived from Renouvier and Hamelin. The concept of 'category', for instance, in the title and body of Mauss' lecture,
relates not so much to Aristotelian or Kantian 'categories' as to
Durkheim's use of category to mean 'fundamental and pervasive form of conceptual organisation'.[17] Durkheim's use,
however, was not entirely consistent. He wished to stress
historical variation and conceptual change; but he also wanted
to depict 'society' as a permanent and pervasive force affecting
men's changing ideas. Durkheim was aware of Kant's distinction of the noumenal and phenomenal self; he was also familiar
with Kant's use of 'categories of thought' to refer to necessary
presuppositions of thinking. Yet his understanding of the self
owed more to the personalist philosophy of Renouvier, which
was based on 'the sacredness of the individual and the fact of
human solidarity'.[18] Renouvier belonged to the neo-critical
Kantian school, which developed Kant's understanding of the
rational self in the direction of practical reason and the ethical
self. He also took over a number of Hegel's ideas, particularly
the view that '*consciousness, or, to use a perfectly synonymous term, the
person*, [italics added] is the synthesis of self and non-self.'[19]
'Renouvierist philosophy used certain themes from Hegel's
philosophy', as Collins observes, 'to transform Kant's unknow-
able transcendental self into the empirically knowable individual – specifically, indeed, the individual of modern liberal
society'.[20] Like Hegel, and unlike Kant, Renouvier emphasised
'both the concrete embodied individual and an historicist view
of categories of thought which allowed for change and development'.[21] Renouvier is thus able to advance the view that every

person is a unique 'original phenomenon'.[22] Durkheim's notion of the person, therefore, recognised the uniqueness of the historical individual. In fact, the sacredness of the individual, Durkheim saw, has become the religion of modern times, a religion in which 'man is, at the same time both believer and God'. It is this idea of the person which lies behind Mauss' lecture.

Confirmation of this interpretation may be found in Durkheim's essay, 'Individualism and the Intellectuals', in which he says:

The human person whose definition serves as the touchstone according to which good must be distinguished from evil is considered as sacred in what one might call the ritual sense of the word. It has something of that transcendental majesty which the churches of all times have given to their Gods. It is conceived as being invested with that mysterious property which creates an empty space around holy objects . . . And it is exactly this feature which induces the respect of which it is the object.[23]

Durkheim acknowledges his debt to Kant in the matter of individualism, but neatly subverts it by deriving individualism from society (cf. 'individualism itself is a social product, like all moralities and religions').

There is in both Mauss and Durkheim a certain ambiguity and confusion, which may be traceable to the transposition of the philosophical (Kantian) term 'category' into a more general and relativistic sociological mode. The varied historical embodiments of the notion of person illustrate not so much the development of a category of thought as the changing content Durkheim would give to the relationship of individual and society. Mauss' category of the person 'concerns essentially the concept of the individual presupposed by or expressed in a society's dominant value system or encompassing ideology'.[24] Yet he appears to have used the notion of category with some fluidity. It is not unjustified, therefore, to say that 'we must learn to distinguish more clearly than he [Mauss] does between a properly philosophical epistemology and a sociologically informed history of ideas'.[25] It is also the case that some of the details of Mauss' reconstruction are less secure than other parts. The emphasis on Fichte and the omission of other features may need to be redrawn, as we shall see in chapters 5–7. Mauss' lecture is still valuable, however, in drawing attention to the idea of 'person' as a social construct, a reflection of ideas about the self which developed over centuries, even if he is unduly influenced by neo-Kantian ideas about the self which he accepted too uncritically from Durkheim and Renouvier. In fact, one of the main reasons for commencing with Mauss is that his view of 'persons' and the relation of self and society is one that has been widely shared by Western liberal thought.

A different criticism of Mauss' reliance on Durkheim emerges in Carrithers' essay, 'An Alternative Social History of the Self', which draws a distinction between the social concept of 'personne' and the individualistic emphasis of 'moi', which Mauss tantalisingly combines, he thinks, in the interests of his Durkheimian liberalism in which social forces are conclusive but which allow for the emergence of the modern autonomous individual. 'Personne' and 'moi' narratives represent different ways of interpreting individual and social life. 'Personne' stories revolve round 'a conception of the individual human being as a member of a i) significant and ii) ordered collectivity'. 'Moi' narratives involve 'a conception of i) the physical and mental individuality of human beings within ii) a natural or spiritual cosmos, and iii) interacting with each other as moral agents.'[26] Mauss' reasons for combining these different features but giving priority to 'personne' can be explained in terms of Durkheim's argument that, not only the forms of social life, but the forms of intellectual life are best understood in terms of the collectivity, but a collectivity which can allow for and support the anti-authoritarian individualism to which he was personally committed and which he saw modern society as reinforcing. Rather than Mauss' grand procession through history, however, there may be only 'distinct episodes moving towards no very clear conclusion'.[27] By pointing to Buddhist traditions which deal with similar themes, Carrithers is able to suggest that Mauss' historical scenario for the development of 'persons' makes too many assumptions about the relationship of individual and society. Even within that scenario, one might add, there is scope for other interpretations of the emergence of individualism. The process by which different aspects of individualism developed (in the legal system; in religious ritual; in family life and social relations) was long and complex, and differed from society to society. Mauss' essay does not present detailed arguments for every contributory phase or every society. None of this, however, would gainsay the significance of Roman–Stoic–Christian influences to which Mauss draws attention in seeking to describe a broad backcloth against which more specific developments in Europe can be understood. If it be granted that Mauss' lecture represents one possible interpretation of the relationship of self and society, there are still questions to be asked about the interests that have been at work to produce this version. Although Mauss draws attention to the importance of Christian theology in section VI, there is a sense in which his own interest in 'the moral person' prevents him from inquiring more fully into the metaphysical grounding of the concept in Christianity. 'Person' can stand for 'human being' anywhere at any time, one might say. What is remarkable is that a term which developed a significant theological use in the early church returned to common speech and philosophy bringing with it this more complex penumbra of meaning because of this theological connection. Mauss' reference to 'metaphysical foundation' seems to serve a mainly historical purpose, since it is seen as contributing to the genesis of individual moral autonomy, which might now be better justified on other grounds. One of the issues which we shall consider later is the possibility of a more robust exchange or dialogue between a living religious moral tradition which makes a close link between divine and human personhood and secular moralities which exalt human personhood.

Mauss helps us to understand some of the important cultural changes which have contributed to a modern understanding of personhood in terms of individual self, but there are a number of points at which his essay may need revision. As already indicated, he is concerned to trace the development of the idea of the person as individual, and in this he may have been more indebted than he realised to the liberal individualism of Durkheim and Renouvier. He recognised that the notion of person is representative of a general framework of attitudes, including moral attitudes and values, which he understood in terms of a structure of beliefs. Fusion and tension between individualistic and social views of the person were then inevitable. Interpretation of intellectual trends in this way also made it inevitable that Mauss, and the modern interpreters who express their own differences from Mauss but attempt a similar task, should employ strategies which attempt to distinguish deep structures of belief from more apparent surface forms. This enables religious belief, for example, to be interpreted as representative of social contours, rather than, or as well as, doctrine or theology, and in this way submerged or subordinated, whereas one of the aims of the present study is to give expression to this theological strand and bring it into relationship with the ethical and social.

The culmination of the concept of 'person' in Fichte is striking and unexpected.[28] It might well be argued that a different conceptual archaeology would be more pessimistic about the emergence of personal autonomy and the sacredness of the individual in the modern world, since the autonomous, rational self has more recently been interpreted as dependent on social forces of unreason and restriction of liberty.[29]

A more significant weakness is Mauss' failure to develop the insights of his social anthropology into a closer examination of the relational nature of personhood. As C. Taylor puts it: 'I become a person and remain one only as an interlocutor'.[30] This emphasis on relationality is now being urged from a variety of directions – in social psychologies, communitarian philosophies and Trinitarian Christian theologies – and it corresponds to one of the earliest uses of 'person' to refer to the relationality involved in speech and communication when one person communicates with another and becomes a member of a language (symbol using) community. It is an emphasis which contrasts sharply with those early modern views which put the emphasis on 'self-consciousness', as in

Mauss, and the interiorisation of personhood. This interiorisation is an important cultural shift which should be viewed with concern rather than simply accepted. Taylor points to a 'post-interiorized understanding in which we could preserve the modern understanding of freedom, responsibility, individual originality, while reinstating the insights about significance and conversation which have been lost'.[31] As we shall see in chapter 7, this emphasis on the relational aspect of speech unites the early uses of 'persona' and 'prosopon' with those modern interpretations which stress relationality in persons.

Mauss compressed his analysis of the modern period (section VII) into two or three pages; Taylor devotes several hundred pages in *Sources of the Self* to a review of this modern period, seeking to interpret and clarify the influences that have shaped modern understandings of the self.[32] He is opposed to reductive views of the self, but wishes to explain how and why such forces have come to play an important part in human self-understanding. 'Strong evaluations' are characteristic of the human agent, and there is an 'ontology of the human', he believes. These two features – the fact that inescapably we regard some things as incomparable in worth and that we are committed to fundamental claims about the nature and status of human beings – suggest to Taylor that morality is best understood, not in terms of human autonomy, but rather as an (objective) response to an order or dimension of reality which is independent of human evaluation. It is not possible to provide a neutral identification of this order or dimension of reality, since our evaluations cannot be left suspended in a neutral mid-air, ready to be activated when the moral dimension has been objectively identified. If this is true, then we need an explicit moral ontology based on a description and assessment of human nature and the nature of the world. In the past this has usually been based on theistic claims. We are in the unfortunate situation today that most of the secular moral ontologies belie the claims they make, in that their theories of human nature are at odds with the ethic they propose. Thus, in the case of utilitarianism, it has 'a reductive ontology and a moral impetus, which are hard to combine'.[33]

Although Taylor does not say outright that he would prefer a religious moral ontology, this is an option allowed by his view and one that we shall commend in the following pages. It will not be claimed that *only* such a view can support the understanding of persons as human beings who are normally and essentially communicative, but that this rediscovered emphasis on communication and relationships with others does, in fact, chime well with the use of 'persona' and 'prosopon' in some of the theological thought of the early church, and can be linked with a view of God as person, which is characteristic of biblical tradition and still relevant to Christian ethics today. How this is to be achieved is disputed, but there are increasing attempts to find a way forward through some form of narrative ethics. Sometimes these efforts have given the impression that in order to succeed they must replace any form of rational ethic based on rules and principles. We shall argue for a narrative ethic which can work in tandem with, and need not displace, a universal ethic which is supportive of the use of reason and rules and principles, provided these are at the service of the love of neighbour/enemy. Before coming to that, however, we must establish what 'person' means in contemporary ethics, and why it has become problematic, rather than the solution it was hoped for.

# CHAPTER 2

# *Meaning and criteria: person / human being*

Before we look at examples of the way personhood is construed by a number of modern moral philosophers, there is one important objection to be countered, namely that personhood is so vague or contested that it is best avoided. Already in 1926, we may note, one German commentator had referred to 'person' as 'a ghastly/awful word' (*ein schreckliches Wort*).[1] Two modern critics who are very sceptical about the use of 'person' to resolve issues in moral philosophy are B. Williams and R. M. Hare. To some extent they are right and support our argument that 'person' has become a term of great value. What is confusing is that the term is attached to different, even conflicting, values. It does not follow, however, that we should simply avoid the term or regard it as signifying great value but with no precise content. It is clear that 'person' is sometimes used simply to refer to an individual human being without any obvious evaluative connotation, as when the notice in the lift says, 'This lift carries up to ten persons' (or a certain weight). In this instance, person means nothing more than an individual passenger or object of weight. This usage is not philosophically problematic but it serves as a reminder that 'person' has a variety of uses.

More significant from the point of view of our study is the way in which 'person' functions both descriptively and evaluatively. It is this combination we shall consider before moving on to examine the sort of criteria that are relevant when trying to understand and define personhood more precisely. We are not starting out with a definition of 'person' and then ruling out any usage which does not conform to the definition. On the other hand, we are not simply tracing the history of linguistic practices involving the word 'person'. We are seeking to understand how personhood has been interpreted in different social, religious and philosophical contexts, and particularly in relation to ethical uses.

R. M. Hare provides a useful starting-point.[2] Towards the end of *Freedom and Reason*[3] he discusses a number of genuine and spurious factual arguments which are frequently used in the consideration of moral issues such as racial conflict. In attempting to display the spuriousness of certain allegedly factual arguments, he begins with illustrations which, he thinks, most of his readers will find obvious. His first illustration is taken from the Nazi persecution of non-Aryans. Nazi claims based on the hereditary make-up of the Germanic races may appear to be factual arguments – there could, presumably, be blood tests. On closer scrutiny, however, no such empirical tests are available; the claim is not supported by factual evidence. Further, no reasons are given as to why certain moral consequences should follow from the state of the blood even if such tests were available. Hare's second example, used, he thinks, by more respectable people but suffering from the same spuriousness as the first example, is the argument that white people ought to treat black people in a certain way because they are 'brothers' or equally 'children of God'. It is not clear, he thinks, what tests are being or could be used to identify someone as a 'brother' or 'child of God'. Further, 'even if it could be established beyond doubt that a certain man was my "brother" or that he was a "child of God", it is not clear why it follows that I ought to treat him in a certain way'. The pride of place amongst spurious arguments, however, is reserved for the claim that we ought to treat blacks in certain ways because they are persons. Hare says: 'As it stands, the inference from "X is a person" to "I ought to be kind to X" is logically no better than that from "X is a non-Aryan" to "I ought to put X in the gas-chamber". . . the argument suffers from the same defects as the "brothers" and "children of God" arguments. No criterion is offered for determining whether someone is a person or not.'

It is not at all clear, however, that Hare's analysis of the

moral features of the situation or of the logic of moral
argument is the only correct analysis. His use of 'person',
particularly, raises issues which are of immediate relevance to
our study. Clarification of the evaluative/descriptive distinction
in relation to 'person' is one of them. Hare's argument that
'persons' are not to be treated morally simply because they are
persons looks distinctly odd. Surely, this is just what one ought
to do – namely, to treat persons morally and, moreover, to do
so because they are 'persons'?

Hare's analysis requires closer examination. He is trying to
illustrate the value of philosophical ethical argument in ordinary life. His examples are chosen, therefore, with an eye to
relevance. His rejection of person-based justification is deliberately provocative because it is the sort of justification often used
by those with liberal sentiments. Indeed, he grants that person-
based arguments may enjoy 'a certain philosophical respect-
ability'. He goes further and admits that, if the argument were
spelt out more fully, it could be made valid. 'But the argument
is nevertheless worthless as it stands, since it suffers from the
same defects as I have already exposed.' Even if the conclusion
is sound, the reasoning is mistaken; to that extent, therefore, it
obstructs critical moral thought, Hare argues.

Central to genuine moral philosophy in Hare's view is the
distinction of fact and value and the need for moral terms to be
prescriptive and universalisable. He recognises two different
senses of 'descriptive', the weaker of which he accepts and
regards as similar to universalisable. He rejects, however, any
strong sense of 'descriptive' which would allow a description to
*entail* an evaluation. The significance which Hare attaches to
the distinction has been challenged by a number of writers (e.g.
Foot; Lee; McDowell; Putnam).[4] Hare's application of the
distinction to the issue of 'person' is instructive. 'No criterion',
he says, 'is offered for determining whether something is a
person or not'. And, even if it were, no moral conclusion would
follow from whatever criterion of identification were offered,
'for no grounds have been given' (i.e. to justify a particular
moral stance). The question would still remain: how ought
persons to be treated?

Hare's argument is as elliptical as the argument he is criticising. The following appears to be the case. Hare objects to the lack of a clear description of what a person is, but then adds that this is immaterial to the real issue (since a clear description will not resolve the moral dilemma), which is the absence of clear supporting moral reasons for treating persons in a particular manner. If 'person' simply individuates one of a class and the class consists of members all of which are purely descriptive, then what Hare says is correct. But, if 'person' individuates one of a class whose members are both descriptive and evaluative, what he says does not follow. One solution, Hare suggests, would be to make the term 'person' evaluative and 'write into the notion of a person some moral content'. It would be only a partial solution, however. 'This will validate the step from "X is a person" to "X ought to be treated in a certain way". But now we are left without a determinate and morally neutral criterion for finding out whether he is a person.' Hare successfully exploits the fact that person has more than one meaning. He starts from the assumption that 'person' means 'human individual'. He then adds the assumption that 'person' must be either descriptive or evaluative. To argue that X should be treated morally because he is a person, says Hare, is analytic (if person has moral content) but vacuous (because we cannot identify who is a person without invoking a moral criterion) or else the statement is contingent and the argument invalid. For Hare, no moral conclusions can be drawn from the argument that someone is a person. Only logical analysis of a moral argument showing that the moral judgements in question are universalisable and prescriptive can logically justify them. By reading universalisability into the term 'person', however, Hare is later able to concede that 'it *is* [his italics] morally relevant that blacks are people. Saying that they are people is saying that they are like us in certain respects.'[5]

Hare's scepticism about moral arguments based on the term 'person' is not fully justified. The fact that 'person' may have a wide range of reference does not invalidate its moral use. Nor is it impossible for the term to have descriptive force if it has evaluative significance. In fact, it appears to share important characteristics with other terms such as 'good', which may be used both evaluatively and descriptively. There seems to be an element of linguistic and logical imperialism in what Hare proscribes and prescribes. If he had examined the concept of person more closely, he would have discovered that 'human individual' is only one of its several meanings. Moreover, even 'human' may function both evaluatively and descriptively within a particular cultural context. Thus, 'she's only human' may embody and support a particular moral judgement, such as 'and deserves, therefore, to be treated leniently, despite the all too human frailty revealed by her action'. We can also say 'truly human', meaning that certain admirable qualities are realised. The evaluative significance of 'human' is particularly clear in the case of the negative 'inhuman', which rarely functions in a purely descriptive sense. To describe conduct as inhuman is to censure it as lacking in desirable moral/human qualities. Inhuman conduct is typically cruel, brutal, or vicious conduct. One of the important uses of 'person', particularly in moral contexts, is 'a being of moral worth'. There are, of course, arguments about the source of moral worth: is it rationality, self-consciousness, autonomous agency, the capacity to choose or some other quality? There are also arguments about the boundaries of personhood. Are all or only human beings persons? Is the foetus a person? Are any non-human animals persons? Is God a person? We shall discuss these issues later.

That 'person' frequently has both descriptive and evaluative force and that this is central to an understanding of the concept is indicated by the following passage from P. Baelz:

*Persons* matter [his italics]. This, we suggest, is a basic moral belief which could provide a common starting point for both secular and religious morality. This is not to say that it is a universal belief. In some cultures persons have not been reckoned to matter very much. Kings may have mattered, but not slaves. Nations may have mattered, but not individuals. Whites may have mattered, but not blacks.[6]

Baelz is using 'persons' to include all, not just some, human beings. All persons are of intrinsic worth and to be regarded as moral agents or patients. This view, he goes on to say, is self-evident in our society, although it has not been universally self-evident. Clearly Hare would not agree with Baelz that it is self-evident that all persons matter. The main question, however, is not whether Baelz is correct in his assessment of our society, but whether Hare's argument about the invalidity of basing moral inference on 'he/she is a person' is correct. One can grant Hare that the argument is something of a short-cut. When the argument that someone ought to be treated well because she is a person succeeds, it succeeds because certain assumptions are being made. But Hare's attempt to uncover these assumptions applies the false disjunction (false even by his own standards) of evaluative or descriptive. Hare's own discussion (chapter 2 of *Freedom and Reason*, especially 2.5) allows the combination of evaluative and descriptive (weak sense); what it disallows is descriptive (strong sense) entailing evaluative.

Elsewhere[7] Hare is equally critical of the use of 'person' in the abortion debate:

In the same way the decision to say that the foetus becomes a person at conception, or at quickening, or at birth, or whenever takes your fancy, and that thereafter because it is a person, destruction of it is murder, is inescapably a moral decision, for which we have to have moral reasons. It is not necessary, in order to make this point, to insist that the word 'person' is a moral word; though in many contexts there is much to be said for taking this line. It is necessary only to notice that 'person', even if descriptive, is not a fully determinate concept; it is loose at the edges, as the abortion controversy only too clearly shows . . . To say that the foetus is (or is not) a person gives by itself no moral reason for or against killing it; it merely incapsulates any reasons we may have for including the foetus within a certain category of creatures that it is, or is not, wrong to kill (i.e. persons or non-persons). The word 'person' is doing no work here (other than that of bemusing us).

It has to be admitted that Hare is writing primarily about abortion rather than the concept of person in the above context, and that he represents the exasperation of many writers with the unclear use of 'person', but to say that 'person' is 'doing no work' seems the very opposite of the truth. 'Person' is being asked to carry a great deal of meaning; enough, in fact, to carry the argument. Hare is entirely justified in pressing for clarification. It may also be true that the concept is being asked to do too much work in this context. But Hare's main point seems unchanged from his earlier comments in *Freedom and Reason*.[8]

Support for the view that the concept of person may be both evaluative and descriptive is to be found in Wiggins' article, 'The Person as Object of Science, as Subject of Experience and as Locus of Value',[9] in which he argues for a way of holding in a single focus three very different ideas:

(a) the idea of the person as object of biological, anatomical, and neurophysiological inquiry;
(b) the idea of the person as subject of consciousness; and
(c) the idea of the person as locus of all sorts of moral attributes and the source or conceptual origin of all value.

If the sense of 'person' is not guaranteed analytically or by public stipulation, the empirical 'human being' may provide a starting-point, suggests Wiggins. Further, if one follows Strawson's view in *Individuals* about person being a primitive concept which combines both M (matter-involving) and P (person-involving) predicates, it becomes possible to see how P predicates can be superimposed on M predicates, although the reverse is not true. (b) superimposed on (a) can then conceivably be superimposed on (c) to give that complex view of persons presupposed in many modern contexts. Beginning with the assimilation of (a) and (b) and (c), thinks Wiggins, may pave the way for the eventual identity of the three different ideas. The article is not directed specifically against Hare, but it does indicate the extent of Hare's assumptions. Other studies (cf. n. 4 above, especially K. Lee) have also cast doubt on the validity of Hare's reliance on a sharp distinction of descriptive and evaluative. It is not necessary for our purposes to enter into the merits of the long-standing debate between Hare and Foot about prescriptivism, but Hare's handling of the person-based argument at the end of *Freedom and Reason* illustrates some of the weakness of his procedure, particularly when it relies upon a kind of linguistic imperialism, which would exclude the use of 'person' altogether. Almost as important as the invalidity of this disjunction of evaluative and descriptive is the narrowing of attention resulting from this particular focus. When we come to theological considerations we shall see that one of the main new features is the change of horizon resulting from recognition of the presence and activity of God. This will inform the possibility that persons are essentially centres of relationship empowered by God. This possibility will allow us to examine more fully in Parts 2 and 3 the implications of Wiggins' important claim that personhood is the source or conceptual origin of all value.[10]

What we have so far, then, is a recognition of the complex usage of 'person' and some indication of the interplay of descriptive and evaluative features when adult human beings are taken as standard-bearers of what persons are. In contexts of personal identity, personal worth and significance, and in debates about the moral rightness of actions that are conceptually related to the creation or killing of possible and actual persons (in contraception, abortion and euthanasia) or other issues where personhood is regarded as morally significant, we need to be able to say what criteria we are using to distinguish 'persons' from non-persons or other entities. There have been numerous attempts to define what a person is.[11] None have met with universal approval. Some try to isolate or emphasise a particular determining or distinctive feature, such as body or brain or soul or rationality or speech or simply sentiency. Others regard 'person' as essentially a term of value, instantiated differently in different cultures and value-systems. One of the most fundamental differences arises over the question whether only or all human beings are persons. In the rest of this chapter we will consider some of the suggested criteria for personhood in order to try to decide this question.

D. Dennett begins 'Conditions of Personhood'[12] as follows: 'I am a person, and so are you. That much is beyond doubt'. He ends his article with these words: 'When such problems arise we cannot even tell in our own case if we are persons.' The problems referred to arise when we encounter someone who is responsible for moral wrongdoing. Perhaps there is something of a rhetorical and literary flourish in his ending. Wrongdoing by persons may even seem inevitable. Wrongdoing on the scale of Eichmann or Hitler does seem to obliterate a great deal of what is associated with being a person. Did Eichmann and Hitler cease to be persons when they embarked on their atrocities? Or do their actions serve as a reminder of what 'person' can include?

There is the further question whether the form of Dennett's concluding sentence is intended as a comment on his opening statement. Wiggins' comment[13] that Dennett's conclusion is a 'desperate expedient' on the part of a normally 'subtle and unsolemn' Dennett, which would have the effect of 'putting in jeopardy the personhood of countless human beings' pays too little attention to the structure of Dennett's article or to the fact that Dennett's conclusion, however overstated, succeeds in drawing attention to one of the significant aspects of person-hood, namely that 'personhood' is something which is not distributed like arms and legs or brains and IQ, but involves self-commitment and the attainment of certain qualities, such as integrity and purpose, which even those beings (viz. humans) who most typically embody these qualities sometimes fail to demonstrate.

In fact, Dennett's and Wiggins' views on personhood are not necessarily far apart. Dennett thinks there are two distinct notions of personhood, one moral, the other metaphysical; the latter is logically prior and a necessary condition of the former.[14] Little is said, however, about the metaphysical notion. Most of the essay is devoted to a consideration of six conditions of moral personhood: rationality; intentionality; the stances of others towards those claimed or claiming to be persons; the capability to reciprocate this stance towards others; the ability to communicate verbally; and a particular form of consciousness, sometimes identified as self-conscious-ness. These are the sort of empirical features which Wiggins regards as supervenient upon the basic features of personhood which he wishes to link more closely with being human. For Wiggins, the human person is properly described as one subject of bodily experience and mental consciousness, who makes moral judgements. It is not entirely clear whether Dennett intends his necessary conditions of moral personhood to be also sufficient, and whether human beings are their most typical embodiment. To these two questions Dennett gives only cautious and somewhat inconclusive answers.

Because the concept of a person is 'inescapably normative'[15] in a way that never allows for the perfect instantiation of the conditions of personhood, there is no way either of saying that all humans do instantiate the concept, or of setting other than an arbitrary mark if we wish to apply the conditions and attempt to include some actual beings and exclude others. One further comment of Dennett suggests considerable unease about all conditions of personhood: 'the moral notion of a person and the metaphysical notion of a person are not separate and distinct concepts but just two different and unstable resting points on the same continuum. This relativity infects the satisfaction of conditions of personhood at every level'.[16]

It is not entirely clear whether Dennett is retracting his view that the moral and metaphysical notions of person are distinct and that priority belongs to the metaphysical. We have noted that he clearly sees them as belonging to one continuum. The reasons for their instability are not stated explicitly, but seem to be related to disagreements about the empirical features which he has listed as necessary features of moral personhood.

Some of his points deserve further examination. Does the idea of a normative concept require that whatever descriptive marks are involved must be perfectly instantiated? A substance like water clearly varies enormously in taste and in the amount of minerals and impurities it contains from one area to another. We have no problem in regarding all the samples as samples of water. But if we demand 'pure water', there may be many people who would refuse to accept what comes out of the tap as 'pure water'. Does pure water exist anywhere, it might be asked, except as an ideal of the mind or text book? Is pure water a normative concept? Does its realisation admit of degrees of purity or is it an all or nothing affair? If pure water

embodies the idea that whatever counts as pure water today by
present standards of measurement may be revised upwards in
the direction of 'purer' water, it is clear that whatever standard
or convention for measuring the purity of water is adopted will
be capable of revision. If, on the other hand, what is to count
as pure water is specified in relation to the absence of certain
impurities, it is quite possible to imagine that even contemporary Water Boards, despite howls of protest from their customers, will be able to advertise quite legitimately that their
water is (normally) pure. If one removes the adjective 'pure'
and simply refers to water, it would be very difficult for
customers to complain that what they were receiving was not
water, although it would still be possible to complain that water
which contained unpermitted levels of lead or such a high
proportion of living creatures (e.g. shrimps, apparently, in
certain water authorities) as to be undrinkable, was not really
water. Is water also, then, in these circumstances capable of
becoming a normative concept? And if so, what are the
implications for instantiating the concept of water?

It is not clear whether Dennett intends 'normative' to
exclude instantiation of 'personhood'. His discussion of the six
conditions of moral personhood suggests not. Why, then, does
he refuse to allow that personhood is (sometimes? normally?)
instantiated in human beings? Why are there more problems
with personhood than with water? It could be argued that
water is not normally a normative concept. It is only when
standards of water control have become problematic that the
description of certain samples of water becomes problematic. If
the nitrates rise above a certain level, then even the Water
Board may agree that what it is supplying is no longer water. In
the case of 'persons', however, particularly in moral contexts,
there is a sense in which the evaluative significance is permanently in question. The evaluative significance is uppermost.
To be a person requires qualities which, although they are in
some senses characteristically human, for example, the ability
to think and speak and relate to others, qualities which appear
to be capable of empirical verification, are also linked with
other less easily verified qualities such as 'free, given to acting

autonomously, possessing a sense of purpose or self-consciousness' and are not automatically possessed by all human beings. If personhood is closely linked with 'being free', for example, are all the problems associated with the concept of freedom to be brought into the discussion of personhood?

None of this need exclude the application of personhood to actual entities. The descriptive/evaluative distinction does not prevent a concept discharging both functions. The descriptive criteria may be complex and difficult to apply. But none of the features mentioned by Dennett are impossible of realisation. Most of his six conditions appear to be realised to some extent by the majority of human beings. To insist on the perfect realisation of his conditions does not follow logically from his argument. Nor does the fact that the conditions may not be realised perfectly mean that any application of the conditions must be arbitrary. In fact, even Dennett seems to assume for the most part that the conditions of personhood which he proposes are relevant and capable of application in a non-arbitrary fashion.

Whether Dennett's conditions for moral personhood are the most fitting or not, their instantiation certainly seems to presuppose an embodied or identifiable agent, even if such embodiment presupposes location in time and space together with some means of communication, features which some writers would have no difficulty in attributing to a disembodied person. A fuller account of what might be involved in the metaphysical notion of person, however, might supply the stability which Dennett desiderates. It is this aspect of personhood that Wiggins deals with more fully. Wiggins represents the view that discussions of personhood and personal identity which emphasise memory and consciousness and a range of mental/psychological qualities presuppose something like an identifiable agent. As Wiggins puts it: 'memory can only have a distinctive part to play . . . in concert with the whole range of faculties that are distinctive of persons'.[17] These faculties cannot be studied in isolation from 'the physical constitution of organisms that experientially remember'.[18] An overrapid identification of 'human being' and 'person', however, is uncalled for. Wiggins puts forward with some plausibility what he calls 'the animal attribute view' of persons. 'Person' is a

concept whose defining marks are to be given in terms of a natural kind determinable, say animal, plus what may be called a functional or . . . systemic component. Perhaps X is a person if and only if X is an animal falling under the extension of a kind whose typical members perceive, feel, remember, imagine, desire, make projects, move themselves at will, speak, carry out projects, acquire a character as they age, are happy or miserable, are susceptible to concern for members of their own or like species . . . [note carefully these and subsequent dots], conceive of themselves as perceiving, feeling remembering, imagining, desiring, making projects, speaking . . . have and conceive themselves as having, a past accessible in experience-memory and a future accessible in intention . . . etc. On this account person is a non-biological qualification of animal.

The strength of this view is that it recognises a clear and important distinction between natural kinds and artifacts, which, however ingeniously invented, remain invented products with no prospect of becoming living organisms. The animal attribute view allows for development and diversity; there may be disagreement about particular extensions that may be recommended (e.g. the extension to non-human animals or the requirement of a particular level or interpretation of rationality). But it rules out the production of persons whose attributes can be accounted for entirely in terms of manufactured attributes (e.g. spare-part surgery; drug control) involving none of the normal features of individuality, desire, belief, autonomy. If persons can be made in test-tubes, the crucial factor is not their origin but their potential to develop into beings who can be said to make their own decisions and lead their own lives rather than function in a machine-like, pre-programmed way. Elsewhere[19] Wiggins argues equally strongly that 'person' is a term which leans on a body of information similar if not identical to that which provides the sense for 'human being'. Just as 'horse' and 'equus caballus' are described in different words yet refer to the same entity, so 'person' and 'human being' may offer two different but related accounts of the same entity.

When searching for a suitable single focus of both person and human being, it is necessary to note that the resulting conception may be expressed more or less accurately, depending on the use made of empirical information. There is no analytic, non-circular definition or publicly agreed stipulation of what a horse or person is, but in both cases an a posteriori conception rests on a shared public understanding of horses and people. In the last resort, if someone did not know what was meant by horse or person we could make use of ostensive definition and point to an actual horse or human being.

It could be objected that up to this point Wiggins has simply assumed the connection of person and human being. Even if ostensive definition plays a part in the way children learn what persons are, it does not follow that ostensive definition captures what is essential to the concept. What, we might ask, is pointed to? There is the further fact that 'horse' and 'equus caballus' are much less controversial than 'human being' and 'person' have become.

Wiggins goes on to argue, however, that if Strawson's account of 'person' as holding together M (matter-involving) and P (person/consciousness related) predicates is now brought into play, then, granting that Strawson's account is not a watertight definition, since it would certainly allow other entities than human beings to be classed as persons, it becomes very difficult to argue either that one could start with P predicates alone or that P predicates could be reduced to M predicates. It becomes necessary to accept that 'persons' are entities whose description involves P properties which then turn out to be M properties also. Wiggins seeks to illustrate this in the case of remembering and perceiving, by showing that veridical as opposed to imagined memories and perceptions can on principle be distinguished by reference to what actually happened. 'Having M properties', however, can mean either 'matter-involving' or 'reducible to matter'. It is the former sense that is applicable to persons, who have both M and P properties. In short, there is an argument for holding together persons as 'objects of biological inquiry' and persons as 'subjects of consciousness'. By carefully chipping away at a possible method for arriving at a concept of person, Wiggins' discussion edges its way forward to counter with some conviction the disjunction of 'person' and 'human being' which has become prevalent in many philosophical discussions.[20] If it is objected, however, that the conjunction of 'human being' and 'person' has been shown to be possible rather than necessary, it can be replied that there is no analytic, non-circular definition of 'person'. It is sufficient to have shown that there are good grounds for holding 'person' and 'human being' together. It is this view, holding 'person' and 'human being' together, which has come under attack from a range of modern moral philosophers whose views we shall consider in chapters 3 and 4. Several of the contributors to *The Person and the Human Mind* (ed. C. Gill) make the point that 'personhood' has become a rather grand abstract concept, which on closer inspection proves elusive. P. Smith is sympathetic to a mild functional view which finds human beings exemplify many, if not most, of the relevant functions, but wishes to leave open the possibility that others than human beings may also qualify as persons. He does not want 'human being' to become an essential substantival pre-requisite for 'personhood'.[21] This important but limited agreement with Wiggins establishes useful common ground over against the claims of Tooley and Singer and those who follow them.

Closer attention to the ways in which 'person' is actually used suggests that person, self and human being may 'represent three different modes of understanding individuals'.[22] One of the sources of confusion is the isolation of properties which characterise a particular understanding, and the subsequent assumption that such properties constitute a complete description. It may be perfectly possible and sometimes very useful to analyse a human being in clinical behaviourist terms, but this should not exclude other interpretations which focus on intentional agency and speech and begin to develop a quite different understanding of the whole person. Moreover, as we have indicated, human personhood is not a purely descriptive matter. And for the religious believer there is the further factor that personhood may apply to both divine and human beings.

Christians would say that their belief in God (whether as triune person or a person) influences their understanding of both 'person' and 'human being'. This will prove important in Part 3, where it will be argued that a Christian perspective on personhood is most relevant, ethically speaking, in terms of a Christian understanding of what it means to be human and how this affects our relations with others and our non-human environment, which is also part of God's creation.

# CHAPTER 3

# Moral personhood in M. Tooley and P. Singer

Modern ethical discussions frequently contain references to 'person' not in an incidental way but implying that, if it is understood what 'persons' are, this will serve as a reason or justification for the behaviour or attitude or policy that is being recommended. A view of 'person' is being appealed to in order to justify the morality of what is being said or done. Some philosophers (e.g. R. M. Hare; B. Williams), as we have seen, are sceptical about this use of 'person' to justify a particular value position. Other writers, however, have taken particular care to clarify what they mean by 'person' in order to be able to use it as a key category in ethical discussion. The writers we shall look at in this chapter are all united in distinguishing sharply between 'human being' and 'person'. They also have certain other features in common. We shall concentrate on Singer and Tooley because they have written at greater length and more explicitly about 'persons', but at least two of the others make it clear that the concept of 'person' is fundamental to their ethical position.

Of these others H. T. Engelhardt Jr[1] makes the distinction of person and human fundamental to his study of health care. 'Persons, not humans, are special.'[2] For Engelhardt, 'persons' in the strict sense are equivalent to moral agents, self-conscious, rational and possessing a moral sense. There is a social sense of persons which includes young children and infants (who have not yet become persons in the strict sense) and the senile and demented (who were once, but no longer are, persons). Permanently comatose individuals, however, should not count as persons even in a social sense; they should be declared dead.

Engelhardt recognises that such a definition will solve some problems but create others. He discusses the implications of the definition for defective newborn infants, sleeping persons, non-human persons and composite persons resulting from brain transplants. His main concern, however, is to show what the effects of such a definition of person might be for health care, rather than to justify in any extensive way this particular understanding or restricted use of 'person'. He makes it clear that he accepts the definition and believes it justified, but he is more interested in the application of the definition than its theoretical justification.

Another writer who is also more interested in the application of 'person' to medical ethics than in detailed justification of its distinction from 'human being' is J. Harris.[3] The chief advantage of 'person' for Harris is that it is not species specific or anthropocentric. It summarises what is of value. A person is any being capable of valuing its own existence. The fact that people value different things and for different reasons is irrelevant. What distinguishes persons from other entities, whether animals or plants or machines, is that persons are valuing entities. The philosophical task of attempting to work out criteria of personhood merges with the task of deciding what is of value in life. It is not necessary, however, to proceed laboriously examining each suggested criterion in detail, when it is accepted that persons give value to their own lives. What is required is a willingness to listen to what persons tell us about their chosen values. The task of recognising a person from a non-person becomes comparatively simple, despite the complexity of what is at stake. A question and answer suffices. 'Language is the hallmark of consciousness'.[4] Harris admits that there are dissenting voices in the philosophical community, but thinks that, if something like his view is not accepted, moral philosophers will find it necessary to put forward criteria for distinguishing between persons and non-persons, between life which ought to be preserved and life which can be terminated, and criteria for answering whether there are other people in the universe and deciding what it is that makes human life valuable. When it is put like this, it is not clear why Harris thinks his solution is preferable. It may not be easy to state criteria of personhood; it will certainly be difficult to obtain agreement; but why should a dichotomy of person/human being be preferable, especially if it cannot deal with the moral complexities involved?

Like Engelhardt, Harris distinguishes between person and human being by appealing to the distinction between fact and value. Some of the arguments are similar to those used by Hare which we noted in chapter 2. Yet, as we saw there, the distinction should not be erected into a dichotomy. To build a new approach to ethical issues involving human beings, particularly in boundary cases, on a definition of person in terms of predicates that further disadvantage the very young and the very old, two groups in society that by virtue of age are normally more vulnerable than other groups in any case, would be to disadvantage vulnerable groups yet further.

The views of Engelhardt and Harris are similar at many points to those of Singer and Tooley and Warren. In so far as Tooley's article on abortion and infanticide, which has now appeared in several recensions, predates the published discussions of personhood in the other writers referred to above, it seems likely that it is the influence of Tooley that has been significant in bringing about a new conception of personhood in recent ethical writing, particularly in relation to abortion and infanticide. Because Tooley has developed his views more fully than other writers, we will discuss him at greater length, although it is probably Singer who has been most successful in popularising the distinction of person and human being through his very readable introduction to practical ethics.[5] Singer draws on Tooley's arguments and we shall consider him first, partly because he is briefer, but mainly because he serves as a useful introduction to Tooley.

The concept of person occupies a crucial role in Singer's development of a preference utilitarian position towards killing. This position is used to underpin his discussions of abortion, euthanasia, and animal rights. He distinguishes two senses of human being – one, 'a member of the species homo sapiens', two, 'a being who possesses certain qualities such as self-awareness, self-control, a sense of the future, a sense of the past, the capacity to relate to others, concern for others, communication and curiosity'.[6] This list of characteristics, which also appears in Warren and Tooley with minor variations, resembles the list put forward about the same time by the American Protestant theologian, Joseph Fletcher.[7] Singer uses 'person' to describe this second sense of 'human being'. He then qualifies this by adding John Locke's definition of person as 'a thinking intelligent being that has reason and reflection and can consider itself as itself, the same thinking thing, in different times and places'. When discussing the killing of non-human persons, he says: 'Some non-human animals are persons as we have defined the term'. He finds support for this view in reports which describe the abilities of chimpanzees and gorillas to use sign language. He adds:

if human life does have special value, it has it insofar as most human beings are persons. But if some non-human animals are persons, too, there must be the same value in the lives of those animals . . . Hence we shall reject the doctrine that places the lives of members of our species above the lives of members of other species. Some members of other species are persons; some members of our own species are not. No objective assessment can give greater value to the lives of members of our species who are not persons than to the lives of members of other species who are. On the contrary, as we have seen, there are strong arguments for placing the lives of persons above the lives of non-persons. So it seems likely that killing, say, a chimpanzee is worse than the killing of a gravely defective human who is not a person.[8]

Singer was influential in bringing the issue of animal rights to the front of the philosophical and ethical agenda in the early 1970s. He made considerable use of the criticism that to model 'person' on 'human being' was 'speciesistic'. His essay 'All Animals Are Equal', first published in 1973, makes use of the term, and a footnote attached to the word acknowledges his debt at this point to Richard Ryder, a clinical psychologist at Oxford and Chairman of the RSPCA in the late 1970s.[9]

In chapter 6 of *Practical Ethics* Singer applies these ideas to the abortion debate. The central argument against abortion is described in terms of a syllogism. The first two premisses are: it is wrong to kill an innocent human being; a human foetus is an innocent human being. From this it is concluded that it is wrong to kill a human foetus. Singer focusses attention on the first rather than the second premiss, and by means of the distinction between 'being a member of the species homo sapiens' and 'being a person' argues that injunctions against killing should only apply to the killing of persons. 'If', he says, ' "human" is taken as equivalent to "person", the second premiss of the argument, which asserts that the foetus is a human being, is clearly false; for one cannot plausibly argue that a foetus is either rational or self-conscious. If, on the other hand, "human" is taken to mean no more than "member of the species homo sapiens", then the conservative defence of the life of the foetus is based on a characteristic lacking moral significance and so the first premiss is false.'[10]

As in Tooley, the argument moves on to justify infanticide, in so far as the 'intrinsic wrongness of killing the late foetus and the intrinsic wrongness of killing the newborn infant are not markedly different'.[11] Singer attributes – probably correctly – the common reluctance to practise infanticide to the influence of Christianity with its teachings about the sanctity of human life, but he thinks 'it is now possible to think about these issues without assuming the Christian moral framework which has, for so long, prevented any fundamental re-assessment'.[12] For Singer 'the grounds for not killing persons do not apply to newborn infants'. Neither classical utilitarianism nor preference utilitarianism, he thinks, offer good reasons why infanticide should be necessarily wrong.

Similar views are found in M. A. Warren. In an article 'On the Moral and Legal Status of Abortion' (*Monist* 1973) she makes a similar point to Singer (and Tooley) when she distinguishes a genetic and a moral sense of being human and restricts personhood to the moral sense. She requires at least some of the following five characteristics as criteria for this sense:

1. consciousness and in particular the capacity to feel pain
2. reasoning

3. self-motivated activity
4. the capacity to communicate messages of an indefinite variety of types
5. the presence of self-concepts and self-awareness.

She is not prepared to say which of these five characteristics, if any, are necessary or what combination might be necessary and sufficient, but she is fairly dogmatic that no other features of personhood are necessary. She concedes that the first feature alone (consciousness and the capacity to feel pain) could be constitutive of personhood and that the foetus at a certain point in its development (somewhere in the second trimester) possesses this feature. She is only willing to grant as certain, however, that a 7 or 8 month foetus is somewhat more person-like than a very small embryo. 'In the *relevant* [her italics] respects, a foetus, even a fully developed one, is considerably less personlike than is the average mature mammal.' She asserts that 'neither a foetus' resemblance to a person nor its potential for becoming a person provides any basis whatever for the claim that it has any significant right to life'.

These views of Singer and Warren represent one extreme in the abortion debate and indicate what is possible when the emphasis on rationality and other features associated with personhood is detached from its moorings within a wider metaphysic or view of the world and human nature. The justification of infanticide offered by Singer in terms of consistent utilitarianism raises questions about the nature of the rationality he favours. Although a definition of personhood in terms of rationality would not automatically justify abortion or infanticide, it is clear that the emphasis on rationality easily leads to diminished concern for certain human beings such as infants, idiots, and the senile, groups of people who have, under the influence of both Christian and humanistic considerations, been given special protection. Singer's argument, which at one level functions as an egalitarian type of argument against speciesism, at another level relies on the 'personalistic' assumption that only or chiefly 'persons' matter, an assumption which has been encouraged by Judaeo-Christian views of *humanity's* place in creation. His attempts to reduce the impact of what he is proposing – no adult should be worried by his proposal, he thinks, because it relates only to those infants whose parents consent; all living adults have passed the stage of being personally threatened by the proposal – suggest he is defective in his understanding of why religious believers and many others find his proposal damaging to both religion and morality. The view that one should assume the moral right to take human life in order to implement a possibly (some would say certainly) mistaken ethical theory, namely utilitarianism, would strike many people as in itself immoral. It is not at all clear that consistent utilitarianism by itself (i.e. when unconnected with restrictive views of personhood) necessarily leads to a justification of infanticide, but there does seem to be a deep incoherence within utilitarianism with regard to life and death. Even when human existence is regarded as a good which should be strenuously preserved, the measuring of present and future utilities is hopelessly complicated and in the case of human life perhaps impossible.

Singer's arguments to elevate the status of non-human animals are counterbalanced by his utilitarian arguments which weigh against the interests of all those he classifies as non-persons, as Hursthouse points out.[13] Singer cannot consistently repudiate the killing of any non-human animals that are not persons in view of his tolerance of infanticide. His utilitarian stance weakens the position he claims to support – namely that persons should be respected. Even when interpreted in terms of person-preferences, utilitarianism seems to lack adequate safeguards to protect personhood. It has also been argued that his rejection of the claims of the foetus is incompatible with his utilitarianism. 'The fact that the foetus in its early stages is incapable of feeling anything at all is no more relevant than that a person under anaesthetic is similarly incapable, or that hibernating bears apparently cannot feel much. The foetus, the anaesthetized person, the hibernating bear . . . are all beings likely to have a happy future and hence (other things being equal) are all creatures it would be wrong to kill, on straightforward utilitarian grounds.'[14]

Despite the initial welcome given by many animal welfare

organisations to the philosophical support of their cause by Singer, many workers in these organisations have begun to distance themselves from his utilitarianism and attacks on the status of the foetus. Many of them are Christians who do not share his religious agnosticism and do not support his utilitarianism or his attack on Christianity. Their concern for animal welfare springs from a love of animals, whereas Singer's campaign seems to be based on a desire for intellectual and ethical consistency. Whether his arguments are consistent, however, is open to question in the light of the considerations raised above. It is also becoming clear in the above arguments that the movement to divorce 'person' and 'human being' on the grounds of ethical clarity is itself riding on the back of assumptions about the comparative status of persons and human beings. The movement to separate the two and to elevate 'persons' seems to lead inevitably to some reduction in the status of 'human beings' *per se*. Those human beings who are also persons will not be adversely affected, but it seems naive not to realise that this pre-judges the position of many (e.g. the very young) who qualify only as potential and not actual persons or who by reason of senility are on the brink of being disqualified through no fault of their own.

Tooley's position is more complex than the views we have examined so far. It is further complicated by the fact that his original article, 'A Defence of Abortion and Infanticide' underwent several substantial revisions before its expansion into a book. Fortunately it is not necessary to examine all of the arguments in the same detail, since many are introduced simply to close off possible escape routes or to demonstrate the possible implications of taking a certain fork in an argument. Our discussion of Tooley's position, therefore, will be directed to understanding and evaluating the main stages in his argument. This is not intended to minimise the value of his thoroughness, but it is important to recognise that, however thoroughly some of the consequences of his position may have been worked out this cannot compensate for major errors or weaknesses in the foundation of the argument.

In his original article, Tooley made it quite clear that he was looking for a satisfactory liberal position on abortion. A clearer understanding of what was meant by 'person' would, he believed, help towards that. His initial moves were directed to showing that 'person' was 'a purely moral concept, free of all descriptive content. Specifically, in my usage the sentence "X is a person" will be synonymous with the sentence "X has a (serious) moral right to life".' He comments on the unfortunate tendency of fellow philosophers to use 'person' and 'human being' interchangeably. For one thing, it makes defence of a liberal abortion position more difficult, if it has to be argued that the foetus is not a human being, and for another it assimilates the question of the foetus' status to a factual question and obscures the moral issues at stake. 'If one says that the central issue between conservatives and liberals in the abortion question is whether the foetus is a person, it is clear that the dispute may be either about what properties a thing must have in order to be a person, in order to have a right to life – a moral question – or about whether a foetus at a given stage of development as a matter of fact possesses the properties in question.'[15] Tooley is unequivocal in his view that the concept of a person is 'a purely moral concept, free of all descriptive content'. His later discussion, however, implies quite strict descriptive criteria. 'An organism possesses a serious right to life only if it possesses the concept of a self as a continuing subject of experiences and other mental states and believes that it is itself such a continuing entity.' This self-consciousness requirement was then analysed more carefully. Revised versions of the original article defend a similar position but in a longer more qualified form. In the revised form, five requirements are listed:

1. the capacity to envisage a future for oneself
2. the capacity to have a concept of a self
3. being a self
4. self-consciousness
5. capacity for self-consciousness.

These requirements are set in a time-indexed context to safeguard the individual who is temporarily unconscious and to distinguish such an individual from someone in a coma suffering from irreversible brain damage. From this brief outline it is clear that although Tooley insists that all persons have a serious right to life this right is limited by his restrictions on the class of persons. In the articles it was not entirely clear what status Tooley attributed to his five requirements of personhood. From his own revisions one must assume that they are capable of being revised and are not final. They have empirical components which are open to testing. Yet it is set clearly within a moral proposal about the allocation of the right to life. How closely related are the empirical features and the moral proposal?

The answer to this question is to be found in chapter 5 of *Abortion and Infanticide,* in which Tooley states his aim 'to formulate a concept of person that is itself purely descriptive and free of all moral and evaluative elements. The choice of content is to be determined, however, by moral considerations.' This appears to be diametrically opposed to his earlier view that 'person' was a purely moral concept.

We shall see, however, that what holds his earlier and later views together is the close link in both between personhood and the right to life. In his more considered judgement, however, 'person' has become a descriptive concept and this is reflected in his method of argument. It is this aim more than anything else which determines the inclusion and exclusion of relevant material content. It proves, as we shall see, to be a restriction which prevents consideration of a great deal that has traditionally been associated with the concept of person even since the time of Kant. It encourages Tooley to seek for ever-increasing precision in determining necessary and sufficient conditions of personhood. It becomes increasingly difficult to connect the semi-technical term that results with traditional or historical usage. When Tooley says, 'this appears to be the way "person" is ordinarily construed', he confuses the fact that there is a descriptive element to the term person in traditional and popular usage with his own attempts to formulate a more precise and much narrower view of person. This impression is reinforced by consideration of the arguments he uses to support his overall position.

He has already pencilled in, so to speak, in chapter 4 what might be involved in the distinction between 'person', as yet undefined, and 'human being'. Properties that give something a right to life will be characteristic of persons. Because of the strictures of R. M. Hare and others on the language of rights, however, Tooley wishes to find an alternative way of expressing the right to life. 'A natural approach is to talk instead about the properties that suffice to make the destruction of something intrinsically wrong.'[16] This might prove too wide, however, since it might be intrinsically wrong to destroy great works of art, which one would not wish to designate as persons. In order to cope with various eventualities of this sort, Tooley finally recommends: 'The descriptive content of the term "person" is to be determined by those relatively permanent, non-potential properties of an entity that, possibly in conjunction with other, less permanent features, make it intrinsically wrong to destroy something, and that do so independently of its intrinsic value.'[17]

What these properties might be occupies Tooley in chapter 5. 'Many answers have been proposed. A natural starting-point, however, accepted by virtually all of them, is the idea that for something to be a person it must, at the very least, be capable of consciousness.' Consciousness, however, which figured significantly in Tooley's earlier articles and which will reappear, suitably modified, in his final version is temporarily set on one side because it is interpreted very differently by materialists, dualists, and others. Tooley simply reaffirms his conviction that ethical issues cannot be resolved without a contribution from the philosophy of mind. He then lists fifteen other candidates that have figured in discussions of personhood, including such capacities as memory, the ability to desire, remember, use language and interact with others. Most philosophers have picked out rationality, autonomy or self-consciousness to describe personhood, because these are attributes possessed by human beings. The question 'which of these properties are the morally significant ones has not seemed pressing', however, in the past because of the apparent agreement to construe person along the lines of human being. The time has now come for a reassessment of traditional Western values. The capacities being looked for must be psychological attributes which are related to those of a normal adult human being but are the capacities of a person. 'Possible connections between the concept of a person and such notions as rights, interests and capacities will be explored. An account of what it is that makes something a person will be set out, and reasons for accepting it will be advanced.'[18] The essential steps in building up the concept of person are as follows:

1. specification of what is involved in the right to continued existence;
2. establishment of a 'conceptual connection between specific rights and the capacities for specific interests';
3. the claim that a single continuing subject of consciousness must have the concept of a continuing self or mental substance.

This leads to four possible definitions of a person as: a subject of non-momentary interests; an entity that possesses rationality; an entity that is capable of action; an entity that possesses self-consciousness.

Despite his earlier (and repeated) hesitation about the language of rights, Tooley reverts to this language on the ground that 'it may be that the only reasons why it is ever intrinsically wrong to destroy things of a given type is that things of that type are intrinsically valuable, or that things of that type possess a right not to be destroyed'.[19]

That there is a connection between 'persons' and 'rights' is an important point which has emerged in both older and more recent studies. Prior to his decision to make 'person' purely descriptive, Tooley wished to define 'person' as 'a being with a right to life'. Despite the appearance of inconsistency in retaining the link between 'persons' and 'rights', this is one of the more welcome features of Tooley's account. Unfortunately, by limiting his account of rights to the right to life and tying this to a purely descriptive understanding of person, Tooley finds himself increasingly hemmed in and circumscribed in his search for features which will support this right to life. Much of his argument is concerned with logical problems related to the connections between desires and interests. The wider context of rights and their justification, and the possibility of an overall metaphysical framework is largely ignored.[20]

Tooley begins his detailed discussion of rights, not with an abstract account of the structure or epistemology of rights, but with the specific right to life or the right not to be destroyed. Epistemological considerations are introduced indirectly through a consideration of the following two claims:

1. A child does not have a right to smoke.
2. A newspaper does not have a right not to be torn up.

The most significant difference between the two cases, Tooley suggests, is that the first claim raises a substantive moral issue, whereas the second can be simply resolved because newspapers lack a property which is necessary to the possession of a right. This property Tooley calls 'the interest principle', following Feinberg. Interests are compounded out of conations and desires. Absence of a specific interest will mean absence or cancellation of a specific right. Presence of a specific interest will not guarantee a right, but will ensure the possibility of a specific right; whether there is a specific right which can be supported will depend on further considerations.

Are there more specific links between specific rights and specific interests? Claim 3. is then introduced:

3. A cat does not have a right to a university education.

Is the cat's case closer to that of the child or the newspaper? Intuitively Tooley opts for the latter and then considers possible reasons for such a choice. A cat does not have any right to a university education because this does not relate to a cat's particular interests. He does not ask whether cats have other rights such as the right not to be ill-treated, or whether they are capable of having rights. Instead he concentrates on the intuitively implausible right to a university education, largely, it appears, in order to arrive at the more basic principle:

It is a conceptual truth that an entity cannot have a particular right R unless it is at least capable of having some interest I which is furthered by its having right R.[21]

The development of this principle by Tooley exposes the

overall weakness of his argument and the concealed value-judgements which are contained in some of his arguments. He asks his readers to compare the killing of a normal adult human being with five minutes of torture for the same being. Killing is a more serious moral wrong than torture in this case. Now compare the killing and torture of a kitten. Here the order is reversed. It would be wrong to torture the kitten, but not to put it to sleep painlessly. There must, therefore, be a property possessed by adult humans not possessed by kittens. Apart from the persuasive use of language (the kitten is not killed but 'put to sleep painlessly'), the question is put in a way that already begins to exclude certain objections. It has already been decided that (only) persons have a right to life. What is it about adult humans and persons that gives them a right to life and denies the same right to kittens? This, it is assumed, will clarify the descriptive properties of personhood that are the object of the inquiry.

This way of formulating the problem is not unproblematic. The judgement that kittens do not have a right to life is already a value-judgement, which, even if it is supported by a majority of adult human beings, is not uncontroversial. There is a growing body of opinion that would assess the rights of the kitten differently. From the kitten's point of view there is plenty of evidence that most kittens desire to survive and have an interest in surviving. In considering the question of interests, whose point of view is to be taken into account? If Tooley is simply making a proposal about how to allocate the right to life, the way is open for further discussion of the issue, including the question of whether the right to life in this case is conceptually connected with other descriptive properties of kittens. There is the further question whether Tooley is right to assume that the possession of an interest by X is dependent on the ability of X to conceptualise that interest. If rights and interests are connected in this way, then it is clear that foetuses, the senile and the brain-damaged will lose any legal and moral rights that they presently possess independently of whether or not the interest on which the right depends has been permanently extinguished. If such a close connection of rights and interests is to be argued for, one would have expected at the very least a more generous interpretation of potential interests and capacities together with appropriate safeguards for those occasions when interests and capacities are accidentally destroyed. Perhaps even more importantly there needs to be some recognition of the fact that 'persons' with a right to life exist within a network of relationships. It is not only the individual person that needs to be taken into account but the social context of which a person is a part.

It is interesting to observe that in his earlier articles, having argued that the kitten has no serious right to life, Tooley seems to have second thoughts about who does have such a right. Having granted that there may be a concept of self prior to the ability to use language, he wonders whether adult animals belonging to species other than *homo sapiens* may not also possess a serious right to life. Has he really produced criteria that justify treating the kitten so differently from adult animals that may, he allows, be persons? For Tooley, the kitten has a right not to be tortured, because of its capacity to feel pain, but it does not have a right to life, because this would require certain desires to be held by the subject of the experiences. Tooley accepts that the kitten does not want to experience the sensation of being tortured. It is not clear why the kitten should not have a desire to live and not be killed. To define rights in terms of what the subject wants rather than what the subject is entitled to seems to omit one of the essential features of a right (see chapter 14 below). It does not seem to be necessary that X recognises or knows he has a right or entitlement, if a third party can legitimate that X has such a right. It may seem odd to say that an entity can have a right of which it is not aware; but it seems even odder to deny that entities can have rights of which they are not aware. The fact that a right can be extinguished or overridden does not mean that the right never existed. The kitten, it could be argued, has a right to life as well as a right not to be tortured. Tooley is not entirely unaware of this in that he wishes to tie rights more closely to interests than to desires.

There are good reasons for justifying the right to life some-

what differently from Tooley. There are other possible justifications, such as intrinsic value, or the value of life itself, or simple
sentiency or rationality, as L. W. Sumner points out.[22] Alongside the paradigm person of an adult human being with normal
capacities of intellect, emotion, perception, sensation, decision,
action, and the like he ranges seven categories of possible
persons – 1. inanimate objects, 2. non-human animals and
plants, 3. non-human extra-terrestrial species of living things,
4. artificial life forms (eg. robots), 5. grossly defective human
beings, 6. human beings at the end of life (e.g. the senile or the
comatose), 7. human beings at the beginning of life (e.g. the
foetus or infant). How do the criteria relate to the possible
candidates? Sumner collapses the first of the four criteria (that
a person is intrinsically valuable) into the other three (life,
sentience, or rationality) on the ground that even if we accepted
it we should still have to find a criterion for what is intrinsically
valuable. He gives serious consideration to the view[23] that all
living things should have a right to life, but decides against it on
the ground that it admits too many into the category of person
and begins to make the category of person virtually impossible
to apply. Is each blade of grass or insect to count as a person?
Attempts to overcome this problem by providing for a hierarchy of persons within the class of persons raise problems
about the hierarchical criterion. For example, should it be
rationality? And, if so, how should it be applied? Would this
not, in effect, undermine the attempt to argue that 'life' itself
was the basis? Not surprisingly, therefore, Sumner rejects 'life'
as the criterion for 'the right to life'.

He also rejects rationality as the determining criterion on the
ground that it is too severe, allowing if not requiring the deaths
of many individuals who may, in fact, continue to enjoy simple
pleasures despite their lack of rationality (e.g. mongoloids,
psychotics, the autistic, the senile, the profoundly retarded).
Rationality may be a good criterion for allocating moral duties,
but it is too restrictive for allocating moral rights, which may be
invoked to protect those who have them and not simply to
assert their capacity for moral action.

Sentience provides a criterion which is more stringent than

life but less severe than rationality. The capacity to feel pleasure and pain is located in a part of the brain that is common to all vertebrates. Only invertebrates and plants, therefore, are automatically excluded. But, since sentience admits of degrees, some animals will be more sensitive than others. '[M]ore developed (more rational) creatures possess a higher degree of sentience. The expansion of consciousness and of intelligence opens up new ways of experiencing the world, and therefore new ways of being affected by the world.'[24] The fact that sentience admits of degrees allows it to be used both as a criterion of 'persons' and the right to life and as a comparative criterion providing for some sort of hierarchy within the total class of persons. On this basis, greater protection of life can be extended to the higher vertebrates than to the lower. This would accord with most people's intuitions that 'in our moral reasoning paramecia and horseflies count for nothing, dogs and cats count for something, chimpanzees and dolphins count for more, and human beings count for most of all'.[25] What Sumner says about the severely abnormal is also very relevant;

A criterion of sentience also requires gentle usage of the severely abnormal. Cognitive disabilities and disorders may impair a person's range of sensibility, but they do not generally reduce that person to the level of a non-sentient being. Even the grossly retarded or deranged will still be capable of some forms of enjoyment and suffering, and thus will still possess (some) moral standing in their own right. This standing diminishes to the vanishing point only when sentience is entirely lost (irreversible coma) or never gained in the first place (anencephaly). If all affect and responsivity are absent, and if they cannot be engendered, then (but only then) are we no longer dealing with a sentient creature.[26]

Sumner's advocacy of the sentiency criterion as the basis for the moral right to life represents a real advance on the views of Tooley and those who follow him. It should be noted, however, that Sumner is more concerned with the right to life than with the category of persons. Persons naturally possess the right to life, together with some other rights, as we shall see later. It is not clear, however, that the moral right to life should exercise such a decisive force on the category of persons. It widens the category of persons in a way that is counterintuitive for many people, and, although there are some gains (e.g. non-human animals receive more consideration than in some other moral theories), these same positive features are capable of being dealt with satisfactorily by views of personhood which focus more particularly on human beings. Sumner's justification of human rights is ultimately utilitarian in character. This appears to ignore the distinctiveness of rights which either trump utility or function as part of the framework within which utility is calculated. Part of the issue, again, is what value is being attached to 'personhood' and 'human being' (cf. chapter 14 below where we argue for a theological justification of human rights). In Parts 2 and 3 it is argued that theology offers a framework within which such values make more sense.

# CHAPTER 4

# Personal identity and responsibility in D. Parfit

Another writer who has made the concept of 'person' central to his understanding and development of moral theory is D. Parfit, initially in a number of articles[1] and subsequently in *Reasons and Persons*. Unlike the previous authors we have considered, he concentrates on the significance of personal identity for an understanding of personhood, which can be applied in a wide range of moral issues, not simply issues which concern the beginning and end of life or non-human animals.

In his earlier articles Parfit argued for a Humean view of personal identity in which pyschological continuity or connectedness between different phases of a person's life exhausts the significance of personal identity. There is no further 'deep' fact, such as the persistence of a separate self over time. Radical discontinuity between our earlier and later selves should be acknowledged even if this seems to imperil the concept of responsibility for earlier actions. Like rivers which go underground, merge and reappear, like volcanoes which erupt, subside, lie dormant, and start again, or like nations, which change their boundaries, their membership, and their character, we are only in a weak sense the same persons that we used to be.

In *Reasons and Persons* he argues at greater length for the adoption of a reductionistic view of personal identity on the ground that this would contribute to a more consistent and effective moral theory. He describes the effect on himself of adopting such a view as 'liberating and consoling', although that is not his reason for adopting it. It is because he regards a reductionist view of 'persons' as true that he puts it forward.

He says: 'it makes me less concerned about my own future and my death, and more concerned about others'.[2] Clearly any theory which confers such benefits ought to be widely welcomed. Parfit is looking for a more adequate moral theory which will enable human beings to deal successfully with some of the unresolved conceptual and moral issues that prevent clear thinking about overpopulation, dwindling energy resources, conservation issues, nuclear defence, unemployment, and famine. Although his proposals do not yet cover all the necessary eventualities, he believes that they go a long way towards such a theory, and that he or others will soon be in a position to deliver such a theory based on his revised understanding of personhood.

How would this new concept of 'person' help? It is a common modern mistake, he says, to imagine that because the bad effects of an action on others are very slight the action may be morally permitted. In small communities in the past we harmed others only if we individually inflicted significant harm. But 'most of us now live in large communities'.[3] The effects of our bad actions are multiplied many thousands of times. In the wake of man-made disasters such as Bhopal, who could disagree? We are, he says, like torturers who individually inflict no great pain, but who together press a thousand buttons which in total inflict equal or more pain. In the bad old days the victim was tortured severely by one individual. Now the victim is tortured by a thousand torturers, each pressing his button and doing only a thousandth part of the harm done by the individual torturer previously; but the result is the same or worse.[4] 'Life in big cities is disturbingly impersonal . . . we need impersonal principles to avoid the bad effects of impersonality.'[5]

Parfit's conclusion is not the only legitimate conclusion one might draw. One might also ask how impersonal principles differ from other sorts of principles. But his decision to relate ethical theory to epistemological questions is worth examining, particularly in his arguments for a reductionist view of persons. By this view Parfit means any view which does not posit an entity which exists apart from or in addition to the experiences of the human subject, such as a soul or mind, and/or the physical body or brain of that subject. He grants that the most plausible unexamined view assumes a form of personal identity which is more than a reductionist can rationally believe in. When the implications of such an unexamined view are considered, however, it becomes more plausible to accept a reductionist view, which is compatible with psychological continuity, but which does not necessarily attempt to find a purely physical criterion for identity. Although there are no conclusive arguments to support the reductionist position, nevertheless, when a number of detailed and related positions are considered, the difficulties and inconsistencies of all views except reductionist views appear to Parfit so strong that a reductionist view becomes the most convincing. It is surprising, therefore, that section 82 ('How a non-reductionist view might have been true') is not argued more strongly. A stronger case for Cartesianism could and should have been made in order to rebut it thoroughly, if Parfit is to carry conviction in his claim that Cartesianism is unsatisfactory. He implies that Cartesian ego theory might have been confirmed in terms of evidence from reincarnation. There is no recognition of the limited value of empirical evidence in relation to theories of reincarnation. What empirical evidence could reincarnation provide, it might be asked. And would there not always be possible alternative interpretations, even if there were empirical evidence, so that the result would always be unclear? As was once said of another survival theory, 'even if someone should rise from the dead they would not believe'. Multiple claims of reincarnation would not strengthen the case as long as there was a widespread conviction that the dead do not survive. What is required for Cartesian ego theory to be true is not empirical evidence from reincarnation, but for the Cartesian view of mind and matter to make more sense than rival views such as materialism or non-materialist views of the self which do not hypothesise individual survival after death. Such a case for non-reductionism is not presented. This inevitably counts against the plausibility of Parfit's reductionism.

In section 79, it had seemed to be Parfit's strategy to make the two rival views a question of overall evaluation ('for a non-reductionist *personal identity is what matters* . . . for a reductionist *personal identity is not what matters*', his italics, p. 215). Instead of pursuing this, he examines a number of examples related to the theme of psychological or physical continuity and concludes that personal identity cannot matter, either because there is no way of resolving the outcome and there is nothing more that we could know that would help us to resolve the situation rationally, or because if the situation were resolved by arbitrary decision such a decision would represent little more than a decision to adopt a particular terminology and 'personal identity cannot be a matter of terminology'. To say this obscures the fact that terminology might be a substantive issue. For example, the debate between those who believe in resurrection and those who believe in reincarnation is both terminological and substantial. There is no means of resolving the dispute empirically. But to classify the dispute as '*merely* terminological' would be to miss the point. It would not represent the stance of either party and might suggest that both parties are simply mistaken. To take such a view is a substantive option, open only to someone who either stands outside the debate or knows something which most of us do not.

Parfit's view that personal identity does not matter seems to function as an evaluation which determines the conclusions he draws from his examples, rather than a conclusion to which he has been drawn by a consideration of relevant data and theories. He draws attention to some problematic data such as unusual combinations of brain cells from different persons together with their resulting psychological complexes in which thoughts and feelings are hypothetically and somewhat randomly redistributed. He also refers, with justification, to the importance of the overall framework of interpretation, usually drawn from metaphysics or theology, and occasionally influenced by scientific speculation. A form of Buddhism would certainly provide an appropriate *Weltanschauung* for Parfitian persons. But, apart from a brief appendix J, this is not argued for. The omission is serious in so far as the plausibility of his view depends not simply on individual arguments but on the overall context of interpretation. For instance, if the concept of responsibility for action requires the concept of a permanent self rather than person-phases, and if the concept of responsibility is fundamental to our outlook on life, this would predispose us not to accept hypothetical arguments in favour of person-phases.

Parfit's detailed arguments about why personal identity does not matter (*Reasons and Persons*, chapter 12) are tested against B. Williams' claim that personal identity must meet two requirements:[6] Requirement 1. Whether a future person will be me, must depend only on the intrinsic features of the relation between us. It cannot depend on what happens to other people. Requirement 2. Since personal identity has great significance, whether identity holds cannot depend on a trivial fact. These requirements, Parfit argues, cannot be met either by a psychological or physical criterion of personal identity. Williams' own arguments, however, undermine Williams' own favoured physical criterion just as much as the psychological criterion. If, on the other hand, we are content with a reductionist view, which offers rather less than personal identity, but something analogous to it (viz. psychological continuity), then it becomes possible to satisfy requirements which are analogous to, though not identical with, Williams' requirements.

The stages of the argument are as follows. For Williams, 'identity is logically a one–one relation. It is logically impossible for one person to be identical to more than one person. I cannot be one and the same person as two different people.' It follows that psychological continuity cannot be the criterion of identity. If it is replied that non-branching psychological continuity would meet the above objection, Williams replies that whether some future person will be me cannot depend on the non-existence of some second person, who is also physically and psychologically continuous, albeit to a lesser degree, with my former self. Once it is realised that there is a possibility of more than one replica, then, even if these possibilities are not realised and only one replica is produced, such a replica cannot claim personal identity with me, but only similarity. Williams uses this argument to support a form of physical criterion and to reject any form of psychological criterion. If it is claimed that a physical criterion might also fail to meet the requirements for personal identity, since it is possible 'to imagine a man splitting, amoeba-like, into two simulacra of himself' (p. 268), it can be replied that the physical criterion can at least be more easily defended because it would be easier to trace physical continuity and so to guard against cases of unsuspected or secret branching. Parfit simply denies this, and assumes that branching is no more of a problem for the psychological criterion than for the physical criterion. He concedes that branching is a real problem for any form of personal identity strictly conceived. He imagines that I have two fatally brain-damaged brothers. If my brain is removed and divided and successfully transplanted into one, it cannot be a condition of establishing personal identity that the other transplant, for whatever reason, fail, or that, in the case of both transplants being successful, one contain more than 50% of my brain, since a difference of 2% (the difference between 51% and 49%) can hardly constitute the difference between my surviving or not surviving. Parfit appeals in part to what is already known about brain-damage:

Many people lose large parts of their brain, but in consequence suffer no more than partial paralysis. These people are fully psychologically continuous with themselves before their injuries. We all believe that these people survive such injuries . . . Less than half a brain would be enough to provide full psychological continuity.

Neither the physical nor the psychological criterion can meet Williams' main requirement about personal identity, but, if the requirement is modified and similarity is substituted for identity, then Williams' stipulation, that whether I am some future person or not should depend solely on my relation to that future person, can stand. 'On this Reductionist View we should take the importance that we give to a judgement of identity, and we should give this importance to a different relation. On this view what is important is relation R: psychological connectedness and/or continuity, with the right kind of cause.' The concepts of identity and exact similarity remain distinct. In some cases the distinction may make little practical difference; in other cases the distinction will be important. But, in any case, it is only a reductionist view which allows one to make sense of Williams' requirements and his examples, says Parfit.

In his discussion of the nature of personal identity and its criteria and of the differences between personal identity and exact similarity, Parfit frequently refers to the problem of an arbitrary cut-off point, which arises particularly in connection with the amount of brain transplant which would guarantee the survival of personal identity. He regards it as most implausible that the difference between whether a future person is me or not me, might be a matter of the difference between 49% and 51%, if the criterion were fixed as simply 'more than half'. There is the further problem that if the criterion is pitched too high, then this may conflict with what already happens when someone continues to exist but with the loss of more than half his brain. In *Philosophical Explanations*, R. Nozick ventures the pragmatic solution that, instead of trying to fix a specific amount or number of surviving brain cells, something more flexible should be sought. His own suggestion is the Closest Continuer Schema, whereby 'to be the same as some past thing is to be that thing's closest continuer'. Nozick is careful to distinguish this from 'the continuer than which none is closer', in order to rule out the possibility of an exact tie, in which two beings equally closely continue X's existence. He explains the asymmetry of identity and similarity in terms of caring and closeness. 'It may appear incoherent to care especially about the closest continuer, but not care especially that there be a continuer that is closest. Focussing on the gap between the closest continuer and the next closest, it is as if I care a lot about this gap when it exists, but do not care at all whether there is this gap. If the gap is important enough to care about when it exists, how can its existing not be important?'[7] Nozick's answer relates to his belief that identity (not similarity) matters, and that it involves a one to one relation between present and future selves. He admits that his closest continuer schema works better in adjudicating the identities of other persons rather than myself, since the schema is difficult to apply without smuggling in unresolved ambiguities in terms of 'I'.

Parfit recognises that Nozick's view has much in common with his own, and to that extent welcomes it. He cannot accept, however, that identity (rather than continuity) matters. Hence he rejects Nozick's asymmetry and his refusal to allow more than one closest continuer. He objects to the apparent arbitrariness of deciding which of two close continuers, both embodying enough similarity to qualify for identity if there had been only one of them, is the closest, and deciding, perhaps by a mere fraction, that one shares identity and the other does not.

It is perhaps inevitable that cut-off points and boundary criteria, of whatever sort, should appear arbitrary. Boundaries are often determined by rules or conventions – length of wicket in the game of cricket, size of pitch in football, age of retirement, school-leaving age, and so on. This does not mean that either the boundaries or the conventions are irrational. Behind an agreed convention may lie a long history of reasoning, negotiation and compromise. Boundary disputes are resolved by appeal to agreed conventions. In the case of personal identity, however, there appear to be no longer any agreed conventions or undisputed criteria. Body and memory have been traditional and rival candidates. Clearly both are relevant. Their relationship, however, and their use are problematic. In recent literature, the body, particularly in terms of the brain, has gained increasing favour as an indispensable criterion, and this has tended to concentrate interest on potential future empirical developments and hence imaginary cases of fusion, fission and transplant in an attempt to clarify underlying principles. If comparison is made with other recently disputed cut-off points in areas related to personal identity such as birth, death, change of sex, it would seem that progress is most likely to be made by a combination of conceptual revision and empirical inquiry. Comparisons have also been made with other entities undergoing rapid or drastic change (e.g. corporate bodies, such as clubs or nations or natural entities such as rivers and volcanoes). It seems likely that these analogies will be less fruitful. Parfit's attempt to push personal identity in this direction seems forced and strained. Whether there can be *degrees* of personal identity seems likely to be the crux of the question.

Serious objections have often been brought against any assimilation of personal identity to the identity of objects (although it was such comparisons that lay behind the discussions in Locke, Reid, Hume, and others). These objections have recently been renewed by Madell in *The Identity of the Self*. He has also urged with some justification that first-person usage constitutes an insuperable obstacle to reductionist views, not simply because 'I' is a token-reflexive word like 'now' or 'you', but because 'I' is 'presupposed' by indexicals such as 'now' and 'you'. 'I', he argues, is a logically proper noun; it is neither a non-referential index word nor a propertyless referential term of self-referral. On such a propertyless view, he argues, it is capable of being combined with an ontology of person-phases 'in which persons, or minds, are just sequences of events which are essentially separable from each other'.[8] He draws particularly on McTaggart and Castaneda to refute the arguments of Vesey, Zemach, Ryle, Boer and Lycan. I is an 'unanalysable, ineliminable, referential term'[9] and 'uniquely so'.[10] 'We recognise that to say of a set of properties that they are mine is to say something more than to say that such a set is instantiated. We have, then, to recognise that I must have an awareness of myself which is independent of the knowledge that a certain set of properties is instantiated if I am to see that set of properties as my own.'[11] Parfit argues that Madell's discussion is mistaken because 'mine' can be translated as 'this experience'. 'Since I can use "this", I do not need to use "mine" – and being "mine" is not a property, anyway. Moreover, the actual cases of divided minds provide an objection to Madell's view.'[12] In this instance Parfit appears to have misunderstood Madell. Although Madell does italicise 'property', his main argument is not about 'mine' being a 'property', but about the significance of 'I' and 'mine'. He is arguing for an anti-empiricist view of the self in which 'I' is not identifiable with a body or with a set of experiences.

Examples of divided minds do not, for Madell, disprove the

unique and unanalysable nature of 'I'. There is no way of identifying a person by means of any particular set of experiences or simply in terms of a body. Parfit agrees with Madell in wishing to dispose of the body as a criterion, but he wishes to retain psychological continuity to relate one person-phase to another. Madell's argument is that this is logically mistaken because every such attempt presupposes or smuggles back in again a use of 'I' which is strictly non-empirical and unanalysable. Both Parfit and Madell agree that two persons may have two simultaneous experiences that are qualitatively identical but straightforwardly distinct.

Fundamentally the disagreement between Parfit and Madell relates to Madell's rejection of all empirical criteria for the self which do not take into account the use of 'I' as a basic, unanalysable logically proper noun. Madell rejects an ontology of person-phases, and Parfit rejects the notion of an unanalysable 'I' and the ontology of a determinate unitary self.

Both writers seem to be strongly motivated by their ontology of the person, although specific discussion of criteria for adopting a particular person ontology is lacking. The discussion revolves round the interpretation of 'I' and the significance of thought experiments based on brain transplants. If the ontological factors are brought more closely into the foreground and the choice of an ontology of the person is examined more closely, it appears that, while both Parfit and Madell appeal to a combination of intuition, rational analysis and empirical evidence each ultimately justifies his view of 'person' by reference to an overall value judgement, which in Madell's case is supported by 'common sense views of a unitary self' and in Parfit's case by a 'rationality' which is at odds with many common-sense assumptions and beliefs. Madell is prepared to concede that, if we are willing to revise many of our ordinary attitudes and beliefs about the unitary nature of the self, then psychological continuity may be a necessary (but not sufficient) condition of personal identity.[13] Such a concession, however, is not strictly required, Madell argues. The importance of psychological continuity is the way it functions as a necessary condition of a range of moral attitudes which presuppose

personal identity over a period of time. Parfit, on the other
hand, is clearly worried that his ontology of the person seems
to conflict with common sense and that a majority of thinking
people favour a stronger form of personal identity than his
reductionist view supports. He has to work extremely hard to
try to show that if the links between the earlier and later self
are weakened, and theories about rational self-interest are
dispensed with, an overall utilitarian view of morality can still
be argued for. A great deal hinges on the results of the
imaginary examples about divided minds. The alternatives
posed by Parfit – when a single mind is divided, then (a) only
one or (b) neither or (c) both of the resulting persons is identical
with the undivided self – do not resolve the issue of personal
identity in favour of a reductionistic view of the self, however.

By drawing attention to elements of discontinuity in the lives
of persons between present and former selves, Parfit seeks to
develop a view of personal identity in which person-phases
replace the single continuous person. The theory of person-
phases is then used to reduce distinctions between individuals
and to argue for an ethical theory which gives more weight to
overall utility and less weight to individual persons. Parfit's
reminder of change, growth, and decay in human organisms is
timely, but his arguments do not add up to the death of the
unitary self. It may sometimes have been too readily assumed
that moral considerations require a continuity of self, but the
issue is more complex than Parfit allows. What is at issue is not
simply the interrelationship of a theory of mind and a theory of
morality, but justifications of different world-views, which may
require discussion at some point of the overall concept of
'person', including issues of death and immortality. Parfit is
searching for a non-religious foundation for an ethic of
altruism, but he is unwilling to allow the requirements of his
ethic to override his reductionist view of persons.

Parfit's case does not rest ultimately on the number of valid
arguments he offers, but on his overall position, which succeeds
or fails to carry conviction not simply by virtue of its detailed
arguments, but because its broad implications tie in with a
number of other important views about the nature of the self

and society. In this respect, religious and theological views may assume great significance. For instance, those who, because of their belief in a Creator-Saviour God, active in the history of humanity, have begun to modify some of their instinctive and learned individualism in favour of a social order in which less weight is given to individual freedoms and more weight to social justice, love, and forgiveness, particularly when this is linked with beliefs about human frailty and sinfulness, will naturally bring these views into their discussion and interpretation of personal identity. Within such a religious view individual exponents will attach different value to some of the empirical features and to specific applications of such views in the fields of medicine, education, national defence or conservation of the environment, but it is important to recognise the part played in such value-judgements by religious, theological and metaphysical considerations. Parfit's view of personal identity and morality not only supports, but is supported by, an overall commitment in which the boundaries of the individual self count for less than common-sense favours. This new picture of the self will find it more difficult to deal satisfactorily with the language of individual human rights and responsibilities, the highly specific and, some would say, unique flavour of personal relationships, and all those views which give prominence to the difference between self and world.

There is value in Parfit's emphasis on discontinuity, however, even for those who radically disagree with him. Those who believe in the resurrection of the body or who believe that a person may in some form survive death still have to wrestle with the radical discontinuity which death brings. Parfit also draws attention to the discontinuities which may develop within a single life. Nevertheless, even the most extreme changes which he envisages do not prove a reductionist view of the self or a theory of person-phases, for the very reason that even when reduced the continuity of personal identity is assumed. Drastic surgery, total or partial loss of memory, and the acquisition of new memory patterns as a result of brain surgery do not alter this picture. Certainly character and temperament may alter, even violently, as a result of physical change, and physical accidents may result in total changes of personality. Even in these cases, however, it seems difficult to argue that personal identity has been destroyed or lost or totally changed. It seems to be a valid objection to Parfit's view that, even when the links between past and present phases of a person's life become very tenuous, they do not normally disappear. Nor do individuals disclaim responsibility for their past actions simply because they have changed. When it does happen, as, for example, when an artist disclaims earlier works or a politician earlier views, this is more naturally interpeted as a statement of artistic or political belief rather than a statement about the logic of personal identity. Even the disclaimer usually embodies the recognition that there is a continuing self, though this self has undergone a radical change in artistic or political sensibility. Neither radical physical change nor radical psychological change means that personal identity must be construed in terms of person-phases.

On the other hand, a non-empirical view of personal identity, which regards first-person usage as unique and underivative, presupposed by other indexicals such as 'you', 'now', 'here', need not deny all recognition of empirical person-phases. What it denies is that personal identity is most satisfactorily interpreted in terms of person-phases. The example of divided minds demonstrates only that there may be cases of genuine uncertainty and that the criteria for resolving some of these disputes are not yet agreed. The content that is given to personal identity is frequently dependent on a wider framework which is influenced by, or takes into account, theories of soul or materialism, which are not, in themselves, open to conclusive proof or disproof.

There is at least one further factor that tells heavily against Parfit's construal. Personal identity is concerned in large part with numerical identity. Without numerical identity some of the subjective considerations involved in examining cases of fission or fusion would not even arise. Identity is normally distinguished from similarity or continuity of character. When this numerical identity is construed from the standpoint of a third party, it is natural to locate one essential criterion of numerical identity in the changing body/brain. The question is complicated in the case of persons because, as it seems to them, their perspective, however much influenced by body/brain patterns, issues in thoughts and feelings which seem distinct from these patterns, so that the person concerned begins not only to refer to her own self-consciousness, but to presuppose a continuous identity in her first-person utterances even when arguing about the criteria of personal identity and aware of features of empirical discontinuity. The numerical identity which is presupposed seems to be logically necessary because without it it would not be possible to use 'I' coherently and consistently. Parfit recognises the intimate relationship between common-sense assumptions about personal identity and philosophical arguments for a determinate unitary self, by arguing both (a) personal identity consists of person-phases, and (b) personal identity does not matter. The only satisfactory way of talking about person-phases is to get rid of talk about personal identity. If, however, the main reason for taking a reductionist view is to be able to deal with divided minds and experiences of discontinuity, it would seem that (b) is unnecessarily drastic, and that (a) is not warranted by the evidence. One is left with the feeling that for an unanalysable 'I' Parfit has substituted an unspecifiable continuity. Perhaps some sort of philosophical health warning ought to be attached to the word 'I' to indicate its dangers. This is no reason, however, for assuming that 'personal identity does not matter'.[14]

Parfit applies his views about personal identity to moral issues in extremely ingenious ways, and there is no doubt that they contribute to the development of an interesting style of utilitarianism. He writes: 'On this Reductionist View, persons do exist. But they exist only in the way in which nations exist. Persons are not, as we mistakenly believe, *fundamental* [his italics] . . . This view supports claims about both rationality and morality . . . It is more plausible to focus not on persons but on experiences . . . My conclusions again give less importance both to the unity of each life and to the boundaries between lives.'[15] At a number of points he criticises views of morality which give preference to self-interest. He wishes to defend a modified utilitarianism which borders on rational altruism. He also supports a view of happiness which maximises the number of beneficiaries. He is worried, however, about the consequences of such views for overpopulation. He is also anxious lest concern for our own immediate futures imperil what he regards as our obligation to future generations.

His discussion of personal identity is set within this context and is intended to contribute to the clarification and solution of the moral issues involved. There is at least a hint, namely in Appendix J ('Buddha's View'), that his combined ethic cum philosophy of mind has or requires a metaphysical context or anchor. He also states in his concluding chapter that 'Metaphysics *can* [his italics] produce the consolations of philosophy.'[16] Unfortunately he does not go into greater detail about the relationship of religion and morality or consider competing anthropologies. He links his own belief in the possibility of progress in ethics with the advances he looks for in 'Non-Religious Ethics'.[17] We have given reasons for doubting this optimism. Later we shall argue for an ethic more closely related to a different concept of person and to Christian ethical traditions that is also capable of taking into account our obligation to future generations and the problems of overpopulation. The concept of persons made in God's image, exercising stewardship on God's behalf, constantly needing to be re-formed so as to conform to His image and respond creatively to His will, showing and receiving love and mercy until the day when God's kingdom is established, suggests an ethic that is no less rational and compassionate and that is capable of coping with the lethargy and despair, technological madness and greed by which we are in danger of destroying one another.

# CHAPTER 5

# Human subject and human worth

We are now in a position to draw together some of the issues that have been considered in chapters 1–4. We have seen the contested nature of 'personhood' and some of the different contexts in which the concept has been used. It appears that one of its attractions to some moral philosophers is the possibility that it seems to allow persons to be distinguished from human beings. In a medical context of scarce resources and new technology which is multiplying the occasions when more human needs can be met only by establishing criteria to determine which individuals and needs should benefit from these resources, a distinction between human being and person which automatically gave preference to 'persons' would seem a great boon to hard-pressed medical teams and their ethical panels. In situations where life can be prolonged almost indefinitely, but only at great cost, on a life-support system, it would seem to be an advantage to know in advance that 'persons' had preference and that human life without the protection of personhood need not be preserved in the same way.

This apparent advantage, however, is also being purchased at great cost, both in terms of the human lives which may be unjustly neglected or terminated and in terms of a mistaken conceptual clarity. We have already referred to some of the problems in the so-called solutions of Tooley and Singer in respect of abortion and infanticide and the treatment of non-human animals (similar problems arise also in the case of euthanasia): the lack of consistency between the utilitarian stance which these writers adopt and neglect of the future potential of the foetus, and between concern for the welfare of non-human animals and a willingness to contemplate the killing of certain human beings. This inconsistency is further compounded by weaknesses in the detail of the argumentation, despite Tooley's strenuous efforts to clarify what is meant by personhood and to develop watertight arguments to substantiate conclusions which he knows are unpalatable to many human beings.

His own indecision about whether to regard 'personhood' as largely if not purely evaluative, conferring the right to life, or whether to regard it as essentially descriptive, should have indicated to him that his attempts to reverse both common intuitions about the preservation of human life and linguistic usage would encounter opposition. They should also have indicated to him that his supporting arguments about animal pain and interests would need both good empirical evidence and sensitive judgement in addition to clear logic. His lengthy argument about the rights of the kitten fails on all counts.

This suggests that a great deal is at stake if philosophers are prepared to go to such lengths to try to substantiate a difficult if not impossible case. This is confirmed by the extreme value which we have noticed is given to 'personhood' in some of the literature, particularly since Kant. Some of the motivation for this trend is quite ancient, associated with the belief that persons are soul or spirit. In modern times, it may be that the reduction of 'human beings' has contributed by contrast to the exaltation of 'personhood', even if that personhood is now associated with some feature such as language-use or moral autonomy, once associated exclusively with human beings. In other words, we are witnessing the increasingly bifurcated understanding of human being/person, which is leading to two different tendencies: an attempt to *exclude* certain human beings who have previously been included as persons (namely, the senile and foetuses), and an attempt to *include* certain non-human animals who were not previously regarded as persons.

The assumption that 'human being' is a purely biological category, unlike 'person' which is a social or moral category, does not do justice to the fact that 'human being' also has evaluative significance. The view that to be human simply means to be a member of a biological species represents a normative view of what it means to be human. In the religious conceptions of most cultures, human beings are regarded as being considerably more than this. In a Christian metaphysic, human beings are made in the image of God. (It may, of course, also be true that the Christian view of human beings as sinners, when separated from its context in the drama of salvation, exacerbates the potential bifurcation between human weakness and the potential glory of true personhood.) To argue now that personhood and being human should not be separated may seem like trying to put the clock back. It is significant, however, that in all the discussions, even including those based on science-fiction or thought experiments, the starting-point and implicit criterion of personhood usually remains the adult human being. Wilkes,[1] writing from an empiricist philosophical standpoint, finds most thought experiments miss the point. She argues clearly and strongly for a common-sense view which would identify 'person' with 'human being' for most practical purposes. She expresses this view as follows: 'Most single human beings just are, unproblematically, single persons. Conversely, we know of no *non*-humans such that any significant number of people regard them as true persons. I have been making the obvious and trivial point that the normal human being is our sole paradigm of personhood.' From this starting-point, which is also her eventual conclusion, she is able, with the help of Dennett's 'conditions of personhood', to indicate what it is about human beings that is associated with their desirable qualities of personhood. Persons are rational subjects to whom we ascribe intentional action, moral agents and patients, language-users with a special kind of consciousness. Wilkes hesitates about adding 'tool-making and tool-using' and leaves the question open, although she gives reasons for thinking that philosophers may have neglected craft-skills and overemphasised language in their interpretation of what it means to be human. These criteria she regards as fairly uncontroversial and clear, although they may need to be made more precise. They would exclude 'most if not all non-human animals'. The moral predicaments involving the killing/use of non-human animals, and the moral issues related to the care of the senile or the protection of the foetus, would be solved more naturally by the use of different arguments, i.e. by typical moral considerations that appeal to benevolence and obligation, than by appeal to the distinction of person and non-person. Any moral predicaments concerning the status of 'intelligent' computers would be handled similarly, noting in this case that, despite their possible sharing of some human characteristics, such as intelligence and language, they lack entirely the ability to form reciprocal relationships and do not have feelings or attitudes. To attribute human characteristics to machines – 'my machine has a mind of its own' – is clearly metaphorical.

It is not necessary to argue that only human beings are (or, more strongly, could be) persons, in order to accept that the two ideas should be kept together and not separated. If one thinks of 'person' as an open cluster concept, with no final agreed instantiation yet most clearly exemplified in most if not all adult human beings, it may make good sense to enquire whether any individuals other than human beings also qualify. To raise the question about other candidates than humans, as Singer and Tooley do, is entirely proper in principle. But, in the end, their arguments turn out to be unconvincing.

Why this is so is related to the normative status of person-hood. Human beings decide who are persons. But is this not a form of 'speciesism' (cf. p. 45 above)? The charge of speciesism only works if the distinction of person-human is accepted and the values that are thought to be associated with persons are transferred – either arbitrarily without reason or as a matter of deliberate but unfair policy – to humans. But, since the values and qualities are ones that characterise human beings anyway, it can hardly be arbitrary or unfair to associate them with human beings, even if it is clear that some individual human beings have lost or not yet gained or never had these qualities. It is more important to recognise any unfairness and lack of rational explanation when it exists in the treatment of non-humans, and the present study does not suggest that there are not plenty of such instances, than to argue that some non-humans are persons or deserve to be treated so. We may, in fact, be doing a real disservice to the dolphin in treating it as a person. As we shall notice later, considerable moral demands may also be made on those who are deemed to be persons. One of the real problems of the anthropological reversal mediated through Kant and Feuerbach is the super-human demands that may then be transferred from divine persons to other persons.

Most of the moral campaigns and victories associated with 'speciesism' do not, in fact, need the help of this unsatisfactory term, which tends to be used as a term of opprobrium but without clear explanation. For example, there are many good reasons for being a vegetarian, which is an ancient practice adopted by the Pythagoreans and other scrupulous groups: concern for the suffering/well-being of animals which are killed to provide food; religious beliefs about how God intended humankind to live; concern for the starving in developing countries today; concern for the future of the planet. But that non-human animals are persons does not seem to be a very strong argument in favour of the practice. This is not to deny that as a teaching strategy it may be a useful way to introduce a number of related issues (e.g. vegetarianism, animal rights) because the issue of personhood remains a lively, contested contemporary issue. Something similar may be said about the extension of personhood and moral standing to trees and stones. Ecological issues related to the person–nature divide do not require nature to become a person, as we shall see in chapter 15.[2]

The claim that 'personhood' can be divorced from 'being human' embodies a huge assumption: namely, that 'human being' is a purely descriptive term, morally neutral or insignificant, whereas 'person' is evaluative and refers to a moral agent. This assumption is then linked with other assumptions about the syllogistic nature of moral argument and the rational nature of moral justification. Not infrequently the ultimate justification proves to be utilitarian, concealing a nest of problems about the *summum bonum* for humans and utilitarianism's inability to calculate the worth of a single human life.

The greater value attached to personhood compared with human life is developed, as we saw (pp. 45, 73), in two different ways. Singer and Tooley focus on the contrast of 'person' and 'human' and link personhood with the right to life, whereas Parfit focusses on the question of personal identity. Singer and Tooley inflate personhood; Parfit prefers to deflate it. Both strategies have the same goal: to influence and change opinion in the moral debates related to the value of human and non-human animal life, the future of planetary life and the use of resources. Both routes are problematic. The issues are complex and the concept of person that is being used is inadequate to deal with the issues posed. A Christian understanding of personhood, as we shall see later, takes account of other important factors, not just the distinction of person and human. In the moral debates about abortion and the moral standing of non-human animals, it is important to give attention to relevant empirical features (such as the development of the foetus, or animal welfare in certain methods of factory farming), definitional issues, other values and the wider moral outlook and commitments of the individuals and communities involved. These may be related to religious beliefs about the createdness of the world or the perception of what is involved in rearing, transporting and slaughtering non-human animals to produce food for humans.

As a result of these considerations, it appears that the case for giving 'person' but not 'human' an evaluative and moral connotation has not been made out, either by the Singer–Tooley or by the Parfit strategy. There is still point, morally speaking, in holding person and human being together and not separating them. Why not, then, identify 'person' and 'human being'? The reason lies in the next part of the study which examines historical usage and the association of personhood with both humanity and divinity.

The historical background which helps to explain this debate about 'personhood' in contemporary ethics is to be located in two very different collections of material: the Christological and Trinitarian debates of the early church; and philosophical discussions from the modern period, particularly in Locke, Kant, Hegel and Feuerbach, to name some representative figures. We begin with these philosophical discussions because they are closer in spirit and time to the contemporary ethical material we have just considered, and help to explain some of the ideas encountered there.

The Reformation and the changed social conditions of the fifteenth and sixteenth centuries paved the way for an important shift in the understanding of 'person' in the thought of the seventeenth and eighteenth centuries. The idea of the individual person reasserts itself, but the theological dimension seems to recede. 'Person' becomes firmly associated with discussions about the nature of man. The transition is most clearly marked in Locke's famous words:

we must consider what person stands for; which, I think, is a thinking intelligent being, that has reason and reflection, and can consider itself, the same thinking thing, in different times and places; which it does only by that consciousness which is inseparable from thinking and seems to me essential to it; it being impossible for anyone to perceive without perceiving that he does perceive.[3]

This is not an isolated passage in Locke. Although he does sometimes use 'person' to mean simply 'human individual' (e.g. *Essay Concerning Human Understanding*, 1.3.3; 1.4.22; 2.25.5)[4] he more frequently distinguishes 'man' from 'person' in order to refer to persons as responsible, self-conscious, moral beings. Elsewhere he distinguishes soul and person. A man is a combination of body and soul. For Locke a person is not simply a soul substance, or a combination of body and soul, but 'a Forensick Term appropriating Actions and their Merit'. The forensic emphasis of 'person' in Locke is closely related to his view that moral responsibility requires rational thought, and to his view of man as a complex, self-conscious body–mind unity. Why Locke used the term 'person' rather than any other, however, has never been satisfactorily explained. Yolton, for example, discusses how rather than why Locke uses the term (pp. 28–32): 'Person [in Locke] refers to a man who can take responsibility for his actions and who is concerned with those actions and their consequences, a man who is vitally interested in his moral worth and his happiness, and who recognises he is God's workmanship. It is the concern – the moral, responsible concern – taken for what he does which Locke stresses in his depiction of a person.'[5] On this view, self-consciousness is part of what is involved in the self-ownership needed for responsible moral action. It is conceptually tied to 'persons'. It is not simply an empirical test, although it is supported by good empirical grounds. (cf. *Essay*, 27.23: 'nothing but consciousness can unite remote Existences into the same Person, the Identity of Substance will not do it. For whatever Substance there is, however framed, without consciousness, there is no Person.')

Responsible action is connected in Locke's view with questions of personal identity, which he explores, at least in part, for their own sake. Even in the puzzle-cases he raises, however, he is concerned ultimately to stress that God will not punish anyone for deeds they 'know nothing of' (*Essay*, 2.27.22; cf. Yolton, *Locke: an Introduction*, p. 31). On the Day of Judgement the sentence 'shall be justified by the consciousness all Persons shall have, that they themselves in what Bodies soever they appear, or what Substances soever the consciousness adheres to, are the same that committed those Actions and deserve the Punishment for them'. As Yolton puts it, 'The person or self is constituted by the actions he performs and by the awareness he has of those actions as his.'[6] Yolton makes the further point that Locke is not primarily concerned at this point to ward off scepticism about knowledge of other minds, but to emphasise that ' "person" is properly a first-person term':

It is this first-person awareness of my actions which is the basis of moral responsibility. That awareness, too, constitutes my identity as a person, my personal identity, my 'personal self'.[7]

None of this, however, explains why Locke selected the term 'person' to convey these ideas. It is hardly likely that Locke invented an entirely new use of the term. Yolton is at pains to play down the theological background of the term and instances Locke's differences with Stillingfleet, Bishop of Worcester. 'His tactic with the Bishop is to argue that his various accounts of knowledge, certainty, ideas, belief, reason, person, have no implications for theology . . . and that the theological language and doctrines invoked by Stillingfleet cannot be found in the Bible'.[8] It can hardly be accidental, however, that Locke used a term which was very much in vogue, particularly in theological discussions of the day.[9] In 1918, C. C. J. Webb ventured the hypothesis that 'the expression "self-consciousness" probably originated in England where we find it used by Locke and other writers of his time and playing a considerable part in the Trinitarian controversy which agitated the learned of that country at the end of the seventeenth and beginning of the eighteenth century'.[10] C. Taylor also refers to 'the seventeenth century epistemologically grounded notion of the subject'.[11] Webb's assumption that the association of the term 'person' and 'self-consciousness' originated in England appears less probable in view of the clear association of 'Person' and 'Selbstbewusstsein' in discussions relating to the Augsburg Confession in the sixteenth century. From this and similar references to 'self-consciousness' in the literature of the period it is clear that the idea of 'person' has become very much associated with the internal workings of the mind. The interest displayed in the problems of personal identity and memory are another sign of this.[12]

The fact that Locke did not agree with the Bishop of Worcester does not exclude theological and metaphysical influence on his choice of 'person' to convey his combination of identity, self-consciousness and moral responsibility.[13] The theological context, in fact, offers several good reasons for his choice of 'person'. It was a term of current but shifting significance, as indicated in his contemporary Sherlock, and it already combined many of the emphases he wished to articulate regarding the human subject. The fact that it had been applied to the incarnate Christ, as the second person of the Trinity, meant that it was not simply transferring to the human subject a term applied chiefly to God. In any case, the old (dramatic?) usage of role-player and the use of 'person' to refer to any human individual was available to be drawn on. Locke did not have to invent an entirely new usage, but he was able to reposition it, applying it primarily to the responsible subject and beginning a process which was to receive more radical expression, as we shall see, in the nineteenth century, particularly in the work of Kant and Feuerbach.

It seems unlikely that Locke would have drawn from his account the consequences that have been suggested by modern writers such as Tooley and Singer or Parfit, but it is clear that, like them, he would not identify 'person' with 'human individual'. By stressing moral accountability, Locke makes freedom and a certain level of rational development a necessary condition of personhood. Since children, according to Locke, lack this ability, they are not accountable and are not persons. In this he reflected the seventeenth-century view that children are incipient adults; but lacking adult powers they are also relieved of adult responsibility. Hence, they do not qualify as 'persons'. There is no sign in Locke, however, of Tooley's drastic remodelling of 'personhood' making it equivalent to 'having a right to life'. For Locke, persons are moral agents; but there is no suggestion that only moral agents have moral worth.

Kant's use of 'person' to signify the quintessential moral subject who is deserving of respect has been even more influential than the Lockean use in ensuring the continuation of discussions of 'person' in modern moral philosophy. And some (e.g. MacIntyre) would find in Kant the source of many of our modern dilemmas. It is necessary, therefore, to examine Kant's views more closely. Without attempting to set out all the ingredients of Kant's moral philosophy, we shall examine the significant but unusual features of 'person' in Kant's thought and consider how these contributed to later views of personhood.

In the *Grundlegung*, Kant moves from ordinary rational knowledge of morality to philosophical knowledge of morality. Only a good will is good without qualification, he assumes. But what is a good will? Not something which is good because of its consequences (e.g. happiness) or because of something outside itself. Consideration of duty, despite its empirical limitations, can help towards an understanding of the good will. The principle of duty derives solely from the principle of volition involved (acting from a sense of duty) and does not depend on the attainment of any ulterior ends; it is essentially the necessity to act out of reverence for the law.

> Since I have robbed the will of every inducement that might arise for it as a conseqence of obeying any particular law, nothing is left but the conformity of actions to universal law as such, and this alone must serve the will as its principle. That is to say, I ought never to act except in such a way that I can also will that my maxim should become a universal law.[14]

Ordinary reason, he thinks, would also agree with such a canon. Eventually (p. 88–421/52) this is formulated as the categorical imperative. In developing this view, Kant assigns a unique status to 'persons'. Persons, unlike things, are to be treated as ends in themselves. Respect is due to persons because they are embodiments of the universal moral law. This brief statement, however, hardly recaptures the paradoxical nature of Kant's theory. Kant is operating with a distinction of persons and things which he did not invent, but which he elaborates in such a way that it begins to represent positions that are peculiar to his moral philosophy. When he says 'respect always applies to persons only, never to things', this may seem unobjectionable, although one might wonder why respect should be limited in this way. Respect for property is different from respect for people, but why should it be excluded or rejected, particularly if the property in question is precious or even irreplaceable? But to think in this way is to fail to appreciate the fairly severe limitations and restrictions which Kant places on 'respect' and 'persons' by integrating them into his moral philosophy.

In chapter 2 of the *Grundlegung*, Kant has argued that for a moral principle to be fundamental it must be more than a generalisation based on experience. It must be a priori. In this sense it will not simply appeal to human reason; 'we . . . ought rather to derive our principles from the general concept of a rational being as such'. Only later, with the help of anthropology, will it be applied to man. Since man is not thoroughly rational, of course, acting in accordance with law is not automatic, as in the case of a divine being, and, therefore, to

bring objective law and subjective will into relationship requires the necessity of imperatives, and, in the case of the
moral law, the categorical imperative a priori, now formulated
as 'act only on that maxim through which you can at the same
time will that it should become a universal law'. All imperatives
of duty, Kant implies, are versions of this Categorical Imperative. Kant restates the necessity in his view for the supreme
principle of morality to apply to all rational beings. Human
nature and its psychology are to that extent irrelevant to the
fundamental principle of morality. It is a metaphysical question
about a necessary law for all rational beings. Is there such a
law? What is it? Kant's answer, beginning in section 428 of the
*Grundlegung*, is that 'something whose existence has an absolute
value in itself, something which as an end in itself could be a
ground of determinate laws, could be the ground of a possible
categorical imperative'. Rational beings, he continues, exist as
ends in themselves and can supply such a law. 'Such rational
beings are called persons, because their nature already marks
them out as ends in themselves . . . Persons, therefore, are
objective ends . . . unless this is so, nothing at all of absolute
value would be found anywhere.'[15] These words deserve to be
printed in red; so powerful has been their impact on later
thought. Commentators are divided, however, over the merits
of Kant's arguments in this section. Aune draws on Kant's
discussion of nature as a system of natural ends in the *Critique of
Judgement* to illustrate how Kant may have been influenced by
the idea that 'man is the final end of creation. Without man the
chain of mutually subordinated ends would have no ultimate
point of attachment.' He regards it, however, as 'an astonishing,
even extravagant view to take of a perverse creature such as
man'.[16] Aune finds no difficulty in thinking that Kant's view of
teleology in nature was at this point thoroughly anthropocentric. P. Haezrahi[17] regards the idea of the dignity of man *qua*
man as gratuitously injected into the argument by the irrational
power of some intuition rather than a rationally demonstrable
deduction. She claims to find intrusions of a similar idea in Mill
and Sartre, which suggests to her that some powerful intuition
is at these points overriding rational argument. She draws

attention to R. Otto's notes on the *Grundlegung*, in which he said, 'It is with great inner emotion that we look upon this eruption of a deep and independent intuition, for we are privileged to witness the birth of the mightiest and most significant of all ideas that were ever pronounced in the domain of ethical inquiry. The idea of a concrete, existent value-in-and-for-itself, an idea moreover which reason can accept and respect.'

H. E. Jones, while critical of certain of Kant's arguments, rejects Haezrahi's view that Kant, like Mill and Sartre, is attempting to argue (invalidly) from the rational agent's own experience to the experience of all other rational agents.[18] 'Kant's argument must stand or fall on the validity of his claims regarding the connection between rationality and dignity.'[19] Jones finds this link in Kant's references to man as an objective end in the sense of a limiting condition for all subjective ends.[20] 'For to be an end-in-itself is simply to be a supreme limiting condition for actions and ends.' Rationality is the supreme condition restricting man's willing and acting. 'To be a fully moral or virtuous being is to be a fully rational one.' Jones appears to be justified in contending that the parallels from Mill and Sartre do not have strict argumentative force, but it is doubtful whether Jones has correctly interpreted Haezrahi's view of Kant, viz. as if Kant was arguing from experience. Haezrahi draws attention to the source of Kant's imagery in Rousseau. In 1764 Kant wrote as follows: 'True virtue can be grown only on principles; the more universal these principles, the nobler and more elevated the virtue. These principles are not speculative rules of reason, but the awareness of a feeling which dwells in every human heart and which is more than mere pity and helpfulness. I think this sentiment is best described as a feeling for the Beauty and Dignity of human nature.' In Rousseau, this feeling is innate in human nature. But Kant later rejected this view in order to locate human dignity solely in rationality or the determination of will by reason.

Haezrahi thinks the possibility of a will determined by reason was deduced from the presupposed possibility of freedom. Jones replies that Kant makes no reference to freedom in the *Grundlegung* at this point. But, although Jones is correct about this detail, Haezrahi is pointing to something overlooked by many commentators, namely, Kant's use of 'person' to refer to rational beings belonging to the noumenal world. Kant invests 'persons' with such attributes that they begin to approximate to divine lawgivers. A 'person' possesses 'dignity', which is elsewhere defined as 'absolute inner worth',[21] 'by which he exacts respect for himself from all other rational beings in the world'. References to the 'absolute', the 'sublime' (*erhaben*) and 'reverence' suggest that Kant is making his rational, autonomous person into a godlike agent in a kingdom of godlike agents. If this were only a reflection of his pietistic upbringing and his moral seriousness, one might regard Kant's usage as a pardonable hyperbole. But Kant is writing with philosophical seriousness to defend an episte-mology which depends on particular links between reality, rationality and morality. Kant seems to be investing the rational moral agent with the attributes of a superman, or the God-man of Christian tradition.

It has been argued by Schrader[22] that one must not import the apparatus of the noumenal/phenomenal world into the *Grundlegung*, but there are enough references to *homo noumenon/ homo phenomenon* in ethical contexts in Kant to suggest that at least the distinction is still being applied by Kant even if it is not central to his metaphysic of morals. In fact, chapter 3, especially sections 106–13, makes important use of the distinction. Moreover, Kant constantly distinguishes in the *Grundlegung* between the fully rational man, who alone can fulfil the moral law by willing that his maxim be universalised, and man as he actually is, always tempted to follow his inclinations and never quite able to do the right thing for the right reason or from the right motive.

It is at this level of principles of morality that one can urge against Kant that his analysis contains confusion and error. This is particularly true in his account of 'persons', rationality and morality. What he says in *Grundlegung*, sections 95–6 and 102–5 is both true and false. His main error is to conflate persons as 'ends in themselves' with persons as 'rational'. What he says about treating persons/humanity as ends in themselves is finely said, although it does not depend on his system or his prior arguments. To this extent, Haezrahi is correct. Man as an end in himself is brought into the argument (section 95/428) when Kant is seeking to ground a possible categorical imperative in absolute value (an end in itself). Kant answers his own question as follows: 'Now I say that man and in general every rational being exists as an end in himself.' To what extent this insight sprang from his pietistic upbringing or his earlier admiration for Rousseau, one can only speculate. Here, as elsewhere, Kant seems to equivocate between man as a potentially rational being and man who actually embodies rationality. As a result, dignity is attributed ambiguously to man as potentially rational and to man as actually rational. But, in either case, it would seem that Kant has begun to replace the view that persons are ends in themselves with the view that rational persons or potentially rational persons are ends in themselves.

At this point Kant's model of the moral self seems inconsistent and unworkable. It is not, in fact, necessary to accept such a model in order to appreciate the validity of some of his insights about the nature of morality and the significance of obligation. A large part of the problem stems from his understanding of persons as essentially rational. It is not that rationality is unimportant in a justifiable concept of the person. But, by isolating rationality and interpreting it in the way that he has, as constitutive of what it means to be a person, Kant has left us with an unsatisfactory model of the 'person'. His exaltation of rationality brought with it overtones of superman. Some confirmation of this interpretation can be found in Durkheim's essay, 'Individualism and the Intellectuals', when he says:

The human person, whose definition serves as the touchstone according to which good must be distinguished from evil, is considered as sacred, in what one might call the ritual sense of the word. It has something of that transcendental majesty which the churches of all times have given to their Gods. It is conceived as being invested with that mysterious property which creates an empty space around holy objects, which keeps them away from profane contacts and which draws them away from ordinary life. And it is exactly this feature which induces the respect of which it is the object.[23]

Durkheim acknowledges his debt to Kant in the matter of individualism, distinguishing himself only (but significantly) from Kant by deriving individualism from society ('Individualism itself is a social product, like all moralities and religions').

In other words, 'respect for persons', which has become one of the pillars of modern moral philosophy and has often been appealed to by Christian writers on ethics, was really about respect for rationality. It is this exalted emphasis on rationality which underlies the attempts of Singer, Tooley and Parfit, among others, to delineate 'person', in contrast to 'human', in a way that would enable personhood to become the touchstone of moral value. The problems associated with applying Kant's somewhat formal ethic of universal maxims have often been noted. By specifying more exactly the content of personhood in relation to the various categories of human and non-human animals, modern commentators may have alerted us to the neglected status of non-human animals reared by factory-farming methods and to other environmental issues connected with human abuse of the environment in shortsighted pursuit of economic gain, but these same issues are capable of being dealt with just as effectively, as we shall see in chapter 15, by means of other arguments and considerations. That some non-human animals are also persons, whereas some human beings are not persons, is a view which raises more problems than it solves. It both extends and restricts personhood in ways that are counterintuitive and difficult to sustain. The solution that is purchased neglects both the foetus and the senile, and fails to resolve the question of *when* some non-human animals become persons, since the criteria (e.g. having a concept of the self) are difficult if not impossible to apply.

Kant's understanding of personhood continued to exert great influence after his death, but it did not go unchallenged. In the wake of Kant, German idealism continued to develop views of the self and its relation to self-consciousness, to sense experience and to God. Metaphysical interests, however, rather than specific arguments, determined what was discussed and written. Although there are discussions which could be relevant to the meaning of personhood, there is no sustained examination of the concept of person. J. G. Fichte's critical philosophy, with its emphasis on the distinction of ego and non-ego, comes very close to it, but even that is directed more to establishing a basis for philosophy as a whole than to an examination of the concept of person. Fichte, according to Mauss, was 'the one who finally gave the answer that every act of consciousness was an act of the self (moi)'. He went beyond Kant in making 'person' a 'category'. But, as we saw (in chapter 1), there are difficulties in substantiating this part of Mauss' thesis. It is true that Fichte attempts to develop Kant by making practical reason fundamental not simply to morality, but to the whole structure of knowledge. The distinction of ego and non-ego is fundamental to this enterprise. The ego, as active, knowing subject, is the presupposition of all experience and knowledge. 'The self is absolutely active and merely active – that is our absolute presupposition.'[24] This represents Fichte's attempt to find an alternative basis for Kant's critical philosophy by avoiding questionable arguments for a noumenal world and by anchoring idealism in an apparently more empirical understanding of the ego and self-consciousness.

Fichte's *Attempt at a Critique of all Revelation* (1792) followed Kant in separating religion and philosophy. Like Kant, he also attached great importance to the ethical subject. In the 1790s, however, his views underwent significant change. Whereas, in 1792, Fichte had agreed with Kant in allowing that morality and happiness, despite their fundamental differences, are held together in practical reason and that this could constitute a moral argument for the existence of God, by 1795 Fichte clearly rejected such a view. This became explicit in the controversies of 1798–9. In March 1799, Fichte was dismissed from his post at the University of Jena for his article 'Über den Grund unseres Glaubens an eine göttliche Weltregierung', which was alleged to be atheistic. Fichte's atheism consisted of his refusal to ground morality on anything but the moral will, subjectively understood.[25] Even in 1792 Fichte was unhappy with the idea of a personal God who underwrites the moral law; by 1798 it was clear he no longer accepted the idea of links between the concept of the moral law and of God. Morality and true religion were identical, he decided. Faith is committed to realising the moral law as the unconditional rule of the good. In 1795, according to reconstructed lectures of Fichte, he still found it necessary to distinguish God as the upholder of the moral law from morality, but, by 1798, this distinction had been replaced: God is identical with the moral order of the universe.

Rather like Kant, Fichte is mainly interested in trying to establish a fundamental perspective which would contribute to the solution of all other problems, rather than in finding specific answers to specific problems. His general insistence on the crucial role of the ego, however, did contribute to that heightening of interest in the role of the human subject in acquiring knowledge of objective reality which is a characteristic of so much post-Enlightenment thought. Along with Hegel and Schelling, Fichte marks an important stage in the development of a modern ideology of the person. It is not clear, however, whether Fichte regards the individual as the source of all reality, as one school of interpretation claims,[26] or whether, as Dilthey and others have argued, he is concerned to develop a theory of man as active being, in which analysis of consciousness provides the starting-point but is not a complete solution in itself.[27]

Although there was no direct borrowing or direct conflict between Kant and Hegel over the concept of 'person', it is not surprising to find that, in a philosophy which regarded the Real and the Rational as identical and which referred to God as the Absolute Person, Kant's reverence and respect for persons was changed from a principle of morality into a principle of metaphysics. Hegel's understanding of 'person' is to be found scattered throughout his *Phenomenology of Mind*, in which he develops his theory of human subjectivity and consciousness. Since his complex understanding of 'person' only makes sense within the dialectic of his overall argument, it is unusually difficult to summarise his distinctive contribution without reference to his thought as a whole. He distinguishes between Substance and Subject[28] and states that ultimate truth must be grasped and expressed from both points of view. 'Substance' is a being constituted by its own necessity, exists prior to its attributes and at one level is also prior to thought, but it is only realised when it is apprehended by a conscious Subject whose activity consists in bringing out what is implicitly in Substance even as the Subject actively realises itself. The Subject is conscious and consciously relates itself to the world of Substance and object. Without them it could not exist. The Subject is constantly in process of becoming itself as it 'mediates with its own self its transitions from one state or position to the opposite'.[29] There is no essential opposition between living Substance and true Subject, but there is a continuous movement towards increasing fulfilment. Hegel consciously defines his position in relation to that of his predecessors. Truth is not to be found in the One Substance of Spinoza, or Kant's separation of the noumenal and the phenomenal, or Fichte's absolute Ego which is itself the synthesis of subject and object. His *Phenomenology* aspires to construct an understanding of the Subject in relation to the world of experience and of rational thought, which is based, not on prior judgements, but on phenomenological analysis of what is the case, in order to arrive at truth.

Like previous philosophers, he searches for fundamentals with which to begin. For him, this means both the conscious subject and what the subject is conscious of, which is not initially itself but the external world. The simple act of perception establishes both the object sensed and the subject sensing. In this way Hegel signifies a very different approach to subjectivity and the world from Descartes, for example. Naive consciousness that an object exists, however, is 'the abstractest and poorest kind of truth'. It says nothing about the manifold nature of the object. Equally the 'I' which senses the object is an abstract universal 'I'. The inadequacy of this initial mode of cognition provokes a need for reflection and understanding which in turn leads to the rise of self-consciousness, which is a decisive step in the self-realisation of the knowing mind.

Analysis of self-consciousness involves recognition both of the self's freedom and its limitations, and this issues in self-estrangement and alienation. It is to rescue the Subject from this precarious state that the next stage of Hegelian analysis examines what is really rational and the identity of rationality and reality. The previous stages are not dispensed with, because Hegel's version of rationality is distinguished from that of his (unsuccessful) predecessors largely because of his attempt to overcome Kant's abstract rational categories and Fichte's Absolute Ego. Hegel engages in a long examination of 'reason as observation' in which he develops a number of acute points about the way we attend to and select and describe particular features of what is observed. The thrust of the argument, however, is concerned with the movement to the formulation of laws and principles and the increasingly complex aspect of organic life culminating in observation and understanding of the rational self. This, in turn, culminates in a consideration of the nature of morality and virtue, but we are left with the search for rational consistency still unsatisfied.

The search then moves to the level of spirit, in which resolution of earlier antitheses can be expected to be found. 'Reason is spirit when its certainty of being all reality has been raised to the level of truth and reason is consciously aware of itself as its own world and of the world as itself.'[30] Hegel states that a phenomenological analysis of spirit begins with existing society in which spirit is realised. He finds the two primal elements of society in family life and national government. This involves a brief consideration of the sexes and the place of law and justice. Together, family and government constitute aspects of divine and human law. The argument is that the Subject can only realise itself in community. The richness of subjectivity lies in becoming a Person, who is not atomistic, or an abstract legal individual with rights; 'to describe an individual as a "person" [in a purely legal context] is to use an expression of contempt'.[31] Unfortunately, the history of society to date has included such grotesque aberrations as the Absolute Person lording it over his subjects, alienating their personality to his. How this can be overcome is examined in the analysis of culture, as reflected in the power of the state, the use and abuse of language, belief and rational insight.[32]

Hegel initiated two developments which were to be important for the concept of person. At the pinnacle of his rational system is the Absolute, which is capable of overcoming the contradictions within finite rationality. The Absolute Idea is also the Absolute Person, whose self-consciousness includes and perfects men's limited knowledge of themselves and their world. The opposition of noumenal and phenomenal worlds is overcome, not by cosmic absorption or reductionism, however, but by the self-realisation of absolute reason in finite human spirits, who retain their rational individuality and existence. This emphasised the significance of self-consciousness in the concept of person. Secondly, by his social philosophy and emphasis on the community Hegel gave impetus to those elements which resisted interpretations of 'person' in terms of the solitary individual.

There is an equally significant but less well-observed development in L. Feuerbach (1804–72), whose correspondence of 1835 suggests an early, intense interest in Fichte's views. Feuerbach is well known as a pre-cursor of the Young Hegelians' critique of Hegel and as the protagonist of a reductionist anthropological theology. He was a philosopher in his own right, and it has been convincingly argued that his ideas deserve further exploration.[33] It has also been suggested that his negative critique of theology is less negative than has often been assumed.[34] Several theologians have noted Feuerbach's interest in personal relationships. Examination of Feuerbach's *Todesgedanken*, it will be maintained, reveals a distinctive and significant concept of personhood which was to have a striking effect on later ideas, although Feuerbach's contribution to this development has up to the present not been clearly recognised.[35]

Feuerbach was converted to the philosophy of Hegel ('the Bethlehem of a new world') whose lectures he attended in Berlin from 1824 after his disappointment with his theological studies at Heidelberg. His dissertation on 'Reason: its Unity, Universality and Infinity' (1828) began to work out some of the implications of Hegel's views. By 1830, his *Todesgedanken* (E. T.

*Thoughts on Death and Immortality*) indicates how he is beginning to reorganise and develop Hegel's views in a rather different direction. The substitution of philosophy and reason for religion and imagery by Feuerbach may be seen as a continuation of Hegelian method and themes. His open, sarcastic attack on the idea of personal immortality, his substitution for it of community survival and his redefinition of 'love' indicate his growing differences with Hegel.

The details, not always convincing, of Feuerbach's arguments against certain conceptions of immortality, which were prevalent both in the religion of the day and in the philosophical schools, are less important than the historical museum of ideas which is brought to life in his writings. What he says about the concept of 'person' is all the more significant for being tangential to the main focus of discussion. It is significant, for example, that his attack on the idea of personal immortality draws so heavily on the idea of 'person'. What he says about 'personhood' tells us, not only what Feuerbach thought, but also what Feuerbach's contemporaries were thinking.

The ideas and terminology of the *Todesgedanken* point to a significant shift in the concept of 'person' compared with what we saw in Locke and Kant. He describes the mood of the times as one of intense individualism, expressed typically in Protestantism.[36] The tendency of Protestantism to moralism and rationalism has been exacerbated by pietism's stress on inwardness, he thinks. The Christ-mysticism of pietism has contributed to this. Belief in immortality now epitomises and encapsulates all this. The reasons, he thinks, are as follows:

Firstly, 'Pure, naked personhood was considered to be the only substantial reality.'[37] Hence, there must be a further life (after death), in which the troubles and disappointments of the present life find no place, and true personhood can be fulfilled. 'In this life the pure person is only imagined, an ideal.'[38] That a real existence for genuine persons, therefore, requires personal immortality, is one of the main reasons why, according to Feuerbach, belief in personal immortality has become so characteristic of the modern age. Secondly, 'true personhood is identical with virtue, free from blemish. Morality, perfectly virtuous personhood, is the essence of the person'.[39] For this to be realised, more time than is available in this life is needed. The realisation of such virtue also raises other problems. Once achieved, such virtue would be the end of the self, and it becomes important, therefore, to strive for unsullied personhood without achieving it. He goes on to make the point that personhood in this sense requires for its identity 'distinctness', and, to that extent, there may be an inner contradiction in personal immortality which prevents the fulfilment of true personhood, since personhood may require the cessation of such distinctness. There are two significant features in this passage. First, personhood cannot be fulfilled in this life, in which it functions as an unrealised ideal. Secondly, personhood is connected with a state of unblemished perfection. If this is the case, it could be argued that personhood is a mirage, or restricted to an elite of divine beings. Feuerbach does not take either of these paths, but argues that there is an inner contradiction in the concept of immortality which requires mankind to strive for something which would contradict itself if realised. This inner contradiction he finds in the distinctness of individuality which is antagonistic to what is universal, namely spirit, soul and essence. 'Over the gap that lies between the present life as it really is and his perception and representation of it . . . the individual erects the fool's bridge of the future life.' The argument against immortality is expressed in terms of a particular view of personhood which Feuerbach regards as characteristic of modernity. Later, he develops these reflections in relation to the personhood of God, in a way that owes something to Hegel's view of God as Absolute Person.[40] 'God is person. But he is more, infinitely more than person. He is person who is pure love' (section 17, p. 20 in Massey's translation). In the edition of 1847, prior to developing the idea that God, as love, must be more than person, Feuerbach analyses human love and argues that it consists essentially of a self-giving which abandons the isolation of the self and chooses community. Community requires self-giving, which is a form of death and, as such, opposed to the desire for personal immortality, which insists on distinctness.

Of itself death is as natural as the ultimate sacrifice, the last guardian of love. Death has its centre in the spirit; it revolves round the spirit like a planet circling its sun. In loving you acknowledge and express the nothingness of your self-existence, your self. You recognise not yourself but your beloved as your true I, as your being and life; as long as you love, you live on the denial of yourself, in the unbroken affirmation of the nought of yourself, and in the affirmation, enjoyment and contemplation of the beloved.[41]

Here, as in several other places, Feuerbach seeks to persuade his readers that death is a natural part of life and that it is not without spiritual significance. He relates this to self-denial and love, both of which have communal features. His description of love is not untypical of the Romanticism of the period. In Feuerbach, however, it is linked with reflection on personhood and with hostility to the idea of individual immortality. Combination of these different emphases in Feuerbach results in a surprisingly 'modern' view of 'person': personhood is important, not simply in terms of individuality or abstract reason, but in terms of relationships and relatedness; insistence on the distinctness of persons prevents the very relatedness on which personhood depends. Feuerbach prefigures so many themes of later discussions of person (e.g. twentieth-century theological personalism; process thought; even, perhaps, a Parfit-type view of persons) that it would be easy to give him credit for ideas which are not really his. There seems little doubt, however, that his anthropological theology touched a live nerve in his own day, and that many of his ideas have become part of the discussions which still continue.

There is an even stronger reason for taking account of Feuerbach's views about the significance of 'person'. He encapsulates the 'secular inversion' which has overtaken the concept since the nineteenth century. This inversion means not simply that a term once applied to God is now applied chiefly to man, but that some of the attributes normally reserved for God have begun to be applied to 'persons' (variously defined). Feuerbach's view that God must be more than person, and yet God is made in the image of the human person, contributes to the ideology of the person which not only exalts the person above the merely human, but gives the person (and what constitutes the person) a sort of ontological priority in contemporary thought. Feuerbach's use of 'person' heralds the breaking of old images. He is also critical of the limitations of personhood as understood in his day. All of which makes him an invaluable source, but one not always easy to interpret. He uses 'person' rather like Prometheus uses fire against the gods. He steals it and then turns it against the God who was designated Absolute Person in Hegel. There is a continuous polemic against Hegel's rationalism and his view of God, even when Hegel is not mentioned. This is especially true of sections 17–49 (pp. 19–49 in Massey's translation).

Feuerbach uses the concept of God's personhood to develop his argument that the human individual cannot be immortal. God is person, but he must be more than person, because otherwise he is nothing more than self-consciousness, freedom, will, decision and purpose, all of which can be attributed to man as person. God would be only a reflection of human personhood if his only attributes were exalted human attributes. It is not satisfactory to say they are realised in God to an infinitely greater degree. If this were the case, death would mean, not new life in God, but a realisation of present human qualities, and death would be understood superficially. The next stage of the argument expresses Feuerbach's disagreement with Hegel's view of God as Absolute Person who self-consciously realises himself in human history through the outworkings of pure rationality. Considerable play is made of the ideas of self-realisation and otherness, which were important in Hegel's system. Feuerbach thinks God must be capable of uniting both person and essence (impersonal). To speak of God as person emphasises God's ability to separate and distinguish himself from nature. This is only half the truth, however. God must include within himself both person and essence. There must be distinction of person and essence within God; otherwise God would lack the energy and stimulus which are essential constituents of joy and pain and all activity. 'For the only self-active essence is one that is distinct from itself within itself, one that is dual in itself'.[42] Human beings are spiritual beings and also embody this distinction. If human beings were only persons, they too would lack all energy. 'Mere personhood on its own is just as spiritless as mere nature on its own.' All of this rests on Hegelian assumptions about the nature of spirit. Consequently, God also must be more than Absolute Person. 'If God were nothing more than personal being, the human truly would be more exalted and more profound than God, for even the human is not just person, not without soul. Therefore, to make personhood into the only determination of God is to make spiritlessness and soullessness into determinations of God.'[43] In the background, again, are Hegelian assumptions about alienation and self-possession, although Feuerbach is critical of Hegelian rationalism and personality.

Feuerbach considers the objection that a better definition of personhood (as 'being-in-self and knowing-of-self') would overcome the above difficulties. He rejects this on the ground that more than self-knowledge is required. God does not simply know himself (as person); he knows his essence and 'in his soul and essence he is everything.' 'As God knows himself he knows and is everything'.[44] The argument points towards a form of pantheism, but this is not Feuerbach's main aim. He is trying to establish that God is more than Person, and that Hegel's idea of God's self-knowing is not adequate. It is not clear that Feuerbach takes sufficient account of Hegel's Trinitarian thought at this point. The distinction of persons within the Godhead allows Hegel to develop a less individualistic notion of 'personhood' than that criticised by Feuerbach.

In paragraph 26 a different argument is used: 'Are there not degrees of personhood?' Self-consciousness is only one aspect of personhood – its driest and most abstract aspect. Personhood includes love – 'the feeling of an essence that is distinct from and yet also at one with the self'. To understand the mystery of love is the key to understanding. Love both distinguishes and unites. In this it is different from every other experience. Love combines multiplicity and unity. The combination of nature and personhood in humanity provides an analogy of the unity of being-for-self and being-everything. When a person sleeps, soul is active without consciousness, and it can be said that 'in his soul the individual is not a person'. To say that God loves is 'already to have transcended your conception of the person-hood of God'. The person 'strictly conceived as person cannot love but can only hate, divide, estrange'. To be able to surrender one's harsh 'being-for-self' requires an 'abode, so to speak, where he is not person'. Love is not 'being for oneself' but 'being together'. 'You love only because you are deeper and more than a person.' 'Love is the unity of personhood and essence.'

Feuerbach is working with at least two different concepts of person: (a) rational individuality which divides (b) loving being which unites. Love, however, requires more than self-love; it needs another to love. Feuerbach's critique of personhood gives priority to love, but does not openly acknowledge the ambiguity on which it is based. His argument here appears to be directed at Hegel's failure to bring his self-conscious Absolute Person, despite the realisation of the divine in the historical process and the overcoming of alienation, into a real relationship with his creation. Feuerbach's theological critique is based on his assumption that 'personhood' is best under-stood from the real relationships of embodied individuals, in which solitariness is overcome through love. This, he thinks, is the true meaning of personhood and the reason why theology must become anthropology.

The conclusion does not follow, of course, if there is a real relationship of persons in the Godhead, analogous to the real relationship of embodied human persons. The question then becomes one of ontological priority. Feuerbach's use of human relationships, however, to develop his theological criticism of Hegel is important, not simply in terms of Hegel, but in terms of later Western thought, both religious and secular. Feuerbach presages that increasingly secular ideology of the person in which what had once been true of divine persons is attributed chiefly to human persons. He represents a shift away from the emphasis on consciousness and rationality as determining marks of personhood to a more material and yet relational view. His clash with Hegel over Trinitarian personhood may foreshadow an unresolved theological debate about personhood and Trinity. Although he attacks traditional Christian thought, his emphasis on embodied love and the need for the other points towards features that will become more apparent in the next chapter. In both Hegel and Feuerbach, there is beginning to appear that movement away from the solitary individual towards a more social emphasis and a sense of persons as not simply agents but as 'interlocutors', to use C. Taylor's expression, and co-respondents. This understanding of persons as embodied, related, reflective and responsible agents who love and serve one another in a society of persons begins to remedy one of the deficiencies found in views which focus too narrowly on the rationality of persons.

CHAPTER 6

# Resituating personhood: embodiment and contextuality

The aim of this chapter is to suggest some modification of Kant's understanding of personhood in terms of rationality by looking at the response of two different currents of thought to issues of personhood: theistic personalism and feminism. As examples of the former, we have taken Boston personalism and E. Mounier's personalism, and, as examples of the latter, we consider feminist attempts to move away from privileged rationality and the attempt of Seyla Benhabib to combine Habermas' goal of undistorted communication with a view of the self as gendered and embodied. They have their own different concerns, but are related by their search for ways of understanding personhood ethically and with more attention to human relationships than Kant gave. They also have an interest in seeing persons as members of community. Separately they may appear slight and even philosophically insignificant compared with Kant, but together they point to a richer alternative.

We have argued in chapter 5 that Kant's account of 'persons' contains confusion and error, in that it conflates persons as 'ends in themselves' with persons as 'rational' (cf. *Grundlegung* 95–6/428 and 102–5) In these passages, as elsewhere, Kant seems to equivocate between person as potentially rational and person as actually rational. In either case, it seems that Kant has begun to replace the view that persons are ends in themselves with the view that rational persons or potentially rational persons are ends in themselves.

Despite the significant role played by the divine and Absolute Person in Hegel's thought and later in Feuerbach's *Todesge-*

*danken* (1830), it was several years before personhood became the centre of debate again. The catalyst in the latter part of the century was the growing influence of the mechanical sciences and the reaction against this in some of the humanistic philosophers of the period. The growing science of psychology was also developing interest in a related concept, personality. To write a complete history of the development of the concept of person in this period, however, would require several chapters in itself. Some of the stages in that history are more clearly marked; others have still to be unravelled. A great variety of personal, social and intellectual influences were at work. Reverberating through them all, of course, are the ideas of Kant and Hegel.

Kant's influence is found not only in philosophy, but also among religious thinkers attracted by an ethical idealism which comports with or supports their overall metaphysical stance. J. R. Illingworth in his Bampton lectures of 1894, *Personality, Human and Divine*, draws on a variety of sources, but refers explicitly to Dean Mansel's Bampton lectures of 1852 which were marked by Kantian epistemology, to support his view of God as person. A large number of idealists, particularly British idealists (e.g. B. Bosanquet; F. H. Bradley; T. H. Green; E. Caird) acknowledged their debt to Hegel.

Some of the responsibility, however, for making the concept of person central to theistic discussion at the end of the nineteenth century lay with R. H. Lotze (1817–81), the Göttingen scientist and philosopher who attempted to bridge the growing gap between the sciences and the humanities, and who, in his *Metaphysics* and *Microcosmos*, developed a system in which the empirical discoveries of modern science, and particularly the theory of evolution and growing awareness of the earth's planetary history, were given an interpretation compatible with theism by making 'personality' the leading shoot of evolution and giving 'personality' a non-reductive interpretation. Although he says comparatively little about 'persons' (apart from *Microcosmos* IX. 4), he does make 'persons' important to his system. Similarly, his emphasis on morality, as indicative of what is most distinctively human, is not new. But he does not, as Kant and many others did, interpret morality as if it were the only (or major) clue to understanding 'religion'. Lotze's influence was particularly strong on a number of American writers, especially B. P. Bowne (1847–1910), and his followers, such as E. S. Brightman (1884–1953) and R. T. Flewelling (1871–1960). The absolute idealism of Josiah Royce (1855–1916) was more influenced by Hegel. There were also other varieties of personalism, such as the pluralistic personalism of G. H. Howison (1834–1917) and the personalistic idealism of W. E. Hocking (1873–1966).[1]

Although the term 'personalism' seems to have been first used in American published writing by Walt Whitman in an article entitled 'Democracy' in 1867, followed in 1868 by an article on 'Personalism'[2] it was frequently used in the late nineteenth century and was given philosophical and theological currency by B. P. Bowne's book called *Personalism* (1908) and the Boston personalists. Bowne, usually credited with having founded the Boston school of personalism, was the first in a line of American personalist thinkers. After graduating at New York University, he studied in Europe (Paris, Halle and Göttingen). At Göttingen he was influenced by the ideas of R. H. Lotze (cf. above) who had attempted to find a way through the religious and scientific conflicts of the period by elucidating the conceptual differences between scientific and humanistic disciplines, and examining the importance of creative mind for persons. Bowne also began from a scientific background, and was attracted by the empirical features of personalism. 'The self itself is the surest item of knowledge we possess'.[3] P. Bertocci, a later personalist, regards Bowne's fundamental thesis as: 'The person, who acts in and makes cognitive claims about the world that his or her acting and knowing do not create, is an indivisible unity.'[4]

Bowne, like later personalists, acknowledged his debt to Kant and his emphasis on 'mind', but he did not assent to Kant's uncompromising separation of noumena and phenomena, which relegated God, freedom and immortality to postulates of practical reason. Despite his respect for Kant, Bowne was clear that 'the law of the logician must yield to the law the mind actually follows'.[5] Introducing a thoroughly non-Kantian category, Bowne puts 'purpose' (essentially practical) alongside time, space and causation. 'Bowne's epistemic dualism, on the whole, followed a Kantian pattern, but his strong emphasis on the person as purposer and actor kept him from the conclusion that we know nothing but the world as organised categorically'.[6]

Another strand in Bowne's personalism was his strong belief in personal free-will, which distinguishes the world of persons from the world of mechanical causation. It was this view of persons that led Bowne to the conclusion that finite, personal intelligence must have its counterpart in a cosmic Person (as Lotze had postulated). With these ideas, Bowne was able to develop a philosophy that took account of science but offered a teleological rather than materialistic view of Nature. Evolution was reintegrated, not as blind process, but in keeping with the larger design of a cosmic Mind. Humean objections to the teleological argument (viz. we have no experience of alternative worlds being made) were redirected into the prior question: how does one select between competing hypotheses about the nature of the universe? The hypothesis of personalism was regarded as a better candidate for truth than materialism, despite problems of theodicy. Provided it was recognised that there could be no intellectual solution to the problem of evil, personalism was itself a way of responding to and overcoming evil. Although Boston personalism may not have produced original thinkers of the calibre of Kant and Hegel, it continues to exert significant influence on American religious thought. One of its more attractive and lively features has been its application to a range of social issues by later writers, such as Martin Luther King.[7]

The currents of personalism and personalistic philosophies have continued to contribute to the shape of the twentieth century. The influence of Martin Buber, for instance, has been incalculable. Religious existential personalism has become, for many, one of those unifying factors across a variety of religious and theological traditions. On a lesser scale, as an example of 'personalism' in European philosophy and ethics, Emmanuel

Mounier (1905–50) is instructive.[8] In *Personalism*, pp. xix–xxviii, he comments briefly on thinkers and developments he regards as significant for the history of personalism and his own ideas – Greek thought ('the Greeks had a keen sense of the dignity of the human being', p. xx); Christianity ('It is Christianity that, first of all, imports into these gropings a decisive notion of the person', p. xx); Leibniz, Kant and idealism (Hegel is the 'monstrous architect of the impersonal', p. xxiv); followed by a long series of modern European writers – Lotze, Scheler, Buber, Berdyaev, Bergson, Laberthonniere, Blondel, Peguy, Maritain, Mansel, Jaspers and Landberg, not to mention British and American writers.

As J. Amato has made clear in a sympathetic treatment of Mounier and Maritain,[9] Mounier's constantly evolving personalism reflected his deep Christian faith and his early encounters, first with Chevalier and subsequently with Maritain. He constantly tried to bring together the theoretical and the practical, so that there is a strong political element in his personalism. He recognises there will be agnostic as well as Christian personalists, but, for him, personalism represents a new and reformed practice of Christian vision and principles capable of bringing about a new world order. The enemies of personalism are the destructive forces of individualism and collectivism (economic, social and spiritual). In 1947, in his introduction to *Qu'est-ce que le personnalisme?*, he says, 'the best future one could wish for personalism is that it should so awaken in everyone the sense of the whole meaning of man, that it could disappear without trace, having become the general climate of our days'.

For Mounier there are five essential marks of the person. Firstly, the person is 'a body in the same degree that he is a spirit, wholly body and wholly spirit'.[10] The great philosopher is attacked by headaches, St John of the Cross vomits during his ecstasies and the great religions spread along the same routes as the major epidemics.[11] But persons also transcend nature, as the failure of determinism to explain human nature and its achievements demonstrates. Consequently, whenever there is a practical problem to be resolved, it is necessary to take into

account both the material and the spiritual sub-structure of
human life. Embodied existence is an essential factor in our
personal and spiritual experience. Human ability to transform
nature, however, does not licence slavery or anarchy or the
technological exploitation of the natural world. The perfection
of the embodied personal universe will not be achieved without
vigilance, discipline and struggle.

Mounier's second mark of the person is to be found in
communication. Persons are essentially relational beings.
Hence, 'personnaliste' is often linked with 'communautaire', as
in 'Révolution personnaliste et communautaire' (1934). 'The
primary action of the person – is to sustain, together with
others, a society of persons, the structure, the customs, the
sentiments and the institutions of which are shaped by their
nature as persons'.[12] Mounier finds this mark of the person in
self-detachment, understanding, sharing, giving and faithfulness. The egocentric stumbling blocks to genuine reciprocal
relationships are numerous, springing from individualistic and
collectivist features of our life. Personalism, however, does not
simply deny or reject these features, which are an inescapable
part of life, but seeks to transform them. The dialectical tension
between the unique individual and the community of persons
sharing a new world order can be resolved, not by positing a
common essence or human nature, but by understanding the
unity of mankind in terms of equality/justice.

Mounier's third mark of the person is 'intimate conversion',
by which he refers to the internal resources of personal being
realised in recollection, self-detachment and the exteriorisation
of our love. The familiar obstacles of unrealistic fantasy and
morbid self-preoccupation are the reverse side of the coin. The
fourth mark he calls 'confrontation', by which he means the
individual's necessity to choose for himself and make explicit
his own values. In the present state of the world, this self-
assertion is inevitably seen as violent or aggressive. There is a
legitimate resistance of violence by violence; otherwise ideals
would become impracticable and simply capitulate to violent
wrongdoing. Responsible choice may be painful, but it should
not be regarded as necessarily leading to self-impoverishment.

The fifth and final mark is 'freedom' – not the mythical, absolute freedom which allows one to do anything one wants, but the measured freedom of persons related to other persons and values anchored in concrete situations. Freedom appears to mean contrary things because it is claimed by warring groups to support their particular views. This is undefined and meaningless freedom according to Mounier. Genuine freedom is not simply spontaneity or autonomy, but the freedom of a community of persons exercising responsible choice.

The example of Mounier alongside that of Bowne may suggest that there is very little that holds all personalists together except their opposition to various forms of materialism. It is significant, however, that interest in what it means to be a person should have developed into a variety of philosophical positions designed to lend support to belief in a personal God. It could also be suggested that personalism, despite the different understandings of personhood it incorporates, remains a flexible response to ethical issues. A fuller history of 'personalism' waits to be written, but several of Mounier's points are picked up in a different strand of thinking in contemporary ethics (feminism), which is of particular interest to discussions of personhood, even when the term 'person' is not used.

Feminist thinkers have drawn attention to the importance of embodiment and gender in ethics. There are increasingly fissiparous tendencies in feminism, but, at its simplest and most profound, feminism regards embodiment as an essential building-block of any theory of personhood. There may be disagreements about the analysis and interpretation of embodiment, but there is no disagreement about its importance. Beginning with the observation that women have been characterised by reference to the body so much more than men, women writers have examined their domestic, childbearing/rearing, family nurturing roles and the importance attached to women's bodies both by themselves and men. The reference to embodiment, however, is not simply an innocent statement of fact, but a deeply ironic comment on the contrasting importance attached in Western thought and culture to the role of the mind or soul, and particularly to the way reason has been understood as if it were something separate from the rest of human nature, superior to emotion and feelings and either divorced from or controlling the human body. Cartesian and other dualisms are regarded as failures in comprehension of the significance of embodiment, which have led to women being ignored, banished to the kitchen or bedroom, abused, marginalised, and even rendered invisible in the public sphere in terms of status, employment and education. Within the family, where one might have expected things to be different, similar injustices have been perpetrated. Even in areas where women's interests were not disputed (e.g. medical care for women, particularly in childbirth), it is men's views which have dictated what is 'good for women' on the basis of arguments which appeal to men. It is clear that this is not the whole picture. There is no single scenario which captures the experience of all women. But it encapsulates a sad truth. Hence, reason itself has been declared masculine, and, to that extent, hostile to women's interests.

Admittedly this rough characterisation of feminist thinking is in need of refinement. Women's interests are complex and diverse; the women's movement and feminist thinking have not remained static; there is now a wide range of feminist theories affecting ethics and the understanding of persons.[13] In their article on feminism and post-modernism, 'Social Criticism without Philosophy', N. Fraser and L. J. Nicholson trace some of the important shifts that have occurred in feminist thinking. On the whole, feminism has found it necessary to treat with suspicion and caution traditional moral and political theories because of dualist assumptions which downgrade material bodies and contingent facts of human experience in preference for timeless, universal truths of reason. Because their experience has so often been ignored, women have sought a contextual ethic related to their situation. Discussion of women's rights and women's liberation, however, has inevitably led to theorising. Unintentionally, these theories became equivalent to the grand 'metanarratives of legitimation' of the dominant Western philosophical tradition (e.g. 'overarching philosophies of history like the Enlightenment story of the gradual but steady progress of reason and freedom, Hegel's dialectic of Spirit coming to know itself, and, most importantly, Marx's drama of the forward march of human productive capacities via class conflict culminating in proletarian revolution').[14]

For example, S. Firestone's use of 'gender conflict', in terms borrowed from Marxian analysis, located the problems experienced by women in the 'biological differences between men and women'. As an explanation, it says too much and lacks discrimination; it is also 'essentialist and monocausal, projecting certain qualities unto all men and women, qualities which develop under historically specific social conditions . . . These problems are only compounded when appeals to biology are used in conjunction with the dubious claim that women's oppression is the cause of all other forms of oppression.'[15]

Other grand causes or metanarratives were developed around the separation of the domestic and public spheres (following Rosaldo, 'Women, Culture and Society', 1974),[16] which excluded women from the power structures of the latter. Again, despite a kernel of truth and the fact that it was more flexible than the biological difference view, the generalisation proved too sweeping, incapable of doing justice to the diversity of human culture and experience. As Fraser and Nicholson note, 'the presumption of an overly grandiose and totalizing conception of theory' was mistaken. Since then, feminist thought has become more differentiated, but 'quasi-metanarratives' continue to appear. As an example, Fraser and Nicholson cite N. Chodorow's (1978) analysis of 'mothering', which tried to relate male-female differences to early childhood rearing and gender identity: 'female mothering produces women whose deep sense of self is 'relational' and men whose deep sense of self is not'.[17] C. Gilligan's *In A Different Voice* (1982) reproduced some of these assumptions in her critique of Kohlberg's moral development theory. She rightly criticised unjustified assumptions in Kohlberg's sampling and conclusions, but her own views were also marred by uncritical assumptions.[18] Her conclusion, that there is an ethic of caring and responsibility (characteristic of women) in contrast to an ethic of rights and justice (typical of men), presumes that the two moralities not only are different, but also are incapable of being combined. A number of feminist writers have acknowledged the exaggeration which this involves.[19] It is not that care is unimportant or that there is no truth in Gilligan's observations, but it is mistaken to convert particular historical truths about human behaviour into gender generalisations and stereotypes. There has been increasing recognition among feminist writers that women's issues are more complex than first thought. Moreover, some white, middle-class, heterosexual women writers have been accused by other feminists of bias and prejudice.[20]

There are, however, important indicators in feminist writing of issues related to Christian ethics and personhood that need to be incorporated in any rounded view. No account of concepts of person can omit discussion of embodiment and relationality. Both of these features also emerge quite strongly in political communitarian thought, which 'rejects liberal individualism in favour of a theory of the social construction both of the self and of social reality – culture, values, institutions and relations. Persons are fundamentally connected with each other and with the world they inhabit.'[21] There are signs of growing intellectual links between feminism and communitarian social theory,[22] in so far as both are critical of liberal individualism and its view of the moral subject as a 'non-embodied, unified individual who is the bearer of rights and interests'.[23]

S. Benhabib (1992) has begun to develop a critical, mediating position on several of these issues. Her discussion has the added advantage that it also focusses attention on a strand of contemporary European ethical thought related to social and political philosophy, as in J. Habermas. Her main aim is to develop a series of arguments and ideas which will support a modified form of ethical and political universalism which is 'interactive not legislative, cognizant of gender difference not gender blind, contextually sensitive and not situation indifferent'.[24]

Although her work contains no analysis of personhood in the

manner of Singer, Tooley and Parfit, it offers a thoughtful and balanced critique of a range of recent theories about the moral point of view and the person as ethical subject. She seeks to establish a communicative concept of rationality which does not try to legislate universally as if from above or outside the world. This communicative rationality would not abandon accepted critical procedures (in this sense it remains universalist in scope), but would attach crucial significance to agreement reached by discussion. This procedure would involve the recognition that 'the subjects of reason are finite, embodied and fragile creatures and not disembodied cogitos or abstract unities of transcendental apperception'.[25] Because the process of human growth from infancy involves interaction with others, she argues that features such as language and relationship with others must be important in the formation of the self. 'The "narrative structure of actions and personal identity" is the second premise which allows one to move beyond the metaphysical assumptions of Enlightenment universalism'.[26] The transition to interactive rationality alters the moral point of view from being a matter of timeless moral truths (and rules) to contingent and conditional universals of impartiality and justice. Instead of looking for an objective and comprehensive ethic for all time, the practice of ethics has to take place in the context of a critical theory of society and culture. She suggests three ways in which communicative ethics can be rescued from its Enlightenment origins: first, by understanding the moral point of view pluralistically and insisting not on specific outcomes of reason but on procedures based on discussion and dialogue as in Arendt's 'representative thinking' (universalisability is not a matter of weeding out logical contradiction, but of getting agents to accept that the other also has a point of view which may be capable of rational justification); secondly, by empowering moral subjects to draw on their experience as embodied, gendered agents; and thirdly, by showing how this new universalist style of moral thinking can be combined with attention to context. Justice and the solicitude of personal relationships are not incompatible, but neither can be reduced to the other. 'My goal is to situate reason and the moral self

more decisively in contexts of gender and community.'[27] These
steps towards a more adequate ethic all involve an understanding of the self as socially constructed, embodied and gendered.
In the first instance, Benhabib qualifies rationality and universality through an examination of Rawls' ethic of justice, which,
as it stands, abstracts from the self (both one's own self and the
self of others) under the veil of ignorance in order to attain
impartiality. She questions 'the assumption that "taking the
viewpoint of others" is truly compatible with this notion of
fairness as reasoning "behind a veil of ignorance". The
problem is that the defensible kernel of the ideas of reciprocity
and fairness are thereby identified with the perspective of the
disembedded and disembodied generalized other . . . The self
is not a thing, a substrate, but the protagonist of a life's tale.
The conception of selves who can be individuated prior to their
moral ends is incoherent.'[28] She argues for a different view of
universality based on acceptance of, and relation to, the other
as concrete, embodied and gendered, allowing the other a
genuine voice and making the possibility of disagreement
explicit so that it can be overcome, not by empathy, but by the
critical procedure of 'reversibility' and 'enlarged mentality',
concepts which she derives from H. Arendt. Her third way
involves bringing together attention to the specific needs of the
concrete other (and the insights of a caring, responsible
attitude) and an ethic of rights and justice, based on the
generalised other.[29]

In order to situate her view of self in context, Benhabib also
considers the disputed nature of community, which can be
given an integrationist or participationist interpretation. She
places M. Sandel and A. MacIntyre in the first group, because
they nostalgically still seek a society which has a single vision;
in the second, Habermas and herself, because they give more
place for pluralism and autonomy. If a communitarian model
according to which values are transmitted socially is adopted,
and, if there is no clear way of subjecting majority traditions to
critical analysis, then, as Frazer and Lacey argue, 'the woman
who lives in a sexist and patriarchal culture is peculiarly powerless',[30] whereas, for all its faults, the liberal individual model

allows a woman to argue for and claim her own rights and to develop a critique of the society she lives in. Moreover, communitarian models constantly bring with them the dangers of unjustified conservatism (e.g. involving a pre-modern world order in which the unified subject is idealised) and even authoritarianism.[31] More fundamental still is the need, as Frazer and Lacey see it, to develop a more adequate definition and methodology of communitarianism. Are communities best defined in terms of shared values and perspectives or in terms of features such as race, religion, geography, gender? When does a community become a loose collectivity and cease to be a community? Is it perhaps preferable to think in terms of specific shared goals, which allow more readily for individuals joining and passing through communities of interpretation and discourse? Should not communitarians distinguish more clearly between public and club (i.e. restricted association or membership) goods? Frazer and Lacey also raise pertinent questions about the nature of ideals of community, such as co-operation, solidarity, reciprocity, fraternity and sisterhood, which posit real differences of practice and allow for some practices which most liberals would find restrictive.

Benhabib gives cautious support to post-modernism's view that the logocentric rationality of the Western tradition has marginalised all those who did not fit its particular standards, but is reluctant to abandon the universalist claims which allow women to become members of a universal moral community. She also attempts to integrate Gilligan's emphasis on the personal more closely with Habermas' communicative ethic based on reason and justice.[32] Frazer and Lacey share Benhabib's concerns in these respects, as well as her confidence that the notion of the relational self is able to meet these difficulties and challenges.[33]

It is, perhaps, presumptuous on the basis of this brief survey to ask whether these attempts to forge a common critique of personhood as construed by liberal individualism succeed. They certainly raise pertinent questions and suggest new approaches to understanding concepts of person. The attack on rationality and rights, and the emphasis on embodiment and relationality, require us to examine more closely traditions which have sometimes been taken for granted. They also have interesting links with aspects of Christian tradition which have sometimes been submerged or given a very different reading because of their connections with God's personal being. In another case, the 'concrete other' which replaces the 'generalised other' is reminiscent of 'the neighbour' in Jewish–Christian tradition. Benhabib's critics have pointed out that she may have assumed too readily that her rational procedure will generate a conversation which is capable of resolving disagreement. Although she acknowledges the strength of 'fierce moral conflict' in modern society, she still has a fundamental optimism that rational discourse is possible and can overcome radical disagreement. It is perhaps a fine distinction to say that the 'emphasis now is less on *rational agreement*, but more on sustaining those normative practices and moral relationships within which reasoned agreement *as a way of life* can flourish and continue'.[34] What does this mean in practice? Should it not be acknowledged clearly that some-times – importantly and beneficially from the moral point of view – disagreements may continue. It is only when this is recognised that one can work towards overcoming disagree-ment. If agreement blurs the distinction between radical alternatives, or the distinction between good and evil, no genuine community can be achieved. As Michelle Moody-Adams has pointed out, there is a real sense in which the moral point of view is not only about securing agreement between conflicting points of view, but about self-understand-ing, self-examination and rational self-scrutiny of our ideals and moral practices,[35] and this may be compatible with a fair amount of disagreement, without leading to the playful free-for-all envisaged by Rorty's vision of the self as simply 'a network of beliefs, desires and emotions with nothing behind it – no substrate behind the attributes'.[36]

When we have examined the historical roots of some of these important modern developments, we shall be in a better position to evaluate their ethical significance. There are good reasons for thinking that it is this very reflection on the nature

and significance of what it is to be human and to be a person
that raises the question of God and the issue of how divine and
human personhood (cf. chapter 9) are related. One of the key
issues in modern philosophical anthropology (e.g. in writers
such as Scheler and Gehlen) is the delayed maturity of human
beings (in terms of a long period of growth and familial–
cultural dependency) which is part of human openness to the
world, and whether such openness and receptivity is part of
human openness to God.[37] In the meantime, it is clear that
Kant's account of persons is open to qualification in a variety of
ways by views which emphasise relationality as well as rationality, communality as well as individuality.

In our discussion of human personhood in Part 1, we have
drawn attention to the complexity of the concept and the
diversity of interpretation, noting both moral and metaphysical
personhood, but concentrating on the former. We have given
reasons for rejecting any sharp disjunction of 'person' and
'human being', while not wishing to obscure genuine difference. Human personhood, it is clear, is importantly related to
relationships and communication between people, as well as
individual rationality and purpose. All of these features are best
understood in a context of moral agency which includes human
biology and environment, rational purpose and social belonging. This does not explain the profound and surprising mystery
of human personhood: free, yet often constricted, influenced
and sometimes largely determined by genetic and environmental factors and always within a social context; capable of
heroic bravery and altruism, yet often selfish, mean and
introverted, capable of tyranny and cruelty. The attempt to
understand human agency in modern philosophical anthropology has been concerned to explore the nature of human
being as concrete, embodied social reality, as the subject who is
responsible for giving value to things by commitments which
link self, ideals and action. This humanistic, often existential,
interpretation may also characterise theistic views, which un-
derscore the importance of the divine–human encounter for
human self-understanding. In either case, it could be said, there
is an attempt to understand what it means to be human by

setting this in the larger context of 'what truly is'. In Part 2 we will examine the contribution made to the understanding of personhood by Christian insights, sometimes stemming from philosophical and theological debate about the nature of divine personhood.

PART 2

# *'Person' in Christian perspective*

Part 2 examines some of the main ideas which have been associated with the development of divine personhood, and attempts a critical analysis of the historical developments as a prelude to examining how this might affect a Christian perspective today. Our historical inquiry into Enlightenment thought has indicated the importance of the seventeenth century as a period of transition, particularly in terms of Locke's usage which appears so clearly rational and ethical, and the monumental significance of Kant in the eighteenth century in establishing the ethical priority of persons, which nevertheless contains dangerous assumptions about rationality within it. It proved impossible from this point onwards to separate discussions of personhood from the currents of German idealism which affect so much later thinking about human nature and subjectivity. Although not complete, the picture is one of contrasting and sometimes continuing conflicting strands, some centred on the personality of God, some on ethical agency. In Feuerbach we saw how ethical and human relationship wins out and is then used to critique the idea of God as person.

Historical inquiry into the previous centuries brings into focus a depth of background not apparent or even suspected in the way moral personhood is used in contemporary ethics. As a result of recent patristic studies, it is becoming clear that 'persona' was used in the Latin West in the first and second centuries CE as an exegetical tool in the interpretation of scripture, and that this led to its theological use in the Christological and Trinitarian debates of the third–fourth

119

centuries. It is sometimes suggested (e.g. by Greek Orthodox and Latin American theologians) that an original emphasis on mutual relationships has been overlooked by later Christians, and that this emphasis should be restored. This raises interesting questions about the sources and methods of Christian theology, and whether God should be thought of as 'a person'.

It was a traditional aspect of theological ethics in the late nineteenth and early twentieth centuries to posit an analogy between human and divine personal being. The understanding of God as personal resonates through many theological treatises of the period.[1] The initial impetus for this way of thinking stems from the Bible in which God is portrayed in personal images and humanity is regarded as being made 'in the image and likeness of God'. Belief in Jesus as God's incarnate Son strengthened this process. Philosophical reflection led to a rather different justification for thinking of God as person. It was argued that 'personality' was the summit of cosmic process up to the present. It was often assumed that personality was closely associated, if not identical, with 'consciousness'. God is personal because only such a conception of deity embodies the moral values implicit in theism. J. W. Oman (1860–1939) developed, in *Grace and Personality* (1917), a theology which based divine–human relationships on the idea of the sacred as personal. Buber's *I and Thou* (1923) was to give considerable impetus to this way of thinking by emphasising I–Thou relationships. In 1935, H. H. Farmer, acknowledging his debt to Oman (his predecessor at Westminster College, Cambridge), organised his understanding of God's relationship to the world round the values of absolute demand (obligation) and absolute succour (benevolence), which he regarded as expressions of the personal nature of the divine. 'The call to seek absolute values even at the cost of life is apprehended as the breaking into human awareness of a higher and more ultimate reality of succouring divine purpose.'[2] This correlation of divine and human in terms of person remains an important feature of theology.[3] We need to clarify, therefore, the meaning of divine personhood and its relationship to what we have determined about the idea of human personhood.

The understanding of divine personhood in contemporary thought involves reference to philosophical debates about divine timelessness and agency. Reasons will be given for thinking that, once it is recognised that concepts of divine immutability and perfection were deeply influenced by Greek philosophical ideas in a way that is no longer necessary or desirable, Christian theology is in a position to resituate significant connections between ideas of divine and human personhood. Support for an understanding of God as person has been traditionally found both in terms of Trinitarian relationships and in terms of the creation of humanity in the divine image. God calls humanity into being and addresses this newly created humanity by name. This view draws on a tradition which takes human address and relationship as the model for divine–human encounter. As between these two ways of conceiving divine personhood, the Trinitarian model may represent the systematic view, but it is logically and chronologically preceded by the model based on creation. Moreover, without the help of Christological and Spirit models, the Trinitarian would never have come into existence. Yet it is this creation tradition that is in danger of being passed over at the present time in favour of the Trinitarian tradition. We shall argue that they are not incompatible, but complementary.

Emphasis on relationships in concepts of person may be desirable irrespective of what is decided about some of these theological issues; and emphasis on relationality in human personhood is not dependent, at least epistemologically, on decisions about divine persons. For Christians, however, the relationship of divine and human personhood remains not only intriguing, but important and relevant to the present.

CHAPTER 7

# The relevance of history and Christology

The concept of 'person' has a long and complicated history in both theology and philosophy. J. S. Mill's comments on the tendency of 'names'(= words) to change their significance with the passing of time are relevant. If usage changes radically, he notes, the name 'can only be made serviceable by stripping it of some part of its multifarious denotation'. This is not the only option, however, especially when accretions enrich or deepen earlier usage, as Mill also notes: 'whoever seeks to introduce a more correct use of a term with which important associations are connected, should be required to possess an accurate acquaintance with the history of the particular word'.[1] From our inquiry into the history of the concept, we aim to show how an understanding of that history can, in fact, throw light on some of the present problems associated with the concept. We shall consider and give some support to the unpopular thesis that ethical judgements, even if not directly derivative from world views (which may themselves form part of an ethical stance), are closely related to overall views of human nature or the world. We aim to show how concepts of person, by virtue of their reference to an understanding of human createdness in the image of God, can play a significant role in the process of ethical justification. Attention is drawn to the role of religious and theological views in overall assessments of human nature and the world. On the other hand, some of the present disarray and confusion surrounding 'persons' stems from the way in which, particularly from the nineteenth century onwards, concepts of person applied to human beings made use, however unconsciously, of attributes and ideas originally connected with divine persons. Recognition of this may help to resolve some of the ambiguities and problems associated with the concept of person and facilitate its clearer use in Christian ethics.

Person language today is heir to a rich diversity of ideas which have developed over many centuries. Some of these developments, it will become apparent, help to explain aspects of current usage and debate. It is not always easy, however, to disentangle what is relevant from what is merely interesting. There are few hard facts, apart from some names, dates and places. Interpretation assumes all the more significance. Faced with a similar problem in *After Virtue*, A. McIntyre contrasts the understanding of virtue and virtues in Homer, Hellenistic philosophy (and the New Testament) and Benjamin Franklin. 'Are we to take these as three rival accounts of the same thing? Or are they instead accounts of three different things?'[2] He draws attention to the problem of distinguishing linguistic and conceptual identity. He concludes that 'it is a complex concept, different parts of which derive from different stages in the development of the tradition. Thus the concept itself in some sense embodies the history of which it is the outcome.'[3]

Something similar might be said about the concept of person. Although there was no exact equivalent for 'person' in ancient Greece, it would be a mistake to assume there was no concept of person at that time. *Soma*, (body) seems to have had some of the connotations of 'person'. Speculation about man's place in nature, his relation to other elements of the universe and to the gods also found a place.[4] Poets, dramatists and philosophers had their anthropologies. At a later date, Plato and Aristotle gave expression to views of human nature, and the relationship of body and soul, which have had a profound influence on ideas about persons. Some writers, like G. Gloege,[5] even divide theological interpretations of 'person' into two fundamental types – Aristotelian–Thomistic, based on the category of 'substance' and regarding person as a rational, independent, autonomous being, and Platonic–Augustinian, in which 'person' is given a more dynamic interpretation as a self-transcendent being which is capable of approximating to, and even participating in, the world of ideal Forms.

Despite their different approaches to the understanding of human nature and conduct and the relationship of body and soul, Aristotle and Plato agree that the good life requires knowledge. For Plato, such knowledge presupposes a world of ideal Forms, in which truth is no longer confused by appearances; for Aristotle, secure knowledge can be had through experience and reflection in a world characterised by purpose and action. Plato's philosopher-king has a vision of the Form of the Good, which enables him to legislate for others; Aristotle's virtuous man is marked by 'greatness of heart', intellectual contemplation and a common-sense understanding of what is practical and appropriate. Their views of the 'soul' diverge quite fundamentally. For Plato, the soul is the immortal, invisible constituent which survives the death of the material body; for Aristotle, the soul can itself be a material thing, since it is the 'form' of a body, and there are different souls (e.g. vegetative, animal, rational) as there are different bodies.[6] There is much debate about the interpretation of Plato's tripartite division of the soul as reason, spirit and appetite. Some commentators, including Martha Nussbaum, have suggested that Plato's *Phaedrus* indicates a major shift on Plato's part, readmitting the sensual and affective and poetic, although others dispute this. Because of their impact on later thinkers, it is not surprising that Plato and Aristotle have been credited with originating two quite different concepts of person. It should not be thought, however, that later views are nothing more than amplifications or extensions of Plato and Aristotle. It would also be misleading to assume that later interpretations of 'person' fall into one category or the other.[7] One of the recurring features of later development is the blending of elements that have at one time been regarded as distinct or even incompatible.[8]

Etymologically, 'person' is connected with the Latin word 'persona', whose derivation is disputed. The medieval derivation from 'per se una' is certainly false. 'Personare', meaning 'to sound through', which is related to the use of the mask in the Roman theatre, is more probable, but not entirely certain. Modern philology links 'persona' with the Etruscan word 'persu', a word found written beside a representation of two masked figures.[9] The word may also have links with the Greek word *prosopon* (face). Despite these uncertain origins, the term is linked from an early date with four different but related uses: as a mask, which one puts on to play a part; a part or role which one plays; the actor who plays a part; and the character represented. It is not difficult to see how such uses can be transferred from a stage context to ordinary life, particularly in the sense of 'role' or 'character'.[10]

H. Rheinfelder, in his detailed study of 'persona' in classical and later Latin, traces the way in which these early associations with the theatre continued to influence later usage. He also describes three other major uses, which are philosophically more interesting: person as individual; person as man or human being; person as someone of worth. The juristic use of 'person' to represent a legal subject, individual or collective, seems to have developed from person as individual. The modern emphasis on self-consciousness and memory, however, does not appear.

It has been widely accepted[11] that it was the theological and Christological debates of the early church which gave prominence to the term 'person', and it was largely as a result of theological developments that the term was taken up by philosophers. This should not be taken to mean that the ancient world had no thought-out concept of person prior to Boethius' definition of 'person' as 'individual substance of a rational nature'.[12] The frequently canvassed idea, that the ancient world could not have produced a metaphysic of the person without the help of Christianity, has been subjected to strong criticism by Christina de Vogel.[13] She has pointed to a wide range of Greek reflection, from Pythagoras and Heraclitus to Plato and Aristotle, on the nature of man. She has also demonstrated that the Stoics, under Panaetius in the second century BC had a developed theory of man characterised by self-determination. Cicero, who was influenced by the Stoics, distinguishes, in *De Officiis* I 30. 107, between the 'persona' which is common to all men, namely rational nature (which also distinguishes man from the beasts), and 'persona' which refers to a man's individual character, including his physical or intellectual make-up.[14] She does not, however, relate these findings to the use of 'person' in theological debate, apart from Plotinus.[15] Responsibility for the introduction of the term 'persona' into theological discussion has usually been thought to lie with Tertullian.[16] It has sometimes been suggested that the term was familiar to him from his legal background.[17] If, however, it was only at a later date (as seems more likely) that the juristic use developed, probably from the use of the word to denote an individual or subject of action,[18] the derivation from legal terminology must be discounted. It is also unlikely that Tertullian was drawing on a use of 'persona' related to the theatre, since he was opposed to theatrical performances, which, he believed, were likely to corrupt morality.[19] As Rheinfelder and Webb suggested,[20] it is more likely that Tertullian used 'persona' of God because of its ability to suggest individual identity without more specific overtones (e.g. of theatre or Stoicism) which he wished to avoid. It may have been the most plastic and neutral term available. On the other hand, it now seems likely that there were other reasons connected with the exegesis and interpretation of scripture for the choice of 'person'. Recent 'prosopological' studies (e.g. Andresen, Linton, Studer, Drobner) have concluded that 'prosopology' was, in fact, a significant exegetical tool in the early church's interpretation of scripture.

It now seems fairly certain that it was from this exegetical background that 'person' developed into an important theological term. Drobner has argued that it was taken up by Augustine in 397 because he saw that it was capable of holding together the divine and human, for instance, in the case of Christ. In other words the term was introduced and used mainly as a tool of exegesis, but, as a result of continued Christological debate, the term began to take on additional meaning. Most significant in this respect was the increasing tendency to use *persona* as a translation of the Greek *hypostasis*, which had acquired the meaning of 'independent or individual reality'. The Latin word *substantia*, which would have been a more literal equivalent of *hypostasis*, was used to translate the

Greek word *ousia* (being). The significance of 'substance' (*ousia*, *substantia*) and related terms such as *hypostasis* in Greek philosophy and early Christian theology tends to be assessed differently by those who see little continuing value in Greek metaphysics, and by those who regard the discussion of that period as still relevant for today.

It is argued by Gunton and Jenson, following Zizioulas, that the Cappadocians managed to break away from the static view of substance which characterised Neoplatonic philosophy and which exercised such a strong influence on Christian theology at this period. By sticking more closely to the biblical emphasis on the distinctions of Father, Son and Holy Spirit, the Cappadocians were able to develop a genuinely relational view of God and the persons of the Trinity. 'For God to be is to be in communion. *Hypostasis* and *ousia* are conceptually distinct but inseparable in thought, because they mutually involve one another.'[21] There appears to be an element of overstatement in what is attributed to the Cappadocians (cf. Pannenberg, *Systematic Theology*, I, p. 279 on certain weaknesses of the Cappadocian solution). It is true that they made a valuable contribution to the development of Trinitarian dogmatic formulae by their use of the phrase *mia ousia treis hypostaseis*, but there is a tendency to read into the Cappadocians a full-blown relational philosophy and theology, when the truth may be that they were simply interpreting scripture in a conservative manner and being faithful to the liturgy. As J. N. D. Kelly notes, the Cappadocians were also hampered by their use of prevailing Greek philosophical terms and ideas.[22]

At least two different claims are being made on behalf of the Cappadocians by Zizioulas. Although they are related, it is important not to confuse them. The first is that the Cappadocians, particularly by their use of *hypostasis* to qualify *ousia* and denote both the particularity and priority of personhood,[23] and by their recognition of the Father as the personal *aition* (cause) of creation, formulated a personal ontology of Being, anchored in baptism and ecclesial existence. This ontology was impossible in the Greek metaphysics they inherited, and was only made possible by adoption of a biblical view of *creatio ex nihilo*, and belief in Incarnation and Trinity. The second is that, without these insights, no adequate ontology of personhood is possible.

Both claims deserve careful examination. Many detailed studies have drawn attention to the Cappadocians' valuable contribution to Trinitarian debate and the construction of dogmatic formulae. Their use of *mia ousia treis hypostaseis* helped to overcome some of the problems inherent in the Nicene *homoousios* by allowing for both difference and unity in God simultaneously.[24] This contribution to the debate in the early church about how to understand the Trinity was undoubtedly very important, but there is also a danger that by seeing it as the foundation of a personalist ontology of Being, Zizioulas (and those who follow him) will read into it an ontology of personhood which reflects modern discussions of personhood. It may be true that modern secular views take no account of Christian views of personhood, but this should not be conflated with the assumption that only a Christian view can establish the importance of relationality in personhood. This latter claim is made by Zizioulas, not by the Cappadocians, although Zizioulas is not alone in deriving it from the Cappadocians.[25] The claim that only a theological interpretation of 'person-hood' anchored in a Christian metaphysic is capable of doing justice to personhood, and that secular interpretations of personhood sell the concept short, is not, in fact, dependent on the Cappadocians. The theological basis for this view, as both Zizioulas and Gunton elsewhere allow, is a Christian under-standing of creation as the act of a personal God, an under-standing deepened by confession of Jesus as Lord and baptism into the Body of Christ, sharing in the divine freedom from nature, without which no one can attain that (absolute) per-sonal freedom which is the essence of personhood.

It is this larger theological claim which has become closely associated with modern discussions about the significance of Trinitarian faith for today. But this is to invite confusion about the different interpretations of 'person' which have existed at different periods of history, and to concentrate too narrowly on one part and period of Trinitarian development. There is something invaluable, as we shall argue in chapters 8 and 9, in a theological understanding of personhood. And it is not unrelated to the development of Trinitarian theology. But the roots and implications of personhood are wider, deeper and more complex than a Cappadocian–Greek Orthodox view, which emphasises chiefly the distinction of *ousia* and *hypostasis*, might suggest. To say, 'If God does not exist, the person does not exist'[26] ignores the very real, but different, claims that non-Christians also make about persons. At this point we reserve judgement on this larger claim. There is a rather more modest claim, which is easier to substantiate and which is all that our ethical inquiry requires, namely that there is a well-established analogy between God as person and human persons. Even this claim is too much for secularists, but it is one that can be urged with more support, as we shall see, than the focus on the Cappadocians allows.

Even among theologians who recognise the historical importance of the discussions, there are those, like K. Barth and K. Rahner, who would distinguish sharply between the concept of person in Trinitarian theology and in modern secular thought. It is clearly necessary to distinguish between (a) what the early church meant by 'person' in Trinitarian and Christological controversy, (b) the significance of early church usage for later theology and (c) the significance of early church usage for later secular thought. With these distinctions in mind, we examine next developments in Augustine and Aquinas.

The importance and limitations of the developing use of 'person' in Trinitarian thought are instructively illustrated in St Augustine, for whom the concept was certainly significant. The following brief examination attempts to recover Augustine's historical meaning, but, in view of the areas of disagreement among modern interpreters of Augustine, it is clear that this must be a tentative judgement. The problems of interpretation and their significance for understanding the concept of 'person', however, will be clearly illustrated.

Augustine's discussion of the 'persons' of the Trinity is directly linked with his ideas about the 'image of God'. The influence of Neoplatonic thought is evident. There is disagreement, however, about how the influence was mediated. Augustine's reference to the conversion and public confession of Marius Victorinus (*c.* 280–363) in *Confessions* VIII 2–5 has suggested to many that the ideas of Plotinus were mediated via Victorinus (and Porphyry). Both Victorinus and Augustine find Trinitarian analogies in their analysis of man made in the image of God. But, whereas Victorinus distinguishes between the image of God which is Christ and what is made in the image of Logos, which is the soul of man, Augustine affirms that man is made in the image of God, who is a Trinity of persons:

For there are some who draw this distinction, that they will have the Son to be the image, but not man to be the image but 'after the image'. But the apostle refutes them, saying, 'For a man indeed ought not to cover his head, forasmuch as he is the image and glory of God.' He did not say 'after the image', but 'the image'. And this image, since it is elsewhere spoken of as 'after the image', is not as if it were said relatively to the Son, who is the image equal to the Father; otherwise he would not say 'after our image'. For how 'our', when the Son is the image of the Father alone? But man is said to be 'after the image', on account, as we have said, of the inequality of the likeness; and therefore after our image, that man might be the image of the Trinity; not equal to the Trinity as the Son is equal to the Father, but approaching it, as has been said, by a certain likeness.[27]

For Marius Victorinus, despite his recognition that God's being cannot be subordinate to the Plotinian One, only the Father's being is identified in this way. Christ, the Logos, is the revelation of such Being, rather than Being itself. This is certainly an expression of Trinitarian theology, but still very much influenced by Neoplatonic ideas.

Augustine's *De Trinitate* was composed over several years. It was already begun in AD 400. Parts of it were stolen and published before Bk. XIII was completed. A quotation from *De Civitate Dei* in Bk. XIII indicates it was still being composed in AD 416. It was completed between AD 416 and 428. The fifteen books of the completed work are difficult to analyse because of overlap, repetition and some inconsistency. Augustine's appeal to the concept of 'person' in Bk. V to illustrate God's Trini-

tarian nature is marked by apparent reluctance to make use of
the term 'person' in this context. 'Yet when the question is
asked, What three? human language labours under great
poverty of speech. The answer, however, is given "three
persons", not that it might be spoken but that it might not be
left unspoken.'[28] But, having established that the term is not
being used univocally of God and man, he develops a number
of analogies to suggest ways in which man as 'person' is made
in the image of God who is three 'persons': for example, 'lover
– loved – love' (VIII 10. 14). Lover and loved, however, could
conceivably be identical (e.g. in the case of self-love) and would
cease to be a genuine trinity (cf. IX. 2. 2). This leads Augustine
to an analogy in which the previous objection would not apply,
namely, the mind, the knowledge wherewith the mind knows
itself, and the love wherewith it loves both itself and its own
knowledge (IX. 3. 3). Another favourite analogy is memory–
understanding–will (eg. X. 11. 18). Because man is made in the
image of God, Augustine looks for Trinitarian analogies in
human experience; but preferably in the spiritual dimension.
The suggestion that 'husband–wife–child' might constitute a
Trinitarian analogy is rejected as false and absurd because it
seems to make the Holy Spirit the wife of the Father. It is also
implied that the whole analogy is too materialistic (XII. 5. 5).
Augustine is at pains to point out that even the better analogies
(cf. IX. 3. 3; XV. 7. 11f.) drawn from human experience are
inadequate when applied to God. The thrust of Augustine's
Trinitarian analogies appears to support the view that he is
using 'person' as a relational term. How valid such an impression is is disputed. There certainly do seem to be aspects of his
thought that anticipate future developments in the understanding of 'person', particularly in terms of self-consciousness and
self-awareness. It would be a mistake, however, to read into
him the ideas of nineteenth- and twentieth-century existentialist writers or philosophers of 'personalism'. P. Henry has
argued strongly for the view that Augustine uses 'person' as a
genuinely relational term.[29] T. F. Driver also thinks Augustine
approximates to a genuinely relational use.[30] But, as R. W.
Jenson and J. Mackey have argued,[31] Augustine's ideas of God

as person remain dominated by Neoplatonic categories, which evacuate God of genuine temporality and relationship. If God's Trinitarian being is best understood by means of introspection, and if the history of the Gospels simply reflects or parallels what has been true all along, the Incarnation is in danger of being overshadowed by timeless Neoplatonic categories.

The work of Andresen, Studer, Drobner and others[32] strongly suggests that person-exegesis of scripture was an important factor in the development of Augustine's theology and that the essential attraction of 'persona' was its ability to hold together 'in one person' body and soul, and, in the case of Christ, the human and the divine. In the matter of the Trinity, Augustine appears to be searching for an analogy that will hold together both three persons and one God. He is aware, however, that 'three persons' appears to move dangerously in the direction of tritheism, and he only accepts the phraseology of 'three persons' because it is already established in orthodox tradition. His own discussion veers towards the unipersonality of God, but he is conscious of the rich plasticity of person terminology, as well as its dangers, and it is possible he is looking for a way to exploit this.

It is sometimes argued (e.g. J. Moltmann in *The Trinity and the Kingdom of God*) that 'person' and 'relation' derive their fundamental importance in Christian theology from the doctrine of the Trinity. This may be true for the systematic theologian, but there is a danger that too much is being read into certain texts, with the result that historical developments and other readings are being neglected. Moltmann illustrates the dangers of emphasising monotheism in such a way (as, for example, the Arians and Sabellians did) that the 'persons' of the Trinity become no more than 'modes' of God's existence. He claims to find this sort of weakness in the Trinitarian thought of Karl Barth and Karl Rahner, both of whom sharply distinguish modern secular concepts of personhood in which the 'I' has a genuinely distinct individuality, from the theological use of the early church in which 'person' denoted an inner relationship. Moltmann is looking for an understanding of person that includes genuine historical relationship and can accomodate

the historical self-revelation of God in Christ without reducing
the Incarnation, Crucifixion and Resurrection to symbols of
God's love. He suggests that Augustine introduced such an
understanding of 'person' in his view of God as a Trinity of
loving relationships. This was later developed by Richard
St Victor and other theologians. It was given a crucial further
dimension by Hegel's historical understanding of person. 'The
substantial understanding of person (Boethius) and the relational understanding of person (Augustine) was now expanded
by the historical understanding of person (Hegel).'[33] In two
earlier passages,[34] Moltmann recognises deficiencies in Augustine's view of the Spirit as 'vinculum amoris', as if the Spirit
were merely the love between Father and Son and not also
'Person'. His criticism of Barth and Rahner[35] for their over-
emphasis on modes of being ought also to apply, at least in
part, to Augustine. In his later references to Augustine, Moltmann seems to incorporate a social notion of person, which is
found in a developed form in the personalism of nineteenth-
and twentieth-century philosophers and theologians, into his
portrayal of Augustine. This overlooks Augustine's Neoplatonic
background and his interpretation of 'person' in largely mental
categories. The influence of Greek philosophical categories on
Christian theology, particularly in terms of timelessness and
immutability, both of which tend to undermine rather than
simply qualify personal categories, is still debated. Augustine
fiercely rejects Manichaean dualism and Pelagian optimism in
the interests of the Gospel. He finds it more difficult to detach
himself from Plotinian ideas of man as essentially soul and
intellect, and in some sense, divine.[36] His Trinitarian ideas
were still influenced by Neoplatonic categories, but his use of
person analogies contained the seeds of something more
thoroughly incarnational.

Something similar can be said of Boethius, whose contribution to the development of the concept of person has been
rated even more highly than that of Augustine. C. C. J. Webb
thought Boethius' definition of person as 'an individual substance of a rational nature' (*persona est naturae rationalis individua
substantia*) established the parameters of all future developments:

The general history of the word Person with its derivatives in philosophical terminology may be said to have moved on the whole throughout on lines determined for it by the process whose result is summed up in the Boethian definition of *persona*. Within these lines there has been a continual oscillation, according as the thought, emphasised by the Greek word *hypostasis*, of independent and fundamentally unchangeable individuality, or the thought of social relationship and voluntary activity, suggested by the Latin word *persona*, has been uppermost.[37]

Boethius (*c.* 480–524), a Roman lawyer and minister to King Theodoric (510) until banished for political reasons, wrote a number of philosophical and theological treatises in exile. The exact scope of his work still awaits more definitive analysis and interpretation, despite valuable recent studies,[38] but he is one of the earliest Christian thinkers to draw heavily on Aristotelian as well as Platonic ideas. He translated and commented on several of Aristotle's studies in logic (e.g. *Prior and Posterior Analytics, Sophistic Arguments* and *Topics*), wrote on geometry and arithmetic, and brought a clear philosophical logic to his analysis of problems in Christian theology, particularly in connection with the Trinity. Embedded in many of these discussions were his attempts to analyse the concept of person by reference to the Aristotelian categories of substance and accident. In chapter 3 of *Contra Eutychen et Nestorium*, individual substance is defined in relation to its accidents. Qualification by accidents distinguishes individual substances from universal essences. The latter exist in and for themselves, whereas individual substances are characterised by accidents. Elsewhere (e.g. *In Librum de Interpretatione*) a distinction is drawn between the singular incommunicable quality which makes Plato Plato, for example, and the humanity which Plato shares with other men. This distinction can be used to suggest that individuality is prior to the accidents which characterise it. Significant for future development was the way in which logical and ontological concepts were combined and distinguished. This was noted by Fr. Bergeron, who argued that Latin views which emphasised the unity of the person were modified as a result of Augustine's psychological Trinitarian views.[39] He interprets twelfth- to thirteenth-century theologians as pulling away from Boethius towards an interpretation of person as relation. Aquinas, by emphasising Boethius' definition and interpreting it in the light of the concept of relationship, was able to reconcile the two approaches, he thinks. Following Bergeron, Schurr also examined whether substance or accidents determine the individual, and came to the opposite conclusion from Bergeron, since it is the accidents which first establish an individual's numerical identity; as Bergeron had also noted, 'individua . . . informata sunt propriis et specificis differentiis' (*Contra Eutychen et Nestorium*).[40] Schurr appeals to the same passages in Boethius as Bergeron but emphasises the logical priority of the individual by reference to accidents. He points out that, according to the second edition of Boethius' Commentary on Porphyry's *Isagoge*, the phrase 'ex accidentibus venientes' applies specifically to what makes Plato Plato ('Platonis proprietates').

M. Nédoncelle attempts to resolve this particular problem of interpretation by arguing that there is no single view in Boethius, only a number of changing perspectives.[41] Boethius made a number of different attempts to define 'person'. It is mistaken, therefore, he thinks, to overemphasise the definition in which individual substance is central. Other researchers (e.g. J. Bidez) have pointed to the links between Boethius' terminology and Porphyry and western Neoplatonism.[42] S. Otto thinks that the idea of person as 'subsisting substance' probably goes back to Marius Victorinus, who was also, as we have seen (p. 131), another Neoplatonic source.[43] There is no agreed definitive interpretation of Boethius' concept or concepts of person. As Webb noted, Boethius' definition contains within it two different emphases: individual and relation. From the researches of Bergeron, Schurr, Nédoncelle, Otto and others it appears that in the following centuries theologians and philosophers gave expression to one or the other of these aspects. These two emphases find their contemporary expression in the debates between communitarians and liberals. Individuals flourish best within supportive communities, but need to be able to assert their independence and integrity. Societies and communities are not simply collections of individuals, but individual freedom needs to be respected. Community and autonomy are both needed; and both are involved in the development of personhood.

The two emphases we have noted in Boethius are brought together in Aquinas' discussion of 'persona' in *ST* 1 q. 29, art. 1–4, in which four topics are examined: the definition of 'persona'; comparison of the meanings of 'person', 'nature', 'subsistence' and 'hypostasis'; whether 'person' applies to God; and whether the term can signify a relation as well as substance. He frequently refers to Boethius and occasionally to Augustine. Boethius' opinions are cited both in support of objections and in support of Aquinas' replies. At no point does Aquinas reject Boethius, although he interprets him in the way that lends most support to his own view.

In art. 2, Aquinas notes passages in Boethius which suggest that 'person' means the same as 'hypostasis', 'subsistence' and 'essence', but goes on to cite other passages which imply differentiation. He reconciles the apparently conflicting usages by arguing that '"person" means in the class of rational substances what these three words mean in general throughout the whole range of substances'. In art. 3, he argues that, despite the lack of biblical precedent for using the term 'person' of God, and despite the need for caution in its use, since it can only be used analogically of God, it is fitting to use 'person' of God because it means 'that which is most perfect in the whole of nature, namely what subsists in a rational nature'. Theologians, he says, have to use appropriate non-biblical expressions in order to rebut heretics. The term 'person' is appropriate if it is remembered that 'hypostasis', when used of God, refers to what subsists and not simply to a support for accidental qualities. Similarly, 'rational nature', when used of God, is not limited to the process of thought or discursive reason. 'Individual', used of God, means 'incommunicable'; and 'substance' means 'self-grounded existence'.

In art. 4 Aquinas indicates how 'person' can convey 'relation' as well as 'substance'. It is important that both should be possible, since Aquinas, like Augustine in *De Trinitate* v. 5. 6, wishes to assert both identity of substance and difference of relationship between the three Persons of the Trinity. Unlike existential relationships (e.g. son of this father), which are accidental and cannot be ascribed to God, logical or essential relationships (e.g. father–son) are not accidental and are appropriate to the Trinity. 'The processions within the Godhead imply real relations, and these are subsisting relations identical with the divine substance or nature.'[44] In claiming that the term 'person' can be used in these ways without contradiction, Aquinas seems to be making an epistemological, rather than an ontological, claim, however. The question whether 'person' is directly or only indirectly relational provides occasion for further linguistic analysis.[45] Aquinas comes down on the side of those who affirm direct relationality. To resolve the matter he refers back once again to the formal definition of 'person' as 'an individual substance of rational nature'. This implies both unity (within itself) and distinction (from others). 'Hence, "person" in any kind of nature signifies what is distinct in that nature.' In the case of human persons, this flesh, these bones and this soul are part of what is meant by this person. 'In the case of God, since each of the divine persons is God, "divine person" signifies relation as something subsisting.' What subsists in this case is none other than the divine nature. Hence, in the case of God, 'person' signifies relation directly. This leads to the conclusion that 'person' can legitimately signify both relation and nature (essence, substance).

Aquinas' discussion makes a number of clear distinctions within his overall framework of analogical thought about God and his general philosophical assumptions about substance and accident. It is also clear that he is attempting to reconcile conflicting interpretations and, where this is not possible, to adjudicate between them in a way that is most harmonious with his other convictions. Sometimes he stresses the overarching concept of rationality, at other times he emphasises the difference between the human and the divine. In terms of historical development, it is significant that he confirms the high status of the concept ('that which is most perfect in the whole of nature'), whether in relation to humankind or God. It is also significant that this status is related to the feature of rationality rather than relationality. Relationality is discussed with reference to the Trinity rather than human nature. Rationality, it is true, is not exactly the same for man and God, but it is predicated of both analogically, whereas relationality is only discussed in connection with God's Trinitarian being. It is constitutive of God's being in a way that is not applicable to man. As W. J. Hankey demonstrates,[46] Aquinas was influenced by the Neoplatonist Proclus to an extent rarely suspected before the twentieth century. His discussion of the persons of the Trinity suffers from many of the same defects as Augustine's view: an assumption of an eternal, timeless substance-deity and a preference for an immanent rather than economic Trinity.

Following Aquinas, medieval thinkers continued to use 'person' in the Boethian sense of 'individual substance of a rational nature', but there were those who followed Richard St Victor in placing the emphasis on the 'incommunicable' nature of persons. Whichever path was taken, 'persons' were inevitably associated with the development of 'individualism' in the medieval period.[47] It is significant, perhaps, that it is only later, when, under the influence of writers such as Feuerbach, theology was identified with anthropology and divine attributes transferred to man, that relationality comes more to the fore and may even become constitutive of human being.

The application of insights drawn from Trinitarian discussions of 'person' in the early church to human persons is taken further by a number of writers from the Greek Orthodox tradition such as V. Lossky and J. D. Zizioulas.[48] Lossky's *In the Image and Likeness of God* examines the implications of Trinitarian discussions for concepts of human person. He regards 'hypostasis' and 'ousia' as normally synonymous, and notes how some of the Church Fathers also thought this in regard to secular philosophy, but attempted to make a distinction in theology because God's being could not be conceptualised in this way. The attempt by Aquinas to preserve and yet modify Boethius' definition of person as 'substantia individua rationalis naturae' and to apply it to both human and divine persons by stressing the idea of 'subsistence' and 'relation', when 'persona' is applied to God, suggests to Lossky that, although the Church Fathers and Aquinas were on the verge of recognising the uniqueness of the human person in relation to the rest of the created order, they failed to do so, because they continued to regard human person as equivalent to individual substance. Since this conflicts with Trinitarian thought about 'hypostasis' and 'person', one ought either to give up calling individual human beings 'persons' or one should recognise that 'person', as applied to human beings, points beyond nature, as in the case of God. Lossky chooses the second alternative because he believes it is implicit in the Christology of the early church.[49] 'Person', whether applied to God or man, signifies the irreducibility of 'person' to 'nature' or 'essence'. Person, as applied to the human individual, means someone 'who is distinct from his own nature, someone who goes beyond his nature while containing it'.[50] The human individual, as person, has to be rethought in the light of Trinitarian ideas of hypostatic union. This leads Lossky to re-examine Genesis i. 27, not in an attempt to recover the original meaning of the passage, but to consider how it can be integrated into a Trinitarian theology. 'Personhood belongs to every human being by virtue of a singular and unique relation to God who created him "in his image."' The significance of this relationship is commented on as follows:

This . . . does not indicate, in itself, a relationship of participation, much less a kinship with God, but rather an analogy: like the personal God in whose image he is created man is not only 'nature'. This bestows on him liberty in regard to himself, taken as an individual of a particular nature. Though not explicit in patristic anthropology, this new category of the human person or hypostasis is nonetheless always presupposed by it.[51]

Like Augustine, Lossky takes up the reference to the 'image of God' in Genesis i. 26–8, because it is important both exegetically and theologically. For the exegete, the plural 'we' raises interesting questions about who is addressing whom. For the Christian theologian, a Trinitarian exposition of creation is both natural and justified. Like Augustine, Lossky assumes an overarching Trinitarian theology. Historically, however, it is worth drawing attention to the importance of this passage in Genesis for the way it describes God as Creator in terms characteristic of human speech and agency. Humanity is made 'in God's image'. Although the interpretation of 'image' is beset with problems, we can safely rule out later views which find the 'image' in rationality. Humanity represents God and is to accomplish the divine purpose. Despite the multiplicity of interpretations of Genesis i. 26–8, there is widespread agreement[52] that the meaning of the passage depends on its context, and that humanity is to rule over God's creation as God's vice-regent. This functional view of 'image' and the dominion tradition is perhaps suspiciously similar to the functional modern outlook, and we should, therefore, be wary. The main rival interpretation, however, the so-called Barthian or relational view, may also be influenced by the contemporary interest in relationships. The two views may not be incompatible, especially if one follows Westermann's understanding of the relational view: 'God has created man in his image to correspond with him, so that something may happen between him and this creature' (see note 52). The relation is not simply between humanity and God, but between God and his creation, with humanity as God's partner in dialogue, responsible to God for the care and replenishment of creation. Personal address, communication and responsibility for the other are important constituents of both views. In that this communication emanates from God it is more than 'humanity writ large', but equally clearly the analogy is based on features of human experience. It will be important to bear this in mind when we come to examine in what sense God may be understood as 'person'.

Within the Greek Orthodox Church, theologians have continued to preserve and rework ideas found in the early Fathers, perhaps more so than theologians of any other Christian communion. A strong sense of tradition runs through their writings. Sometimes this leads to suspicion and rapid distancing of themselves from other Christian theologians, particularly Protestants. Even where there has been some convergence of theological ideas, as in the matter of the human person understood primarily as a related being, the differences rather than any similarities are emphasised. This is largely true even of J. D. Zizioulas' *Being as Communion*, although there is a brief acknowledgement that some Western Protestant theologians have begun to develop views which are not dissimilar. In an earlier article, in which he investigated theological aspects of personhood, he divided anthropologies into those based on introspection (a category which included Tertullian, Augustine and the Scholastics) and those in which man is approached as 'an indefinable being which can be grasped only by being put in the light of his ability to relate to extra-human realities' (a category represented chiefly by Eastern and Orthodox theologians and a number of Western thinkers such as Martin Buber, John Macmurray and Wolfhart Pannenberg).[53] His fundamental conviction that personhood is relational, and that God is the source of all such personhood, is applied in a searching manner both to secular philosophy and to religious claims and beliefs. Such personhood is inescapably ontological, he thinks. In the light of the criteria which he advances, a great deal of philosophical and theological thought is found wanting; it is ontologically deficient, or, worse, demonic. His fundamental presuppositions, however, are assumed rather than argued for. It is not enough to show what the early Fathers believed. The continuing adequacy of their views must be argued for. It is not clear how Zizioulas justifies the connections he makes between patristic ideas and modern discussions of personhood. In this respect, Pannenberg and others make a more extended attempt to deal with some of the epistemological and ontological questions by grounding them in an understanding of human nature which combines attention to empirical factors with theological interpretation.

Zizioulas makes it clear that he is not concerned simply with personal relationships. Such an emphasis might conceivably be associated with a rather limited view of reality and personhood. He comments: 'Methodologically, the issue under discussion cannot be decided on the basis of human nature as such.'[54] The human nature important for Chalcedon is not empirical human nature, whether in Christ or others, he thinks, but personhood, which is characterised by communion with God in freedom and love. Man's highest capacity is to be God's image, but this is not a fixed capacity, so to speak. Man's divinisation, which Zizioulas welcomes like Orthodox theologians in general, is to be found only in his communion with God, a communion which allows for difference without division and individualisation. 'In communion with God man is capable of everything (Mark ix. 23; Philippians iv. 13; etc.) – though only in the incapacity of creaturehood which poses itself clearly in such a communion.'[55] He is right to draw attention to inadequate notions of personhood in Western thought,[56] but his claim that everything needful was anticipated in the hypostasis-person concept of Greek theology in the fourth century requires further scrutiny. The attempt in both Lossky and Zizioulas to interpret 'person' as more than 'individual' (whether human or not, characterised by rationality) is a step in the right direction, but whether the idea of 'persons in relation' depends quite so entirely on the Trinitarian context is a question we shall examine further in chapter 9.

CHAPTER 8

# *Divine embodiment and temporality: is God a person?*

Our historical survey (chapters 5–7) suggests that the concept of person underwent a remarkable development from its early grammatical and exegetical usage via Christological and Trinitarian speculation to its Lockean use as both a forensic term of responsibility and a term for personal identity, its rational and ethical emphasis in Kant, its use in Feuerbach to subvert Hegel's idealism and some of the theological ideas of the period, and its almost purely evaluative use in many contexts today to signify approval of status.

The present chapter will analyse more closely the idea of God as person, and important objections to the idea. Although it is assumed by Lossky and Zizioulas and others, as we noted, that the idea of human personhood is influenced by, if not derived from, the idea of God as person, we need to explore what is meant by this, particularly in relation to Trinitarian usage. Our historical survey has indicated how members of the early Christian church made use of the concept for theological purposes, because it enabled them to relate their exegesis of scripture to their experience of God in Christ and their common life in the Body of Christ. It was flexible and could be related to prevailing Greek philosophical ideas, yet, at the same time, it was free from some of the alien connotations of substance philosophy, and allowed them to bring out the distinctiveness of historical revelation, i.e. what God had done in Christ.

This early Trinitarian usage, however, can be a source of confusion for modern thought in which reference to persons is based almost entirely on ideas of self and consciousness and individual ethical agency stemming from the seventeenth century. It is also confusing for those who have been deliberately open and receptive to earlier theological views of personhood, especially when this is linked with a conscious or unconscious desire to preserve earlier theological formulations as representing the tradition or orthodoxy of the church.

In what follows, we shall examine the arguments for thinking that the nature of divine personhood in its relation to human personhood has a direct bearing on the ethical implications of personhood if it is accepted that God is understood as person and that humanity is made in God's image. In earlier chapters, we have argued that person and human being should not be sharply separated; that there was a certain amount of interaction between ideas of human personhood and Christological and Trinitarian speculation in the development of Christian thought; and that in the modern period, particularly in the thought of Feuerbach and later, humanity became the *locus* of ideas and values once associated with divine personhood. It would be quite possible to argue on the basis of a (religious) conception of the human person (even without reference to Trinitarian thought) that such a conception affected ethical outcomes. In this case, although it would matter greatly what our theological understanding of human personhood was, it would not matter that divine personhood was something very different. There is also a stronger thesis, namely that the conception of divine personhood should be, or, even more strongly, is determinative of, the understanding of human personhood and that this should also influence ethical stances. It is this stronger thesis that we now wish to examine.

Two obstacles faced by this stronger thesis are represented by the view that:
(a) God is a disembodied person
(b) God is a timeless person.
If God is disembodied and/or timeless, how can God be a model for human personhood which is embodied and temporal? We will consider these objections in turn. It has normally been assumed by classical theism that God is 'without body, parts or passions'. Yet human personhood is normally

understood by reference to an embodied, material agent, even if agency as such requires intentional action and no agent can be understood in purely materialistic terms. One of the most interesting and developed attempts to counter the idea that personhood requires material embodiment is R. G. Swinburne's analysis of the concept of person in *Coherence of Theism*, part of a larger programme which seeks to justify a form of theism. The aim is to show that, if one can demonstrate that the concept of a contingent god, based on the idea of an omnipresent person, is itself coherent, this would be an important stage in any attempt to show the reasonableness of belief in a non-contingent God of the sort envisaged in several versions of classical theism. One of the crucial steps in the argument is to show how the description of a contingent god as a non-embodied person aptly prepares the mind to understand what is involved in the worship of a non-contingent God, also described as a non-embodied person. This defence of theism is executed with great imagination and thoroughness, but we shall examine only that part which is relevant to our purposes, namely Swinburne's analysis of what is meant by 'person'.

Swinburne's discussion[1] gives a clear account of how he thinks the concept of person is acquired. As children we learn what 'person' means by being given examples of actual persons such as parents, brothers and sisters and ourselves. References by Swinburne to 'our normal concept of person', however, are unhelpful and misleading, since this suggests a far greater degree of agreement than actually exists. He makes use of Strawson's discussion[2] of 'person' as a primitive concept embodying both M (material) and P (person) predicates, and concludes with many other writers that Strawson's formulation, although useful so far as it goes, is insufficient to distinguish 'persons' from other animals possessing both M and P predicates. He supplements Strawson's account, therefore, by reference to persons as language users (cf. Wittgenstein), as having second-order wants,[3] and as forming moral judgements. 'If a thing is characterizable by all of the above predicates, then it is a person; and if it is characterizable by none it is not.' Borderline cases are put on one side temporarily. This account, says Swinburne, would differentiate persons and animals, and would correspond to the way in which 'medievals following Aristotle' would say 'persons have rational souls'. Can this account be applied to a non-embodied person? Swinburne devotes most of the rest of his analysis to this particular question. Could there be an individual who 'thought and perhaps talked, made moral judgements, wanted this and not that, knew things, favoured this suppliant and not that etc., but had no body?'

Swinburne's exposition of what it means to have a body draws on Harrison's account,[4] which lists five essential features: the body may be a source of pain and other sensations; the inside of the body is experienced (e.g. empty stomach); I can move some parts of my body directly; my body forms my vantage-point in observing the world; my thoughts and feelings are affected by bodily stimuli (e.g. alcohol). Although God is not embodied in all of these ways, he is embodied in some of them, for example he can move any part of the universe directly, he knows everything that has happened or is happening in the universe. Swinburne argues that it is coherent to suppose God is a person without a body. The strongest counter-arguments, he thinks, come from discussions about personal identity in which the body plays a crucial role. In response to such arguments he asserts that:

1. all empiricist theories of personal identity lead to absurd conclusions and are to be rejected;
2. the identity of a person over time is something ultimate, not analysable in terms of bodily continuity or continuity of memory and character.

In order to establish the first point, he examines a number of problems posed by recent discussions of personal identity. He regards the second point as either an intuition (like induction) or an analytic truth. He makes it clear that he is not talking about evidence for personal identity, which is most naturally understood in terms of bodily continuity and continuity of memory and character. The real issue is the coherence of the concept of person, which, he maintains, does not necessitate a body.

Swinburne's view, however, is to be rejected. There are good reasons for the emphasis on embodiment. The persons we are most familiar with, other human agents, are, without exception, embodied. And the body plays a crucial role in philosophical discussions of personal identity. It can be argued[5] that, in opting to defend the idea of God as a bodiless person, Swinburne is turning his back on one of the most essential features of a person. G. M. Jantzen[6] has made a good attempt to argue that the world is analogous to God's body, and that God, being a person, is inseparable from his body, which may, of course, assume different forms. She criticises Swinburne for failing to see the force of his own comments on embodiment. God's direct control of the universe is an argument, she says, 'not against God's having a body but in favour of it – only, his body must be understood as the whole universe, not an individual part of it'. It would certainly have been open to Swinburne to make greater use of those references in Harrison's article which point to non-corporeal embodiment to argue that embodiment is necessary but need not be material. Jantzen's argument, however, requires such a close relationship between God and the world ('there are strong theological reasons for saying that God and the universe must be co-eternal')[7] that some theists may object and argue that the distinction between God and the world should be more clearly stated. What is required is some means of identifying God non-corporeally. Can this be accomplished in terms of other features (e.g. his unique relationship to parts of an empirically grounded narrative)?

Strawson gave good reasons for construing 'persons' in such a way that the stronger forms of mind–body dualism are avoided and the individual person is thought of as a unified and embodied personal agent. Swinburne, on the other hand, argues that, even if normally associated with a body, both human and divine persons are essentially non-embodied (i.e. they can be understood in the final resort as non-embodied).[8] Swinburne's overall strategy for defending Christian theism by putting forward the picture of a divine agent, who can be understood on the analogy of a human person, discounts the crucial role of the body for the human agent, and then argues that, by analogy, we can do the same for God. It is doubtful, however, whether the idea of a human agent without a body does successfully get off the ground, since it appeals to several vestiges of a body which are only made compatible with non-embodiedness by reliance on ideas drawn from empirical embodied agents, for example, the idea of a non-embodied voice. It is true that people claim to hear voices in the head or above or around them (some of which turn out to be imaginary), emanating apparently from nowhere, but the whole idea of non-embodied voices possessing a reality which is entirely unrelated to embodied agency is parasitic on the twin features of a conceptual distinction of voice and body and a long tradition (oral and literary) of the capacity of human beings to hear discarnate voices (from a spirit world). Whether there are such spirits and voices is no more testable than the question whether God does, in fact, exist. What is quite clear is that Swinburne cannot (logically) appeal to such voices to affirm the existence of disembodied agents. He can only argue that, if such voices turn out to be veridical, then the idea of a disembodied agent could be equally veridical. It is not enough to argue that such voices are conceptually possible, since he wishes to defend the strong thesis that persons (human or divine) are, in fact, essentially disembodied.

More serious, however, is the damage which the idea of disembodied agents does to our ideas of persons, human or divine. It flies in the face of a great deal of human experience, and is not consonant with the main tenor of biblical revelation. (Strictly speaking, it is anachronistic to say that a particular form of dualism is biblical, since the question had not been raised in these terms for the biblical writers, but, presumably, Swinburne means that this form of dualism is compatible with, and logically required by, biblical teaching about an after-life. Others would no doubt dispute this on the grounds that biblical teaching points to other possibilities.) It is an expedient which ought not to be considered unless there are extremely strong reasons for ignoring the crucial importance of the conceptual link between body and person.

Such a reason might perhaps be found in the tradition that God is spirit. But this appears to misunderstand the nature of 'spirit' in Hebrew. Closely connected with ideas of breath and wind, the Hebrew *ruach* significantly contrasts the power of spirit with the weakness of flesh (cf. Isaiah xxxi. 3). God is spirit; man is flesh. But God, who breathes his spirit into men and women, does not rob them of their bodies, nor does the fact that God is spirit mean that God cannot be referred to by means of human form and features of the human organism. The horses of the Egyptians, in Isaiah xxxi, are 'flesh', signifying their weakness or lack of power. If God had breathed life and spirit into them, they would have been strong and full of power. H. W. Wolff's discussion of *ruach*, aptly sub-titled 'Man as he is Empowered',[9] makes it clear that *ruach* ('spirit') is not identical with disembodiedness.

The philosophical questions that troubled the early Fathers, who were familiar with the ideas and thought-forms of Platonism and Aristotelianism, and the medieval doctors of the church, are not, of course, raised in the Old and New Testaments. To that extent, we have to allow the questions raised by later philosophy to stand in their own right. But it is not necessary to accept all the presuppositions of Greek views of body and matter. The nature of identification and embodiedness may now be understood in different ways.

Strawson suggests that normally 'spatio-temporal relations provide an indispensable network of individuating relations'. There are other modes of identification, however, which are particularly relevant in the case of God. These are: 'story-relative identification'; 'logically individuating description' (e.g. the particular mother of a particular child; the winner of a specific sporting event; or the sole creator of the universe); and 'non-transferable ownership by a single person'. These three criteria together make possible a very different approach from that argued for by Swinburne. The first criterion by itself simply points to the identification of a particular within a narrative framework, in which all the characters may be fictional. 'The identification is within a certain story told by a certain speaker. It is identification within his story; but not identification within history.'[10] This would only enable us to identify God within the Jewish or Christian stories as 'Creator and Redeemer' for Jews and Christians, or as 'the One who raised Jesus from the dead' for Christians. It would not enable us to go further and locate the Jewish-Christian stories within history without further criteria. The reference to 'story' and 'narrative', however, can be given an empirical reference by means of the second and third criteria, so that we are no longer dealing simply with a story-relative identification, but with a narrative clearly rooted in history and a narrative-related identification that relates to God's actions experienced in history. There is still the subjectivity of God's actions having to be experienced in history. And who is to say whether that which was experienced as God was truly received and interpreted? But the links between the person God is and the character of God can be developed in narrative terms in a number of fruitful ways. If narrative-relative identification offers a promising way forward, then, although there is no neutral identification of God – how could there be? – we can understand divine embodiment and agency on two different levels: in terms of Incarnation and the narratives reporting this. It is true that, on this view, God is not embodied in exactly the same way as the human person, except in the Incarnation, but the numerous problems of substance dualism can be genuinely overcome, and it is possible to attribute personhood to God and human agents in a non-equivocal sense.

We turn now to the second objection to God's personhood: that God is timeless. W. Kneale's article on 'Time and Eternity in Theology', questioning God's alleged timelessness, was instrumental in setting light to a slow-burning fuse which eventually led to a great explosion of academic interest in God's timelessness.[11] At issue, it came to be seen, is the nature of God. Not so much whether God is eternal, but in what sense God is eternal. On the one side, God's eternity is taken to be timeless; but such a timeless eternity removes God from real contact with the world, it was claimed. Hence, rival views interpret God's eternity as time-filled. As Wolterstorff has commented:

All Christian theologians agree that God is without beginning and without end. The vast majority have held, in addition, that God is eternal, existing outside of time. Only a small minority have contended that God is everlasting, existing within time.[12]

He then argues that:

God as conceived and presented by the biblical writers is a being whose own life and existence is temporal . . . they present him [God] as acting within *human* history . . . God the Redeemer cannot be a God eternal. This is so because God the Redeemer is a god who *changes.* And any being which changes is a being among whose states there is temporal succession. Of course, there is an important sense in which God as presented in the Scriptures is changeless; he is steadfast in his redeeming intent and ever faithful to his children. Yet *ontologically* God cannot be a redeeming God without there being changeful variation among his states.[13]

Wolterstorff contrasts the difference between biblical pictures of God as eternal in a timeless sense and God who is everlasting, enduring through all time, but involved and active in time. Kneale argued that one of the reasons why the biblical pictures of God acting in time were replaced by a view of God as above time or outside time was the Greek view that time and change represented something less than perfection. How could a perfect being change? Because change and perfection were thought to be fundamentally incompatible, it was assumed that God, who had to be perfect, must also be impervious to temporal change. But, for many modern philosophers and theologians seeking to challenge the assumptions of Greek rationalism, 'every attempt to purge Christian theology of the traces of incompatible Hellenic patterns of thought must fail unless it removes the roadblock of the God eternal tradition'.[14] It could also be argued that there are close links between ideas of perfection and ideas of power. The discussion of God's perfection almost inevitably draws on ideas of God's omnipotence. Not only can God not do what is logically impossible; he cannot be unfaithful to his character as a just and loving God. What this means in the light of revelation is clearly of fundamental importance.

There are at least four different areas of conceptual inquiry involved in the issue of God's timelessness from a philosophical point of view: the nature of time; the nature of religious language; the relation of omniscience and free-will; and God's knowledge of the future. The question of omniscience illustrates many of the problems, and we shall concentrate on that. When it is said that 'God knows everything' and therefore knows in advance what the future will bring, the question is raised: if this is true, what happens to human freedom? A God who is omniscient, who knows everything, must know past, present and future. If such a being knows the future before it happens, there appears to be a sense in which the future is already determined, because it is known to God. In this case, since all future events and actions are foreseen by such a God, they are all predetermined. No one is free. No actions are free. We can try to wriggle out of this by denying the efficacy or importance of such foreknowledge. Since no other being is omniscient, and unless God reveals his knowledge to another, no one does, in fact, know the future, except God. But all such palliative proposals are worthless in that they do not affect the basic position that, if God is omniscient, even if uniquely so, he automatically knows the future and human freedom is compromised. It was, in part at least, to meet this dilemma that the doctrine of God's timelessness was developed. Boethius (*c.* 480–524) defined 'eternal' as 'complete, simultaneous and perfect possession of all its life'. By removing the characteristics of 'before' and 'after' from God's timeless omniscience, it seems possible to remove the problem of foreknowledge. God does not foreknow what I will do, although all my actions, past, present and future, are known to him. He simply knows (timelessly) what I have done, am doing or will do. Because God is not involved in the time process, the process of change, the process of cause and effect, he does not foreknow or predetermine anything. This is a sophisticated answer to a theoretical theological problem about God's omniscience and human freedom. In order to rescue human freedom, I make God's omniscience timeless. The solution has been adopted by many Christians since Boethius.[15]

Unfortunately, in solving one set of questions it raises others.

If God is outside of time, what is one to make of other descriptions of God which attribute time-related features to him? As J. R. Lucas says:

To say that God is outside time, as many theologians do, is to deny, in effect, that God is a person. The Absolute, *to on*, the Form of the Good, or even, perhaps, the Ground of our Being, may be outside time, and timeless in a full-blooded Platonic sense, but they are not persons: they neither see what we are, nor hearken unto our prayers, nor care what we do, let alone intervene in the course of the world's events. If we think of God as a living person, who acts in the world, or even who is merely conscious, we must seem to be ready to apply temporal expressions to Him, because the applicability of temporal predicates of some sort or other is a necessary condition of activity, even the inactive activity of consciousness.[16]

If I try to resolve the problem of God's omniscience by making him timeless, I may create a worse problem by denying to him the essence of what it means to be a person.

In fact, it is not only philosophers who have become worried about the idea of God's timelessness. Theologians are also concerned. What happens to the idea of God's providence and ability to answer prayer if He is timeless? And, for the Christian, there are further issues raised by Incarnation and Crucifixion. It may seem at first sight that a God who is involved in time is limited. His omniscience is restricted to past and present and whatever future events are already determined. Not even he, on this view, knows the undetermined future except as a possibility. But is not a timeless God even more limited? It is conceivable that God is timeless in the way that numbers and logical truths are timeless. But what advantages are there in regarding God as timeless? And, more importantly, is it true? What is to be made of the tradition that regards God as operative in time?

One possible answer is to distinguish between God and His effects. God, it is said, causes things to happen in time, without Himself being in time. Recent study of indexicals does not encourage this solution, however. Take, for example, the word 'now'. When I say, 'it is now 4 o'clock', the truth value of this statement is relative to a point in time. At 5 o'clock the statement will be false, although it was true when uttered at 4 o'clock. The importance of 'now' and other time-index words is that, although God can know 'it is now 4 o'clock' at 4 o'clock, he cannot know this always, because at other times it will be false. Moreover, if God is outside time, he can never know 'it is now 4 o'clock', because now relates to a position in time. It is not possible to escape this dilemma by trying to invent a tenseless but dated speech by arguing that 'it is now 4 o'clock' is equivalent to 'it was 4 o'clock' uttered with reference to 4 o'clock on a particular date. As A. N. Prior comments, when considering the statement that the 1960 final examinations at Manchester are now over, 'It's true now, but it wasn't true a year ago . . . what we know when we know that the 1960 final examinations are over can't just be a timeless relation between dates, because this isn't the thing we're pleased about when we're pleased that the exams are over'.[17] Against this view, which maintains the importance of indexicals like 'now' and 'here', it has been argued that, although this is partly true, what is known at one particular time by a particular person can be known at a later time by another person and all that is necessary is to change the way of expressing it. Thus, 'It is now June 10' known by me today, could be equally known by you tomorrow if you claimed to know on June 11 that 'yesterday it was June 10'. But 'it is now June 10' uttered on June 10 is not equivalent to 'it was June 10 yesterday' uttered on June 11. The debate about indexicals continues, and is not yet settled, but its relevance for theology is clear. It casts doubt on the view that an omniscient being can timelessly know what a time-related being knows at a particular time.

Two groups of theologians who have argued strongly for the view that God's knowledge and actions must be time-related in order to make sense of other claims about God are process theologians and eschatologically oriented theologians. Process theology is significant in this context because time is a central feature of process thought. Applied to God, it means that Becoming rather than Being is the best way to understand His nature. God's being is not self-complete and separate from the world, but interacts with it and is influenced by it. Much of what process theology says about love and the lure of God's love is relevant to discussions of personhood. As persons, we are always in process of becoming. God, too, is in process of becoming. He is not uninfluenced by the world he is involved in creating. It is not clear, however, that process thought is able to do justice to other aspects of God's character, such as his creative and redemptive power. God becomes a part of history rather than lord of history. He becomes indistinguishable from the future. 'Neither God, nor the World, reaches static completion. Both are in the grip of the ultimate metaphysical ground, the creative advance into novelty. Either of them, God and the World, is the instrument of novelty for the other.'[18]

Eschatological theologians have been more aware of the dangers of this line of thinking, and have tended to concentrate on the newness of the resurrection of the dead and the relation of this to other eschatological (and sometimes apocalyptic) themes in Christian thought. They fall into two groups. Those who stress the universality of a Christian scheme (cf. Pannenberg) and wish to relate Christ's resurrection to an overall philosophy of history somewhat in the manner of Hegel, and those who distance themselves as completely as possible from idealistic philosophies of history (cf. Moltmann), believing that only God and Christ can usher in the End. Some of the former group also share some of the ideas of process theology.

There is no clear conceptual examination, however, of time and timelessness in major eschatological theologians such as Moltmann. The influence of Barth, who contrasted God's time ('the fullness of time without the defects of succession') with human time which is characterised by the succession of past, present and future, perpetuates the assumption that divine time without succession is more real and fails to clarify what is involved in God's relationship to human time.

Philosophers (of religion) continue to expend great energy on the topic, and, although theology is sometimes only a minor conversation partner, there is evidence of clear progress in some recent discussions. For example, A. Padgett,[19] after a careful examination of the relevant literature and the main discussions about the nature of time and timelessness, concludes that, even if timelessness is formulated in a way that is internally coherent, so that it may be attributed to God, the theory of time which it involves is not necessary and does not do justice to what can be known of God, particularly in the light of biblical statements about God acting in time.

Since God really changes in relationship with the world, God must in some way be temporal. For whenever a change occurs the subject of the change goes through some interval of time. Therefore, God is not absolutely timeless, and the traditional doctrine of eternity must be abandoned. (p. 122)

This involves the rejection of Neoplatonic immutability, but allows for constancy of character, nature and perfections in God. God is not in time as creatures are in time, however, and it is important to note significant ways in which God transcends time. God is to be understood as the ground, or creator, of time. Although God could logically have chosen to live in a timeless universe, he 'has chosen eternally to have a temporal universe in which to live. This choice is an eternal one . . . Time need not have been in God's creation. This is one way in which God transcends time' (p. 123). Moreover, God is the Lord of time, not subject to its vicissitudes in the way that human beings are. Although he does not determine the details of every event or prevent free agency, he is not limited by the passage and ravages of time. 'For the Lord of time and eternity, time is a servant and not a master' (p. 124). God does not die and his existence is not threatened by time or by any state of affairs outside himself. It is important, however, not to confuse this truth with the Greek view of immutability and perfection. God, as understood by Christians, is a God who intervenes in history and is capable of exercising initiative in relation to our temporal existence. This means that God's relation to time is not adequately conveyed by 'timelessness', at least in the most common sense of that term. On the other hand, 'it is far more appropriate to say that we are in God's time, than that God is in our time' (p. 126). God is not subject to measured time, but neither is he simply above time or timeless.

Can one still think of such a temporally active but 'relatively timeless' God (Padgett's phrase) as a person? In terms of embodiment and temporality, it is clear that God is not physically embodied or literally in/subject to time. There are good reasons, as we have seen, for not thinking of God as 'a person' like other persons, even if we revise the understanding of timelessness to take account of God's temporal relationship to the created order. God is not 'in time' or 'subject to time' in the way that human beings are. He is not 'a person' without qualification. The idea of God as 'a person' remains genuinely problematic. And yet there is a sense in which God may be construed as the primordial person – in terms of the sort of agency and character which human beings often set before themselves as ideal. Divine agency is not limited and encumbered by the restrictions of time and space, whereas human existence and agency frequently has great difficulty in making any impact at all on a hostile and recalcitrant environment of natural and social forces. Moreover, God's character is not flawed or lacking in virtue, as the character of the human person so often is. Human goodness is often ambiguous and fragile, despite the best of intentions.

Time and space are not defects in themselves, yet, in terms of human experience and apprehension of them, they fail materially to realise the hopes and ambitions that human creatures have for the world and themselves. Hence, the longing for an existence not subject to the conventional limitations of time and space, a longing which is sometimes expressed in the relentless urge for technological change, is reflected in a way of thinking which posits personhood without these limitations.

Such a view of divine personhood, however, encounters all the strictures of a theological hermeneutic of suspicion, which wants to have nothing to do with such a projection of God in superhuman terms. Although it should not be assumed that the idea of a deity embodied in narrative and revealed in the ambiguity of history is put forward in order to reduce the (metaphorical) distance between God and the world or to imply that divine personhood is simply human personhood writ large, it is important to respond to this particular theological criticism.

What can be said about God is clearly vital. It is generally recognised by theologians that there can be no direct speech about God, if this implies direct human access to, or experience of, God. All our access is mediated and our experience indirect. Talk/speech about God is similarly indirect. But the language used about God is language that can be, and frequently is, used about human experience, and is applied to God analogically or metaphorically in order to give expression through symbol, narrative, poetry and ritual to human intimations of a transcendent dimension to reality. Can the language of divine personhood do that?[20] And what theological commentary would such a use require?

It is clearly necessary to be aware of the material and social conditioning of theological utterance. The idea that both God and the human subject are 'persons' seems suspiciously like an attempt to place humanity in a privileged position at the centre of the universe. The language of personhood applied to both divine and human persons is ideologically suspect.[21] Can the suspicion be defused? Recognition of the dangers in the idea of God as a disembodied and timeless person is the first step. We have given good reasons for thinking that God is neither disembodied nor timeless in any straightforward sense. In chapter 9 we suggest that a necessary second step is closer attention to the question of relationality in the analogy between divine and human persons.

In the remainder of this chapter we try to clarify what is involved in the analogy of personhood applied to a God who is not disembodied or timeless in the traditional sense, but who is embodied in Incarnation and the narratives about divine embodiment and temporal activity. This will involve further consideration of Trinitarian personhood and why theologians are often willing to regard God as a Trinity of persons but not as a person. Our earlier discussions made it clear that Trinitarian debate and the idea of God as three Persons influenced later ideas of person as a relational being. From both the philosophical and theological side, there are good reasons for starting with the human person in exploring what the concept of person can mean. But there is also a Trinitarian theological tradition which regards human beings as persons chiefly by virtue of the fact that they reflect divine–human nature. The essence of what it means to be a person is found primarily in God's Trinitarian nature. These discussions have in turn influenced later ideas of person as a relational being. A clear example of this line of thinking is J. D. Zizioulas' *Being as Communion* (see p. 184 below). Other theologians, less impressed by the importance of Chalcedonian categories, would construct their anthropologies on more existentialist lines, but might still use personalist and relational categories which are closely related to Trinitarian ideas and biblical views of God as personal. Literalistic intepretations of the Bible, which argue that God is a person because the Bible portrays God as seeing, hearing, speaking and acting, should not prevent recognition of the fact that it was this sort of language about God which was partly responsible for the growth of more reflective views which continue to see God as person.

What are the more positive reasons for thinking of God as 'person'? Underlying the view that God is person is the emphasis on the personal, and the willingness to use personal language about God. God remembers, has feelings, judges, is angry, repents, sees, speaks, listens and acts. That God does such things can hardly be construed literally, even from the perspective of writers who had a pre-scientific world-view. The God who sees is also all-seeing; nothing is hidden from him. Even in the womb he knows all about me (Ps.139). His sight is not dependent on physical organs of vision. Or, as H. H. Rowley said, 'we can hardly presume that when God asks Adam what he has been doing, he is ignorant of the answer until Adam confesses. In the following chapter Cain avoids confessing his sin, but finds that God already knows. His power to control the forces of Nature and the kingdoms of man is assumed everywhere . . . There is no place from which he is excluded. All this is taken for granted in the Bible and there is no need to cite texts to establish it.'[22] Some of the language may be more anthropomorphic than linguistic analysis would prefer (e.g. God walks in the garden in the cool of the evening), but poetic metaphor is not a linguistic defect. Running throughout the Old Testament is the fundamental recognition of God as Creator and Redeemer, ideas which receive their most sublime expression in Isaiah 40–55. God is Spirit. When these affirmations coalesce round the mission and identity of Jesus in the New Testament, we are not far from Paul's conviction that 'God was in Christ reconciling the world to himself' (2 Corinthians v. 17) It is not surprising, therefore, that theological reflection on God's nature and character should concern itself with the Trinitarian thought of the early church, particularly in respect of temporality and impassibility. In Christian tradition God is not *a* person, for the simple reason that He is One God in Three Persons. This oneness of God in a plurality of persons means that the personhood predicated of God, analogous to that of human persons, who are essentially related to other persons and cannot be understood as isolated individuals, although their individuality is unique and precious, has to be expressed in a paradoxical way which gives expression both to the oneness and threefold embodiedness or self-actualisation of God. Moreover, God is also intimately related to creation, which is empowered with a certain independence and autonomy yet remains God's creation. God's relationship to humankind, the divine steward, within the created order is distinctive and special, but the whole of creation is part of the paean of praise responding to God's fruitful blessing.

In examining how the concept of 'person' developed, we noted that its importance in Trinitarian and Christological discussion in the early church may have contributed to the status and value of the human person in later thought, especially under the influence of theological references to humanity 'in the image of God'. With Feuerbach, some of the self-transcending powers of the divine person are transferred to the human person, and the divine person is made in man's image. It is noticeable, however, that theologians rarely refer to God as 'a person' in these discussions. C. C. J. Webb notes, as possible exceptions to this, the heresiarch Paul of Samosata in the third century and Durandus a Sancto Porciano in the fourteenth century. Durandus observed that, if God is not a Trinity, this would make him a person.[23] Webb dates talk of

God as a person to the eighteenth century, and gives as examples Schleiermacher and Paley.[24] Kant's use of the term in moral contexts, although referring to the ideal rational moral agent, contributed to a burgeoning ideology of the 'person' which has led to a situation today where the concept is readily inflatable to take on board almost any ideological claim.[25] Nineteenth-century German Romanticism, the idealistic philosophies of Fichte, Schelling and Hegel, and the dialectical materialism and humanism of the neo-Hegelians all played a part.[26]

References to God as a person begin to increase during the nineteenth century, although the tendency is to refer to God as person or personal. It is perhaps a comment on the current assumptions that R. G. Swinburne can write 'That God is a person yet one without a body seems the most elementary claim of theism.'[27] A. E. Taylor, writing in 1921 in Hastings' *ERE* vol. 12, pp. 261f, was able to devote more than twenty thousand words to theism without mentioning the idea of God as person or a person. Writing in 1982 on theism, H. D. Lewis regards the idea of God as a person as one of the major claims of theism.[28]

Modern philosophers are perhaps more inclined than modern theologians to describe God as a person. One of the reasons for this has been their concern with the intelligibility (or lack of it) of religious language. Traditional attributes of God have been re-examined to test their meaningfulness. Theological emphasis on God's perfection and immutability has begun to be seen as an unfortunate legacy of Greek metaphysics. The view that God is a person may also commend itself to some because it avoids talk of a Trinity of persons in God. God is understood as a person analogous to other persons. It is assumed that we can know what persons are and that this reduces the scope for ambiguity in talk about God. Since we cannot dispense with analogy, however, in talking about God, then, even if we say that God is a person, we do not necessarily mean that God is exactly like a human person.

In general, modern theologians have been cautious about referring to God as a person. Tillich at one point refuses to call

God a person.[29] The passage makes instructive reading in relation to God as Being and as symbol. Tillich alleges that 'God became a "person" only in the nineteenth century in connection with the Kantian separation of nature, ruled by physical law, from personality ruled by moral law.' Ordinary theism, he continues, has made God a heavenly, completely perfect person who resides above the world and mankind. 'The protest of atheism against such a highest person is correct. There is no evidence for his existence, nor is he a matter of ultimate concern.'[30] Later, in the *Theology of Culture*, distinguishing God as symbol and God as ultimate reality, he wrote, 'Thus all of these discussions going on about God being a person or not a person . . . could be overcome if we could say, "Certainly the awareness of something unconditional . . . is not symbolic." We can call it "Being Itself", *esse qua esse, esse ipsum*, as the scholastics did. But in our relationship to this ultimate we symbolize and must symbolize. We could not be in communication with God if he were only "ultimate Being". But in our relationship to him we encounter him with the highest of what we ourselves are, person.'[31] In *Biblical Religion* (lectures from 1951), Tillich had said, 'Against Pascal I say: the God of Abraham, Isaac and Jacob, and the god of the philosophers is the same God. He is a person and the negation of himself as a person.'[32] Whatever one makes of these varied expressions of Tillich's thought, it is clear that calling God a person does not dispel all ambiguity. What is meant by 'personhood' is a major part of any attribution of personhood, whether to human or divine being.

In a somewhat similar manner, Hans Küng, Wolfhart Pannenberg and Heinrich Ott, among others, emphasise that God cannot be a person in the sense of one being amongst other beings. 'God is not the supreme person among other persons. God transcends also the concept of person. God is more than person.'[33] Equally, God cannot be less than personal. God is not an impersonal It. No term is adequate, but 'transpersonal' or 'suprapersonal' would be a more appropriate description. Pannenberg advances a line of reasoning similar to Tillich and Küng, seeking to avoid any assertion of the existence of God that would make God seem to belong to the same category as other existent beings. God is the source of all being. He wishes to say that the term 'God' is inescapably personal, but without saying that God is 'a person'.[34] 'Anyone who says "God" says "person".' Unlike Tillich and Küng, however, Pannenberg argues that 'a person is the opposite of an existent being'. Human beings are persons by the very fact that they are 'not wholly and completely existent for us in their reality, but are characterised by freedom and as a result remain concealed and beyond control in the totality of their existence'.[35] Another way of expressing this might be to refer to a quality of self-transcendence which characterises persons. Although Pannenberg does not call God 'a person', there are aspects of his thought, related to his understanding of man as a creature of infinite possibilities, who is open to the future in a way that no creature determined by instinct or genetic and environmental factors could be, that point in the direction of God being a person, in a sense analogical to the way in which the human being can become a person. Pannenberg does not mean that persons are not existent beings; but they are always capable of being more than simply that. In his *Systematic Theology*, (vol. 1, pp. 300f, 319f, 422f, 430–1), he makes clear that, although he welcomes the analogy of divine and human persons, he refers to God as a 'trinity of persons' but not as 'a person'. He also makes it clear that he is not using the concept of personhood equivocally.[36]

There are similarities here with Ian Ramsey's brief reflections on the language of 'personhood' in relation to God. Noting that the two main problems of religious language are reference and preference, i.e. what does 'God' refer to and what language is most appropriately used about God, Ramsey suggests on at least one occasion that the value of the term 'person', as compared with say 'father' or 'king' when applied to God, is its wide range of extension. It is a term that is capable of being quantifiable to the nth degree or until the ice breaks and the penny drops and cosmic disclosure takes place; that is, it is capable of evoking what is meant by 'God', who is transcendent.

A not dissimilar line is taken by Heinrich Ott, who in his book, *God*, not only calls God 'a person',[37] but argues that this is central to his theology. He qualifies the whole discussion, however, by saying that God is an infinite Person. His reasons for regarding God as a person are as follows: firstly, all I–Thou relationships are reciprocal; secondly, I–Thou relationships are fundamental and primary; thirdly, such relationships preserve an important interpersonal 'between' character; all of these three features characterise human relationships with God. He regards it as important for Christian theology to construe the whole of reality in personal terms. His use of personalist and existentialist motifs, particularly Buberian ideas, does not, however, confront the theological and philosophical objections raised by those who want to resist referring to God as a person. These objections focus upon whether the knowledge which is claimed to be distinctive of interpersonal relationships, both human and divine, does not need a more empirical foundation in the sort of knowledge which only a body or its equivalent can supply. Without such a foundation, interpersonal knowledge may still be in the position of having a Cartesian basis, i.e. in the mind alone.

It is perhaps for this reason that at least one modern theologian, Karl Rahner, has taken the very different line of arguing that God *is a person*, whilst at the same time drawing a sharp distinction between modern and Trinitarian views of 'person'. Rahner is concerned to relate traditional theological concepts and ideas to the thought world of modern man. Accordingly, he finds it necessary to approach the question of God via anthropology, since it is man who raises the question of God. The anthropology he develops could be regarded as an essential form of Thomism. He draws on a range of insights about human nature from various scientific disciplines, not unlike Pannenberg, but, whereas Pannenberg finds one of his major clues in historical existence which achieves its meaning only when the total picture becomes clear at the eschaton, Rahner concentrates on an analysis of man in his subjectivity. 'Personhood' is the key term, and this is expounded in terms of 'man's transcendence, his responsibility and freedom, his orientation towards absolute mystery, his being in history and the world and his social nature'.[38] He aptly distinguishes theological anthropology from what he calls more regional anthropologies based on the physical or human sciences, which deal with aspects (or regions) of human nature. Theology and philosophy, by contrast, draw attention to the human subject *qua* subject. Regional anthropologies and analyses often imply man's affirmation of himself as subject, despite their sometimes deterministic stance which may omit or exclude human freedom, transcendence and self-affirmation. 'To say that man is person and subject, therefore, means first of all that man is someone who cannot be derived, who cannot be produced completely from other elements at our disposal. He is that being who is responsible for himself.'[39] In his discussion of God as absolute mystery, Rahner also considers what it means to think of God as Person.[40] Language about God is essentially analogous, but 'the statement that God is a person, that he is a personal God, is one of the fundamental Christian assertions about God'. Rahner recognises the problematic character of such an assertion. What is being meant by it? Is God a person in himself or only in relation to man? If the latter, is his essential nature hidden from us? And how, in any case, does the assertion that God is a person relate to Trinitarian language about three Persons?

Rahner is quite clear that any personhood attributed to God is analogous and not to be confused with finite human personhood which is subject to innumerable constraints, but he regards this qualification as inherent in all talk about God. Despite this qualification, 'if anything at all can be predicated of God, then the concept of "personhood" has to be predicated of him. Obviously the statement that "God is a person" can be asserted of God and is true of God only if, in asserting and understanding this statement, we open it to the ineffable darkness of the holy mystery.'[41] The content of this transcendental personhood still remains to be determined in accordance with 'our historical experience'. Rahner is opposed to any philosophical pre-judgement of what this could be: history, he indicates, includes 'our individual histories, the depths of our conscience, and the whole history of the human race'. Religious experience is also part of such history. He is anxious to distinguish this concept of person from Trinitarian usage, on the ground that 'when in our secular use of language today we speak of one "person" as distinct from another person, we can hardly avoid the notion that in order that they be persons and be different, there is in each of these persons its own free centre of conscious and free activity which disposes of itself and differentiates itself from others, and that it is precisely this which constitutes a person. But this is the very thing which is excluded by the dogmatic teaching on the single and unique essence of God'.[42] God cannot be three different centres of consciousness, and, since personhood involves consciousness, God cannot be three persons.

Rahner had prepared the way for this position in his 'Remarks on the Dogmatic Treatise "De Trinitate"',[43] where he argued that there is an 'almost unavoidable danger' of thinking of three different consciousnesses. Usually there is an attempt to modify such a conception when it is realised that it does not fit with what must be said about the simplicity of God. 'But, in all honesty, one must ask oneself with some embarrassment at the end what right one has to call the surviving remnant of the triune "personality" in God a person, if one has had to eliminate from these three persons precisely what one began by thinking of as a person.'[44] Rahner's reluctance to make use of a Trinitarian concept of 'person' has been severely criticised by Moltmann,[45] on the ground that he operates with a modalism similar to that found in Barth. Both Barth and Rahner are critical of the terminology of 'three persons' because it too easily suggests tritheism. Barth prefers instead a phrase such as 'modes of being', and Rahner 'modes of subsistence'. Moltmann disputes Rahner's view that the modern concept of 'person' implies an independent, free, self-disposing centre of knowledge and action. Rahner has drawn his concept of person from possessive individualism, says Moltmann.[46] Admittedly, this is one of the modern options, but it is not the most modern or appropriate in view of the tradition of philosophic personalism in Hölderlin, Feuerbach, Buber,

Ebner, Rosenstock and others. Some of Moltmann's criticisms of Rahner's idealistic modalism and his uncritical assumption of God as the Absolute Subject, seem valid. There is no reason, for example, why Rahner's initial concept of 'person' as individual, self-conscious and responsible should not be qualified substantially to emphasise relationships with others. At the same time, it is clear that Rahner (and Barth) are drawing attention to the very different views of personhood that are possible. The basis of Moltmann's own concept of personhood, however, is not altogether secure, because it conflates different views. It needs to be clarified and supported by further analysis and argument.

Moltmann's theological interpretation of the character of God could be said to begin with his *Theology of Hope*, and is continued and developed in all his subsequent theological writings. Characteristic throughout is his attempt to recover significant features of the biblical witness which have been overlaid by Greek philosophy and rationalism and to re-express the Gospel in terms that are relevant and meaningful in today's intellectual climate. The *Theology of Hope* picked up the debated question of a theological interpretation of history[47] and argued, against Pannenberg and others, for a less Hegelian view of the future. Eschatological (apocalyptic?) hope and trust in the living God who raised Jesus from the dead was distinguished from the seemingly more comprehensive but almost deterministic horizon of a self-unfolding God whose future contained the future of the world and was revealed in Christ. This was followed by the discussion of theodicy and the centrality of the crucifixion, not only for Jesus and mankind, but also for God. God also suffers. The saving God is also the crucified God. The God-forsakenness experienced by the Son can only be understood in the context of Trinitarian relationships. The Son freely gives himself up. 'This deep community of will between Jesus and his God and Father is now expressed precisely at the point of their deepest separation, in the godforsaken and accursed death of Jesus on the cross. If both historical godforsakenness and eschatological surrender can be seen in Christ's death on the cross then this event contains community between Jesus and his Father in separation, and separation in community.'[48] Later works extended and developed these and related insights in relation to the Holy Spirit and the Trinity, the church and the world, in order to demonstrate how all creation and history are affected by this Trinitarian history.

Philosophically, however, ambiguities and obscurities remain. Moltmann clearly wishes to defend a view of personhood which places a high value on 'relationships', and he also wishes to retain a connection between theological–Trinitarian views of 'person' and modern ideas about persons in relationship. In doing this, he looks for allies in the history of theology and includes, among others, St Augustine. But, as we have seen, although Augustine is an important figure in the history of personhood, it is very doubtful whether he can be said to have voiced the form of existential personalism which Moltmann attributes to him. Nor can one simply take Hegel's dialectical philosophy with its emphasis on alienation and reconciliation within Absolute Personhood as indicating that Hegel is continuing a biblical–Augustinian–existentialist view of 'personhood'. Moltmann's ethical application of personhood, in *On Human Dignity*, reveals a Reformed position which in the final analysis attributes personhood primarily to God and only derivatively to humanity. Moltmann might argue that this is, in fact, the dominant view of the Bible. But, as we will argue, there are good theological reasons in terms of a doctrine of creation for allowing humanity more autonomy and independence than this view does. Moreover, it has been one of the main contentions of our historical overview that there has been interplay between different historical periods and views, and that we need to be careful not to read ideas back into the past. Modern views are heir to a variety of influences from the past. We agree with Moltmann in not wishing to make a total break between Trinitarian views of 'person' and the more individualistic views of the modern period. But we cannot simply conflate them, or trace a clear pedigree which overlooks significant differences. Despite our attempts to support the view that God is a person by allowing for a certain embodiment and temporality in our concept of God, it seems impossible to draw directly on Trinitarian personhood in order to derive human personhood from it. This does not detract from the important analogy between divine and human personhood. We need to re-examine, therefore, what sort of links between divine and human personhood are conceptually feasible and desirable and how these might affect ethical positions. We shall argue in the next chapter that more indirect links are in order.

# CHAPTER 9

# Divine and human: relationality and personhood

The analogy between divine and human personhood derives much of its strength from two different quarters: rationality and relationality. They are not incompatible. Either alone may give a skewed picture. Traditionally, however, rationality has been emphasised, in line with a long philosophical tradition which has also been influential in theology. This view would make personhood primarily a matter of rational qualities of soul and mind.[1] Materiality and embodiment would be discounted. Relationality is much broader in its scope. It need not exclude rationality, but, in emphasising that individuality by itself omits a significant and distinctive feature of personhood, namely relationship with others, it also allows for embodiment and temporality to be taken into account. Rationality need not be interpreted narrowly as 'discursive reason' or 'intelligence', but should include the broader 'capacity to decide and act freely'. Even so, the rational model remains too narrow. Relationality, which includes, not only the ability to communicate success-fully with others and the qualities needed for such communi-cation, but the simple fact of being in relationship, must form an important part of the total picture of personhood. This fact of 'being in relationship' will include, not only the foetus and the senile, but so-called inanimate nature. This will not involve an extension of 'personhood' to trees and mountains, but will allow the relationship of persons to trees and mountains to be taken into account when trying to understand personhood.

The decision of some modern thinkers to regard personhood as a purely moral category, not tied to humankind in any way, suggests a paradoxical transfer and inversion of previous uses of the rational model, in that it is being used, as we saw in chapters 3 and 4, to exclude a group of human beings who appear to lack this necessary quality. The focus on relationality, on the other hand, appears to offer a point of comparison that is more in keeping with modern anthropological studies. A number of cautions, however, are needed. First, the differences between God as Creator and human beings as created should not be blurred. This is fundamental. Secondly, direct inferences should not be drawn between the inner life of God and human relationships. This point is also of fundamental importance, particularly since the revival of Trinitarian theology has sometimes given the impression that the importance of relationships to personhood is both epistemologically and ontologically dependent on the immanent (i.e. intra-divine relationships within) Trinity.

There are good reasons for preferring the language of Three Persons in respect of God, as we have indicated. In insisting on the significance of the differences between divine and human persons, we are also resisting the compromising tendency to gloss over hard reality by spiritualising the transfer of relationality from divine to human personhood. The doctrine of the Trinity is not intended as a blueprint for human sociality and Christian ethics. It is more like a health warning about the dangers of making personhood conform to the latest doctrine of social theory or psychology. Good and bad relationships exist side by side, like the wheat and the tares, until the harvest. The doctrine of the Trinity is not part of a campaign to improve human relationships, although the knowledge and worship of God should cause us to reflect and act on the practical issues involved in creating a more just society in which human relationships are less fearful and inadequate, more positive and joyful.

The analogy of divine/human personhood raises problems similar to those of divine/human agency. Discussions of the latter may help us to understand the former. There are issues of meaning and issues of reference. What does it mean to speak of God as person (or a person, or Three Persons)? If God is not identifiable by means of a physical, material body, how can he be identified? God's agency is understood by analogy with human agency. Human agency presupposes an agent with knowledge and purpose. Overt action (and a material body) is normal but not necessary to the meaning of agency. To restrict divine agency by requiring overt action and bodily movement is unnecessarily demanding on the meaning of agency, even if it is typical of human agency. Nor is it necessary to assume that all human actions are governed by strictly causal laws which leave no room for the agent's freedom. When we attribute an action to God, this may be compatible with it also being a human action, since divine and human agency are not mutually exclusive. It is widely believed that God acts through ordinary events and human agency, as well as through miracles and special events.[2]

It should be apparent by now that, in the rich and diverse history of human thought about the concept of person, the analogy between divine and human persons is complex. This is not simply because modern concepts of person have become thinner and more individualistic. It is also because of the sea-change in patterns of thinking and terminology which defy straightforward translation from their context in Greek philosophy and patristic theology. For those who, in the modern period, think of personhood in terms of rational, self-conscious individuality or personal relationships, there are inherent difficulties in relating these views to philosophical and theological ideas of personhood, which are bound up with a conceptuality in which 'substance' and 'relation' are primarily logical terms within a metaphysic of substance.

Various strategies are possible. One might try to defend a form of substance metaphysic and claim that it still has some plausibility. It is difficult, however, to avoid the impression that a universe of spiritual substance is a 'something we know not what'.[3] Moreover, even if it were conceptually possible, it is not what is required by a Christian faith seeking understanding in the late twentieth century. The Christian faith need not be tied to a substance metaphysic. In fact, it is important that the Christian faith should be free to pursue the search for truth in this area as in any other. Aristotelian or Thomist ideas of substance are not an essential part of Christian truth, and there may be better ways of expressing this truth.

Another alternative would be to remove from Christian doctrine whatever cannot match agreed criteria of truth. In one sense, this is a process that is going on whenever theologians debate issues of doctrinal importance, but, since there are usually strong arguments on both sides of an issue, doctrinal changes take place only slowly. The fascinating issue of doctrinal change is high on the theological agenda, but there is no agreement even about the shape of the process or the relevant criteria, despite much useful academic work on the subject and ecumenical statements on faith and church order.

Problems of this sort may lie behind the confusion and disagreement in modern theology between those who appear sceptical of all talk of God as a Trinity (e.g. J. P. Mackey; M. Wiles) and those who want all Christian theology to begin with the Christian doctrine of the Trinity (e.g. K. Barth; J. Moltmann; E. Jüngel). Since 'the doctrine of the Trinity simply is the Christian doctrine of God',[4] how did this disagreement arise and what does it signify? It seems to have arisen, in part at least, because certain developments in the doctrine of the Trinity suggested that the internal relations of the Trinity exist in a perfect form apart from God's relation to the world. The doctrine of the Trinity has been assumed to include both a doctrine of an immanent Trinity (God in himself) and an economic Trinity (God for us), with the implication in many writers that the latter is somehow derived from, or dependent on, the former. But the truth is that we have no direct or sure knowledge of this inner divine life. All that we have and can have is faith and speculation. Such speculation might conceivably fill a useful heuristic role occasionally, but not if it detracts from an overall understanding or leads to confusion, as in this case.[5]

If we exercise appropriate discretion and agnosticism, however, about God's inner life, are we depriving ourselves of a valuable theological insight and resource? Are we in danger of severing the links between ancient and modern concepts of person? The answer to these two questions requires us to reconsider the notions of 'relation' and 'person'. In an interesting article 'Why Three? Some Further Reflections on the Origins of the Doctrine of the Trinity', S. Coakley suggested a rough typology of five different, but not mutually exclusive, ways of classifying recent literature on Trinitarian thinking: dismantling the Trinity by not hypostatising the Spirit (e.g. Wiles, Mackey); identifying the 'economic' with the 'immanent' Trinity (e.g. Rahner); construing the Trinity from reflection on the death of Christ (e.g. Moltmann, Jüngel, von Balthasar); understanding the Trinity as prototype of persons-in-relation (e.g. Zizioulas, Gunton, Moltmann); and, finally, emphasising the Holy Spirit as a means of incorporation into the Trinitarian life of God (eg. A. M. Ramsey, von Balthasar, Lossky and Congar).

Coakley suggests that the fifth and final way, suitably modified to give fuller expression to the experiential, mystical and doxological, would at least point in the right direction and might even allay some of the concerns of those who, like Wiles, favour dismantling the Trinity. She also accepts that the fourth way, understanding the Trinity as the prototype of persons-in-relation, modified to take account of Richard of St Victor, has 'considerable potential'.[6] This fourth type has, in fact, resulted in a far greater response than her brief discussion indicates. For this reason, and because it is particularly relevant to our overall theme, we shall examine it more carefully.

Broadly speaking, the fourth type is a social doctrine of the Trinity, appealing to roots in Cappadocian patristic theology and later Greek Orthodox thought, in contrast to Augustine's more psychological view. Although social doctrines of the Trinity have a long history[7] and W. R. Matthews could say in 1930 that the time had come to combine the social and psychological views of the Trinity,[8] there has been a resurgence of interest in Coakley's fourth type in recent years, partly for the reasons we have indicated in respect of the ethical aspect of personhood. J. Moltmann, L. Boff, P. Wilson-Kastner, C. Gunton, J. D. Zizioulas, E. Yannaras and C. M. LaCugna[9] have all written with enthusiasm about the renaissance in theological thinking about Trinitarian 'persons-in-relation'.

Moltmann's contribution, beginning with his *Crucified God* and his persuasive argument that Christ's suffering and death on the Cross must be integrated into Christian thinking about the Trinity and that the doctrine of divine impassibility must be revised to take account of that, cannot be overestimated. We have already indicated, however, (p. 167 above) that in *The Trinity and the Kingdom of God*, despite his shrewd criticisms of Barth's and Rahner's modalistic interpretations based on imperfect understanding of 'personhood', he tends to read later developments into earlier texts, linking Augustine, Hegel, Feuerbach and Ebner as precursors or allies of his own view of 'persons-in-relation'. In a perceptive article, R. Olson[10] has drawn attention to a number of places where Moltmann's exposition leaves serious questions unanswered. Apart from the frequent references to the intra-divine relations, which we have noted as speculative and problematic, Moltmann tends to assume there is a toing and froing between the economic and immanent forms of Trinitarian life.[11] The immanent Trinity is waiting to be realised through Trinitarian history, yet there is an eschatological determination about this history which seems to defeat the openness of a historical process characterised by the interaction of persons. Another important feature of Moltmann's interpretation of divine personhood relates to the question of gender in the Trinity. God has both 'fatherly' and 'motherly' aspects, and even 'gives birth' to the Son.[12] Moltmann's emphasis on *perichoresis* (interpenetration), used of the relations of persons in the Trinity to express 'communication which is free from domination' and to apply this to the relationships between human persons, has attracted a number of feminist writers.[13] This perichoretic relationship within the Trinity, because it also applies to God's relationship to the world, entitles us to say that God is in the world and the world in God, according to Moltmann, but this seems to take insufficient account of the real and important differences between God and creation.

The analogy between divine and human personhood has to take account of these real differences between God and creation. What is the basis of similarity that enables any sort of divine/human personhood analogy to get off the ground, so to speak?[14] It is clear that behind the analogy lies the *imago dei* (Genesis i. 27–8) motif. Humanity (*'Adam*, male and female) is made in the image of God. If God is a Trinity, and conformity with Christ is the goal of Christian personhood, this means that relational being, reflected in human nature, is central to what it means to be in the image and likeness of God. Gunton has pointed to the twin features of otherness and relation. 'To be a person is to be constituted in particularity and freedom – to be given space to be – by others in community.'[15] Despite the plural 'Let us make man in our image', it is unlikely that the idea of a Trinity which was still seeking ecclesiastical confirmation many centuries later was already at work, although it was one of those many passages used by the early church as evidence of that differentiation within the godhead, which impressed itself on them following the resurrection of Christ and Pentecostal transformation of the church. Much more important are the narrative accounts of Jesus' ministry, which give us insight into the new relationships which accompany the coming of God's rule, and suggest what is involved in the new creation: 'unless a grain of wheat falls into the earth and dies, it remains alone; but if it dies it bears much fruit' (John xii. 24). There are eschatological overtones in the image analogy which bring together new creation and the gift of the Spirit through the life of the Son, and point to the transformation of both church and creation through the Spirit. Although we have no words to express the inner life of the Trinity, the Gospels will help us to recover fundamental aspects of divine and human personhood.

We have noted that the concept of human personhood is normally associated with rationality, sentience, embodiment and relationships with others.[16] It is a characteristic of human persons that they are incomplete, historical beings, always prospectively situated towards the future, never completely determined by their past or present environments or hereditary factors, and, to that extent, free. From a theological perspective, it is also important that such persons are created and sustained by God to live together in society as God's stewards or vice-regents, answerable to God and capable of being redeemed by God. This is in marked contrast to views which see 'soul' as the identifying substrate of personhood.[17]

A number of theologians, including K. Barth and T. Torrance,[18] go beyond the analogical use of personhood and seek to *derive* human personhood from divine personhood. This is all the more surprising since Barth is opposed to any 'analogia entis' between the divine and human. It corresponds, however, with Barth's theological starting-point and his view of revelation. Theology is reflection on the being of God. God has revealed himself as Father, Son and Holy Spirit. As E. Jüngel notes: 'The *Church Dogmatics* is the ingenious and diligent attempt to think the proposition "God corresponds to himself" through to the end.'[19] But, despite the comprehensive manner in which this is worked out by Barth from his Trinitarian beginnings, there is some doubt as to whether the initial Cartesian assumptions about 'personhood' are ever overcome.[20]

A determined effort to overcome this flawed starting-point is made by LaCugna. Along with others (cf. p. 175 above) who see themselves as part of the renaissance of Trinitarian theology, she argues that, despite the changes in substance philosophy and terminology, the crucial issue is that relationships of a personal kind are common to both the Trinitarian conception of God and to concepts of human persons. But, whereas, for Aquinas, God's relation to creation was only logical, not real, because being related to creatures was not part of God's nature (although the creature's relation to God was real because creation is constituted by its relation to God), for La Cugna, the relationship is both real and logical. By Trinity she normally means the economic Trinity, and at one point comes close to abolishing the distinction of immanent and economic Trinity.[21] She does, however, continue to assume that there is an essential analogy between human experience of what it means to be a person, in terms of relationships to others, and God's relatedness and differentiation as Father, Son and Holy Spirit and God's relatedness to the rest of creation.[22]

LaCugna considers four different ways of thinking which

might contribute to a sounder understanding of personhood: the personalist philosophy of John Macmurray; the thought of Orthodox theologian John Zizioulas; feminist and Latin American liberation theologies; and explicitly Trinitarian ethics. Within the wider context of the book as a whole, which argues strongly and with some plausibility, for a revival of economic Trinitarian thought, LaCugna tries to show how these four developments avoid some of the limitations of previous discussions of personhood and may contribute to Trinitarian theology. She warns explicitly of the dangers of reading ideas into the immanent Trinity. Moreover, it is not enough to show that the economic Trinity makes relationality fundamental to personhood. Her treatment of Farley is a good illustration of her critical method.[23] Farley's article, 'New Patterns of Relationship: Beginnings of a Moral Revolution',[24] attempts to construct an egalitarian ethic on the basis of *agape* and ideas from Trinitarian theology. This requires critical analysis of gender stereotypes to prevent misuse of *agape* to reinforce existing mistaken stereotypes, in which women are seen as submissive and passive, compared with men who are active initiators. Both men and women, Farley argues, are 'actively receptive'. *Agape* requires 'full mutuality of persons'. The perfect equality and reciprocity of relations in the immanent Trinity then become the model for human personhood. LaCugna comments: 'it is not enough to argue from a nonsexist interpretation of divine persons to a nonsexist vision of relationships within the human community' (p. 281), and warns against a literal translation of divine relationships into human terms.

Yet LaCugna seems to misconstrue the direction of Farley's analogy. Most of Farley's article is devoted to showing that the relationship of men and women has already had to change as a result of changes in society and changes in human knowledge. The old order did not do justice to the relationship. Without trying to discover or assign responsibility for past mistakes, Farley simply notes that Christians and the church were also implicated in these mistakes, and are still implicated. Even when *agape* is recognised as central, there is a tendency to interpret it in such a way that women are given subordinate or

passive or servant roles. Hence the necessity for equal regard
and equality of opportunity:

Now it is just here that Christian ethics has suffered from an
inadequate theology of the human person; for as long as the reality of
woman is considered to be essentially lesser in being than the reality
of man, she can be affirmed as personal but as essentially subordinate
to men (in much the same way as children . . .). (p. 633)

Farley argues that a large part of the problem is the inadequate
definition and understanding of self-sacrifice and servanthood,
which have been interpreted as passive. This passivity has been
mistakenly linked with gender difference, because of imperfect
knowledge of human sexuality and lack of awareness of the
active role of women's bodies in the reproductive process (i.e.
the tendency to see women as passive receptacles of male
sperm and biological ignorance about the role of the ovum
until the nineteenth century). *Agape* has been similarly miscon-
strued. Humans receiving God's *agape* have been construed as
wholly passive, those showing *agape* to the neighbour as wholly
active. In both cases, the mutuality of giving and receiving is
overlooked. Women have begun to rediscover this mutuality in
the process of taking their own bodies seriously (but not too
seriously, cautions Farley). Associated with this is a growing
recognition that receptivity is 'at the heart of Christian love'. It
is not entirely clear whether these are simply parallel movements, or whether reappraisal of Christian ideas has been
influenced by rethinking what it means to be human and
feminine in Farley's view. She continues: 'But it may be that we
can grasp the meaning of receptivity in Christian *agape* only by
seeing it in the broader context of Christian faith' (e.g. in the
incarnation, resurrection, indwelling of the Spirit in the
Church, and 'in the life of grace which is the sharing of human
persons in the life of the triune God').[25]
   Apart from what may be concealed in 'the life of the triune
God', there is no reference here to immanent, as opposed to
economic, Trinity. Support for references to Trinitarian doctrine is found mainly in Rahner, who identifies immanent and
economic Trinity. Farley does not argue from a model of the

Trinity to human relationships. Rather she finds confirmation in divine revelation for what she already understands and believes about the human situation. She suggests that this new model of interpersonal relationship might be compared with the doctrine of God to discover whether 'God's own self-revelation includes a revelation of a model of interpersonal love which is based upon equality and infinite mutuality.'[26] God is essentially transcendent and gender images may be a distraction, but it is worth asking, she thinks, whether the *imago dei* which is most fully represented in the Trinity 'can be imaged in feminine as well as masculine terms'. She argues that it can in terms of a 'feminine principle of creative union' in which 'both the First Person and the Second Person are infinitely active and infinitely receptive'. The metaphor becomes a model. 'Do we not have here, in any case, a model of relationship which is not hierarchical, which is marked by total equality, and which is offered to us in Christian revelation as the model for relationship with Christ and for our relationships in the Church with one another?' It almost seems at this point as if we are back to a model of the immanent Trinity and inner Trinitarian relationships, in which we imagine how the different persons of the Trinity relate to each other in complete mutuality and equality while retaining the self-differentiation necessary for personhood. Whereas initially Farley argues from human to divine personhood, at this point the process is reversed. Perhaps such speculation is allowable, provided it is recognised for what it is. But there is still good reason, it seems to me, to emphasise the features which led to the idea of Trinity in the first place, namely that God's self-revelation in creation was part of a larger story which includes God's self-revelation in Christ and the work of the Holy Spirit. It is this threefold activity of divine being in creation, redemption and renewal which is characteristic of God's Trinitarian being and divine *agape*. Farley's argument, on the whole, is not that we learn about such *agape* from inner-Trinitarian relations within God, metaphorically speaking, but that, having observed such *agape* in human life and history, from whatever source – but not excluding the life of Jesus or the story of God's creating and redeeming love, we can see how such *agape* typifies the relationship of Father, Son and Holy Spirit. This approach avoids many of the problems we have noted in Rahner's reluctance to acknowledge any links between modern personhood and Trinitarian persons, and in Moltmann's overenthusiastic identification of personhood in different periods and writers.

In the light of this assessment, it seems that LaCugna is mistaken in trying to assimilate Farley to a view of personhood which starts from the Trinity and works towards human personhood. Clearly there is interaction, but, as one might expect, the analogy works mainly in the opposite direction – from human experience to theological symbol. LaCugna argues that Farley would have a better case if she were to appeal to the economic Trinity rather than the immanent Trinity, and suggests making more play of what we know about the life of Jesus.[27] Although she is right to identify the Gospels as narratives in which divine–human personhood is embodied in the life and death of Jesus, her discussion of his sexuality is clouded by abstract doctrinal formulations. What she says about his sexuality as the creative overcoming of the antinomies of maleness and femaleness 'because of the perfect coincidence of *hypostasis* and  *ousia*', to demonstrate that 'the body is not ultimately determinative of nature',[28] suggests that we are still trapped in the assumption that we can move directly from divine to human personhood. To argue, as LaCugna does, that Jesus' sexuality was creative because of the perfect coincidence of *hypostasis* (person) and *ousia* (nature) in him makes it seem like an a priori deduction rather than a comment about Jesus' human nature. In short, does not LaCugna still assume an a priori link between divine and human personhood? Otherwise how could one ever establish 'the perfect coincidence of *hypostasis*  and *ousia*' in Jesus Christ? It is surprising, in view of her careful assessment of the dangers of reading subjective wishes into intra-divine relations, that she is not more sensitive to similar problems involved in any attempt to model an understanding of the human person on a concept of divine persons and intra-divine relationships.[29]

Is it possible to develop a more modest and realistic view of the analogy between divine and human personhood? God's ontological priority, and the fact that he is the creator of all that is, does not determine how we make epistemological and conceptual distinctions. The belief that God is the supreme example of personhood or that God is 'person' to the nth degree, in Ian Ramsey's terms, should not mask the process of analogy involved. From an initial understanding of personhood (cf. the fatherhood of God) applicable primarily to human beings, we use the term of God subject to important qualifications. God is like a human father in that he cares for his children; but he is more capable and caring than any human father; he is our heavenly father, and thus like no earthly father. It may be appropriate for the believer in these circumstances to say that understanding of fatherhood (including earthly fathers) is based on our understanding of the fatherhood of God. But that should not hide the starting-point of the analogy, which remains firmly rooted in our knowledge of earthly fatherhood. This experiential knowledge of earthly fatherhood is direct and may differ significantly from what is later determined about divine fatherhood with the help of theology and religious experience. This latter image (sc., of divine fatherhood) becomes the correcting image or lens through which we see (and correct) our starting-point. Our image of divine fatherhood is dependent on a range of other religious beliefs which we acquire and systematise over a period of time.

What we propose is that the economic Trinity can be a significant factor in the understanding of human personhood (and its ethical implications) provided it is recognised as a self-conscious theological extrapolation from the Gospel records and the life and teaching of the early church, rather than the starting-point for thinking about human personhood. The reason for proposing this is that attempts to derive human personhood in any straightforward way from divine personhood obscure the stages of thinking involved. The steps by which we arrive at a view of divine personhood are even more complex than those involved in the case of divine fatherhood. The economic Trinity projects a view of (divine) personhood in which relationships are characterised by mutual giving and receiving in love, such that anyone who has seen the Son has seen the Father (John xiv. 9). The Father sends the Son; the Son reveals the Father. There is perfect communion and undistorted communication with no hiatus or misunderstanding. As the Father sent the Son, the Son sends the disciples. Father and Son together love the world, but the world does not recognise God's love for it, until the work of revelation is completed in crucifixion and resurrection and the sending of the Spirit, who has power to forgive all sin and to guide into all truth. If it is granted that human personhood operates at a creaturely level, often shrouded in the fog of sin, and that the influence of ideas from divine personhood is more indirect, we shall be less likely to confuse ideas about, and links between, divine and human personhood, and be in a better position to formulate a more modest, yet also more constructive, view of the links between concepts of divine and human personhood. This may seem *too* modest in view of Christian claims to share in the divine life itself through worship, prayer and service. Some answers to this objection will become clear on pp. 186–8 and in chapters 10–12.

At the end of chapter 7 we referred to the work of V. Lossky and J. D. Zizioulas on personhood in Greek patristic theology as pointing in the right direction, namely relationality. We refrained from more wholehearted endorsement of Zizioulas' position, since our position does not depend on speculation about an inner divine life. Some of his insights, however, are too important to be lost sight of, and in what follows we adapt some of his ideas and conclusions to support our own proposals. In *Being as Communion*[30] Zizioulas contrasts a social understanding of 'person', which can be found in Graeco-Roman culture, with an ontological understanding which is found in patristic theology influenced by the Cappadocian distinction of *ousia* and *hypostasis* (see. p. 128 above). Whereas Greek tragedy gave expression to the unfulfilled and tragic nature of human existence, Christianity points to the new being of resurrected existence in Christ. Zizioulas argues that the inability of Graeco-Roman views to develop a more complete view of

human personhood was the result of two factors: their cos-
mology, which was overdetermined by physical and biological
necessity; and their ontological assumption that true being is
essentially rational mind or spirit. Without endorsing all the
claims that Zizioulas makes for fourth-century orthodox Greek
theology, we are sympathetic to his view that the distinction of
divine *hypostasis* and divine substance provided the context and
terminology for a significant advance in the ontology of personhood, by grounding personhood in the personal being of God
(e.g. as Father), which was characterised by differentiation and
communion of persons, rather than in a monistic essence of
divine being.

It is not necessary to determine the origin of the distinction
of *ousia* and *hypostasis* to accept that Zizioulas' insight about the
primacy of 'person' over 'substance' is one that makes good
theological sense, particularly in relation to modern discussions
of personhood. It also points in the same direction as our
discussion of personhood and relationality, and has wide appeal
to Christians of diverse church affiliation. Further, it has links
with what secular thinkers have been saying about the importance of human freedom as a characteristic of personhood.[31]
Zizioulas argues that the crucial feature of what is still an
obscure development, historically speaking, is the identification
of 'person' and 'hypostasis'. In the case of divine personhood,
this means that, instead of positing a divine substance or
essence, which is later understood in terms of triune personhood, Christian theology interprets divine essence in terms of
its faith in God who has revealed himself in history as Father,
Son and Holy Spirit. Vital to this view is the Hebraic understanding of God's relation to the world as creator *ex nihilo*,
rather than as the Greek Demiourgos of pre-existent matter.
This understanding frees the world from 'necessity' or conformity to pre-existing physical laws; it also frees God to be the
sovereignly free, loving Creator and Redeemer, attested by
Christ and experienced in the fellowship of the Holy Spirit.
Participation in the Spirit, if it were allowed in Orthodox
thought, would also provide an empirical sounding board in
Christian experience: 'The being of God is identified with the

person.'[32] Christians believe the Holy Spirit enters into their experience, drawing them into fellowship with the triune God, exposing their shortcomings, holding out the offer of forgiveness and reconciliation, and calling them to a life of Christian holiness and love. 'When we cry, "Abba! Father!" it is the Spirit himself bearing witness with our spirit that we are children of God, and if children then heirs' (Romans viii. 15–17; cf. Romans v. 5). There is also a strong community dimension. Christians are members of the Body of Christ, members of God's family, sharing in the life of the Holy Spirit and love of the brethren. For Paul, the Christian life is a life in the Spirit, as opposed to the flesh. It is a life which is constantly renewed by the Spirit, which he describes in Galatians v. as marked by love, joy, peace, patience, kindness, goodness, faithfulness, gentleness and self-control. This life points forward to the time when God will transform all things – by the resurrection of the dead and the consummation of all things in Christ. Taken together, this means that the Christian ethic must be an ethic in which the Holy Spirit, the spirit of Christ and divine love, is embodied in thought and action in the life of the Christian community and the world.

If God's freedom were located in a divine essence, there would be no prospect of humanity sharing in that freedom, since human nature is not part of divine nature. But, because God's way of being God is essentially personal, i.e. one of personal communion, as Father, Son and Holy Spirit, in uncoerced love, this encourages the hope and allows for the possibility that human beings may also become free for personal communion with one another. Such freedom may remain incomplete in the case of created human beings, who are hemmed in by introverted individualism (sin), finitude and death,[33] but the Christian hope is one of ultimate freedom and transformation. As Moltmann notes,[34] there is an important distinction between freedom understood in terms of lordship and ability to exercise one's own freedom competitively over against others, and freedom which is essentially freedom as fellowship, when 'the other person is no longer the limitation of my freedom, but an expansion of it'. Christian freedom understood in this way also reaches forward into the future to realise the possibilities inherent in divine love.

This interpretation of freedom is linked with a contrast between biological and ecclesial existence. Human personhood remains subject to death at the biological level. But divine personhood has opened up new possibilities. Baptism into the life of divine communion in the Body of Christ is the beginning of that resurrection to eternal life which constitutes salvation. Zizioulas calls this the hypostasis of ecclesial existence. Biological existence is not without elements of the love and freedom of ecclesial existence, but is essentially constrained by biological necessity. The life of the body and erotic love at their best prefigure a more unconstrained existence, but cannot achieve it.[35] This failure or weakness of biological existence is constitutional and endemic, not dependent on individual moral strength or weakness. But baptism into the death and resurrection of Christ means entrance into a new life (cf. p. 53 'a new hypostasis'.)[36] This ecclesial existence is clearly not realised everywhere or perfectly within the life of the Christian church. It points to a future realisation. In the meantime, Christians share in a eucharistic existence which sustains them as they move towards their ecclesial goal. LaCugna summarises Zizioulas' view as follows:

The deified person, conformed to the person of Christ, is an authentic expression of ecstasis toward communion, and thus an icon of God's own mystery of communion, which originates with the Father and subsists in Christ and the Spirit.[37]

If this interpretation of divine and human personhood and their interaction is sustained, it would qualify significantly the model of ethical thinking and decision-making based on personhood. Whereas, for example, natural law type thinking and divine commands have been prominent in Christian ethics, personhood characterised by the dynamic of freedom in love and community suggests a rather different stance for Christian ethics (e.g. related to realising the potential of personal being in communion).

This view of personhood is both suggestive and instructive. It resonates with some of the views we have already advanced in chapters 6 and 7. Certain qualifications, however, are in order. The very relevant and important distinction between 'person' and 'individual' is unnecessarily extended into an attack on 'individuality', whereas in our view personhood enhances rather than destroys individuality. The claim to find in Greek patristic thought a theology and terminology which answers all modern problems, is often part of a theology which remains patriarchal in thought and language and indifferent to the position of submerged groups in society. The persistent resistance to Western theological rationalism is not without some justification, but it is a view which needs more cautious and differentiated expression (cf. pp. 238–47 below). La Cugna observes that 'The ontology of personhood is the strong suit of Orthodoxy. Personhood is understood as receiving oneself by ecstasis toward another.'[38] The emphasis on love and freedom is certainly important in any account of personhood, and represents a valuable aspect of the view represented by Zizioulas and Yannaras (e.g. 'Love is the supreme road to knowledge of the person, because it is acceptance of the other person as a whole. It does not project onto the other person individual preferences, demands or desires, but accepts him as he is, in the fulness of his personal uniqueness'). It should not be overlooked, however, that a similar view can be found in other Christian traditions. Some of the work being done by secular psychologists also affirms persons in community. What is distinctive about Christian views of personhood is the link between divine and human personhood in terms of the personal nature of God's self-revelation in creation, Christ and Holy Spirit. In the case of Orthodoxy, however, this is concentrated in a particular view of Trinitarian relationships, with especial emphasis on *hypostasis* and its distinction from *ousia*. Whether it is possible to build so much on this particular feature, is a matter of debate. The proper recognition that morality requires more than the making of impartial decisions and has to take account of a wider context (including views of God and the world) should not be confused with making morality simply a reflection of ontology. Morality has its own work to do, and decisions have to be made in the light of expanding empirical knowledge as well as ontological commitments.

# CHAPTER 10

# Religion and morality: personhood, revelation and narrative

We are now in a better position to examine how a theological ethic can take account of both divine and human personhood. In the present chapter we examine some of the important theoretical issues involved in the development of moral practices based on faith commitments. How do religious believing and belonging influence conduct? These issues are not new, but they are articulated from a fresh perspective in relation to our understanding of divine and human personhood within a religiously plural society. The chapter deals with the relation of religion and morality in terms of: the influence of religion on the content and context of morality and the scope of revelation; the significance of the human subject in morality; and narrative ethics. We develop the idea that the cultural and religious narratives which are to be found in the major world faiths can serve to qualify our shared humanity. Being qualified or distinguished in this way does not detract from a common humanity and shared rationality. Faith commitments do not erase or replace reason; on the other hand, the activities of reason and the shape and content of morality may be influenced and even determined by religious narratives.

The relation of religion and morality is sometimes discussed as if it were a matter of logical priority or derivability. Whether an action is right because God wills or commands it, or whether God commands or wills it because it is right, is a dilemma often associated with Plato's Socratic dialogue, *Euthyphro*. Euthyphro's father has thoughtlessly caused the death of another peasant. Should Euthyphro prosecute his father, or would this be an act of unnatural piety? Socrates asks Euthyphro whether pious deeds are pious because they please the gods, or whether they please the gods because they are pious deeds. The dilemma assumes there are two mutually exclusive choices. This assumption is arbitrary and unjustified. There are other alternatives. For example, the action may be right but God does not command it, or God may command it but not because it is right. Only if the action is right, and God commands it because it is right, does it satisfy one horn of the Euthyphro dilemma. The other horn of the dilemma is that God commands it and it is right because God commands it. As put, the two horns of the dilemma are incompatible and mutually exclusive. One can only unpack the presuppositions to allow the full implications of the dilemma to emerge. Underlying the dilemma, are genuine issues connected with the relationship of reason and revelation and the basis of morality.

The nature of the contribution of religion to morality has been the subject of much debate. One important aspect of this debate has been the discussion whether this contribution affects both content and context. Within a religious ethic is there specific moral content which is directly attributable to religious belief or influence and which is not found in other contexts? Or is the content of a religious ethic largely identical in content with that of a secular ethic ? Does religion influence the context but not the content of morality?

Those who have stressed universal or common features in the ethical process and the similar content of ethical judgement have tended to argue that religion supplies vision, motivation and support for an ethic which is essentially autonomous. Even a religious ethic has to be understood primarily in moral terms, it is argued, and a religious ethic should be understood to make universal moral claims, applicable to believer and unbeliever alike. One of the most influential theological traditions regarding the status of ethical reasoning is that, like other aspects of human reasoning, it must be subject to normal rational criteria. It occupies no special or privileged position. It is not dependent on special revelation. What is morally right for Christians or Jews or Muslims is what is morally right for others also. There is a universal moral law which is accessible to all. Sometimes this was linked in Christian theology with a distinction between the spheres of creation and salvation. Morality was part of the created order.

Those seeking a more distinctively Christian ethic have argued that a universal ethic fails to capture some of the most distinctive elements of a Christian ethic based on the teaching of Jesus. Despite features which it shares with a secular ethic, a Christian ethic contains specific features which are the result of Christian belief, it is contended. Agreement on what these features are is not easy to demonstrate, but frequently cited are such matters as attitudes to wealth and poverty, sexuality (especially virginity, abstinence and rejection of abortion), power, suffering and *agape*.

In the earlier part of this century, particularly under the influence of the renewal in biblical theology, which was sparked off, at least in part, by the various social and religious factors that led to the breakdown of liberal theology, dissatisfaction with reliance on natural law and neo-Scholasticism led to a number of proposals in which a theme of biblical theology or Christian tradition was used as an organising principle for a Christian ethic which reflected Christian themes more clearly – covenant, discipleship, salvation, the Kingdom of God. Although the emphases were different, there were similar developments in both Catholic and Protestant circles. But, as MacNamara notes,[1] even when God's will or the imitation of Christ became primary, very little was said about a specific new content required or made possible by the new emphases. 'The very sparse description of the Christian moral life comes as an anti-climax after all the rhetoric about the new ontology and the morality which is said to correspond to it.'[2]

Although there is some truth in this assessment, it should not cause us to overlook the underlying positive influence of the analogy of divine and human personhood. There is a persistent strand of biblical thinking which is based on the *imago dei* motif and its implications for human nature and conduct: 'You shall be holy, for I am holy', says the Lord (cf. Leviticus xi. 44; xix. 2; xx. 7, 26; I Peter i. 15–16; I Corinthians iii. 16). Children of the Father are to be perfect (*teleios* – whole and unblemished) as He is perfect (cf. Matthew v. 45–48). Christians are to forgive as they have been forgiven (Colossians iii. 12f). The coming of Christ modifies but strengthens the analogy. Christians are baptised into the body of Christ, who is the very image of God (cf. Colossians i. 15). The goal of baptismal life is Christ-likeness (cf. Romans viii. 29; Galatians iv. 19); incorporation into the body of Christ means that the Holy Spirit of God is active in assisting the baptised to become like Christ. The Decalogue remains valid, but is now part of something greater.

The imitation of Christ is part of the same context of ideas. Christians are to follow Christ's example (cf. I Peter ii. 21f). It is unfortunate that imitation may suggest mere copying. However perfect the copy, it can never replace the original. Even an exact copy lacks something of the original: the vitality, the flair, the historical depth. Despite these drawbacks, 'imitation' has retained an important place in religious ethics. It refers not so much to copying, certainly of the more mechanical sort, as to the close personal relationship of disciple and teacher, mediated through study, worship, discipline and fellowship. The disciple may imitate, but more than copying is required. As E. J. Tinsley notes, 'It is a pity the word "imitation" suggests uncreative copy.'[3] Imitating Christ in the New Testament is 'conceived to be the work of the Holy Spirit moulding the life of the Christian into some likeness of Christ'. One of the ways used by the early church to encourage this was to recall and retell narratives about Jesus, keeping alive the freshness of his life and teaching so that others might come to know him and share in his sufferings and the joy of his resurrection. The Hebrew scriptures that Jesus used and followed also became the scriptures of the early church. These narratives were part of a life of worship and service in the community of other Christians. Buried with Him in baptism, says Paul (Romans vi. 3), Christians share in a new life of resurrection, having put to death their former way of life. Moreover, imitation is forward-looking: the goal is a transformed existence, not the recollection of a past which is no longer available. If one thinks of the way in which a gifted performer puts herself into the words or music she is re-creating (but did not compose) so that others can share in the original, it becomes clear that there is a great gulf between meagre copying and vital yet faithful performance, which involves qualities of heart and mind, integrity and even autonomy. Called to identify with God's holiness, the Christian is called to surrender whatever is incompatible with God's will. Holiness is what marks out God as God. Originally it may have had little specific ethical content. It was synonymous with the otherness of God and his *kabod* (glory), the dazzling and 'burning splendour of the presence of the Lord . . . the positive activity of that Personal Other'.[4] Over the centuries, it was combined with the prophetic emphasis on social righteousness. In the life of Jesus, it became associated with compassion and an attack on idols of holiness – sabbath-keeping, temple purity, ritual laws and social ostracism from table-fellowship.[5] Holy love is God's very self. The disciple is invited to share that life.

The analogy of divine and human personhood presupposes that there is a quality of life and broad community of purpose shared by the person God is and the persons human agents are. The analogy also suggests that human conduct will be influenced by this. It does not assume that we can read off from divine personhood exactly what the shape of human morality should be. We need to be clear about what is implied in referring to God as (a) moral being and to human agents as moral subjects. Can one discern a pattern of morality consistent with, and possibly fundamental to, divine and human personhood? Whether God is 'person' or 'three-personed' is, in this context, relevant but subsidiary to the analogy between divine and human personhood and the consequent inference that divine personhood has a bearing on the moral nature and agency of human beings. In the process of drawing an analogy between divine and human personhood, the original conception of human personhood is deepened and enriched. Thus, the fatherhood of God, experienced fully only by the eternal Son, becomes the correcting lens for our understanding of fatherhood. The mutuality of Trinitarian relationships lies beyond direct human experience, but, from our understanding and experience of willing and feeling in harmony with another person, we draw an analogy between human and divine mutuality, which, in turn, deepens and enriches the original insight. In this limited sense, the Trinity may become the correcting lens for our understanding of human mutuality, particularly if we find this insight corroborated in prayer and worship.

From our discussions in Parts 1 and 2, it is clear that a variety of views about personhood are involved. We have given reasons for thinking of persons as rational and communicative in a broad sense, members of a community of persons and part of a wider environment, embodied in time and gendered. In all of these personal characteristics, what is true of God must be significantly qualified. God is Creator and Redeemer of all that is. Yet the attribution of personhood to God remains valid and is significant for human personhood. What bearing do these considerations have on a religious ethic? They require, it seems to us, two responses: an account of the revelational complex which is characteristic of the religion whose ethic is under consideration; and an account of how God (Person) communicates his moral demands and wishes, together with an account of the persons with and to whom God relates and communicates.

The first requirement stems from the nature of the exercise: on what basis are commitments about moral values made and justified in the context of a religious ethic? This may include such fundamental issues as whether the idea of revealed moral truth makes any sense, and, if it does, whether it makes any difference. More particularly, however, it affects the way in which religious communities organise their attempts to perceive and understand moral truth. Some rely on revealed scriptures, and the interpretation of scripture may then become central to the understanding of morality. Others focus their understanding of revelation on the community (or individual) that receives and interprets God's wishes. This may lead to a range of interpretations, depending on what priority is assigned to reason, individual experience, and structures of community and communication.

The second requirement is not unrelated to the first, and

may even be seen as prior to it, in that it crucially affects how the originating source of a revealed ethic is thought of. If God is thought of as like the Plotinian One ('absolutely undetermined and uncircumscribed, the Good who always lies over the edge of our thought so that it can only construct a multiplicity of inadequate images which may be means of his presence to us if we do not turn them into idols, but can never give a description of him'),[6] we shall almost certainly arrive at a different pattern of moral truth compared with the Jewish-Christian revelational complex in which God is undetermined, in the sense that he cannot be limited by our thoughts and words, but *has revealed himself* through the law and prophets and in the last days through his Son. How the new fulfils the old covenant remains a matter of some debate, but, despite varieties of intepretation and practice, there is broad agreement among most Christians that their scriptures are fundamental to their understanding of God's self-revelation and that these scriptures are couched in narrative form. Some examination of what is involved in narrative ethics, therefore, will be appropriate, together with a critical view of society (i.e. the social context of persons in community), particularly as this relates to society now.

The significance of revelation for the complex relationship of religion and morality lies in the fact that Christianity, like Judaism and Islam, bases its understanding of the world and of morality, not simply on human reason and experience, but on divine revelation. Interpretations of revelation underpin and support accounts of the relationship of religion and morality. This does not mean, however, that there is any 'innocent return', least of all in terms of fundamentalism, to a dependence on uncontested or revealed moral truths. Consequently, it is important to understand the significance of this revelation for the interpretation of religious morality. 'Revelation' is itself a multi-faceted concept which requires careful handling if it is to clarify rather than confuse.[7]

One of the functions of revelation in the past has been to effect a contrast with reason. Whereas reason brings together whatever is logical or capable of empirical examination and analysis, revelation points to a content from a different source, namely God, whose existence cannot be observed or proved. In this sense, Aquinas could say that 'theology uses the authority of canonical scriptures as being that proper to it and reasons from it with necessity'.[8] Hence, revelation was based on the truths revealed in scripture. Revelation in this sense (A) is expressed in propositions whose truth value is capable of determination. This understanding of revelation has come to occupy a prominent position since the Enlightenment, even when it is a view under attack, as it frequently is in modern theologians who wish to point to what they regard as a more fruitful understanding of revelation (B) in terms of God's revealing of himself in various forms of personal encounter, where the propositional element is either absent or muted. Buberian-type understandings of revelation as 'encounter' are influential, for example, in many modern theologians. If revelation has to be capable of being shown to be true, it is not surprising that it came to be viewed as chiefly or simply another avenue to truth alongside science and other disciplines. It may simply confirm what can be discovered more securely, and possibly more quickly, by other methods (e.g. logic, rational analysis and empirical observation). If, on the other hand, revelation deals with mysteries which are not capable of rational elucidation, it pays a heavy price for such self-understanding in modern societies: neglect, suspicion and rejection.

This neglect of revelation was often based on the assumption that truth is chiefly or only a characteristic of propositions. The stranglehold of this assumption is loosened, however, when it is acknowledged that revelation (B) may have propositional force, but that true propositions are not exhaustive of truth and that scripture and other sources of revelation are themselves in need of interpretation as testimony and narrative, not simply as evidential propositions.

Attempts to ground revelation (A) in religious experience or rationality usually fail, as Thiemann has shown in *Revelation and Theology* (chapters 1–2), because they fail to provide a satisfactory analysis of the relationship of revelation and reason by their search for a rational justification and defence of theology's main premiss, the existence of God, and by their attempt to ground such a justification in a foundational-type theology dependent on the use of non-inferential intuition. A more fruitful approach to revelation and its relation to reason can be developed when it is accepted that divine revelation includes all of the ways in which God reveals himself. Divine revelation is not limited to specific propositions or key doctrines found in scripture and sanctioned by the community of believers or governing hierarchy. Revelation embraces the totality of God's self-revelation in creation and history and at the end of all things, through reason and experience as well as faith. In the light of such an understanding of revelation as given to all (cf. Romans ii. 14), it is possible to speak of general revelation (as in conscience) and special revelation (as in faith). The importance of truth is not overlooked, but the emphasis is on relationship with God. In many Protestant churches, revelation was accordingly understood in terms of a quadrilateral of scripture (usually accorded primacy), tradition, reason and experience. The historical aspect of revelation related both to founding documents (scripture – hence the significance attached to the inspiration of scripture and to historical criticism and interpretation of scripture) and to persons in community (e.g. Jesus Christ and His Body, the church – hence the significance of debates about Christology and ecclesiology in the light of changing epistemologies and sociologies). Neglect of God as Holy Spirit, and the attempt to find unchanging formulations of divine truth, have continued to plague 'revelation' (B), but there has been a growing recognition that 'revelation' (B) offers a more hopeful way forward, particularly when this is associated with recent thinking about the nature of narrative and the human subject in revelation.

Such a perspective characterises the analysis of K. Trembath[9] who has distinguished between divergence and convergence theories of revelation. Divergence theories (e.g. those of W. J. Abraham; C. F. H. Henry; K. Barth and J. I. Packer)[10] support an evangelical Christian view, which emphasises the gulf of sinfulness between God and man, and locates revelation, not in God's creation, but in the Bible or Jesus or the church or miracles. Trembath criticises the main methodological weakness of this approach as a failure to take God's creation seriously and a persistent attempt to find criteria which themselves become the authorities behind revelation (cf. 'these criteria function as ultimate revelation but are shrouded in mystery; revelation then becomes in practice whatever those in authority say it is').[11] As J. P. Mackey notes, the whole revelational complex can be quite damaging to morality when the original revelation becomes ossified in outdated religious systems and power structures.[12] In addition to recognising that revelation is closely linked with salvation and the transformation of what is human, we need to be able to 'define and defend a formal notion of what would and would not count as a disclosure from God'.[13] Some attempt must be made to express, however inadequately, the nature of God and how God and humanity are related. God works through the natural, and revelation is located, not in one particular source, but in a variety of processes, events, personal interventions and qualities. No part of reality on this convergent view is, in principle, excluded from becoming a means of God's self-revelation.[14] Theologians and philosophers examined under this heading by Trembath are: A. Dulles; J. Macquarrie; G. O'Collins; I. T. Ramsey and M. Polanyi.[15] In *Models of Revelation* (1985), Dulles puts forward criteria for evaluating theories of revelation (such as faithfulness to the Bible and Christian tradition) and then formulates various models or types of revelation focussed on doctrine, history, inner experience, dialectical presence and new awareness. Revelation is symbolic communication which affects our understanding of what it means to be human in relation to the divine, and Dulles explores the use and meaning of symbols, without, however, – and this is Trembath's chief criticism – making clear how symbol mediates truth and meaning to us, without indicating how revelation is 'intrinsic either to what it means to be human or what it means to be God'.[16]

Trembath himself concentrates first on what it means to be human and finds this in the moral nature of humans: 'To be human is to be moral.'[17] ('To be human is to be able among other things to recognise, understand and implement a moral theology; such values are involved in other attributes such as speech and thought, which are also fundamental to being human.') He rightly insists that this moral nature is not limited to being morally good, but must also include the possibility of moral evil, but his attempt to include under 'moralness' all the attributes of human knowing and living blurs the very characteristic which he draws attention to by the term 'moral nature of humans'. His argument, which goes on to draw an analogy between the moral nature of humans and the moral nature of God, would be strengthened if he were to argue first for the analogy of divine and human persons and the way in which his view of revelation supports this, before going on to draw out the importance of morality as one of the most important features of being a person.

What, then, of the distinctive contribution of 'revelation' to an understanding of the relationship of religion and morality? Have Jewish, Christian and Islamic morality been reduced to 'human moralness' or the morality of persons in community? All three religions have traditionally recognised that morality is not limited to believers, and have tried to account for the 'good pagan' in a variety of ways, sometimes by stressing the close links of reason and morality and developing a form of natural theology in which there is a common foundation in reason, even when revelation goes beyond, if not against, reason.

Unfortunately, this has frequently led to a blurring of the distinctiveness of religious morality and to a misunderstanding of the intimate links between faith and morality which transform morality from being a purely human or rational enterprise to a vision and praxis which is, throughout, religious in character. The advantage of what is proposed above by means of revelation (B) is that it allows for genuine input into morality and moral debate from the different faith positions and does not imply that moral debate can be settled on purely rational or secular grounds. At the same time, it allows for and encourages dialogue in matters of morality both between believers of different faiths and between believers and non-believers. This is important in democratic societies aspiring to openness and religious tolerance. The Enlightenment compromise and the attempt to find a common denominator in rationality needs to be broadened to allow for recognition of the significance of revelation. Those who insist on the absoluteness of divine law should also be prepared to interpret their religious heritage within a framework which allows for differences and moral debate if model (B) of revelation is accepted.

If this view of revelation is accepted, it becomes possible to see how a religious ethic may satisfy both universal and distinctive claims. It is a view which is particularly appropriate for a Christian ethic which recognises both the important differences between divine and human personhood and their similarities and points of comparison. The relationality which is characteristic of Trinitarian personhood cannot be exactly reproduced in human personhood in this life, but the influence of understanding God as personal is profound and, for Christians, determinative.

It has been common ground between both sides in the autonomy–heteronomy debate that morality has traditionally formed an important aspect of religious faith and belonging. There were, however, some major differences. Those stressing ethical autonomy and often relying on a form of natural law to support their view have tended to locate the religious contribution, not in content, but in motivation, without, however, being too explicit about what is meant by 'motivation'. Motivation has been used loosely to cover reasons for action and intentions as well as motive. The effect of context on content was not always appreciated. It is not the case that religious believers and secular humanists are committed to the same moral policies but with different motives. They sometimes commit themselves to different moral policies and courses of action. At the same time, the alleged links between religion and morality do need careful empirical investigation; clear conceptual distinctions are also needed; most important, however, is analysis and discussion of what is being claimed in the dispute between those who argue that a morality based on religion has significant advantages over a secular morality based solely on reason.

Another important reason why an understanding of the human subject is relevant to the relationship of religion and morality is the way human nature functions as both a theoretical and a practical concept. It has frequently been pointed out that ethics builds on a view of human nature. There is no agreed view of human nature, but, as recent discussions have begun to indicate, this is not essential for recognition of the role that 'human nature' legitimately plays in questions of morality and obligation. Developing ideas of Putnam, Midgley and Foot, C. J. Berry has argued for the recognition of 'human nature' as both a theoretical and a practical concept:

> The concept of 'human nature' provides a criterion for acting or not acting in the world. This means that the conceptual context within which the facts of human nature are identified is orientated towards practice. Such facts establish a context within which it is possible to identify what it is appropriate for humans to do . . . This factual establishment of what is appropriate is thus also the establishment of a context of normative significance. The concept of human nature is . . . at once descriptive and prescriptive.[18]

The understanding of human nature in Christianity, as in other religions, is shaped by an understanding of God as revealed in their scriptures. Christians believe humanity was created in the image and likeness of God. God speaks and gives instructions about the right way to live. Confronted by disobedience, God takes steps to change what is happening. In short, we are given a picture of divine–human interaction in which the understanding of what human nature is, can and should be is related to an understanding of God as one who communicates through speech and action.[19] The faith communities of the different world religions contribute different understandings of the human subject, and these interpretations influence the outcome of moral ideals and practices in the different religions. It is necessary to plot the descriptive differences. It is not necessary, however, to get complete agreement at the descriptive level.

D. Brown's *Choices* will serve as an example of how differences may be compatible with common ground within a tradition. He contrasts a truly Christian ethic with counterfeit

Christian stances such as Joseph Fletcher's 'situation ethics' and certain forms of 'liberation ethics', nicely illustrating that this descriptive task includes differentiation between different 'Christian' claimants. Brown regards both situation ethics and liberation ethics as religious versions of utilitarianism or Marxism which neglect fundamental features of a truly Christian ethic. 'Any satisfactory account of Christian ethics requires a concern for both love and justice – in a way that is compatible with respect for each and every individual having a unique worth in their own right, and must be built on the assumption that God's creation is fundamentally good.'[20] For this reason, Brown pays particular attention to conscience and natural law, holiness and love in a Christian ethic. His account focusses on Catholic and Anglican tradition (he finds Lutheranism and other forms of Protestantism deficient in respect of the criteria he has listed above) to illustrate a significant pattern of Christian (Anglican) response to various moral problems and situations, without, however, trying to argue that there is a uniquely Christian response to every moral dilemma. He makes an excellent attempt to describe what he regards as normatively Christian, but his account also indicates the impossibility of securing moral agreement even within one religion. It is common ground that the Christian is called to love his/her neighbour. But what does this mean? Christian love is not 'generalised, impartial benevolence'.[21] Individuals who may appear to be worthless are to be loved because of their God-given potential. Scripture supplies an additional motive, gratitude for forgiveness in Christ. God has made human beings in such a way that this loving constitutes a form of personal fulfilment. What ought to be is anchored in what is. The so-called 'naturalistic fallacy' is not necessarily a fallacy. An ethical naturalism which stops short of trying to *derive* values from facts is both reasonable and desirable. Brown's account of Christian love, particularly his restrictions on neighbour-love, might not command the assent of all Christians, but his discussion would be accepted by most Christians as a clear example of how a particular faith commitment may rightly influence the ethical judgement.

The importance of the human subject and the autonomy thesis in ethics has been amply recognised by numerous writers, including Gustafson[22] who is anxious not to introduce religious and theological positions into the ethical sphere precipitately. He is concerned, however, as a religious ethicist, that the theological dimension should not be overlooked or misrepresented. 'How do the ideas about God and God's relation to the arenas in which we live and act qualify our valuations of things?' His characterisation of a religious ethic as asking 'What is God, the ultimate ordering power in the Universe, enabling and requiring us to be and do?' makes the theocentric perspective quite central. He is concerned to emphasise the sovereignty of God and its significance for ethics. Only in this way is he able to express the religious and spiritual context of his own upbringing and continued, albeit modified, confession. Yet, throughout his writing, the human subject is equally clearly in the forefront of the picture he paints. Ethics is concerned with 'what agents do' in medicine, politics, war and peace and the business of living. Terms such as 'perspectives' on ethics and 'discernment' of truth suggest the combination of objective and subjective features which characterise his approach. He lists eight features, such as a focus on humanity, what is natural, interaction with others, concern for the totality of things and self-restraint, which, he believes, typify his 'theocentric construal of reality'.[23]

If one takes the view that Gustafson's points are not intended to delineate what is distinctive about a theocentric construal of reality, but represent rather the way in which he proposes to carry out his 'theocentric construal', one has to look elsewhere (e.g. his outline in chapter 2 of *Ethics from a Theocentric Perspective* of the different views of human nature held by Barth, Aquinas, Rahner and Paul Ramsey) for what he regards as distinctive. His theocentric construal of reality simply states the context and, to some extent, the method of a religious ethic and, in this sense, is a useful reminder that content alone is not the issue.

A more concise attempt to formulate the essentials of a 'will of God' ethic can be found in MacNamara's *Faith and Ethics*, which makes specific reference to God as Creator and the goal of moral striving, but appears to *subject* God to rationality. God 'wills whatever is the demand of right reason'.[24] If God is identical with right reason, the sentence is tautologous; if God is not identical with right reason, it appears that right reason is superior to God (i.e. the Euthyphro dilemma in another guise).

As in Gustafson, aspects of a natural law approach are retained. There is an emphasis on the totality of things; the frailty of human reason is recognised; there is an emphasis on the human subject. Each point is clearly linked with God's will or divine reality. The coincidence of divine will and human rationality, however, must strike one as remarkable. Too much is conceded to human rationality. On the basis of these assumptions it would be strange if the contextual features did not make a difference to the content of an ethical system or set of ethical principles; but the content remains unspecified. Depending on how the context is elaborated in relation to other features (e.g. the empirical facts of a moral issue; detailed theological exposition, for example, of doctrines regarded as relevant to a particular ethical issue), different ethical responses will be justified. These different responses will also reflect the ethical subject's faith commitments. Consideration of the context or network of other beliefs that usually accompany belief in God, requires that the religious or believing moral subject should also be taken into account, and this will give a certain prominence to the subjective pole of moral discourse. The moral subject or agent is often overlooked in discussions of morality which focus on topics such as moral principles, levels of moral thinking, the nature of moral language, ethical theory and meta-ethics. This comparative silence about the moral subject is encouraged by features of moral discourse which underline the significance of impartiality, reason and universalisability. The emphasis of classical utilitarianism on the maximisation of pleasure, and the need for equal consideration of all those involved, each one to count for one and only one, does nothing to ameliorate this tendency to bypass the irreplaceability of the individual human person. Variants of utilitarianism which substitute individual preference tend to regard this 'preference' as a 'vote' which can be measured and added together with other votes, rather than as a personal agent interacting in a historical situation with other agents.

Another source of misunderstanding about the nature of moral agency may be traced to a dualistic Cartesian view of the self. Dissatisfaction with the Cartesian 'ghost in the machine' unites many commentators.[25] The concept of agency becomes impossibly unrealistic and obscure if one starts from an assumption that effectively prevents consideration of the agent as a body–mind unity or embodied self. Yet Descartes' influence has been fundamental in turning the attention of later philosophers to the centrality of the subject.

Recent studies have begun to qualify the interpretation of Descartes which gave priority to the mental aspect of agency.[26] Recognition of the role of empirical observation in his theories and his desperate desire to relate his rational speculations to the empirical universe, and even to find a physical link, such as the pineal gland, between mind and body, together with closer attention to his philosophical correspondence have suggested that, even if Descartes was mistaken on a number of epistemological issues, what divides him from his more empirical successors is more a matter of degree than the absolute difference sometimes posited.[27] If self-consciousness is interpreted against the background of Descartes' other ideas (including his inquiries into the development of speech and personal growth), it can be argued that self-consciousness 'depends on the exercise of cultural skills' and interaction with other persons. 'Persons essentially are second persons, who grow up with other persons.'[28] On this interpretation Descartes is not far from recognising conversation and relationality as vital marks of personhood.

Whether or not this is the correct interpretation of Descartes, the 'turn to the subject', which is certainly indebted to Descartes, has, under the successive influence of many different schools of thought, many of them in conscious opposition to Descartes, such as materialism, romanticism, dialogical personalism among others, made it imperative that the moral subject should not be overlooked in discussions of morality, despite the continued neglect of this point in many works on ethics.

From the religious point of view, this is all the more important for several reasons. The so-called 'object' of religious life and experience, God, is not an empirical reality open to observation and study in the manner of other objects. Even without adopting Schleiermacher's decisive turn to the subject, which seems to give priority to human religious experience over divine existence, the study of religion makes it necessary to attend carefully to the subject of religious life and speech in such matters as belief, ritual, morality, social belonging and spirituality. From whatever standpoint the religious moral subject is studied (e.g. phenomenology, anthropology, philosophy), scholarly attention can no longer focus simply on abstract slices of the moral subject. The religious beliefs, attitudes and practices of the moral subject as a whole person cannot simply be ignored. A 'richer notion of the moral agent than has been traditionally employed' is needed, it has been suggested, if the scope of a religious ethic is to be appreciated.[29]

Since religious commitments run deep, one might well expect them to have a profound influence on people's values and the way they live. One clear way in which such an influence might make itself felt would be through the religious person's belief system. There is research, for instance, showing the effect of Seventh Day Adventist beliefs about not eating meat on their rates of illness and longevity. This illustration, however, might also suggest that it is not simply a matter of cognitive beliefs. The web of beliefs in question is held in place by a wide range of communal activity and support sytems.

Another way in which a richer notion of the moral agent might be developed is hinted at by MacNamara, when he refers to 'the myths and stories and symbols that shape my consciousness' and to the 'controlling key images of the person, of reality and of society'.[30] This is similar to J. P. Mackey's concept of formative 'picture ideals', as instanced in the apocalyptic world-view which led to moral withdrawal and detachment from the world, in contrast to the creation-affirming attitude of most of Jesus' teaching, for instance. Mystery, symbol, picture and story are not enough, as MacNamara recognises, to serve as substitutes for a richer notion of the moral agent, but there is material here that can be developed. It is clear that cognitive belief is too thin to support the whole gamut of religious moral diversity. There is an important place for moral imagination and recognition of the contextual nature of moral experience. If myths, stories and symbols are to be given a greater role, more attention also has to be paid to the detailed contours of the different world faiths.

One writer who has discussed how the moral agent is affected by faith is D. D. Evans. In a series of essays probing the relationship between language expressing convictions of faith and commitment and the language of morality, particularly in relation to the ideas of contemporary thinkers with whom he feels some affinity – Ian Ramsey, Sam Keen, Gregory Baum and Paul Ramsey, Evans develops his earlier ideas about 'onlooks'[31] by extending his analysis of attitudes, especially the attitude of trust, on existentialist lines and with the help of depth psychology and his own experience. He suggests that one of I. T. Ramsey's weaknesses was his failure to develop a philosophical anthropology. He uses the same term that Ramsey sometimes uses for his most unlimited metaphor or model, viz. 'person', and suggests that a more Buberian understanding of the self in relation should be the key to understanding a religious ethic:

What I meant by 'person' was something 'metaphysical' in the sense that it cannot be explained by reference to observable or introspectible characteristics of human beings, but only by reference to an *attitude* which is appropriate towards human beings as persons. In every human being there is something which, as I said, 'claims my concern, reverence, personal involvement and acknowledgement of value – my *agape*, to use the New Testament word. This attitude does not depend on his particular observable qualities. A person is a being such that *agape* is the appropriate attitude.'[32]

Later this becomes stage 1 of a 2 stage argument. 'Human nature is such that attitude X is necessary for human authenticity or fulfilment or personality; therefore we ought to cultivate and live by attitude X.' The second stage consists of the argument that expressions of attitude X imply belief in God and would be logically inconsistent with expressions of atheism. Attitude X may be basic or pervasive trust, or respect for the moral law, or absolute dependence depending on one's normative anthropology.

This position is refined in a number of ways. Basic trust or receptivity is argued to be the fundamental attitude in the development of a person and to be a necessary condition for other religious attitudes and moral virtues. This view is qualified yet further by reference to a set of attitude-virtues or stances which combine religious attitude and moral virtue and correspond to the attitudes noted by Erik Erikson as appropriate responses to life-crises in an individual's psychological development. 'According to my earlier proposal religion and morality, while having *different* constituents, have a common origin in the divine activity which is at work in the receptive person. According to my new proposal, while the common origin is still affirmed, religion and morality have the *same* constituents, the set of attitude-virtues which are constituents of human fulfilment' (my italics).[33]

The emphasis on basic trust or receptivity in the formation of the religious believer/moral subject represents a significant move away from an interpretation of Christian beliefs in terms of their content. The insight should not be lost sight of, and can be incorporated into discussion of Christian symbol and story. But Evans is immediately plagued by the realisation that there are other positive attitude-virtues. How should these be accounted for? There is also the underlying deep-seated problem of epistemological justification: on what basis is the role and scope of attitude-virtues being supported? Evans' position clearly rests on a particular view of human fulfilment. This view, in turn, rests on several supports which, although clearly identifiable, are not easily evaluated. One of these supports is to be found in depth psychology and Evans' own response to psychotherapy. It is not presented as a logical deduction (from psychology) or as a purely personal intuition, but as a reasonable empirical inference. He argues, on the basis of his own experience, that this is a reasonable view of human nature, which gives a more adequate account than linguistic analysis or studies which focus on the cognitive aspects of belief. In effect, he appeals to his readers to examine whether their experience chimes with his. He is aware of the gaps and difficulties in his account. Even if one concurs with the emphasis he gives to 'basic trust' in human nature, it does not follow that it entails religious belief. There are, moreover, many different articulations of basic trust, 'since trust is essentially pre-linguistic'.[34] Despite his justified criticism of I. T. Ramsey for undue reliance on a too Berkleyan model of the ego, and despite his own stress on relationships and the interpersonal, Evans places the culminating cosmic stage in contemplative detachment, and operates throughout with a model that is essentially neo-Kantian and preserves a cognitive ego that remains remote from other enfleshed interacting selves. Many of the difficulties in Buber's dialogical and existential personalism,[35] particularly his ban on objectivity and spatio-temporal characteristics and absence of distinguishing contextual features which result in the I–Thou relationship becoming a somewhat abstract concept, are reproduced in Evans. The language of encounter becomes a metaphor without foundation. What Evans says, however, is important, and it is possible to give a different interpretation of what he calls 'pre-linguistic experience'. That there are experiences which are difficult to express in words is clear: deep joy, deep sorrow, for example. *Sunt lacrimae rerum et mentem mortalia tangunt.* It would surely be understood if we said that some feelings cannot be put into words. It is also clear that, as a matter of human development, infants can feel pain, hunger, happiness and distress long before they can talk. What he says about 'trust', however, can be accommodated more satisfactorily both in relation to his own insights about relationship with others and in relation to other evidence and theories (see chapter 11), not by stressing pre-linguistic experience, but by developing the account of linguistic practices and the nature of human communication, which he himself was so interested in. One such aspect of human communication is narrative, which gives scope for consideration of the subject and, at the same time, gives public form and expression to the subjective.

In recent discussions, great weight has been placed on the

idea of narrative, both in theology and ethics.[36] This would allow a Christian ethic to develop links between personhood and narrative and community, thus softening any rigid distinction between scripture and tradition, although this is not necessarily intended or necessary. It is proposed, therefore, to examine some of the discussions of narrative ethics in relation to our concern with persons and personhood. It will be found that many of the traditional concerns about the analysis of Christian moral judgement reappear: are values inherent in the human story? What is the role of the Christian community and the teaching of Jesus? Is a Christian ethic to be located only in the Christian story? It will be found that, although some of those who wish to emphasise the importance of narrative ethics do so in order to recover the lost distinctiveness of Christian ethics, as they see it, there are also those who take narrative ethics seriously and yet would not wish to separate Christian ethics so sharply from a more universal ethic.

The prominence of narrative in many recent discussions of theology and ethics is the result of several different factors. Dissatisfaction with more traditional views which are sometimes characterised as one-sidedly rationalistic and analytic is clearly part of what has happened.[37] Desire for more holistic approaches, which take account of the whole person and the social contexts in which individuals and communities share, is also clearly involved. But perhaps the single most important factor has been the increased recognition of the significance of language and the linguistic context of theology and ethics. These different concerns are given expression in P. Nelson's view that: 'The fundamental idea underlying the variety of claims made on behalf of narrative is that narrative, or story, is ingredient to understanding the self, social groups and their histories. The moralities into which we are socialized are not so much sets of rules or principles as they are collections of stories about human possibilities and paradigms for action.'[38]

Although there is no agreed analysis of 'narrativity' and narrative theology, it is widely accepted that narrative has a significant function both in terms of what human beings are like (they tell stories about themselves and others – to themselves and to one another – to understand, amuse, educate, inform, deceive, betray, pray, believe, in fact, to stay alive and remain human or become more human; even the processes of dehumanisation and victimisation of others are accompanied by stories), and in terms of fundamental analysis of human discourse and speech-acts (laws, poetry, history and even mathematical-scientific discourse are usually embedded in a narrative, and the analysis of forms of speech also underlines the significance of narrative).

Narrative also gives expression to an even more crucial aspect of human personhood: existence in time and history. Who we are not only depends on others, but on the fact that we think and plan, live and act in time. Without time neither action (events, plot) nor character would mean very much. What would it mean to contemplate an action (such as a journey) which has no ending or purpose? The importance of this temporal quality of narrative for moral personhood can be illustrated from discussions about respect for persons in medical ethics. Professionals are often tempted to pigeon-hole the patient and find a solution before hearing what she is saying. 'We cannot ever cross the divide between ourselves and others but we can pay attention to what they tell us they see on their side . . . In order to stay in that no-man's land between professional detachment and personal involvement, we need to be clear as to what we understand by the patient as person.'[39] Reason, communication and personal identity are aspects of personhood, but not the whole. An essential dimension is time. Without time, so necessary for growth and development, for understanding where we have come from and where we wish to go, we cannot know another person. Admittedly this is a point about medical case-work. But it has wider applicability. It is one of the main reasons why personhood is linked with narrative. A meaningful life, like a story with its movement from beginning to end, is one that has coherence over time, so that even interruptions and contradictions, while remaining just that, can be inscribed into a purposeful whole. It is also one of the features of biblical narrative that God's self-revelation is attested over time; who God is is not immediately obvious. Only when his promises are fulfilled in acts in history do we begin to glimpse the reality that undergirds the future.

It is perhaps not surprising, therefore, that moral discourse should be found to be closely related to narrative, both in context and in expression. In the case of Jewish-Christian ethics, it has long been recognised in traditional teaching that the outstanding ethical sequences of the Old and New Testaments are set within a narrative context. The Decalogue is not simply a list of laws, but instruction for a body of people delivered from slavery on their way to God's promised land. The Torah as a whole takes the form of a narrative. The Sermon on the Mount is not simply a list of impossible ideals, but guidance for those who want to know what it will mean to follow Jesus' call to repent and believe since the Kingdom of God is at hand, and to live already as those who willingly accept God's rule. The parenetic passages in Paul's letters, which advise Christians to pay their taxes and love one another (among other things), are also closely related to being baptised (into the death and resurrection of Jesus) and becoming members of a community, the church, which lives in the faith that the story of God's people, delivered from slavery and sin, has found its fulfilment in the coming of God's Messiah, Jesus of Nazareth, and continues in the blessing of the Spirit which continues to transform the church and the history of the world.

This concentration on narrative as the means to a better understanding of a religious ethic may have been overstated and exaggerated occasionally. Narrative context does not exclude rules, laws and principles, some of which may have universal application. By examining some of the claims made for narrative ethics, particularly in relation to personhood, we hope to advance our inquiry into the relation of personhood and a Christian ethic. We shall examine four different ways which have been used to link Christian story and morality, focussing our examination on the third and fourth ways. We shall use these to advance the outline of a communicative Christian ethic, which incorporates insights from several of these ways.

An example of the first way is R. B. Braithwaite's 'An

Empiricist's View of the Nature of Religious Belief'. Writing as a scientist in 1952 when linguistic empiricism was dominant, Braithwaite suggested that earlier debates about the significance of religious and ethical propositions had benefited greatly from R. M. Hare's analysis of the logic of moral language with his emphasis on universalisability and prescriptivity as the twin criteria of what is essential to moral utterance. This movement away from the unduly relativistic and subjectivist positions of emotivism espoused by Stevenson and Ayer, to a position which characterised morality analytically in terms of significant features which could be examined linguistically, appealed to Braithwaite's scientific outlook. His attempt to apply this new perspective to religious ideals and religious moralities led him to suggest that religions were, in effect, expressions of intention to behave in a certain sort of way together with a story or set of stories which acted psychologically to motivate and sustain the believer. Braithwaite's claim that religious assertions are primarily moral assertions was widely challenged, both at the time and since, as too sweeping and inadequate. It was, in effect, a form of reductionism. There was equal criticism of his attempt to differentiate between religious and secular moralities and between different religious moralities by means of 'story'. His understanding of story was ill-defined and elusive: 'The reference to the story is not an assertion of the story taken as a matter of empirical fact: it is a telling of the story, or an alluding to the story, in the way in which one can tell, or allude to, the story of a novel with which one is acquainted. To assert the whole set of assertions of the Christian religion is both to tell the Christian doctrinal story and to confess allegiance to the Christian way of life.'[40] He went on to say that 'the language expressing the story is given a meaning by the standard method of understanding how the *story-statements* can be *verified*' (my italics). 'The empirical story-statements will vary from Christian to Christian.'[41] Similarly for other religions. 'Story' in Braithwaite is sometimes interchangeable with 'story-statement' or 'doctrine' as well as 'novel' or 'parable' or 'myth', and it is clear that his main interest was not in the analysis of narrative. The 'story' did not have to be believed to be true, but it exercised a psychological role. A work of fiction, like Bunyan's *Pilgrim's Progress* or Hindu epic, would do equally well if it could exercise a profound influence on how people thought and believed and behaved.

As an account of Christian belief or Christian ethics, Braithwaite's view appears dated and somewhat eccentric. It bears the stamp of its period – clear, confident and amazingly short-sighted, since even then the works of Wittgenstein were being translated and there was an awareness of the range of language and the importance of metaphorical language (e.g. in the writings of I. T. Ramsey and A. Farrer). It was, however, an attempt to explain the distinctiveness of a Christian ethic in a way that would be understood by adherents of linguistic empiricism in a situation where the plausibility of a religious ethic was under attack (cf. M. Knight, *Morals without Religion*). Moreover, despite all its faults, it retains the virtues of Hare's characterisation of morality in terms of universalisability and prescriptivity, which represented a marked advance on emotivism, as Braithwaite claims. The attempt to combine the formal features of Kantian ethics within a utilitarian framework remains a significant factor that a religious ethic needs to take account of,[42] but, in general, the model functions as a warning how *not* to treat narrative in a religious ethic. The narrative has a 'glued-on' quality as far as the ethic goes. This may reflect the dissonance between life and narrative which some commentators feel. Narratives have a wholeness not found in real life; they are superimposed on events to create meaning where none was experienced. Whether or not this is true, the choice of narrative seems to require more 'fit' and cohesion with what events are about. The whole point of narrative, one might say, is to make sense of life.

Like the first way, the second way of relating narrative and morality tends to regard the narrative as somehow secondary or illustrative rather than integral to the meaning of events, but existential meaning now moves to the centre of the frame. Morality is no longer the command or will of a supernatural lawgiver. The supernatural is part of a 'mythical' universe. Morality is essentially autonomous, when the subject acts in freedom. Bultmann's theological existentialism is a good example of what can happen when a philosophical anthropology based on shrewd phenomenological analysis is wedded to an interpretation of the gospel narratives as essentially kerygmatic representations of the early church. 'Once one has understood the unity of the eschatological and the ethical preaching of Jesus, one also has the answer to the real meaning of the eschatological message . . . Jesus "dehistorized" God and man; that is released the relation between God and man from its previous ties to history (history considered as the affairs of nations).'[43] Heidegger's analysis of the structure of being and human existence, with its themes of the need to escape from care-death-nothingness by authentic decision, and Herrmann's 'contrast between the past history researched by historians and a personal, inner, existential "history" (*Geschichte*), which is said to be the locus of faith', were the presuppositions which determined the shape of the gospel which Bultmann attributed to the gospel writers. It cannot be said that Bultmann failed to find meaning in the Gospels, but it was a theology read into the text as much as out of it. As R. Morgan concluded, 'When Kierkegaard is supplemented by Marx, and Heidegger by Freud and Bloch, Bultmann's framework will allow theology's concern with human existence to include a more positive relationship to real history and society.'[44] This may seem a rather strong verdict, but it indicates the extent of what Bultmann omitted. Existentialism retains a strong attraction for those seeking to make sense of human existence. Throughout history, religions have contributed to the existential quest for meaning and purpose. One of the ways in which this has been achieved has been through narratives – of religious experience, faith and service. The constant weakness, however, of fusing past and present horizons is that present concerns begin to dominate and the scope of history is neglected or narrowed. By his focus on 'myth' Bultmann directed attention to one particular sort of language and away, for example, from realistic narrative. And, even in the case of 'myth', his exposition confused different senses.

A third, and more historically nuanced way, of relating

narrative and morality is proposed by theologians and philosophers such as J. B. Metz, Hans Frei and Paul Ricoeur. Although
influenced by earlier existentialist theologies, such as Bultmann's, and by Rahner, Moltmann and Pannenberg, who had
pinpointed the importance of history and eschatology but were
still strongly drawn towards producing an overall view of
history, Metz pointed to the influence of post-Enlightenment
rationalism on Christian theology and the problems resulting
from a privatisation of religion and religious meaning. Concerned to counteract these tendencies, he began to develop a
critical political theology in *Theology of the World* (1969) and *Faith
in History and Society* (1977). Since religion is concerned with
human liberation in its totality, it must enable believers both to
understand who they are, not only as individuals, but in
relation to society and institutions, and to act with faith,
courage and integrity in their various circumstances. A great
deal of attention is focussed on the world because prevailing
ideologies have masqueraded as 'true' or 'Christian' and
genuine Christianity has been hidden and is suffering from an
identity-crisis. The church has to release the genuine memory
of Jesus Christ and his message of freedom. This cannot
happen if its theology continues to rely on the rationalistic
categories of an outmoded idealist philosophy, which pays
insufficient attention to history.[45] Metz uses the story of the
hare and the hedgehog(s) – the second hedgehog, identical in
appearance with the first, is always ahead of the hare in the
race, until eventually the hare collapses with exhaustion – to
suggest that something akin to the hedgehog trick has been
perpetrated by the church and Christian theology in its attempt
to defeat the stratagems of unbelief. Despite all appearances,
Christianity has claimed, the universal meaning of history is
guaranteed, because at the end of the race God and Christ will
triumph.

Is there not a better way to present Christianity and its
genuinely risky involvement in history, without opting for
idealist or other inadequate solutions, such as reducing salvation to the salvation of the individual? Metz puts forward his
proposal for a narrative and practical theology in this context.

It is post-idealistic in that it no longer accepts the rationalistic criteria and categories of Enlightenment thought. It allows for universal meaning without guaranteeing this in advance, and takes account of the suffering and experience of individuals. He points to the forgotten importance (in idealism) of the narrative structure of the Bible. Narrative allows for new experiences; it evokes a personal response; it has an emancipatory role.[46]

This may seem to suggest an apologetic role for narrative in terms of applied theology, but Metz wishes to use narrative more fundamentally. He sees in narrative a way of reconciling history and salvation, which is important for Christians. 'History', he says, 'is always a history of suffering'.[47] The only way to preserve this lies through stories rather than abstract thought and reason. The theologies of Pannenberg, Moltmann and Rahner, he argues, only maintain a Christian character, if indeed they do, through their use of narrative reference.[48]

Metz's concern with history and narrative finds more developed expression in Frei and Ricoeur, both of whom delve much more deeply into the hermeneutical issues raised by modern historical and literary theory, although Metz's pronounced ethical concerns are not matched in either. Both Frei and Ricoeur explore the significance of narrative for Christian theology, involving analysis of the nature of revelation, anthropology and scripture, particularly the Gospels and the significance of Jesus Christ. Despite convergence on many issues, however, there are fundamental differences.[49] In *The Eclipse of Biblical Narrative* (1974), Frei argued that, from the eighteenth century, critical biblical studies, focussing on what actually happened and attempting to dissect the biblical narrative into a variety of sources, began to read the Bible in a new way, which resulted in a form of 'eisegesis'. Presuppositions were read into the text, as if it had been intended as a quarry for objective history instead of a meaningful narrative, intended to be read as such. Frei is critical of biblical theologies which ignore this and seek to interpret the biblical narrative primarily in terms of objective history or philosophical categories, such as anthropology. Frei has since developed his position (e.g. in 'The "Literal Reading" of Biblical Narrative in the Christian Tradition: Does It Stretch or Will It Break?', 1986) to make clear that a fruitful hermeneutic does not first develop a category of 'realistic narrative' and then subsume the gospel narratives within it. The interpreter's prime task is to understand how the Gospels were used in the believing community, rather than to relate them to general categories of human experience drawn from philosophical reflection.[50]

Ricoeur, on the other hand, *is* concerned to relate the biblical narrative to more general philosophical categories, although he would deny that he is imposing alien categories. He regards the use of symbolic and poetic language in the Bible as part of a wider significant use of metaphorical language to enable us to understand the human situation and human experience. Indeed, his detailed, sensitive explorations of the way language is used have made a massive contribution to the interpretation of narrative and temporality. Narrative is connected with the essential temporality of human existence. It is not possible to do justice to the scale of that contribution in the context of this study, but two examples will illustrate how his understanding of personhood operates. In 'Narrative Identity', he uses the distinction between identity[51] as sameness (*idem*) and identity as selfhood (*ipse*) to mount a powerful critique of Parfit's *Reasons and Persons* (cf. chapter 4 above), in terms of its methodology ('which allows only an impersonal description of the facts whether relating to a psychological criterion or to a bodily criterion of identity') and its conclusion that personal identity is not what matters. In Parfit's science-fiction cases, the subject suffers alone; 'in fictional narrative, on the other hand, interaction is constitutive of the narrative situation'.[52] The most important difference between Parfit's narratives and historical/fictional narratives, however, lies in response to the question *who* is the self? If we say with Parfit, 'Identity is not what matters', 'it is still someone who says this'. 'Many conversion narratives bear witness to such dark nights of personal identity. At these moments of extreme exposure, the null response, far from declaring the question empty, returns to it and preserves it as a question. What cannot be effaced is the question itself: who am I?'[53] Ricoeur employs his dialectic of the unity and continuity of a person combined with the change and diversity experienced by persons in time to develop his views about narrative identity.

In *Oneself as Another*, Ricoeur moves towards an understanding of the self with the help of a threefold dialectic, which regards the self as 'only mediately available' (i.e. by explanation and understanding rather than by introspection); as constituted between the existing or sedimented self (*idem* – sameness) and future, undetermined initiatives of the self (*ipse* – selfhood); and in relationships between the self and the other, which may include the other as body or the experience of passivity/the voice within (conscience) as well as intersubjectivity. The ontological grounding of this view of the self is located, not in consciousness or empirical verification, but in 'attestation', the voice of witness and promise which reaches out beyond the self with 'ontological vehemence'.[54] This is a view of the self which is able to take embodiment, rationality and relationality seriously. It is a view of the self which is deeply indebted to his interpretation of the gospel narratives, particularly those of the Passion, which throw into relief the symbolic nature of the Creation and Fall narratives. Cosmic evil is overcome and hope reborn in the Garden of Gethsemane. Although it may seem that Ricoeur is not primarily interested in ethics, in that ethics is swallowed up in the discipleship of the suffering servant, his emphasis on temporality is important for understanding personhood. It is also important, as we shall see, in a Christian ethic.

A number of questions, it is true, are left unanswered: does Jesus of Nazareth inaugurate or merely illustrate what human personhood might encompass? What criteria are being used to establish what is humanly possible? Is every believing community allowed to establish its own criteria of meaning and human possibility? Are the differences between fact and fiction simply blurred? Does the surplus of meaning discovered in language simply imitate or reflect a prior surplus of meaning in ontology? The questions are testimony to the effectiveness of narrative as a vehicle of inquiry and understanding, however, rather than empty or impossible questions. In all of these ways of using narrative, except perhaps the first, religion and morality are closely associated by means of narratives which belong to the revelational complex of a particular religion or faith. This is particularly true of the fourth way of using narrative, which we will examine in chapter 11.

# PART 3

# Implications for a Christian ethic

No single moral theory has been able to capture all that is required of a universally acceptable moral theory. Even the staunch defenders of utilitarianism and Kantianism usually recognise as much. Utilitarianism has prided itself on reducing morality to a single principle, but finds it impossible to give a clear answer to the question of what a life is worth. In fact, in more recent modified versions, such as rational preference utilitarianism, there is an attempt to feed off an underlying sense of moral obligatoriness. Utilitarianism is best understood as an attempt to relate morality more closely to empirical circumstance. Kant's emphasis on respect for persons in their own right, on universalisation, and on duty for the sake of duty, clearly represents important aspects of morality, but at the cost of leaving much of the content of morality non-specific. Dissatisfaction with aspects of utilitarianism has led some to search for a rights-based ethic that would incorporate features of utilitarianism.

Christian ethics has never attempted to provide an overall ethical theory. The theories of Plato and Aristotle were already in the field when Christianity arrived with its new way of life and will of God ethic. Now, as then, it brings to moral theory an overall vision of life, a way of relating to God and others, a concern for specific values such as loving kindness, justice and mercy for the weak and defenceless. Translated into action, however, these concerns make a radical comment on claims of self-sufficiency which are sometimes attached to either teleological or deontological ethics. In fact, there is a sense in which Christian ethics subverts ethics totally, because it is always advancing towards an open future, in which God's initiatives of grace in continuing to embody incarnation, death and resurrection confound human calculation and expectation. But, although some versions of Christianity have deliberately sought to give expression to the workings of God's spirit in a non-rational way, most mainline versions of Christianity have attempted to hold spirit and reason together, as being more in keeping both with scripture and tradition. From this standpoint, there is no exclusively Christian ethic (cf. Romans ii. 14 and chapter 10 above), although a distinctively Christian ethic is clearly possible.

The ideas of divine and human personhood we have investigated lend support to the view that some of the rational models of contemporary ethics (chapters 3 and 4 above) are based on a limited although important strand of Enlightenment thought stemming from rational-utilitarian philosophies. Reservations and criticisms already apparent in Hegel's successors have multiplied. One of the most significant developments is the attention being given to ideas of relationality, community and embodiment. We have noted the emphasis on mutual relations in Trinitarian thought. It is also significant that speech-relations, as evidenced by prosopological studies, seem to have played an important role in developing ideas of personhood in Christianity from the beginning. There is a recognition of the importance of speech-relations in modern analytic philosophy, and we shall consider the use made of this in the social philosophy of Jürgen Habermas, whose rational discourse ethic incorporates a theory of society relevant to 'persons in society'.

In Part 3, we draw on our discussions in Parts 1 and 2 to formulate a number of hypotheses and conclusions about the content, style and shape of a Christian ethic which makes critical use of personhood.[1] This will involve both philosophical and theological considerations. It is not our intention to develop the whole of Christian ethics round the concept of personhood, although that sometimes seems to be the intention of those who believe that a patristic ontology of personhood should be central to a Christian ethic. Nevertheless, we have argued that 'personhood' should be important in a Christian ethic, since it has implications for the understanding of human beings made in the image of God. Our discussion in Parts 1 and 2, therefore, governs the selection of topics in Part 3. In chapter 11, we bring together the narrative ethic of Hauerwas with the discourse ethic of Habermas in our search for a suitable vehicle for an ethic of personhood. In chapter 12, we examine the 'love command' which has traditionally summarised Christian ethical teaching. This allows us to develop the understanding of community, tradition and narrative from chapter 10. The inclusion of 'the enemy', so often silenced rather than subsumed in 'neighbour', points to the radical, but not irrational, nature of a Christian ethic, which is taken further in a discussion of forgiveness in chapter 13. Forgiveness, perhaps more than any other quality, distinguishes a narrative ethic based on 'persons in community'.[2] By contrast, the same tradition of persons in community includes 'human rights', often neglected in Christian ethics because of its secular, individualistic emphasis in the past, but having a clear connection with modern, rational views of 'persons'. Issues where personhood has been centrally involved (e.g. abortion; animal rights), some of which were discussed in Part 1, will be reconsidered in chapter 14. Finally, the issue of how Christians should care for the environment, of which they are in part co-creators, is considered in relation to our argument that divine and human personhood are related through creation.

# CHAPTER 11

# A communicative ethic: Hauerwas and Habermas

Previous chapters have illustrated how speech, communication, embodiment and relation to others, as well as autonomy, rights and interests have been integral aspects of personhood in more than one period of history. Persons are not solitary individuals, but persons in relation to others. This is also true from a Christian perspective. In examining the implications of personhood for Christian ethics, therefore, it is appropriate to make use of insights drawn from theology and social theory, as well as from philosophical ethics about the nature of ethical discourse. In this and the next chapter, we consider what is involved in developing a communicative Christian ethic and seeing the church as a community of ethical difference.

Despite the secularisation of intellectual disciplines since the Enlightenment and the privatisation of many aspects of religious life, religion and theology still make a strong contribution to public and private values. The religious pluralism of modern societies has made it more difficult to link such values with a single religious tradition, but all the major religions with their several million adherents have a particular interest in the ethical dimension. The interaction of religious and secular interpretations of morality is of critical importance in the modern world.

'Community' is sometimes contrasted with 'society'.[1] 'Society' may refer to a fairly loosely connected set of individuals and groups for whom belonging to the same society means little more than adherence to the same laws. Language, education, religion and occupation may be differentiating rather than uniting factors. 'Community', on the other hand, requires greater social cohesion, in terms of linguistic practice, shared commitments and personal relationships. In modern societies, characterised more by choice and differentiation than warmth and cohesion, such community may be found in various places: at home, at work, at church, or in a variety of voluntary associations, such as sport with its frequent emphasis on teams and team spirit, or campaigning groups (e.g. for the environment or the handicapped). Even in competitive capitalist societies, where self-interest often seems to rule, individuals express themselves, not only as individuals, but as relational beings who may participate in a variety of communities. Self-interest alone has difficulty in creating a community. There is fierce debate in political philosophy between communitarians who desire a politics of the common good, and liberals who stress the rights and freedoms of the individual.

A. MacIntyre made a strong case for recognising the communitarian nature of ethical traditions in *After Virtue*.[2] His haunting picture of a world desolated by catastrophe, lacking coherent knowledge of scientific thought and practice and attempting to piece together from scattered fragments a scientific conception of the world, and his comparison of this to our present disjointed understanding of morality has found a wide response:

What we possess are the fragments of a conceptual scheme, parts which now lack those contexts from which their significance derived. We possess, indeed, simulacra of morality, we continue to use many of the key expressions. But we have – very largely, if not entirely – lost our comprehension, both theoretical and practical, of morality. (p. 2)

His suggestion, however, that what we lack is the sort of ethical community which the Greek *polis* provided for Aristotle or the religious community for St Benedict, is less convincing. The small city-state with its dependence on slavery and the strictly ordered religious community are in no position to provide an ethical model of social differentiation and cohesion for a modern, pluralistic society.

MacIntyre is not alone, of course, in emphasising the importance of community and tradition for morality. Other communitarians (e.g. M. Sandel and C. Taylor) also emphasise the importance of context, community and tradition, in contrast to liberals (e.g. Rawls, Nozick and R. Dworkin) who emphasise reason, individual rights and interests. Not all the details of this debate need concern us, since it is not about religion and theology directly. It has significant implications, however, for a religious ethic concerned with personhood, and relates to those movements in the history of personhood that we have examined. Whether a Christian ethic is understood chiefly in terms of individual discipleship or a social ethic (of justice? liberation?) is related to the issues raised in the liberal–communitarian debate and will clearly affect the outcome.

This debate is also relevant in other ways, since it is concerned with the place of traditions, narrative, the nature of language and hermeneutics, all of which are lively issues on the theological agenda. As a community called into being by the word of God, it would be surprising if the church were not drawn, at least initially, to espouse a communitarian position of some sort. Yet its claims to possess and communicate universal truth draw it in the other direction also.

One of the aims of the present chapter is to show that, if we examine what is happening in social theory and in philosophical ethics, we find signs of a converging trend to give more weight to tradition and community in ethics, and that this corresponds with our understanding of persons in relation and with the ethical insights of Christian faith. If we can show that it is possible to hold context and universality together, this will lend support to the idea that Christian ethics is not a ghetto ethics, but is relevant to society as a whole.

It has been argued[3] that neither of the two main types of ethical theory, teleological utilitarianism and deontological Kantianism, are adequate to resolve the problems encountered in applied ethics. Although the derived principles of autonomy, beneficence and justice appear to offer guidelines for hard-pressed practitioners, it turns out that clear thinking alone without careful attention to context and detail is insufficient, and that, once the practitioner embarks on a specific case, it is the context and details that begin to matter

far more. Contextual understanding is not simply a matter of
filling in the descriptive details. The context itself has to be
evaluated. 'Optimism like Hare's, that with philosophical
clarification the problem would not seem as perplexing, rapidly
faded.'[4] One response to this situation has been to put forward
a contextual ethics model. Winkler, for example, has argued
that the applied ethics model puts the cart before the horse
because it proceeds deductively and tries to fit the case to the
principles, instead of starting with the situation, admittedly
within an overall theoretical framework of cultural values
which may not be dissimilar to the moral principles of the
applied ethics model, but which function differently in terms of
expectations and moral argument. The applied ethics model is
overambitious about the role of ethical justification. Contextualism is generally more sceptical; 'justification is essentially
continuous with the case-driven inductive process of seeking
the most reasonable solution to a problem'.[5] Clearly the two
models can be brought closer together by reducing the role of
principle in applied ethics or by making principles equivalent
to 'generalisations' which are developed from reflection on
particular cases.[6]

Contextualism by itself, however, is hardly sufficient to
ground a community of ethical interpretation. Criticism of the
applied ethics model may be justified, but contextualism seems
to rest its case on assumed cultural and community values.
What resources does it have for dealing with conflict? How
does it justify its own position when the society of which it is a
part is divided and unable to agree? This is a question, not only
of sufficient detachment and distance, but of genuine independence. Utilitarianism and Kantianism at least have their own
articulated principles and procedures for dealing with this
when the need for fundamental justification arises. And, ultimately, each appeals to a different view of society or the
individual or 'what is human'.

These views and the rational study of morality, at least in the
West, have their origins in the philosophical traditions of
ancient Greece. And that constitutes a dangerous legacy in the
eyes of those who are dissatisfied with the emphasis on rational

criteria in modern philosophical ethics, which has managed to embrace almost as many theories and shades of opinion as there are moral choices to be made: egoism, hedonism, relativism, emotivism, utilitarianism, prescriptivism, objectivism and so on. Despite this diversity, one could argue that one of the major debates of modern philosophical ethics is that between those who argue for some form of non-cognitivism, the position that moral claims do not represent objective values but the attitudes and feelings of those who express them, and those who believe that moral values represent, in some sense, objective values which correspond with the way the world is. Whatever view we take of this particular matter, however, it would be common ground to both parties that the proper way to resolve moral differences is through the exercise of reason and rational considerations. Although emotivism has its defenders, modern discussions about the logical structure of moral discourse have tended to favour those who argue – on logical grounds – that moral judgement cannot be assimilated to expressions of personal taste. There is something to be disagreed about, and rational arguments, which presuppose some views are morally right and others morally wrong, are involved.

This assumption of rationality is now being challenged by those who argue that the so-called rational arguments are frequently expressions of concealed power and prejudice masquerading as objective truth. Objections to logocentric rational individualism, as we saw in chapter 6, have been made by feminist writers who wish to see a larger role being given to gender and women's experience in ethics. Rationality mistakenly claims to be not only a method for resolving moral problems, but an avenue to substantive principles and objective values. Kant's discussion of rational persons as the ground of value, as we saw in chapter 5, had as its aim to establish a rational and universal basis for ethics. We also noted (in chapter 10) how a religious ethic diverges from a purely secular ethic by drawing on sources of revelation and interpreting human experience in the light of beliefs about God as creative and redemptive in relation to the whole of life, by its practice of worship, and by the deliberate construction and constant reformation of emancipatory communities which embody and sustain commitments of justice for the poor and underprivileged. These include patterns of living based on divine forgiveness and reconciliation and hopes for the future. A Christian ethic has traditionally drawn on the resources of its scriptures, Christian tradition, personal and social experience and human reason. In Christian traditions which regard the Fall as total and interpret original sin as total depravity, human reason has a more precarious status, but, in any case, reason is not normally the final authority for a Christian.

Depending on whether scripture, tradition, experience or reason is given most weight, different types of Christian ethic result. When scripture has primacy, as frequently, the natural tendency is for a Christian ethic to emphasise God's will or command.[7] The interpretation of God's will/command revealed in scripture then assumes a significant role. The history of warring Christian factions and their different ethical stances is contained in the history of the interpretation of scripture. What could have been a somewhat barren absolutisation of the past, however, has been redeemed by the resurfacing of deep simplicities from Old and New Testaments ('What does the Lord require of you . . . but to do justly, love mercy and walk humbly with your God?' Micah vi. 8) and by the ways in which Christian communities have been challenged and encouraged by the same scriptures to find ways of applying God's will to ever new situations (cf. Bengel's 'te totum applica ad textum; rem totam applica ad te', which became John Wesley's simple hermeneutic). The appeal to experience is clearly under suspicion in present discussion (cf. chapter 10), which is not surprising in the aftermath of Joseph Fletcher's *Situation Ethics*, where 'the situation' was arbitrarily defined in relation to either legalism or antinomianism and a thinly disguised utilitarianism did duty for *agape* in order to loosen up Christian attitudes to sexual morality.

In recent writing on Christian ethics, attention has been focussed on narrative, and links have been suggested between personhood and narrative. At the same time, it is not possible to overlook the tradition of rational ethical reflection, as expressed, for instance, in natural law traditions. Christians are human and, since the ethical is concerned with what is human, we would expect a Christian ethic to have important elements in common with a rational ethic, even when that ethic is also secular.[8] The concern for a distinctive Christian ethic, however, deserves fuller consideration. The fourth way of relating Christian ethics and narrative, which we held back from the last chapter, is relevant at this point. The proposal, which has aroused considerable interest in its own right, is that of Stanley Hauerwas in *The Peaceable Kingdom* for a 'qualified' and narrative Christian ethic. We will relate it to a revision of Jürgen Habermas' communicative ethic by Seyla Benhabib[9] in order to suggest further developments. Hauerwas voices important Christian ethical concerns, but his reluctance to engage with the universality of rational ethical reflection seems to be a real loss if it prevents the Christian community from engaging with the wider community in which it is situated. For this reason, we consider whether Benhabib's modification of Habermasian ethics may not point the way to a more constructive Christian communicative ethic.

First, then, the way of relating narrative and ethics exemplified in Hauerwas. Although Hauerwas is unwilling to accept that narrative is 'the central focus' of his position,[10] he does regard it as 'an extraordinarily fruitful concept'. It will become clear in the following discussion how important an understanding of narrative is for his position. Much of his work has consisted of essays on particular topics, such as abortion, euthanasia, pacifism, the care of the mentally ill, the role of virtue, character and vision, the role of the community and community narratives in forming and sustaining a particular morality. He has written 'against the stream' to challenge the apparent complacency of moral theologians whose recommendations seem to vary hardly at all from those of secular moral philosophers. We will summarise Hauerwas' views as he expounds them in *The Peaceable Kingdom*, where he has been explicitly reflective about his way of doing ethics and about the way his views have developed, before moving to an evaluation of them and some suggestions of our own.

There is something profoundly disturbing and unsatisfactory, thinks Hauerwas, about the concentration of modern ethics on right and wrong decisions and actions or on moral quandaries, if this 'obscures the fact that they make sense only in the light of convictions that tell us who we are'.[11] 'Our most important moral convictions are like the air we breathe: we never notice them because our life depends on them' (ibid.). One of the main reasons for this unhappy concentration on decisions and actions has been the separation of the language of religion and the language of ethics in modern times. He draws on the work of MacIntyre, with whom he has collaborated on many occasions, to express this forcibly:

What we possess, if this view is true, are the fragments of a conceptual scheme, parts which now lack those contexts from which their significance derived.[12]

In order to supply this missing context, Hauerwas regards it as vital that Christians should anchor their morality in Christian belief and belonging rather than be concerned, as many Christians influenced by Kantian ethics have been, with a universal ethic. Hence, he speaks of a 'qualified' ethic (an ethic qualified by Christian faith and belonging). It would be a mistake to think that the main task of Christian ethics is to supply the secular world with values which will hold back the floodwaters of chaos. To do this is to subordinate truth to function, and fosters the futile notion that Christian ethics can supply an essential ingredient for secular morality, while allowing the secular world to continue otherwise unchanged. A truly Christian ethic requires the discipline and support of a Christian community. For this reason, Hauerwas conceives of theology and ethics going hand in hand. Ethics is not a late appendage to theology; ethical considerations are important from the beginning and all the way through. The narrative character of Christian ethics as expounded by Hauerwas is his attempt to demonstrate how this works.

His exposition begins by attacking the abstractness of what he calls an unqualified ethic. He includes here a number of separate issues: the use of meta-ethics to establish a sort of 'mid-air objectivity'; and the assumption and use of rules in both utilitarianism and Kantian ethics. The alleged defeat of popular moral subjectivism, which moral theorists often claim by pointing to the nature of moral disagreement, which, whatever it is, cannot simply be a matter of taste, leads only to a pale objectivity, which has to be compatible with subjective autonomy. On the use of rules he agrees with E. Anscombe's claim (1958) that modern moral philosophy tries to talk of laws without a lawgiver. Despite their differences, the two main accounts of moral rules, utilitarianism and Kantianism, 'share the common assumption that ethics, first and foremost, should embody an adequate theory of moral obligation derived from or involving in a fundamental manner, rules and principles. They differ only about what single principle best supports and orders our rule-determined obligations.'[13] This assumption he regards as mistaken. In both there is a concentration on moral quandaries and problems instead of a deepening awareness of what is involved in the moral life. There is a mistaken attempt to separate actions from the self which does them, as if the moral self was simply a 'series of actions lacking continuity and unity'.[14] This has a further unfortunate consequence for Christian ethics. It makes us unprepared for moral tragedy (i.e. irresolvable moral conflict). Moral tragedy is a fact of life, and a Christian ethic ought to prepare us to handle such conflict. What may be needed is not a moral answer, but the strength of conviction to go on living a moral life. Such conviction should not be abstracted from life in a Christian community. This involves that community's account of the good life, 'and that account necessarily takes the form of a narrative'.[15] This is illustrated from both Old and New Testaments, where God's laws are always set within the framework of a narrative and the life of a community. The Decalogue and the Sermon on the Mount, for example, 'are unintelligible when treated as sets of rules justifiable in themselves', although they are often used to illustrate the importance of law in a Christian ethic. The Bible does not put forward an abstract ethic of obligation, but a life of growth and development, a journey with God. Both Old and New

Testaments are stories of that journey and of the virtues needed for that journey.

The narrative is complex, with subplots and digressions, but it is not something that could be removed without loss. Nor is it purely illustrative, something which could be articulated without narrative. Neither is it fictional. 'There is no more fundamental way to talk of God than in a story.'[16] Narrative is more fundamental than doctrine, which, though important, is usually an abbreviation and refers back to a story. Doctrines are not the heart of stories, but a form of shorthand, like creeds. To understand the story, liturgy would be a better guide. But there is no substitute for story. God, world and self are interrelated concepts and their relationship is best seen in story. Just as we know ourselves through the stories we tell, 'we know who we are only when we can place ourselves – locate our stories – within God's story'.[17] The story of God is the story of His giving of Himself to us in His Son. As we receive Christ we are drawn into God's story and become part of *His* purposes, members of His family. To know God in this way requires constant resubmission to His will, the reaffirmation of our obedience and the constant renewal of discipleship.

The centrality of narrative for theology involves three crucial claims: we are contingent, created beings; we are historical beings who communicate with one another by means of historical narrative; 'God revealed himself narratively in the history of Israel and the life of Jesus' which is continued in the story of Jesus and the church. 'Narrative is the form of God's salvation.'[18] A Christian ethic, therefore, is a qualified ethic, based on narrative, not primarily concerned with rules but with helping us to form a vision of how things are. This transformation of the self means learning to live as sinners, and the Christian story must include language that gives an account of this transformation through the Cross and resurrection of Christ. We have to learn to see ourselves, not only as friends of the Crucified, but as among those who crucified *Him*. 'We . . . learn what our sin is as we discover our true identity through locating the self in God's life as revealed to us through the life, death and resurrection of Jesus Christ.'[19] When we discover ourselves as sinners we discover our calling to share in God's salvation, to become *His* people. Ethics, therefore, is 'not primarily about rules and principles, rather it is about how the self must be transformed to see the world truthfully. For Christians such seeing develops through schooling in a narrative which teaches us how to use the language of sin not only about others but about ourselves.'[20] Such an ethic would be of universal significance, but it would be a qualified (i.e. revealed) ethic.

In further reflection on the task of Christian ethics,[21] Hauerwas points to the failure, as he sees it, of traditional Catholic and Protestant conceptions of this task. Both have misread the practical nature of the undertaking. Ethics is 'at the heart of the theological task. For theology is a practical activity concerned to display how Christian convictions construe the self and the world.'[22] Roman Catholics have been particularly prone to confusing 'being Christian' and 'being human'. They have done this in the interests of 'natural law' on the assumption that there must be a common human morality intelligible to reason which Christians and others share. The specific Christian content of morality has been replaced by the 'believer's fundamental Christian decision to accept God's love in Christ and respond to it as one who believes and loves, as one who assumes the responsibility for life in this world in imitation of Christ, that is, as one who has died with Christ and is risen with him in faith and sacrament thus becoming a new creation'.[23] This *reduction* (italics added) of Christian content 'distorts our moral psychology since it presupposes that virtues . . . can be "objectively" characterized'[24] without reference to the process by which virtues are learned. This destroys the character required for moral agency, since there is no longer a clear relationship between who we are and what we do. It is mistaken to regard the Christian faith as supplying the motivational factor but not any content for Christian living. Hauerwas recognises that his procedure, at this point, is liable to be challenged by those who argue that 'to be Christian is but an intensification not a denial of what it means to be human'.[25] He acknowledges the force of this objection, but claims that there is no valid way to arrive at a purely objective ethic. There is a concealed tendency in the 'human is ethical' view to assume that Christian ethics will somehow support the prevailing cultural view. 'Why . . . assume that Christians should be able to contribute to the "public forum" on its own terms?' (i.e. instead of using Christian criteria). 'By virtue of the distinctive narrative that forms their community, Christians are distinct from the world. . . . recent attempts to identify Christians ethics with a universal human ethic fail to recognize that all accounts of the moral life are narrative dependent.'[26]

Hauerwas' overall position will commend itself to those who are looking for a reassessment of modern developments in moral philosophy and a clear statement about the distinctiveness of Christian ethics. His criticism of recent trends, his contention that narrative has been overlooked in Christian ethics, and his attempts to put forward a narrative Christian ethic will be welcomed in many quarters. One can also admire (without accepting) his determination to let a Christian ethic speak on its own terms. Some of his views, that ethics and theology belong together, that morality involves a community's account of the good life, that doctrine, creed and morality depend on a story about how the world is, are compatible with earlier parts of our study. There are, however, a number of worrying confusions, obscurities and ambiguities in his presentation which prevent wholehearted support for his position. We shall detail and examine these.

Hauerwas' polemic against rational analysis does not make it clear whether he is seeking to exclude or downgrade all rational ethical analysis or only certain types of rational analysis which take for granted certain presuppositions that have been common since the Enlightenment about the possibility (and some would say necessity) of justifying ethical norms in ethical terms. It will be clear from earlier chapters in the present study that the exclusion of religion and theology from the ethical arena is one feature of a rational ethic that stands in urgent need of reconsideration by religious ethicists. But Hauerwas' views seem to go much further and push Christians into a sectarian attachment to particular norms (e.g.

separation from the world; pacifism) without any recognition
that there may be legitimate disagreement among Christians
about some norms. Moreover, any discussion about the relationship of a Christian ethic to the ethic of others with whom
Christians share the world seems to become problematic. Is
there any bridge at all? Is there any scope for rational ethical
analysis? The position he adumbrates in chapter 4 appears
resoundingly unfavourable to all claims of reason, although
there is no reason, in principle, why an emphasis on narrative
should exclude rational analysis.[27]

The concept of narrative is not self-evidently clear, and
Hauerwas' use of 'story' can be quite confusing. What does he
mean when he talks of our story intersecting with God's story?
In what sense is scripture God's story? Who is the narrator?
What does it mean for one story to become part of another?
On occasion, Hauerwas recognises that 'much of Scripture
does not take narrative form',[28] and he refers to an excellent
analysis of the dialectical relationship between scripture as
narrative and scripture as praise in P. Ricoeur,[29] but this
recognition of the laws and psalms and prophecy is not carried
through into the understanding of the role of narrative. There
is a constant danger of all discourse being subsumed as
narrative. Ricoeur preserves better the interaction of narrative
and non-narrative forms of discourse. When discussing the
intersection of narratives, Hauerwas is in danger of assuming
what he has to establish. He does not make clear the transition
which he refers to between 'self' and 'narratives about the
self', on the one hand, and 'God' and 'God's narrative' on the
other.[30] He regards the Christian ethic as requiring us to set
our own story within God's story. But he does not say how. Is it
an act of faith? If so, what is involved? The relation of faith and
reason could again be of major importance. How are faith and
reason related to the art and use of narrative? Elsewhere he
talks of 'learning to be disciples' (which presumably might
involve the use of rational argument and discussion, and even
ethical analysis) and of 'being faithful' to the life, death and
resurrection of Jesus. At other times, he appears to go further
and argue that all ethics puts 'being' before 'doing' and that

every ethic presupposes and is nourished by life within a community which shares that ethic. At its strongest, this seems a very deterministic thesis about the role of individual and community. And are all communities really so unbending and monolithic? Scripture is fundamental and final for the Christian community, but, tantalisingly, scripture becomes virtually indistinguishable from the church, not the institutional church, but the living church of all those who truly believe. 'The authority of Scripture is mediated through the lives of the saints.'[31] 'To know what Scripture means we must look to those who have most nearly learned to exemplify its demands through their lives.'[32] How do we tell who are the saints? Perhaps reason is needed after all? There is, he concedes, some truth to this. 'We do need to try to say why some exemplify God's story better than others.'[33] But the reason or principle we are looking for is part and parcel of the lives of the saints; in short, another story or narrative. By virtue of this answer, Hauerwas seems to wish to make narrative watertight and impervious to analysis and reason. But can the Christian moralist avoid the work of ethical analysis pursued by his secular colleagues? Do not the narratives themselves require considerable interpretation, about which Christians may sincerely differ?

In a probing, balanced examination of Hauerwas' narrative morality, P. Nelson has suggested that Hauerwas should consider implementing a two-tier approach to the use of reason and narrative, allowing both to operate more freely. He finds signs within Hauerwas of a desire to retain elements of a natural law ethic. 'Such a narrative-independent account of common morality is more modest than that furnished by traditional (ontological) natural-law theory. Nevertheless, it supplies a "natural" basis for perduring universal moral norms. As long as such a description of the narrative independent features of morality does not purport to be comprehensive, thereby obviating attention to narrative-dependent features, there is no good reason for Hauerwas' continued resistance to a bi-level theory of morality.'[34] Hauerwas' proposal for a qualified ethic of forgiveness gives insufficient attention to the role of both procedural and purpose-oriented reasoning in ethical interpretation. This leads, among other things, to a neglect of human rights within a Christian ethic and to an indifference towards all those areas in which it has seemed good to many (Christians and non-Christians alike) that co-operative action is desirable and called for. In view of his negative attitude towards the secular agenda,[35] it is not at all clear how Hauerwas would deal with ecological issues, for example, except in terms of a qualified ethic for Christians. The fact that Christians and non-Christians inhabit a common world, and often share ideals and values, must raise serious questions about such a stance. A Christian ethic associated with these particular religious and theological claims would certainly not be accepted by large numbers of people. This makes a communitarian justification (e.g. 'a Christian ethic for Christians') more attractive to some. It has the serious drawback, however, that it drives a wedge between religion and the world, and is likely to provide only a temporary solution. A more positive attitude to theoretical and practical reason would give his 'qualified ethic' a much stronger basis.

By contrast, one of the outstanding features of Habermas' discourse ethic is its underpinning by a carefully elaborated theory of social structure and communication theory. 'Habermas replaces Kant's monological reflecting moral subject with a community of subjects engaging in moral discourse.'[36] In the remainder of this chapter, therefore, we explore the possibility of using a modified version of Habermasian ethics (cf. chapter 6) as a suitable vehicle and partner for a narrative ethic that takes seriously the positive features of Hauerwas' view, while avoiding the problems we have pointed out. Among the strengths of Habermas' position are his commitment to a form of universal ethic, an analysis of society that even those who disagree with it find realistic and sensitive, a theory of language and communication which is less about the truth of specific moral views and more about a procedure for reaching agreement,[37] and, finally, a utopian undercurrent that emerges as a clear commitment to emancipation, releasing individuals and groups from oppressive socio-political and moral practices.[38] If critical theory is 'a process without content', as Lakeland maintains, it is worth considering whether it can be adapted to serve the needs of a Christian ethic.

S. Benhabib's version of Habermasian ethics has a number of relevant things to say to a Christian ethic which takes the idea of persons in community seriously.[39] At the risk of some simplification, it can be said that Habermas''discourse ethic' is a natural development of his critical theory of society, which builds on the work of Weber, Adorno and Horkheimer in depicting modern society's captivity to bureaucratic, instrumental reason, which is in turn dominated by a system of monetarisation and power rather than by consensus. In contrast to this *Zweckrationalität* (instrumental reason), Habermas sets the lifeworld of shared meanings, norms and practices, which represent humanity's emancipatory search for a noninstrumental rationality and understanding that will contribute to an ideal speech community, characterised by freedom and equality. In modernity, the different aspects of reason have become separated, so that Habermas can speak of an 'uncoupling' of 'system' (which symbolises instrumental rationality and all its works) and 'lifeworld' (which represents human values and symbolic discourse generally, including the aesthetic.) Traditional world-views (and religions) are increasingly dissolved as a result of this uncoupling, and consequently, teleological moralities decline. Religion and morality become separate and independent. Rather than simply regretting these developments, however, Habermas seeks to move away from the subjectivity, as he sees it, of previous rational systems towards an intersubjectivity of communicative speech and action, including a communicative ethic, in which universal rational ideals can find their fulfilment as a result of a new realisation of the power of undistorted communication and the institution of rational procedures.

In developing his theory of communicative action into a theory of discourse ethics Habermas was responding both to Kant's maxims of universalisability and to Hegel's criticism that they were purely formal and lacked content. Habermas holds a mediating position in which he attempts to transplant

Kantian emphases into a community context of universal rational procedures which avoid the danger of conforming to the values of a community which may itself become corrupt. Habermas co-operated closely with Karl-Otto Apel, and drew on the ideas of J. L. Austin and J. Searle (speech-act theory), C. S. Pierce (the scientific community as the source of validity of scientific judgements) and L. Kohlberg (the use of developmental psychology to support a theory of post-conventional moral maturity) in developing his communicative ethic. There are also obvious similarities with the work of J. Rawls. Both men regard justice as the central issue of ethics in the modern world, and both seek to generate canons of justice internally, so to speak; but, whereas Rawls has responded to communitarian critiques which allow for the contribution of particular cultural arrangements (e.g. democracy), Habermas has continued to emphasise the possibility of generating universal value procedures from the understanding of moral language. Whether Habermas has really succeeded in avoiding reliance on cultural assumptions about the nature of the good life is one of the questions his critics frequently pose.

S. Benhabib is both supporter and critic of Habermas. She supports his emphasis on rationality and is reluctant to dispense altogether with universalisability, but she seeks a more communitarian standpoint, as we saw in chapter 6. Unlike other communitarians, she does not focus on the dearth of genuine moral communities in the modern world brought about in large part by the Enlightenment project (of autonomous reason and morality, individual rights and freedom), but adopts a more positive attitude to the achievements of liberalism and democratic pluralism. She welcomes, therefore, Habermas' emphasis on intersubjective rationality, but wishes to overcome some of the polarities that have developed between Habermas and his critics in order to present a version of Habermas which gives more emphasis both to communitarian interests and to the contexts of personhood.

She distinguishes three strands in the objections of neo-Aristotelian communitarians (e.g. A. MacIntyre; M. Sandel; C. Taylor; and M. Walzer) to Habermas: 'a neo-conservative

social diagnosis of the problems of late capitalist societies',
which she finds somewhat backward-looking and nostalgic; an
anti-Enlightenment resistance to liberal individualism and
liberal democratic welfarism, which is destructive of genuine
communities; and 'a hermeneutical philosophical ethics' based
on Aristotelian *phronesis* (practical wisdom) and Gadamer's
'powerful synthesis of Aristotle's ethical theory and Hegel's
critique of Kant'.[40] She is concerned mainly with the third
objection which she wishes to rebut by means of a 'dialogically
reformulated universalist ethical theory'. It is true that the
principle of universalisability can become purely formal. For
this reason, contemporary neo-Kantians have adopted different
strategies to try to shore up Kant's position. Kantian rationality
has to be combined with empirical and possibly utilitarian
features, or intersubjectivity is subordinated to the rational
individual. Benhabib combines intersubjectivity and universalisability, and gives this combination priority. 'Instead of asking
what I as a single rational moral agent can intend or will to be
a universal maxim for all without contradiction, the communicative ethicist asks: what principles of action can we all
recognize or agree to as being valid if we engage in practical
discourse or a mutual search for justification?'[41] From this,
Benhabib infers that universalisability should be seen, not as a
test of non-contradiction, but as a means of communicative
agreement. But is this a solution? Is not the problem simply
pushed back into the conversational situation? Will not the
preconditions of the conversation determine the outcome?
Either the ideal communication community is defined so
minimally as to be practically worthless, or substantive conditions are introduced unwarrantably. At this point, Benhabib
introduces a normative claim to underpin her argument: 'The
way out of this dilemma, I suggest, is to opt for a strong and
possibly controversial construction of the conversational model
which would nonetheless be able to avoid the charges of
dogmatism and/or circularity.'[42] The ideal speech situation
entails, in her view, 'strong ethical assumptions': universal
moral respect for all conversation partners; and egalitarian
reciprocity. Apel argues that these assumptions are logically

required by discourse ethics; Habermas thinks they can be justified in terms of an empirical description of post-conventional morality. There is, however, no agreement among commentators about these empirical features; their alleged a priori nature has not commended itself. Benhabib suggests that a 'historically self-conscious universalism', not established in a priori fashion nor purely empirically, but based on 'reflective equilibrium' (a philosophical process of careful judgement) might function somewhat like the Golden Rule to support this procedure. She recommends the following steps: an account of what it means to 'justify a moral judgement'; an account of how a moral dispute could be 'reasonably resolved'; procedures for 'fair debate'; procedural rules; 'mutual respect'; 'social practices embodying the discursive ideal (the principle of egalitarian reciprocity)'.

Universalisability requires members of the moral community to be able to reverse perspectives, she argues, in order to be able to understand the position of others and engage in reciprocal activity. The distinguishing feature of a 'modern' as opposed to a 'pre-modern' social ethic is that its community of moral agents is coextensive with all beings capable of speech and action, i.e. potentially all humanity. This presupposition can be challenged from within the conversation, but the ground rules cannot simply be suspended, since they function to enable the conversation to continue. 'It is up to the critic of such egalitarian universalism to show, with good grounds, why some individuals should be effectively excluded from the moral conversation.'[43] She responds to the sort of problem we encountered in connection with the personhood debate in Tooley, Singer and Parfit, where personhood is restricted to those who possess certain rational attributes, by saying that the linguistic community must be taken to include those who lack the normal features of linguistic competence and rationality.[44]

Can a universalist ethical theory of this sort meet the objection that it is either true but trivial (because it has no content) or relevant but inconsistent (because it makes use of empirical factors)? Habermas' formulation tries to avoid any statement which smacks of the isolated individual, but the way he expresses the intersubjective allows in utilitarian criteria which undermine the deontological strength of the theory. Moreover, it is still quite abstract; as A. Heller said: 'we cannot obtain any positive guidance from the Habermasian version of the categorical imperative'.[45] Too much is assumed about the ideal speech community in which reciprocity actually works.

This leads Benhabib to regard universalisability as less important than dialogue and agreement about what to do. Habermas' formula guarantees consensus, but at the cost of making it true by definition. What is really required is a way of securing a process of consultation and agreement which will allow for a plurality of goods and a way of keeping the conversation going in the face of practical disagreement and conflict.[46] She makes use of H. Arendt's idea of 'representative thinking' (adopting another's point of view) to fill out the concept of dialogue. She argues that Habermas does not set out to depict the good life, because he is more concerned with the processes that are rationally and morally required if there is to be any sort of good life: hence the focus on justice. This also means that the criticisms of Rawlsian justice are not applicable to Habermas, because, unlike Rawls, he does not put forward an allegedly neutral justification of justice as 'the basic virtue of a social system';[47] rather, he argues that 'after the transition to modernity and the destruction of the teleological worldview, moral theory in fact can only be deontological'. Benhabib accepts that Habermas' attempt to restrict the moral domain to justice in this way is needlessly limiting, but suggests that a broader conception of discourse ethics, which allows conceptions of the good life to be considered, can still be based on a weaker form of deontology (i.e. allowing discussion of which conception of the good life ought to be pursued). Her real enemy, at this point, is the view of MacIntyre that one can only argue deontologically about the good life from within a particular moral community. She wishes to safeguard both individual and community, reason and other sources of tradition, and to preserve the widely accepted ability of individuals and communities to speak across existing boundaries, even where there is disagreement. She recognises the utopian element within her version of communicative ethics, but regards that as a small price to pay, compared with the communitarian view which sees moral subjects as having only the internally accepted criteria of their own moral community and being, to that extent, imprisoned within their own community. She is willing, however, to make concessions to the communitarian case, and recognises that, 'by ignoring the genealogy of the moral self and the development of the moral person out of a network of dependencies, universalist theorists often view the moral agent as the autonomous, adult male head of household, transacting in the market place or in the polity with like others'.[48] It has been a defect of rational, universalist theories that they have ignored women's experience, for example.[49] It is not, however, a necessary weakness in such theories, which can be revised to incorporate what has been neglected or omitted.

Benhabib's revised version of Habermasian rationalism does not require the moral point of view to be regarded as a court of appeal, in which points of view are approved or rejected, but as a conversation 'in which we seek to come to terms with and appreciate the others' point of view'.[50] The moral point of view requires the participants to acquire the skills of listening, understanding and responding. 'Discourse ethics projects such moral conversations, in which reciprocal recognition is exercised, onto a utopian community of humankind.'[51] The contextualisation which is sometimes alleged to be missing from Habermas' procedural method, Benhabib finds in yet another skill of moral conversation, namely 'representative thinking' (Arendt), the art of wise judgement which is able to enter into the perspectives of others. This version of communicative ethics has a number of strengths which make it an improvement on the original version of Habermas. The reciprocal dialogue even allows for the 'point of view' of the inarticulate, including the foetus and the senile, although it is not clear how these are arrived at. She also makes significant improvements with regard to embodiment and gender.

There is, however, at least one important issue which requires further discussion in the context of the present study, namely Benhabib's attitude to what she calls 'conventional morality', which includes religious moralities. The issue is linked with the question whether communicative ethics, despite its attempts to be even-handed, 'privileges the institutions and principles of secular, western democratic societies'.[52] Although she has moved towards those critics of Habermas[53] who complained that a theory of transformative relationships must include more than 'the force of the better argument', it is not clear that she has carried this through consistently. She argues (pp. 42–3) that communicative ethics is characterised by 'comprehensive reflexivity' in a way that is impossible for a conventional and religious morality. At this point, she seems to be either overoptimistic about the utopian nature of the universal moral community, or less than fair to the critical and cross-cultural thinking which can take place in moral (religious) communities. Benhabib is critical of Aristotle's commitment to slavery and his view of the 'barbarian',[54] and makes the point that moral judgements cannot be justified simply by appealing to the customs of our own community. She also refers to polygamy in Mormonism and Islam as examples of the inadequate conventional moral justifications (i.e. in terms of the teaching of Joseph Smith or Muhammad) sometimes offered by religious believers. She argues that those who hold these views have 'a cognitive barrier beyond which they will not argue . . . they have to withdraw from the process of reflexive justification in order not to let their world-view crumble'.[55] If such believers were willing to concede that they could be wrong, and were willing to consider other points of view, this would indicate that they have ceased to believe in conventional morality and had begun to adopt a post-conventional morality or communicative ethic. There are a number of questions that need clarification. How do Benhabib's strictures here square with her notes on the procedures of communicative ethics, which exclude only those who exclude themselves by seeking to suspend the ground rules of procedure? When presenting the Mormon lawyer who has chosen to be the ninth wife in a Mormon extended household on the ground that it allows her to combine career and family, Benhabib says: 'Obviously this woman's self-esteem is so far removed from traditional biblical accounts of female weakness and dependence that she can conceive of polygamy as some version of a 1990s "Hippie commune".'[56] Benhabib prevents the Mormon lawyer from presenting her case, in effect. Elsewhere, she is sympathetic to contextual features of a moral situation, but, at this point, she appears unnecessarily dogmatic, as if she were responding to a presumed (but not clearly documented in the text) dogmatism on the part of the Mormon. At the same time, she gives the impression that communicative ethics is always willing to re-examine its own value positions, provided that this does not involve suspension of the ground rules of procedure. It is perhaps this question which bothers Benhabib about her Mormon lawyer and also about the Muslim. Perhaps she suspects that they will only use the process of communicative ethics as long as they get their own way. This may or may not be true, but it raises a further question about the nature of religious moralities and the problem of religiously motivated moral fanaticism. The problem is similar to that of Popper in *The Open Society and its Enemies* (Routledge, 1962): how does democracy defend itself against those who operate within democratic societies and use all the facilities of democracy to try to overthrow it?

On our account of revelation (chapter 10), attempts to con-strue sacred texts in the literal, uncritical way, which may characterise some religious sects, are not typical of mainstream Christianity. Moreover, the religious fanatic, who claims that his terrorist suicide mission involves killing members of another religion simply because of their religious profession, is acting contrary to the teachings of all the major world religions. R. M. Hare was similarly troubled by the possible universalising qualities of the Nazi fanatic who wanted to murder all Jews – including himself if he were shown to be of Jewish descent.[57] Self-interest, others' interests, the value of individual and social freedoms and human life itself are all brushed aside by the fanatic. Words change their meaning. No moral philosophy can deal with such crazy logic. One can only point to the inconsist-encies and illogicality of the various parts of the fanatic's claims and hope that he will see reason, says Hare.

A single fanatic can do a great deal of damage, especially with the help of modern weapons technology, but the more persistent theoretical and practical problem is not so much the moral fanatic as the issue of what 'limit situations' can be tolerated by, or allowed to exist within, a communicative ethic. The impression is given that, although not everything can or will be justified in the moral pluralism of a communicative ethic, there are no limits that can be prescribed in advance. This is part of Benhabib's objection to the communitarianism of Sandel and MacIntyre. But her objection to the limits of conventional religious morality seems to undermine an important feature of morality itself, namely that individuals and communities do have limit situations – based, not only on community tradition, but on experience and reason. Such limit situations (e.g. no adultery) may not find universal acceptance in the wider society of which the religious community is a part, but they are not arbitrarily or irrationally invented. The 'private' position given to religion by both Habermas and Benhabib cannot be accepted as it stands, since it does not adequately represent what is involved in a living religious tradition. The distinction of private and public needs further consideration. Moral (and non-moral) issues occur in *both* domains as aspects of a single event (e.g. the religious education of children). F. S. Fiorenza rightly draws attention to the problems caused by Habermas' failure to develop 'an adequate institutional base for discourse ethics',[58] particularly in relation to religion.

Habermas' view also underestimates the amount of agreement that may be found between religious and secular moralities. On the whole, there have been periods of considerable moral agreement in civilised societies about the wrongness of killing innocent human beings, an agreement which many would like to extend to other members of the non-human animal kingdom. In many areas of ethical disagreement, legitimate peaceful discussion and protest – particularly where powerful bodies like departments of government and powerful sectional and commercial interests are involved – are beginning to have an effect. We are a long way, however, in most democracies from the forms of ideal speech communication which would allow such differences to be resolved co-operatively. Nevertheless, a modified version of Habermas' communicative ethics, if developed further to give a more nuanced account of a critical religious ethic, could offer an attractive alternative to the rationalistic utilitarianism of Singer and Tooley and make a suitable partner for a Christian understanding of personhood. It would avoid the anti-rationalism of Hauerwas, while allowing a more careful use of narrative. It would also be receptive to contextuality and pluralism in ethics, while retaining sufficient 'meta-critical ranking of norms' to avoid the ethical relativism of Rorty.[59]

The relative lack of specific moral policies in communicative ethics is a procedural strength, which may, however, generate relativist arguments. If confronted with the radical difference of the *lex talionis* and forgiveness, say, how would communicative ethics decide which to apply? Is either less universalisable than the other? How might dialogue resolve disagreement? Each position would need to be stated as unambiguously as possible. Some differences might become more pronounced; others might fade or become irrelevant. Dialogue presupposes the two parties are willing to listen to each other. It does not mask existing differences. At the end of the process, both parties will have been influenced by the exchange. But it is possible they will have been confirmed in their views rather than converted. In a discussion of the relative merits of *lex talionis* and forgiveness, each will adduce other views, some closely related (e.g. about punishment: how it is carried out; how effective it is; and so on), others less closely related (e.g. the formation of a just society; the goal of human living; divine justice and mercy; human wickedness and the possibility of reform). Internal consistency will be a mark of rational belief and conduct even in religion. Evidence from empirical studies of crime and punishment will be addressed; genetic and environmental factors will be considered. Yet, ultimately, it may be argued, our information will be processed, analysed and fed into an evaluative system which determines our choice of moral policy. This evaluative

system, which may be story-related, will determine the
outcome, goes the objection. Have we really overcome the
fact/value dichotomy (chapter 2) or the Euthyphro dilemma
(chapter 10)? Does communicative ethics help?

It is important not to let cultural and moral difference,
however real and profound, either imprison us in separate and
incommensurable moral camps or undermine justifiable confidence in our own value-system.[60] A genuine communicative
ethic will help if it clarifies that disagreement need not lead to
total scepticism. To understand other moral systems does not
require us to abandon our own. We can also learn from others.
If it is suggested that two moral systems are totally incommensurable, we can point out that, unless our moral systems had
something in common, we would not even be able to express
our differences. Cultural and moral diversity is clearly not
excluded, but there is no evidence to suggest that difference
should prevent dialogue. How the discussion is enfleshed may
require a larger narrative. We might think, for instance of
Shylock's contract in *The Merchant of Venice*: the business
venture; Jewish–Christian relationships; his daughter's marriage; the pound of flesh; and the quality of mercy. How is a
process of moral reflection translated into moral life? When
disagreement is real and profound, as it is here, critical
reflection may face acute choices. Should a whole moral system
be scrapped in favour of another? Arguing against the Cartesian temptation to start with a clean slate and put aside all
presuppositions, McNaughton advocates what most of us
would probably do most of the time: we should revise and
adjust our beliefs and principles gradually until they are
rationally confirmed and consistent. 'Our system of beliefs may
be compared . . . to a ship at sea. Any rotten plank can be
repaired or replaced, but to take up all the planks at once in
order to check them for rot would bring the voyage to a speedy
end.'[61] Gradual, systematic reform is also the method of
communicative ethics. There is, however, an important footnote to be added. It relates to conversion. There are occasions,
both in religion and other parts of life, when we do see things
in a completely new light, when we turn around and go in the

opposite direction. The Christian faith asks us to 'repent' and turn to God – not once, but eternally. What mental baggage we take with us will be influenced by the process of sanctification referred to in chapter 10.

At this point, the issue of dialogue in a communicative ethic has similarities to the issue of inter-faith dialogue. There are many forms of inter-faith dialogue, and it is true that some of them are more concerned with strategies of practical humanitarian co-operation than with ventures of theological understanding or faith. Dialogue, however, presupposes a certain measure of trust, as well as openness, and strategies of practical co-operation (e.g. projects of medical, agricultural and environmental aid and development) may help to build such trust. Once it is recognised that dialogue is not simply another form of mission and colonisation, there is scope for an extension of horizons of understanding and faith and mutual sharing. If it is understood that dialogue need not diminish loyalty to one's own faith, there can be a more open and fresh exchange between individuals and groups. Most importantly, dialogue does not seek to hide or obscure differences or try to arrive at a false or shallow consensus. John Cobb gives a good example of how, in the early stages of Christian–Buddhist dialogue, attempts were made to equate 'God' with Buddhist 'emptiness'.[62] It was some time before it became clear that 'God' and 'emptiness' do not necessarily have a common referent. They are not contradictions. They are not even trying to say the same thing in different ways. Both may be transcendent without being identical. The claims are not mutually exclusive. This does not exclude the possibility that a patient search for truth will bring contradictions to light. But, as one writer has put it: 'dialogue . . . is about learning who the other is in order to find out who I am.'[63] This dialogical model goes beyond inclusivism or pluralism, and reflects more accurately the context in which members of different world faiths share a common world. Something similar is true of ethical dialogue and the plural context in which all ethical discussion and action now take place. The different ethical theories and different ethical norms cannot be reduced to variants of a common master theory. They are genuinely different. But there is hope for increasing convergence, at least in terms of principle and action, as they learn to share their different insights and narratives.

There is, of course, a big difference between those who regard moral pluralism as implying some form of relativism (there are a number of irreconcilable, different views and there is no means of ascertaining whether any are ultimately more true than others) and those who believe that rational discourse can promote ways of moving beyond incommensurability (e.g. through dialogue) and difference to a reconciliation of conflicting views. When proponents for the ordination of women or the acceptance of homosexual relationships and their physical expression clash head on with fellow Christians who regard these views, not only as mistaken or wrong, but an affront to God, it is important to be able to decide what is negotiable and what is not. Arguments for a metacritical ranking of norms, allowing for the provisional nature of such a task, since Christian theological claims are formulated by fallible human beings, are put forward by Thiselton to avoid inconsistency with fundamental principles of Christian theology, which would 'lose their currency if they are deemed to operate only in relation to given cultures and contexts'.[64] These principles he lists as: the prohibition against idolatry together with the reality of the Cross; the illocutionary force of biblical texts which do not simply describe but involve the reader/hearer as they address, promise, liberate, pardon and commission her; the universal horizon of eschatological promise. His argument is that without such principles Christian theology would cease to be Christian.

Adopting Habermas' distinction of lifeworld and system to contrast our lived reality of shared meanings, norms and practices with an objective system of interpretation which transcends the lifeworld, Thiselton argues – against Rorty and those who see no possibility of establishing a universalist metacritical position – for a rational hermeneutic which is capable of doing justice to both lifeworld and system. Despite Thiselton's support for hermeneutical pluralism, there seems to be a subtext which assumes the incompatibility of pluralism and universality. His illustration of the mutual transformation of attitudes involved in the case of two lovers assumes that they will overcome their differences and move to a position of new understanding and agreement, and their former interests come to seem 'narrow, ill-informed and self-centred'. He appears not to accept that love may be compatible with genuine difference and that the success of the illustration is dependent on the view that a single outcome is desirable. This arises from his implicit assumption that pluralism, although inevitable for now, must eventually be overcome. So it may. But is it not possible that, in the ethical sphere, divine truth is pluriform? Forcing it into a single channel may be a perpetuation of the human tendency to hegemony and other forms of human error. Values such as justice and mercy may sometimes clash, but they are not always incompatible; it would be a mistake to think that if justice is right, mercy must be wrong. Sometimes attempts to harmonise the different ethical traditions reflects a mistaken reluctance to accept diversity. It is more important to interpret the diversity with historical accuracy and with ethical aware-ness. Later in the same chapter, when dealing with the eschatological horizon, Thistleton is more realistically cautious about our interim evaluations which remain 'provisional and open to misunderstanding and to revision'. This distinction between reality and our perception of it should also apply to the idolatry criterion. The history of religion is frequently the history of mistaken and misplaced idolatries.

A theological ethic has to make haste slowly, boldly but without presumption, to set out the basis of its ethical under-standing. There is no direct word from God in scripture, church or tradition – or private experience – which excuses the Christian from taking proper thought about what ought to be done now. The words most often appealed to in this context as a moral ready reckoner, the Ten Commandments or the Double Commandment to love God and neighbour, do not function as simple absolutes which can be translated without remainder or ambiguity in the contexts of human living. In issues of war, human sexuality, medicine, the environment, unemployment and the many thousands of adjacent issues, not only do complex facts have to be interpreted and evaluated in relation to individuals and societies, but the basis and contexts of the moral judgements have to be scrutinised and evaluated. This does not mean that there is no clear rejection of what is clearly wrong. But there will be many occasions when it is not clear. As recent church declarations on a number of social issues such as contraception, abortion, human sexuality and unilateral disarmament illustrate, there is no agreement among the churches about what should be done in cases of sustained ambiguity, or insufficient evidence or conflicting interpretation. It is this element of dispute and ambiguity which raises most discussion about what may legitimately be called 'moral personhood'. The question we turn to next, therefore, is: what are the central moral convictions of the Christian community and how do we ascertain them? What determines the limits of moral reflection and praxis exercised by a Christian community?

# CHAPTER 12

# A community of ethical difference: including the 'other'

In the last chapter we outlined elements of a communicative ethic based on two very different sources: Hauerwas' narrative ethic and Benhabib's development of Habermas' discourse ethic. Although not intended as a religious ethic, Benhabib's attempt to develop a 'dialogically reformulated universalist ethical theory' contains structural possibilities for a dialogical Christian ethic that is potentially universal in scope, combining narrative and rational argument, and yet true to its own historical particularity. Her corrections to the understanding and place of rationality and gender could be welcomed by Christians who are looking for fresh approaches that will enable the whole Christian community to respond positively to more egalitarian patterns of Christian community life in the organisation of the church. Furthermore, she is not unsympathetic to a utopian element in her ethic, which might prove amenable to an eschatological adaptation. As we shall see shortly, the ethical outlook of the primitive church was strongly influenced by eschatological thinking. Above all, her emphasis on the 'concrete other' represents a move that should commend itself to Christian ethicists who are dissatisfied with combinations of teleological and deontological ethical theories, yet wish to adopt a more universalistic stance than Hauerwas' 'qualified ethic', which reduces communication between Christians and their non-Christian neighbours and results in 'a Christian ethic for Christians only'.

Not surprisingly, there are other features of a Christian ethic that find either no recognition at all or only critical comment in Benhabib: the relationship of religious and moral outlooks; the influence of worship on patterns of living; the tendency to regard religious moralities as conventional and uncritical. There are also some features by which a Christian communicative ethic may enrich Benhabib's account, particularly through the Christian faith's embodiment in concrete emancipatory communities, sustained by 'dangerous narratives' of reversal, of slaves delivered, the poor made rich, the blind given sight, the deaf made to hear and the dead resurrected.

In order to appreciate the ethical difference brought about by a community committed to a gospel ethic, but to avoid any idealistic re-construction, we shall, in drawing on the narratives of the New Testament, make use of relevant critical sociological and historical studies. The account that emerges is impressively different from narratives of other associations and societies of the period, in that the community depicted draws its strength from one who was crucified for disturbing the land with a message of God's approaching kingdom and the forgiveness of debts/sins.

The definition of a Christian ethic can be elusive for reasons we have already seen, relating to context and content, and the description and evaluation of what is human/natural. We have argued that a Christian ethic cannot be based solely on rational considerations, but must take account of revelation and narrative. These features, however, raise further issues about the diversity of Christian faith and practice, even in the New Testament, and even more so if we look across the centuries and take into account the adaptation to many different regions and cultures, which makes it impossible to select simply one version as wholly representative. Occasionally there is genuine uncertainty about what is distinctively Christian and what is compatible with or shared with other ethical belief systems and practices. Moreover, it is no longer possible to start naively with an unreconstructed historical Jesus. 'It is Matthew, not Jesus, who is the author of the Sermon on the Mount.'[1] It is not just Jesus' enemies who construct him in their own image.[2] A great deal more is now known about Jesus and the early church than in previous centuries, but more is also known about the complex process of transmission of the source materials. There is no need for unnecessary pessimism, however. We can be confident that John the Baptist's call to repentance was followed by Jesus' call to disciples to enter the kingdom of God before it was too late. It was a message that was both religious and ethical.

Since it is one of the more assured areas of gospel criticism, we begin with the message of the kingdom. The Kingdom of God was not a new concept to Jews of the first century. The prophetic teaching which Jesus and his fellow Jews inherited had schooled them to read the signs of the times as God's immensely powerful but concealed commentary on all materiality and history, good and bad. Jewish Torah and prophetic teaching relate God's kingdom to his covenant with Israel and the outworkings of that in conduct. The Decalogue is the expression of a covenant based on the rejection of idolatry, on single-minded worship of God and on genuine respect for one's neighbour. The context and the narrative are as important as the rules and principles. When prophets such as Amos refer to this covenant, they criticise Israel for idolatry and shallow religious practice on the one hand, and for killing, stealing, war crimes, commercial greed and dishonesty on the other (cf. Amos viii). Hosea goes further and, like other prophets, relates the profaning of the covenant to the state of the land and environmental disaster: 'There is no faithfulness or kindness and no knowledge of God in the land. There is swearing, lying, killing, stealing and committing adultery. They break all bounds and murder follows murder. Therefore the land mourns and all who dwell in it languish.'[3]

The times in which Jesus lived were turbulent: Roman occupation; peasant debt and agricultural unrest; religious sectarianism.[4] Even if eschatological expectation among the sectaries of Qumran and other literate Jewish groups has been exaggerated, it is clear from Josephus that there was popular expectation of an eschatological Messiah figure and that various individuals set themselves up as 'king' or 'prophet' of the new age. The new covenant promised in Jeremiah (xxxi. 31) looked forward to a time when God's law would be written on the heart, and all would know God and God would forgive their sin.

Jesus' teaching about the kingdom is rooted in the covenant traditions of Israel. Before we examine that teaching more closely, however, a sociological account of the early Christian communities in the first century will provide us with a context for understanding the important role played by concrete communities in the Christian ethic of difference. G. Theissen, *Social Reality and the Early Christians*, and Wayne Meeks, *The Moral World of the First Christians* (1986) together provide a critical and perceptive analysis of those first communities.

From the beginning, the early Christian communities displayed a variety of responses, both in worship and conduct, to their experience of Jesus Christ as their risen Lord. The Gospels and the communities which shaped them indicate that their faith and practice contained both common features and differences. Diversity in belief and practice was a characteristic of the early church. Sometimes the differences may have been regarded as minor, in the same way that Paul allows that some of his teaching is his own view, rather than a 'command of the Lord' (1 Corinthians vii). Yet differences could be contained within the fellowship without having to be ironed out or excluded. Theissen plausibly argues that the transmission of the gospel traditions and the epistolary activity of the early church correspond to different forms of social life and organisation within the early church. The relative absence of radical Jesus logia from the letters to urban Hellenistic congregations, and the presence of household codes of conduct, reflect, at least in part, the social setting of these congregations. He notes that the radical Jesus logia which were transmitted by wandering charismatics were mainly preserved within the framework of the Gospels, whose Palestinian setting allows for some distancing between the original traditions and their application in contemporary urban Hellenism. The apocryphal gospels, such as the Gospel of Thomas, and other gnostic literature, however, indicate how these same radical logia could find a home, when modified, in gnostic circles. 'These groups were probably often made up of men and women who were fairly prosperous. A radicalism of perception without any practical consequences was not unduly costly even for these people.'[5]

Theissen refers to the early church as an 'interpretative community with shared fundamental convictions',[6] deriving from its experience of the holy and expressed ethically in specific conduct. He concludes his sociological analysis of the early church with the help of three different theories: a phenomenological hermeneutical theory; a functionalist, integrationist theory; and a conflict theory. These theories, we suggest, may also help to explain the different constructions of a Christian ethic both in the early church and today. The phenomenological view lends itself most readily to a transformational ethic: the functionalist view to either a natural law type ethic or a communitarian ethic, depending whether the wider or narrower community is regarded as normative; and conflict theory to a form of liberation ethic. In fact, all three emphases can be found within the New Testament.

According to the phenomenological approach, the early Christian communities are characterised by their living experience of Jesus Christ and the Holy Spirit. Jesus is the way to God and the beginning of a new society, a whole new world. Christians have been baptised into the death and resurrection of Jesus and now form a new community in which the old hierarchies and distinctions have been 'relativised in a setting of mutual service'.[7] The essentially charismatic structure of these early Christian communities led to innovation and conflict, particularly in terms of conversion and martyrdom, because it allowed for radical reorientation to traditional values. Galatians iii. 28 expresses something of this. By breaking away from traditional patterns of behaviour, however, the early Christian communities were exposed to conflict with the dominant culture of their environment and to divisions within their own ranks. Not surprisingly, these charismatic conversionist traits were sometimes modified in order not to antagonise the political authorities. All forms of oppression and slavery may have been overcome in principle, but there was no support for a rebellion of slaves against their owners or for wives wanting to assert their independence over against the *paterfamilias*. Charisma was gradually routinised and attached to particular offices, eschatology was diffused and toned down,

conversion became equivalent to church membership, love of
the enemy was redirected to love of the brethren and the
abolition of social hierarchies became a purely internal mark
of Christian communities. This disappointing decline in
fervour of thought and action, however, cannot conceal the
importance which attached to these early Christian groups as
communities of ethical interpretation and action. And, as
Theissen notes, they were remarkably successful in beginning
to break down the division of Jew and Gentile and the barriers
between those possessing wealth and power and the poor and
powerless.

From a functionalist viewpoint, the same phenomena can be
understood rather differently as part of a pattern in which
religion enabled its practitioners to be integrated into society,
even when they were not consciously aware of this or seeking it.
Instead of starting with individual groups, this view seeks to
relate Christian belonging to membership within the wider
society of the Roman Empire, in which power was in the hands
of ruling élites, yet peasants (urban and rural) and slaves made
up a large proportion of society. 'Socially the Christian congregations were deeply rooted in the lower classes',[8] with little
or no connection with the imperial upper class, although a few
individual Christians among upper-class families were active in
local government. 'Most Christians with a relatively high status
were on the periphery of the local upper class because they
were women, *peregrini* or *liberti*.'[9] On this interpretation, Christians rejected some of the main values of society and functioned
as a society within a society. At odds with the imperial cult,
they created a counter-cult, expressing their loyalty to Christ in
his kingdom/family/church, their new supraregional community. Like Jews they could not be assimilated. They remained a
'monotheistic heresy in a pluralistic world',[10] but they began to
create for many a community and an ethic, which enabled
them to live and work within the Roman Empire and adapt to
the changing economic and social realities with hope for a
better future. This was significantly expressed in a 'compassion
ethic' (pre-Christian in origin but encouraged by both Judaism
and Christianity) which worked to counteract social inequalities

by stressing the obligations of the rich and powerful towards the poor and underprivileged.

Theissen's third interpretation, based on conflict theory, allows more scope for the elements of conflict which clearly existed in the relation of the early church to its environment. Primitive Christianity represented a 'revolution of values' and at the same time a struggle for survival in relation to the dominant environment, so that overenthusiastic conflict where there was no hope of winning was suppressed (e.g. in the matter of slavery). Theissen gives an excellent summary of this 'revolution of values':

In the Jesus tradition 'sovereign' ideals are transferred to ordinary people in some passages: the 'peacemakers' are called blessed (Matt.5.9). Like the rulers of antiquity, they are to be called 'sons of God'. In the commandment about loving enemies the *clementia* of the sovereign is required of everyone – even the people who are persecuted (Matt.5.44f.) But above all, in Christianity an ordinary person – a carpenter's son – himself assumes the role of the king to whom all power belongs. Christians are his 'household', his 'body', his 'kingdom'. They participate in his power and therefore form a community which is as universally organized as the worldwide power of their ruler . . . In the distribution struggle about chances for living, the early Christian faith takes up an unambiguous position. We find here the attempt to win power for the powerless, possessions for people who possess nothing, wisdom for the uneducated.[11]

A not dissimilar picture emerges in Wayne Meeks' *The Moral World of the First Christians*, which seeks to relate the 'grammar' of early Christian morality to the major traditions of Greek philosophical ethics and the traditions of Judaism. Christian ethics was very much influenced by the various social contexts (urban-cosmopolitan, rural, rich, poor, Jewish diaspora) and interests of the early Christian communities, as well as by religious beliefs and doctrines. In its beginnings, the primitive church can be characterised as a Messianic Jewish sect with strong apocalyptic interests and a 'very particularistic ethos'[12] calling for separation from the condemned world. The standards of the church were naturally regarded by its members as 'universally valid'. What began as a way of life for a tightly knit sect soon became the way to salvation incumbent on all who wished to be saved. It also soon became clear that the gospel was called to address a variety of social contexts and interests (cf. the issues about eating meat sacrificed to idols in I Corinthians). As several scholars have noted, the second generation of church leaders was already making use of old household codes going back to Aristotelian civic virtue as part of the way of life for the Christian family. It might be thought that this fatally compromised Christian standards, but it is difficult to deny that 'something new was emerging in the private homes where believers in "Jesus the Christ" gathered'.[13] Even when the early Christians drew on previous ethical traditions they were conscious of the great difference made by the coming of Christ.

Wayne Meeks illustrates this clearly in his discussion of the 'grammar of early Christian morals'. Paul's first letter to the Thessalonians begins with a conversionist emphasis on their changed way of life. Idols and former habits have been rejected in order that they might serve 'a living and true God' (I Thessalonians i. 9) A process of resocialisation based on their new identity in Christ has begun. Baptism into the body of Christ, the church, means death to the old self and former way of life and resurrection to a new way of life, marked by 'putting on' Christ. Conventional virtues are not necessarily spurned, but the crucial difference is their allegiance to Christ, who has delivered them. By following him they will please God (cf. I Thessalonians iv. passim). This is very different from both Greek and Jewish ethics.[14] Something similar could be said about a number of passages in Paul's letters (cf. Romans vi. 3; xii. 1). S. Fowl has made a similar point about the use of hymnic material by Paul in ethical contexts: 'Paul's aim is to present each community with a story of its founder – a story to which they are committed by virtue of their community membership – and then to spell out the implications of this story for their everyday faith and practice.'[15]

It is clear from these analyses and reconstructions of the life of the primitive church that, despite all the differences of context, each of these communities was profoundly affected by what they regarded as the teaching of Jesus. It is because of their faith in him as crucified and risen for their salvation that his teaching has such an impact. We need now to look more closely at that teaching. Since the present study is not primarily an exegetical study of the New Testament or even of the ethical teaching of Jesus, we shall concentrate on two contrasting but characteristic parts of that teaching: the command to love neighbour and enemy; and the household codes of the early church.

We have already noted that Jesus' ethical teaching seems to be rooted in the covenant traditions of Israel. Commentators on the Sermon on the Mount are not agreed as to whether Jesus is presented by Matthew as the giver of a new law or the true interpreter of an already existing law. W. D. Davies, in his study of the Sermon on the Mount, relates Jesus' teaching to several important historical contexts – eschatological, prophetic teaching, rabbinic practice and the beliefs of the Qumran community. None of them, however, satisfactorily explain the striking summary of the law and the prophets in the double commandment to love God and neighbour. Davies says: 'Whereas for Judaism the Law expressed the will of God, for Jesus his immediate awareness of the will of God became Law.'[16] We cannot know what went on in the heart and mind of Jesus, but it seems clear that the kingdom was associated for him with the love of God and neighbour. He teaches his disciples to pray: 'Thy kingdom come, thy will be done'. This includes God's purposes, clearly revealed in the prophets, for the transformation of society and the regeneration of the land, respect for persons and respect for nature, when God's new world order is realised. No theory of ethics is worked out, but the foundations are laid for a normative personal and social ethic. A renewed society and a renewed earth is the reason why the poor and outcast figure so significantly in his message. Their salvation is a sign of God's care for all his creation and his desire to transform the world.

Matthew records Jesus as saying: 'Think not that I have come to abolish the Law and the Prophets. I have come not to destroy but to fulfil' (Matthew v. 17). Like the other synoptics, Matthew also records Jesus as commanding his followers to love their enemies (Matthew v. 44; xxii. 39). This love is linked with the love of God for his creation, which the disciples are expected to emulate. Going the second mile, turning the other cheek and forgiveness up to seventy times seven are character-istic of this new way of life. Strict justice and consequentialism are turned on their head. Individuals and minorities come to the fore instead of majorities and the big battalions. Although there is no single organising principle which will allow us to structure the ethical teaching of Jesus within a comprehensive sytem, which is perhaps as well, since all systems have their *aporias* and tend to reflect contemporary blind spots, there is a common emphasis in both Judaism and Christianity, in their founding scriptures, liturgies, doctrines and ethical practices on the concrete double commandment to love God with all one's heart and mind and soul and to love one's neighbour as oneself, and this seems to be an accurate reflection of Jesus' own life and teaching.

This 'love of neighbour' ethic, it might be thought, is not incompatible with self-love, since we are to love our neighbours as ourselves. Apart from uneasy questions about the assump-tions of compatibility which begin to surface (can I really accomplish both in one breath? Is there no conflict or tension between them?), the context in the Sermon on the Mount raises other doubts about who exactly my neighbour is. If my neighbour is anyone who is close to me, does this include those whom I could wish were less close, including those not at all well-disposed towards me, namely my enemies? Does love of enemy not sound more like the original gospel ethic, radical and uncompromising? Do not the conflict stories of the Gospels (e.g. Luke vii etc.), which show Jesus rejecting the apparently high moral standards of the Pharisaic community as part of his insistent campaign for a new understanding of religious com-munity and a new understanding of God, recall the original message of Jesus? In Luke x. 29f when Jesus is asked, 'Who is my neighbour?', he tells the story of the good Samaritan, who unlike the priest and Levite, goes to the help of the injured traveller. The 'enemy' becomes the 'neighbour'; the neighbour is not whom we thought. It is open to anyone, even those regarded as enemies, to become neighbours to those in need. Not surprisingly, therefore, neighbour-love in the teaching of Jesus also includes the enemy.[17]

A similar argument is developed by P. Ricoeur[18] when he contrasts the Golden Rule of Matthew vii. 12 and traditional morality ('whatever you wish that men would do to you, do so to them; for this is the law and the prophets') with the command to love one's enemies. There is no credit in loving those who will love you in return. Even sinners do that. Disciples of Jesus are to do good and lend, 'expecting nothing in return' (Luke vi. 35).

There are issues of exegesis related to the different contexts of these sayings in Matthew and Luke. Does Matthew quote the Golden Rule more approvingly than Luke appears to? Ricoeur argues plausibly that, despite the real contrast between the 'logic of superabundance' ('give without expecting anything in return, go the second mile, turn the other cheek') and the 'logic of equivalence' ('do as you would be done by'), and despite the apparent victory of the logic of superabundance, the morality of justice is being recast rather than rejected.[19] 'A much more interesting situation obtains concerning the status of ethics in a religious perspective if the Golden Rule, instead of being denied, is rather re-interpreted, not only according to its potential intent, but according to the new scope which the logic of superabundance conveys to it.'[20] There are a number of reasons for preferring this interpretation, according to Ricoeur. The position of the Golden Rule within the carefully structured Sermon on the Mount suggests that it is being 'integrated into a new ethics' rather than simply quoted or queried. 'This would be unthinkable if it could not be re-interpreted according to the new logic of superabundance sealed by the love of enemies.'[21] Even more telling, however, is the fact that, if the Golden Rule is seen as being repositioned to reflect the analogy between God's generosity and the conduct required of faithful disciples, we have a more fundamental and accurate appraisal of the tension inherent in Christian ethics between the logics of superabundance and equivalence. These logics are not identical. There is genuine

contrast and paradox. This paradox, says Ricoeur, is essential
to a Christian ethic. 'The ethical paradox is intended to
disorient for the sake of re-orienting . . . In the moment of
disorientation ethics is suspended rather than grounded, as
Kierkegaard understood so perfectly. Then a crisis is generated
in the midst of ethics. A doubt is cast about its claim to be
ultimate. At best, ethics is only penultimate.'[22]

This is a timely warning and represents an important strand
of Christian thought. The subsequent reasons which Ricoeur
gives in support of this view, however, seem much more like
accommodation to a secular viewpoint and retreat from
paradox. It would be impossible, he argues, to base a social and
economic order on love of the enemy without regard for merit
and fairness. Love of the enemy is not an ethical but a 'supra-
ethical' standard.

At this point, it seems to us that Ricoeur goes beyond his
perceptive delineation of the tension between the Golden Rule
and the love commandment and begins to unravel what he had
established. This could be avoided if he were to take more
seriously what is involved in a 'neighbour' ethic, which not only
acknowledges the tension in question, but sustains it into a
positive ethic which can be translated into action without
surrendering the vitality of the religious ethic and without
involving Kierkegaard's suspension of the ethical.[23] In chapters
13 and 14 we pursue this in terms of forgiveness and human
rights.

'"Neighbour" is an inclusive category. Someone is my
neighbour before she or he is a woman or a man, a Christian
or a Muslim, of Afro-Caribbean or Anglo-Saxon origin, a
member of this or that class.'[24] This is an important point
which is easily overlooked. It is a category which, without
appearing to do so, can subvert any ethic, but yet at the same
time confirms the ethical domain. Who is my neighbour?
There are no limits. The category of neighbour understood
from a Christian perspective involves not only who I am, but
also who God is. Hence the double reference to both the
human being and God as person.

There is a very pertinent contribution to the interpretation of 'love of the enemy' in Matthew v. 39–44 by L. Schottroff.[25] She takes issue with those interpretations (e.g. Bultmann and Braun) which focus on the attitude required by the disciple, but ignore the social context and the enemy who is to be loved. She is critical of exegesis which makes assumptions about human dignity or the love of humanity. The love of enemy is a 'concrete social event.'[26] She finds a good example of this more appropriate exegesis in Martin Luther King: 'it is a struggle in which the enemy is conquered without the use of military weapons'.[27] The socio-historical context in Matthew is the conflict between Christians and their persecutors. Similar sayings are found elsewhere in Greek and Roman literature, but the crucial factor is the context, which imparts a distinctive meaning to Matthew v. 39–44. Matthew v. 38f is not about a superior power's charitable attitude to a subordinate or the resigned deference of a powerless but high-minded individual such as a philosopher. The words are addressed to members of the Christian community. 'The Christian is challenged to include his persecutor in his own community . . . the command to love the enemy is thoroughly aggressive though not in a destructive sense . . . The command to love the enemy is an appeal to take up a missionary attitude towards one's persecu- tors . . . Even the enemies of the community are to be given a place in its common life and in the kingly rule of God.'[28] This sort of analysis is equally necessary, she urges, if we wish to apply the command to love our enemies today. Generalisation inevitably invites ambiguity. The only way to avoid this is to relate the love of enemy to specific situations. In that way we shall be less tempted to misconstrue the nature and use of power and what is ethically required.

The above analysis suggests that the neighbour ethic of Jesus must be one of the most important features of a Christian community of ethical difference. The concrete other, even the actual enemy, is brought within the scope of Christian love. The relevance of this to forgiveness will be considered in chapter 13. There is another equally characteristic aspect of New Testament ethics, however, which seems to present a more introverted view, more concerned to uphold the status quo and

existing patterns of social life: the household codes found in the
letters of Paul and the early Christian communities.

These household codes are relevant to one of the problems
that confronts a modern Christian ethic which takes persons in
community seriously: the distortion and inequality caused by
patriarchal attitudes. In chapter 6 we referred to the changing
attitudes within feminism to the causes of patriarchal oppression and the possibility of developing a critical understanding
of the self in relation to community, which preserves a proper
concern for embodiedness and relationships. Post-biblical feminism has excavated similar issues in biblical texts and tried to
develop an 'evaluative hermeneutics' of biblical traditions and
their expression in contemporary communities. Do the household codes acquiesce in the inequalities caused by patriarchal
attitudes? What is their bearing on controversial ethical issues
in the life of the modern church? There is no disagreement that
women should not be abused, manipulated or treated unfairly,
but, when issues of equality are raised, there are some who
appeal to a divine order of creation which establishes as
normative for all time that women are excluded from certain
roles within the church, on the ground that Adam preceded
Eve.[29] Even commentators who interpret *'adam* as inclusive of
male and female in Genesis i. sometimes argue for male head-
ship (sacramental) in marriage.[30]

To review this whole debate is not our purpose. But we
cannot avoid the question whether the household codes represent a more legalistic and conformist view than the love of
neighbour-enemy ethic. We shall examine the household code
of ethics, which is found in its full form in Colossians iii. 18–iv.1
and Ephesians v. 22–vi.9, less completely in I Peter ii. 18–iii.7; I
Timothy ii. 11–15; v. 3–8; vi. 1–2; Titus ii. 2–10; iii. 1–2 and in
a number of other passages, to discover the position of wives,
slaves and children in the Christian household and to decide
whether the household code upheld or modified the teaching of
Jesus.

The interpretation of the codes has attracted an extensive
literature.[31] It is usually accepted that the codes use terms such
as 'fitting' or 'natural' which were found in Stoicism and

Hellenistic Judaism, and relate to groups (women, slaves, children, for example) who were the subject of conventional ethical wisdom. It is also clear that this traditional material was modified by the addition of words such as 'in the Lord'. For some commentators, this changes everything: 'The added words [in the Lord], simple as they are, transform the whole approach to ethics.'[32] This by itself does not prevent disagreement about their meaning, however. Previous interpretations, which attributed the form of these codes to Stoic influence and sought to uncover Christian features in their expression, are now widely discounted in the light of studies which seem to have established that these codes were based on an Aristotelian view of patriarchal relationships in household and city, which begin with marriage as the union of natural ruler and natural subject. In contrast to such patriarchal households, it is argued, the early church established communities of equals in which women and slaves, as in Philemon, were given full moral standing (cf. Galatians iii.28). In the words of sociologist R. Nisbet: 'The strategy from the Christian point of view was thus a vital and almost obvious one: to denigrate so far as possible the historic and still deeply rooted kinship tie and offer the community of Christians itself as the only real and true form of kinship.' Commenting on this, Fiorenza says: 'By offering the community as the new kinship structure, the Christian movement disengaged women from their traditional patriarchal family roles and limitations.'[33] By contrast, it seems that the household codes attempt to reinstate to some extent the patriarchal pattern of women's submission to authority. Even if the codes are tempered by genuine Christian consideration for women, slaves and children, acceptance of the Aristotelian framework deprives the Christian communities of their ability to transform the patriarchal order in family and state. 'From the perspective of women and slaves, however, the household code ethos is a serious setback, since it does not strengthen Roman cultural tendencies to equality and mutuality between women and men.'[34] She describes how this unfortunate development has been justified by commentators as being necessary for survival in the prevailing society; or, more positively, as repre-

senting a genuinely Christian engagement with the existing
structures of society; or, paradoxically, as showing how Christians can continue to display Christian virtue while being
submissive. Such theological justifications she regards as misplaced. 'They support the postbiblical feminist claim that
Christian theology and the Church are inherently sexist.'[35] The
church has taken over an inherently flawed model based on an
Aristotelian political ethic of natural inequality. Genuine Christianity favours 'communities of equality and mutual inter-
dependence' and 'co-equal discipleship.'[36]

There is another aspect, however, to these household codes.
D. Lührmann has pointed to the way that these household
codes are often misunderstood as referring to the church and
not to the *oikos* (household).[37] His evidence indicates very
clearly that the reference is to actual household organisation,
which was the focus of the economy in the ancient world. From
this, some very significant conclusions follow in our view. The
codes represent an attempt by the early church to bring their
new-found faith and ethic into the mainstream of their daily
existence. Theirs was no ghetto ethic. Further, from the very
beginning, the Christian ethic aimed to become a universal
ethic. This ethic for Christians, frequently living in mixed faith
households, had relevance for others also. This strongly suggests that the household codes do not represent a diminution of
Jesus' ethical teaching, but its application. They were *household
codes*, not a new Mosaic law. They were modelled on Christ,
who gave new meaning to the idea of 'servant' (cf. I Peter). 'On
this model all are servants; all are subject to one another. There
is no more ruling over each other in the church or outside the
church. But there is equality; there is mutuality and the gifts of
each person (I Peter iv. 10) are honoured.'[38] Following Christ
and being a good citizen in a particular society, however, are
not identical. Sometimes they cohere; sometimes they clash.
The citizenship required of a Christian has to be responsive to
a pattern of discipleship which has priority. The household
codes represent an attempt to apply the love of neighbour in
the new household situation. On the other hand, one cannot
help feeling that the seeds of legalism were there and that the

logic of superabundance ('love your enemies') was gradually being displaced by the logic of equivalence ('love the brethren'). There is a 'lagging conservatism' at work.[39]

The interpretation of these early household codes is only the tip of the iceberg. They point to a much bigger issue: to what extent was the gospel ethic, in its mediation through social contexts, affected by more conservative and reactionary forces? The letters of Paul, the *Didache*, and other evidence from the early church suggest a mixed picture: radical ferment on the one hand; clinging to old ways, on the other. There is certainly no hint of a golden age of Christian ethics in Paul's letters to the Corinthians. There were communities of ethical difference; but we should not exaggerate the differences. Aristeides' *Apology* and the *Letter to Diognetus* in the second century illustrate something of this. Christians are said to 'follow the customs of the land in clothing and food and other matters of daily life, yet the condition of citizenship which they exhibit is wonderful and admittedly strange'. The world survives by their intercessions. 'And if there is among them a man that is poor and needy, and they have not an abundance of necessaries, they fast two or three days that they may supply the needy with their necessary food.' It would be an exaggeration to think of the early church transforming the society of the whole Roman Empire. But it made a significant difference both in practice and ideal. The way of Jesus opened up new possibilities. Christians were learning to forgive as they had been forgiven (cf. Colossians iii. 13), as we shall see in the next chapter. 'The early Christian ethos of coequal discipleship in community could provide a model for the "new family" as an adult community of equality, mutuality and responsibility for the home and for the "world" . . . A feminist critical hermeneutics of liberation seeks to reactivate this early Christian ethos for today so that it can become a transforming historical model for the ordering of interpersonal communities, society and the churches'. It is not limited to feminism.[40] Such a hermeneutic of liberation will pursue justice, freedom, human rights for all persons and societies. It is important that this ethic should find embodiment in actual communities. It exists only sporadically among the churches, but it is the goal of all Christian communities. This view of the aims and style of a Christian ethic is complementary to our understanding of divine and human personhood and its relevance for ethics. Christians are not offered a blueprint for all the ethical issues of the future, but a way of life is set before them which is anchored in the life and teaching, death and resurrection of Jesus. This Jesus was a complete human person. He was also, in the eyes of those who worshipped him, the revelation of God and divine personhood. He embodied a freedom which was rooted in his love for God and all God's creation. It points to the destiny of all who are made in God's image. The costly love of God excludes none. The logic of such superabundance is most clearly exemplified in the practice of forgiveness, which we explore in the next chapter.

# CHAPTER 13

# The logic of superabundance: an ethic of forgiving love

Closely related to the 'love-command', which is at the centre of a Christian ethic, confirming its concern with 'persons in community', is forgiveness. Christians are to forgive as they have been forgiven (Colossians iii. 12f); Jesus teaches his disciples to pray, 'Forgive us our debts, as we have forgiven our debtors.' On the cross he prays, 'Father, forgive them, for they know not what they do.' Forgiveness is characteristic of God's generous love in creation and redemption. It is also meant to characterise human relations. In this chapter, therefore, we inquire into the logic of such superabundance. We examine what forgiveness means; how it acquired a community dimension; and how this might relate to contemporary social applications.

At the point where the human and Christian stories intersect most significantly in the view of Christians – in the life and death of Jesus of Nazareth – morality is plunged into darkness and might appears to be established as victorious. At the same time, Christians point to this event as the most crucial demonstration of God's love for sinners. Healing and forgiveness and reconciliation are made possible by Christ's action, in which human categories of justice and morality are transcended. Evildoers are forgiven, and the human attack on God's representative and God's justice is transformed into a new beginning for all those who will follow in the way of love and repentance and forgiveness, and be baptised into the death and resurrection of Christ (cf. Romans vi. 3). This new beginning applies to the whole of creation which is, so to speak, in the final birth-pangs prior to the birth of a new creation (Romans viii. 19).

Christians have no monopoly of forgiveness, but forgiveness is one of the distinctive marks of Christianity, which promotes an ethic in which justice alone is no longer regarded as adequate to deal with the confused web of human greed, murder and injustice. Just dealings between individuals and as a mark of social order remain a desirable goal, but it is recognised that such a goal is humanly impossible of achievement. And yet it is replaced by a goal that is even more impossible, humanly speaking – forgiveness and love. This new creation becomes possible because of what God has done and is doing through his Son, Jesus of Nazareth. God, creating and redeeming, is personally involved in the human story in the person of his Son who suffers and dies voluntarily for the sake of others and who, in so doing, transforms the web of deceit and injustice, taking the place of the victim and establishing new possibilities of response and relationship. The former religious machinery set up to deal with sin and reparation for sin is set aside as a gigantic but unsuccessful attempt to cope with the weakness and frailty of the human condition. The sacrificial system only leads to ever more intractable awareness of failure and sense of guilt, although it was set up to insure against guilt. His death on the Cross was an act of institutional injustice. But it is also recorded as a clear demonstration of what divine–human personhood means. Jesus represents both God and humanity, both divine and human personhood. It is for this reason that a Christian ethic revolves so completely round the person and work of Jesus, and that his teaching, however difficult to separate from that of the earliest Christian communities, is so important for a Christian ethic. Because of this coming together in Christ of the human and the divine, a Christian ethic which takes account of this claims to be capable of dealing with the complexity of the human situation, in which a variety of human concerns and values, including rights and responsibilities, have to be brought into a creative relationship with other values, particularly love and forgiveness.

How to characterise this forgiveness is not easy. Philosophers do not often examine it, and theologians tend to take it for granted. 'To err is human, to forgive divine.' It is not the only test of concern for another, but it is a good test. It is interesting and perhaps significant that one philosopher who does discuss it argues that it is illogical to think of God exercising forgiveness, given his other attributes.[1] If forgiveness means retraction of a judgement following new evidence or recognition of mitigating circumstances or just turning a blind eye to something still regarded as wrong, it is clear that none of these can apply to God. Nor, if God ordains a particular punishment, does it seem logical for God to remit it, since he would have known the outcome beforehand; either his omniscience or his justice would be impugned if he changed his mind and remitted the punishment. Forgiveness conditional upon repentance strikes Minas as an unworthy bribe. A third sense of forgiveness, giving up resentment, also seems inapplicable to God. Giving up resentment may be one of the most common ways in which human beings exercise forgiveness, and it is usually made easier if there is an admission of guilt and expression of regret or repentance by the offending party. Such conduct and such attitudes, however, do not seem compatible with God's perfection. If God were not involved, Minas thinks a change of heart on the part of the offending person(s) would be perfectly intelligible. But no change is needed or possible on God's part. Finally, Minas notes that forgiveness is 'appropriately directed only towards actions which have wronged the forgiver'. How, she asks, can an omniscient, omnipotent, eternal and perfect being forgive? To speak of God forgiving sins seems to make the rightness or wrongness of an action depend on God's say-so, and to allow that things which are, in fact, wrong are somehow changed simply by the act of God's forgiveness. This seems like magic, and is impossible to reconcile with a righteous God. Divine forgiveness, she concludes, is 'morally and logically absurd'.[2]

Minas' arguments depend on a number of questionable assumptions about the attributes of God, and her interpretation of what is meant by timeless, omniscient and perfect. The absolutely perfect Being of Greek philosophy may be incapable of forgiveness, but the God of Abraham, Isaac and Jacob, who creates and redeems and intervenes in the affairs of the world, should not be assimilated automatically to Being conceived as perfect.

Minas' arguments have been subjected to careful scrutiny by M. Lewis, who develops two major criticisms.[3] Firstly, the practice of forgiveness requires a context in which moral qualities and human relationships are understood in a certain way. If there have never been bonds of affection or ties of mutual good will between the parties involved, then forgiveness may seem irrelevant and out of place, even if one party, offending or offended, comes to feel a need for it. It is not simply an alternative to punishment or compensation. Where the wrongdoing is experienced as a betrayal of former friendship or shared values, however, a request for forgiveness is 'inseparably connected with remorse (not just guilt); it is an expression of repentance, a recognition that harm has been done, evil committed'.[4] Because Minas fails to explore such a context, her comments fail to get to the heart of what is meant by forgiveness. Lewis' second and main argument is directed to showing how a different understanding of love, as in Kierkegaard's analysis of the qualitative difference between Christian and secular love, would lead to a different understanding of forgiveness. Minas fails to appreciate this because of her understanding of God as essentially timeless and perfect. We have referred (cf. chapter 8) to other problems associated with this way of conceiving God. Christian love is undeterred by hostility, and is permanent and unconditional. It is based on God's love and God's command to love. Secular love is based on personal preference, and is subject to all the variations and idiosyncrasies of such preferences and the limitations of human affection and knowledge. Forgiveness in the religious context is 'not a concession but an eternal obligation'.[5] Lewis admits that it is no panacea for the world's problems. 'If unconditional forgiveness were to be universalised, then the result would be total anarchy.'[6] Divine forgiveness is not simply a moral matter. Nor is the believer's prayer for forgiveness simply a request for a moral judgement to be modified, as Minas implies. In short, there is almost total disagreement between Minas and Lewis about divine forgiveness.

In an attempt to answer some of these difficulties, we shall examine a range of meaning which is common to cases of divine and human forgiveness. We can agree with Minas that forgiveness does not mean condoning or overlooking an act of wrongdoing. Talk of forgiveness also seems better avoided in cases of accidental injury or minor mishaps. Supposing someone spills a cup of tea on my jacket. An apology and expression of regret follows. I recognise it was an accident, not deliberate. I may have a right to some compensation. As an expression of regret, it would be an appropriate gesture, perhaps, to pay for the coat to be cleaned. I may insist on something like this; on the other hand, it may be more appropriate to overlook the matter. Forgiveness does not enter into the matter. Supposing, however, someone goes out of their way to destroy my character. Later he experiences genuine regret and tries to remedy the wrong done to me. He withdraws what has been said and offers an unreserved and public apology. This seems to be a case where forgiveness is certainly a possibility. A deliberate injury has been done and there is an attempt to put it right. Whatever is decided about reparation, the question of forgiveness seems distinct. What would forgiveness mean in this situation? That I should not harbour resentment or hold the matter against the other person? That I should let go of the wrong done me and start again? I cannot pretend that it did not happen. I may find it difficult, if not impossible, to forget. But if I act in such a way that the action which has wronged me does not rankle and cause bitter feeling, is this forgiveness? Can I alter my feelings?

In her book, *Suffering, Innocent and Guilty*, E. Moberley says, 'Forgiveness is a change of heart in the wronged, *vis-à-vis* the wrongdoer.'[7] She points out that 'it cannot compel the wrongdoer to change . . . it is not dependent on penitence . . . it may or may not include the remission of an external penalty'. Most importantly 'it implies acceptance of the wrongdoer as a person, but with full awareness of the horror of wrong'.[8] Whether or not reparation has been made, forgiveness goes beyond a legal settlement or the attitude that, because damages have been paid and the offence punished, there is no more to be said. Forgiveness is on a different level from punishment and retribution. It is true that even punishment cannot be fully understood simply in quasi-legal terms. It is a moral act which asserts moral responsibility and restores the moral offender to the moral community. But there are feelings and sensibilities associated with wrongdoing and guilt and reparation in human relationships which punishment cannot satisfy and where nothing less than forgiveness seems adequate to restore personal relationships. In these circumstances, the ability to forgive and the willingness to be forgiven are not simply matters of feeling. Nor are they solely matters of will. Forgiveness may be metaphorically described as the healing of a wound, the restoration of communion and fellowship or even of life and health. It points to a restoration of a positive state of affairs, as signified by health or love. In this, it constantly seeks to lift morality beyond obligation and utility.[9] It is certainly mistaken to regard forgiveness as a soft option which replaces punishment. Rather, it points to a source of goodness and morality which is normally excluded from consideration by moral philosophy. Its affinities lie with religion and theology. Religion preserves and sustains those values like forgiveness and mercy which may, on occasion, reverse and overturn what may otherwise appear reasonable and rational moral judgements. This is not to deny the possibility of a utilitarian justification of forgiveness. Such a justification, however, appears out of character with the concept in question. Just as, when punishment is denied all retributive character and given a purely utilitarian or educational justification, we seem to end up by considering something which is not punishment at all, so, when forgiveness is given a utilitarian justification, it ceases to be forgiveness and becomes a means to an end, a social or psychological resource. From the standpoint of consequences, forgiveness could be understood as something generally desirable in human conduct on the ground that it is usually better to forgive than not. Without forgiveness, human relationships would be consumed in hatred, jealousy and bitterness. One might develop a psychology of human conduct showing how forgiveness is in keeping with other qualities of civilised behaviour. Unfortunately, forgiveness which is justified in purely utilitarian terms tends to be something rather less than forgiveness: general benevolence, perhaps. From the standpoint of Kant and duty, it could be argued that forgiveness is a human obligation like truth-telling. It is part and parcel of what it means to be a moral human being. One ought always to forgive. Again, this has the effect of making forgiveness into something rather different – and rather less. When it is said that God ought to forgive, 'it is his duty', then we know we are in the world of deism, not Christianity.

In ancient Israel, where law and religion were more closely associated than in modern society, the Torah provided both legal penalty and sacrificial expiation. It was clear that, although human beings exercise forgiveness, there is a sense in which its source is God. Only God can forgive sin.[10] The cultus provided the appropriate machinery. In the course of time, and under the influence of prophetic criticism, the inadequacy of the sacrificial system was increasingly realised and the process of interiorisation, which had never been wholly missing, was underlined. What God required was more than a burnt offering; nothing less than a contrite heart would do. What separated man from God was not simply the wrong act, but a wrong relationship. Sin was not just a deed, but a whole relationship.

The early Christians found the key to a deeper understanding of forgiveness in the person of Jesus of Nazareth, in his life and death and resurrection. They drew on a variety of images and metaphors from their religious and cultural heritage, such as the Jewish sacrificial system, slavery and martyrdom, to interpret the significance of his death. One of the metaphors used was 'justification', and, as Ziesler notes:

> even if a legal background is pressed, the legal system in question was less concerned to pronounce innocent or guilty than to put wrongs right and to restore people to their proper place, no more and no less, in the covenant community. Justification in Paul is thus the act of restoring people to their proper relationship with God. It comes close to forgiveness, with which it is indeed equated in Rom. iv.6–8.[11]

Paul's teaching about justification seems to have originated

with the Galatian debate, and Ziesler thinks 'Paul first pro-
pounded it not to answer the question, "How can I find a
gracious God", but to answer the more immediate question,
"How can Jews and Gentiles live together in one community?".' The question of circumcision, however, could not be
answered except in religious and theological terms, and so 'the
community issue leads straight into the issue of the way to
God'.[12] In other words, one of the main factors in early
Christian conceptions of forgiveness was their understanding of
God's character and purposes, particularly what he had done
in and through Jesus Christ. 'Christ's death is central, not only
in the traditional sacrificial sense, but much more as something
in which believers participate so that his death because of sin is
appropriated and shared in as their death to sin.'[13] Another
important feature was its community reference.

Forgiveness represents a vital part of a Christian ethic.[14] It
points to a fundamental level in the understanding of right and
wrong, supplementing and revising rational interpretations of
obligation and utility. When a wrong act has been admitted
and corrected so far as that is possible, the need for forgiveness
may still be felt. To dismiss such a feeling as subjective or
irrelevant to moral philosophy is to dismiss an important aspect
of moral and religious experience. It marks the recognition that
wrongdoing spoils something fundamentally good, whether in
terms of human relationships or other possible goods. Where
there is a belief in God's creation and sustenance of the
universe (including moral values) and of his ability to redeem
evil, it is natural to ask God for forgiveness.

This is not incompatible with taking steps to overcome the
wrongdoing at the human level; 'so if you are offering your gift
at the altar and there remember that your brother has something against you, leave your gift there before the altar and go;
first be reconciled to your brother, and then come and offer
your gift' (Matthew v. 23). Forgiveness cannot make wrong
actions right, or prevent all the consequences of wrong actions.
What it can do is to snap certain links in the connecting chain
of evil and make a new start possible. Forgiveness restores a
person to fellowship with others, and, in the case of the

Christian faith, this is understood in the context of God's family.

The role of divine forgiveness in Christianity expresses awareness of both human potential and human limitation. To exercise forgiveness requires unusual qualities of courage and humility and also an awareness of first having been forgiven. The confession of sin and the prayer for sin's forgiveness implies that it is inadequate to consider human wrongdoing simply in terms of the number and variety of wrong acts. Since God has revealed his hostility to wrong thought and desires, as well as to wrong actions, and also has demonstrated a way of breaking the power of evil at key points, such as the death of His Son, by not allowing his love to be deflected or reduced by evil, it is incumbent upon those who trust in Him to turn to Him for the forgiveness they themselves need and for the strength to show the same forgiveness to others.[15] It requires great spiritual resources to be able to forgive without becoming paternalistic or falling prey to other similar attitudes. Perhaps for this reason the church has seen itself as a community of forgiven sinners; the support and encouragement of others sharing the same convictions makes it easier for weaker members of the community also to forgive as they have been forgiven.

There are, of course, interpretations of Christianity in which forgiveness occupies a rather different role. In his interpretation of a Christian ethic, Reinhold Niebuhr characterises Jesus' ethical teaching as rigorous, absolutist and perfectionist: 'the ethic of Jesus does not deal with the immediate moral problem of every human life – the problem of arranging some kind of armistice between various contending factions and forces'. Jesus' ethic represents an 'impossible ideal'; the ethical demands of the kingdom are 'incapable of fulfilment in the present existence of men'. It is precisely this which makes it valuable and always relevant. This is not an apocalyptic interim ethic, which writes off the world because the end is imminent. It is a sober, Augustinian theology which has turned its back on his earlier pacifism in the direction of a more realistic estimate of what is humanly and Christianly possible in this world. The eschatological vision constantly beckons. Forgiveness is part of the eschatological vision ahead. 'Forgiveness is a moral achievement which is possible only when morality is transcended in religion.'[16] Human beings can forgive, but there is no absolute or forgiving perspective possible in this life. The emphasis is on sin and the complexity of society and social justice. 'The society which punishes criminals is never as conscious as it might be of the degree to which it is tainted with and responsible for the very sins which it abhors and punishes.'[17]

It is difficult to resist the conclusion that, despite his testimony to the power of *agape* and forgiveness, Niebuhr's 'pragmatic ethic in which power and self-interest are used, beguiled, harnessed and deflected for the ultimate end of establishing the highest and most inclusive possible community of justice and order',[18] defers the need for forgiveness and its power. The transforming power of forgiveness is projected into a more distant future. This world is subject to the restraining influences of sin in all its various forms. Niebuhr clearly recognises the important role of forgiveness in the ethics of Jesus, but it is not easy to see how this becomes effective in the life of contemporary Christians or society.

One way of appreciating the religious dimension of forgiveness and its relation to other attitudes is to compare the operation of forgiveness with instances of reprisal and revenge. In one of Maupassant's short stories, *Une Vendetta*, a Corsican widow revenges her son's death in a most gruesome way. She cannot sleep for thinking of her murdered son. She has no other male relative to avenge his death, so she devises a cruel substitute. She makes a figure in the likeness of her son's murderer. She starves her dog until it is ravenously hungry and then offers it sausages strung round the neck of the figure. Eventually food and ravenous attacks on the figure are inseparable. When she judges the dog is trained for its mission, she goes to church and prays to God to help her. She goes to the shop where her son's murderer works and sets the dog upon him. He is torn to pieces. That night she sleeps soundly once more.

However much one might sympathise with the widow in her loss, what she does adds to the poison of violence and vengeance that has already been released into the life of the community. What is required are steps that will bring the violence to an end. Such steps have to begin within the human heart and will. This is the profound difficulty, the virtual impossibility that Niebuhr points to. But a Christian understanding of human nature, in which divine purpose and power play a crucial role, allows for, and indeed, requires the exercise of forgiveness.

Situations of tragic conflict and violence often cry out for the release that only forgiveness can confer. Conflict in Northern Ireland is a continuing testimony to the power of unforgiving memories as well as yesterday's bombs and guns. When citizens remember their war-dead, and families remember loved ones who died, sometimes after torture, in captivity, can forgiveness exorcise the buried bitterness? What does forgiveness mean in circumstances where the object of hatred is no longer the original offender but descendants of descendants of the offender? It has been said that forgiveness begins with 'memory suffused with moral judgement',[19] rather than with forgetting and overlooking blame. Without the cutting truth of memory, forgiveness would lack the strength to change things; memory alone would prolong the bitterness. Perhaps the most telling initiatives to re-establish peace come from those who have experienced conflict and have realised that without forgiveness there can be no renewal of community.

It is worth recalling here Parfit's attempt to replace the continuous person with a series of psychologically connected selves. If the links between earlier and later selves are weakened, as Parfit suggests, it would seem that even the original war criminal could no longer be regarded as responsible for atrocities committed in his youth. If a criminal can escape detection for long enough, no one can be held responsible, it seems. On a 'simple' view of Personal Identity, which regards the self as enduring over time, it is clear that we are responsible for our earlier actions, even when the law acquits. Parfit argues that 'psychological continuity carries with it desert for past crimes'.[20] 'Suppose', he says, 'that my past crime showed me to be a homicidal maniac. Since he is psychologically continuous with me, Lefty [my future self] would also be a homicidal maniac.' This makes certain assumptions about crime and psychological continuity that would need empirical confirmation. If it were discovered that a purely causal sequence operated and the genes X Y Z produced crimes A B C, one might prefer to revise one's ideas about crime and responsibility. It is not clear why Lefty should be imprisoned for my crimes. Even if society decides it would be safer to imprison Lefty, does not punishment require the notion of responsibility and closer links than Parfit assumes? Is psychological continuity enough? Despite the agnostic assumption that the Christian scheme of things imposes too many unrealistic demands, does it not require an even greater feat of imagination to accept Parfit's complex view of personal identity and its consequences for morality?

Another aspect of forgiveness is that it relates to the parties intimately involved. Even though the offended party has an identical twin brother, who may identify very closely with him, forgiveness has to come from the offended one, not from his twin brother, although the twin can clearly respond with forgiveness to any wrong done to him through the accusation of his brother. In situations where communities are involved, however, the individual may be so closely associated with other individuals that one may represent the whole community. What is done to or by one is done to or by all. The one is representative, as when a country or community acts through an individual. Although this is mainly reserved for representative occasions, something similar seems to be the case when a family member, usually a parent, speaks on behalf of another member of the family. In cases of tragic accident or loss, the family representative speaks on behalf of the injured or dead person. There are a number of examples relating to forgiveness following accidents arising from terrorist violence. Gordon Wilson, whose daughter was murdered by the IRA in Enniskillen, says that he forgives the IRA. Clearly, Gordon Wilson in this case is not simply a bystander. His daughter's death is a severe loss. He has every right to hold it against the IRA. When he forgives, he speaks not only for himself (although that must be very important in this case), but for his family and his murdered daughter. Clearly we do not know what his daughter might feel or do, if she were restored to life. It is as if we transfer the dead person's prerogative in this matter to someone (e.g. the father in this case) who acts in their stead.[21]

Forgiveness cannot be neatly fitted into a utilitarian or deontological framework. It goes beyond what is characteristically human. It has something divine about it. This is important. If forgiveness is nothing more than an exalted form of benevolence or duty, the argument that it is characteristic of Christianity and fits naturally into what we have said about personhood will be deflated if not defeated. On the other hand, it is not a practice which only Christians are capable of pursuing. It commends itself across a wide spectrum of moral opinion. If forgiveness has this extraordinary quality, then it is not difficult to see why it expresses something significantly Christian and yet universal about personhood.

If it is allowed that forgiveness is an important moral quality of the sort I have suggested, then we may begin to find that our conventional ethical stances and theories are in need of such revision that we experience something of an upheaval in our ethical systems. This upheaval or subversion of ethics may be both linguistic and practical: words slip and slide; moral certainties are undermined and changed. Leonardo Boff tells the following true story:

One day in 1981, nineteen farmworkers from Colonia and Rumo, two small hamlets, were abducted by the police acting on the orders of several large landholders. They were evicted from their tiny plots of land and held prisoner. To celebrate, the victors held a barbecue, in the course of which they decided to send some of the food to the poor peasants who were being held prisoner. The peasants 'politely refused'. In the course of the celebration, one of the victors, a Dr Sebastiao, ridiculed the prisoners for refusing food from the barbecue. 'If it had been up to me, I'd have had you filled with the lead of a machine gun', he swore. Later that night the peasants were released. Returning home through the night, they came upon a stalled pickup truck. And by the side of it someone asking for help. It was Dr Sebastiao. What should the peasants do? They had every right to teach Dr Sebastiao a lesson. But that was not their way. They had learned in their community that Christians should be merciful and love their enemies. Do good to those who hate you. Do not be overcome by evil, but overcome evil with good. 'So the workers decided to help Dr Sebastiao. They helped him to get his truck going again.'[22]

It is, of course, possible to interpret the story in different ways. When forgiveness is taken seriously, it begins to prick and eventually bursts the norms of standard ethical theories. Boff's true story, like our earlier example from Northern Ireland, raises the question whether forgiveness, which clearly has a community dimension in its essential reference to relations between individuals, may also have a political community dimension. Boff tells his story as an example of what it means to be a good Samaritan in Latin America today. The church is meant to be a community of good Samaritans. Whether there is a duty on the part of ordinary citizens – and their political leaders – to be altruistic in this way is a question that has generally been answered in the negative by philosophers. Charity may be a virtue, but it is not usually a duty. If a doctrine of charity were exploited by political opponents, it might prove damaging rather than emancipatory or healing. How to apply forgiveness in politics may not only strain credulity, but imply gullibility. And yet a Christian communicative ethic which is committed to a vision of a redeemed humanity can hardly avoid the question. 'Jesus perceived that the orientation of the heart – its most deeply seated commitments – had historical-political consequences. He saw that the most fundamental commitments of his culture were leading to a collision course with Rome. Finally, the basic quality of a heart centred in God – inclusive, embracing compassion – was to be the mark of the people of God as a historical community.'[23]

In his brief but very clear treatment of forgiveness, C. R.

Bråkenhielm rejects the suggestion that politics is amoral, or that some form of dualism, which would make forgiveness a purely personal matter, having no reference to political structures and decisions, is necessary. He finds a way forward in what he calls 'the multidimensionality of forgiveness'.[24] In this way he is able to select elements of political life, which, even if they are not the clearest examples of forgiveness, yet suggest ways in which approximations to forgiveness may become important and operative in political life. He begins with 'forgetting the past', admittedly some distance from the pain and new beginning that is usually associated with overcoming the breach in communion that needs forgiveness. 'To let time do its healing work may be political wisdom in the service of forgiveness.'[25] His reference to Shakespeare's *Richard II* captures the same idea:

> This we prescribe, though no physician;
> Deep malice makes too deep incision;
> Forget, forgive, conclude and be agreed;
> Our doctors say this is no month to bleed.
> (Richard II, I. i. 154–7)

Perhaps if this were extended to a more deliberate, active overcoming of the past, the association with forgiveness would be clearer. Such overcoming of the past, made explicit in negotiation and treaty, as instanced recently in South Africa's constitutional reversal of apartheid, and followed up in programmes of social reconstruction and rehabilitation, affecting all the areas previously marked by discrimination and oppression, would count as the political equivalent of forgiveness. Even here, however, one might hesitate to call this 'forgiveness' itself. What is more clear is that, without an attitude of positive acceptance of the other, which is an ingredient of forgiveness, the treaties and processes will never be able to deliver what they promise.

But what is one to make of even more momentous political events like the Holocaust? Can forgiveness apply here? And does 'overcoming the past' mean keeping the memory alive rather than trying to bury the past? The fiftieth anniversary of

World War II presents many of these dilemmas. One simply cannot forget, if one was involved. It seems doubtful whether those who were not involved should be allowed to forget such events, in the sense that they receive no education about these events. The younger generation cannot be held responsible for what a previous generation did, nor should they be tarred with collective guilt. But no one – even those not involved – can read about and look back on these events without feeling a sense of shame and horror that these things were done by human beings/persons to other human beings/persons. And what is true of the Holocaust is true of so many other atrocities that are still being committed – in Bosnia, Tibet, Rwanda, Chechnya.

Is there a legitimate response which refuses to forgive? Elie Wiesel's words, 'Do not forgive those responsible', echoing round the world from Auschwitz in 1995, recall Psalms 69, 109 and 137. What can a mere observer say to this survivor of Auschwitz? Words truly fail. But there is an important theological issue that has to be addressed. The Pauline interpretation of 'Vengeance is mine, say the Lord; I will repay' (Romans xii. 19) suggests that those who trust in God have to leave vengeance to God. The human task is to seek to do good, even to overcome evil with good (cf. I Corinthians xiii. 4–8; cf. Luke vi. 27f). Such actions may enrage and infuriate the Dr Sebastiaos of this world. Whether this leads to repentance or more violence, we do not know in advance. No one should dispute the (Jewish) right to keep the memory of the Holocaust alive, but memory alone will not save the next generation. Theological responses among Jews to the Holocaust have led to death of God theologies (Rubinstein) and to Deuteronomic type theodicies (Fackenheim). There is also a legitimate response which argues against drawing theological conclusions from the Holocaust, particularly if it causes us to overlook the founding traditions of Judaism in Creation, Exodus and Day of Atonement. Somehow, despite all the difficulties, it is these theological considerations which must determine Judaism's response to the Holocaust. The Day of Atonement has never been a ritual of purely individual forgiveness. It is a day of mourning and new beginning for the whole community.

Bråkenhielm refers to several other approximations to forgiveness in political life: to the forgiving use of memory, 'so that it serves to release us from the burden of the past';[26] to acknowledgement of wrong actions, as in the case of American soldiers in the war in Vietnam; to explicit decisions 'not to repeat a morally wrong act';[27] to avoidance of rancour and ill-will; to positive efforts to be free from destructive structures of social and political life (as in the founding of the United Nations in an attempt to avoid future wars); to the remission of punishment and the use of amnesties; to formal ceremonies and treaties which declare the end of hostilities; to activities which seek to rebuild trust and co-operation between groups and nations. His references to cultural anthropology and the peace-making of primitive tribes are perhaps more difficult to relate to modern society. Whether any of these initiatives amount to forgiveness in political life would require much more analysis. It seems to us that they deserve serious consideration as one of the consequences of a communicative ethic committed to a vision of universal peace and undistorted communication. In so far as they tend to obscure the transcendental and unconditional quality of divine forgiveness, we would want to preserve the importance of recognising how incredibly *different* forgiveness is from the ordinary run of ethical life. It is this transforming aspect, however, that *is* characteristic of Christian faith and *agape* and which is constantly at work within a communicative ethic of persons in relation, working from within like the yeast in the dough.

It will be important for the future of international and national politics for this to be communicated in a way that makes sense beyond the strict boundaries of religious communities and individuals, as long as we live in a world with a diversity of values. We should not be surprised, however, if a Christian ethic, which emphasises love of enemy and forgiveness, sometimes clashes with purely ̓rational and secular systems of morality. Forgiveness is at the heart of the Christian way of life. Translating this into the life of communities is

frequently thought to be the work of justice, and justice is
sometimes contrasted with forgiveness. In the next chapter,
therefore, we examine the place of rights to illustrate how
justice and rights are also needed if forgiveness is to be given its
proper place. Forgiveness and rights are allies, not enemies,
even though forgiveness ultimately transcends rights. In situations of conflict, it would be wrong to expect good relations to
be restored while injustices remain. In the numerous cases of
political conflict we have mentioned, grievances have to be
addressed, violence curtailed and social and political solutions
devised, but without forgiveness and neighbourliness no long-
term solutions will emerge.

It is instructive that, despite the constitutional abolition of
slavery in America in 1865, the reinstatement of social and
economic and educational inequalities in the years that followed led to a system in which black Americans, despite
citizenship rights, were denied vital aspects of personhood,
especially the freedom to participate fully on equal terms with
others in American society. Behind this inequality was a moral
judgement which implied both second-class citizenship and
imperfect personhood. This, together with aspirations for a
fuller share in American society, fuelled the sense of injustice
that led to the Civil Rights Movement in the 1960s. The years
of slavery and inequality, the denial of personhood, are still
taking their toll, argues Shriver, because the majority of white
Americans have not perceived the political significance of
forgiveness: *'the willingness to count oneself as neighbour and fellow
citizen with enemies in spite of the latter's continuing resistance to
reciprocating'* (his italics).[28] With some justice, Shriver traces the
decline of the community dimension of forgiveness to developments in the early church (e.g. the settlement with Constantine;
Augustine's willingness to use force in reprisals against the
Donatists; and, most importantly, the privatisation of penance
and the focus of forgiveness on the confessional). Although the
Reformation led to reform, forgiveness continued to be a
matter for the individual soul in relation to God. Against this
background, it is perhaps not surprising that Locke and Kant,
both of whom understood the language of religion and were

sympathetic to Christianity, developed a rational and moral individualism characteristic of the Enlightenment, and drew back from embracing the personal centre of Christian faith with the zeal which would have allowed them to appreciate the place of forgiveness in a Christian ethic.[29]

CHAPTER 14

# Rights and persons: the religious ground of human rights

Persons have rights, and they have them because they are persons. This is perhaps the most basic statement about the connection of rights and persons. What are these rights? Who are the persons who have them? On what basis do they have them? And what is their ethical significance, particularly from a theological viewpoint? In this chapter we explore these questions in order to return afresh to some of the practical issues raised in chapters 3 and 4 about the rights of the foetus and non-human animals which were discussed in relation to concepts of personhood advocated by many contemporary ethicists.

The presuppositions for a theory of rights are to be found in a combination of early Christian thought, Stoicism and Roman law, but the first anticipations of the developed theories of the seventeenth century cannot be found before the medieval period, in the writings of theologians and philosophers such as Aquinas, Scotus and Ockham.[1] Richard Tuck draws attention particularly to the creative thought of Jean Gerson in 1402, based on the idea of the reciprocal relationship of God and man, involving a covenant which generated rights on both sides.[2] This view was not shared by the Reformers, since it seemed to compromise the sovereignty of God and under-estimate the force of human sin. Implicit in these early theories we can see the seeds of later conflict and debate about the basis of human rights and the nature of a religious ethic.

Dissatisfaction with religious and sectarian justifications of human rights came to a head in seventeenth-century England with civil war and the rejection of the divine right of the king.

294

Civil society looked for a less autocratic and feudal foundation. Hobbes and Locke offered different solutions, but both thought in terms of a social contract. For Hobbes, it was a matter of power and sovereignty, if chaos was to be kept at bay. For Locke, the rights to life, liberty and property were self-evident, based on reason and experience. Locke assumed there was order in the universe, reflected in morality which had no need of revelation and existed prior to all revelation. The Lockean rights to life, liberty and property influenced the assertion of ancient rights and liberties in the Bill of Rights (1688) and the American Declaration of Independence (1776), where the right to property is significantly replaced by the more intangible but far-reaching 'right to the pursuit of happiness'. These liberal-political formulations, revised and qualified in the light of both individualism and socialism, find their natural continuation in the Universal Declaration of Human Rights in the United Nations' Charter of 1948. The rights have now multiplied, but much of the justification remains the same: 'all human beings are born equal and free in dignity and rights. They are endowed with reason and conscience' (article 1).

The story of how early rights' theories were converted into modern political theory, where the 'rights of the individual' become a significant article in political discussion and a feature of moral philosophy which takes no special account of God, is not unconnected with those historical changes we noticed in relation to ideas of personhood (cf. chapter 5). As M. L. Stack-house observes, human rights are both the product and the enemy of religion. They might even be said to represent a new religion.[3]

Rights are frequently asserted; but it is not always clear what the assertion amounts to. Some moral philosophers wish to shun all talk of rights, often citing Bentham who dismissed talk of rights as nonsense and talk of inalienable rights as 'nonsense on stilts'. R. M. Hare, in his article 'Abortion and the Golden Rule', says, 'nobody has yet proposed an even plausible account of how we might argue conclusively about rights. Rights are the stamping ground of intuitionists, and it would be difficult to find any claim confidently asserted to a right which could not be as confidently countered by a claim to another right, such that both rights cannot be simultaneously complied with.'[4] Similarly, R. Young has argued that appeal to rights is otiose and jarring in relation to other moral sensibilities. Like Simone Weil, he thinks rights have 'a commercial flavour' and are asserted 'in a tone of contention'; moral rights are attractive to minorities, but, unlike legal rights, they are redundant because all that can be achieved by moral rights can be more securely achieved by reference to the moral principles which undergird them.[5] But, as others have pointed out, moral discourse would be seriously impoverished by abandoning rights talk and referring only to the good or duty which is the basis of the right.[6] 'Rights enable us to stand with dignity, if necessary to demand what is our due, without having to grovel, plead or beg or to express gratitude when we receive our due and to express indignation when what is our due is not forthcoming.'[7] They act as a constraint against utilitarian manipulations of individual worth. And they keep alive the question whether moral principles are objectively grounded. In the extensive and growing literature on 'rights', recent discussions have focussed on: the nature of rights (are they best characterised as entitlements or claims? Are they correlative with duties?); the justification of rights (are they based on some form of social contract? Or on the nature of the individual? What is the relation of utility and rights?); and the claims of rightholders (do babies, idiots, animals and future generations have rights?).

One of the most influential classifications of rights, particularly for legal theorists, is Wesley Hohfeld's analysis of rights as: (a) claim rights; (b) liberties or privileges; (c) powers; and (d) immunities. As Finnis[8] points out, (a) is the most crucial, and someone who wishes to apply this analysis must first stipulate whether a claim right correlative with B's duty to A requires simply that there be an A for whose benefit the duty has been imposed, or whether A must have the power to take appropriate remedial action at law if B fails to comply with his duty.[9]

The nature of a moral right has sometimes been described as a valid moral claim or entitlement.[10] The claim element in rights has frequently been regarded as primary, but, since unjustified claims are not rights, some qualification such as 'valid claim' seems to be necessary. McCloskey[11] disputes that rights are claims, even valid claims, on the ground that 'valid claim' is in part synonymous with 'right' and yet fails to capture all that is meant by 'right'. His own view, emphasising that rights are 'entitlements', has also been criticised as simply another synonym for 'rights'. In any case, it does not differ substantially from Feinberg's analysis in terms of valid claims, although the two views lead to different responses to the question whether rights and duties are correlative.

It is sometimes argued[12] that 'right' and 'duty' are different designations for the same normative relation, according to the point of view from which it is regarded. Even if the terms 'right' and 'duty' are not used, a society in which people have obligations towards each other, which are the ones that correspond with rights, can be said to have the concept of a right.[13] There is no doubt that rights and duties sometimes are correlative, particularly in the case of contract rights, where the right in question is the basis of a corresponding duty on the part of a specific person or institution. If A has a right to repayment by B of a loan from A to B, this implies B has a duty to repay A, even if, because of bankruptcy or other causes, the duty cannot be fulfilled. Such rights and their corresponding duties may be extinguished by a competent authority, but the relation of right and duty is clear. It is equally clear, however, that not all duties (e.g. duties of charity) create rights. And there are occasions when the existence of rights is not paralleled by any clear counterparts of duty. It is largely for this reason that McCloskey prefers 'entitlement' to 'valid claim', since a claim is normally against someone. Feinberg also recognises the problem, and puts forward the case of the starving, fatherless child of a poor, illiterate mother in a Mexican slum. 'Doesn't the child have a claim to be fed, to be given medical care, to be taught to read? Can't we know this before we have any idea where correlative duties lie? Won't we still believe it even if we despair of finding anyone whose duty it is to provide these things?'[14] In discussing rights against others and attempting to counter McCloskey's view that a right (e.g. the right to life) may not be against others, Feinberg says:

> If a general rule gives me a right of non-interference in a certain respect against everybody, then there are literally hundreds of millions of people who have a duty towards me in that respect; and if the same general rule gives the same right to everyone else then it imposes on me literally hundreds of millions of duties – or duties towards hundreds of millions of people. I see nothing paradoxical about this, however. The duties, after all, are negative; and I can discharge all of them at a stroke simply by minding my own business.[15]

Such a multiplication of duties, however, even negative duties, suggests that the correlativity thesis is being stretched unnecessarily. Rights and duties are often correlative. But must a right always imply a valid claim against someone? Does the starving Mexican child have a right against the state, irrespective of the state's ability to meet this requirement, or against the world community or only against those who are aware of the existence of the child and are in a position to help? It seems clearer to speak of such rights as entitlements in the way that McCloskey does, without making rights and duties necessarily correlative. Certainly rights are not reducible to duties, whether they are basic moral rights or welfare rights, or what Feinberg calls 'manifesto rights', rights which he regards as 'emerging' rather than being fully developed, as, for instance, animal rights or disputed human rights. Such claims are 'permanent possibilities of rights', 'the seed from which rights grow'. When established, they may give rise to duties, but their characterisation as rights does not seem to be dependent on ascertaining correlative duties.

The characterisation of moral rights is related to the grounds on which such rights are attributed. At this point, moral considerations can hardly be separated from wider judgements which have an ontological or metaphysical character in that they make claims about the nature of reality and are themselves the basis or foundation for other moral claims. The fact that the ground of rights may be attributed to a religious viewpoint may be significant for both rights and persons. Even if the relation is one of enrichment rather than logical entailment, it should not be simply dismissed as another version of the naturalistic fallacy.

The ground of human/moral rights has been variously ascribed to: human nature as such, distinguishing humans from all other individuals, so that if animals, for instance, have moral rights they have them derivatively, by virtue of their relationship to humans; rational human nature, distinguishing between individuals who count as rational and others and allowing, therefore, for some humans to be excluded and for other rational creatures, if there are any, to be included; to sentience, such that any sentient creature can be said to have interests; and even to utility, despite the obvious potential for conflict between rights and utility. There are two other grounds which are of particular interest, namely personhood, which sometimes overlaps with features of previous categories; and divine creation, which may also be linked with previous categories and may operate in conjunction with other categories but at a different level.

The idea that rights are owed to human individuals by virtue of their humanity, but not to non-human animals, plants or things, may reflect both Greek and Judaeo-Christian thinking about human nature, but, essentially and explicitly, neither rationality nor divine activity is being put forward as the ground of such rights. It may also have a democratic tendency and be related to the idea of a social contract, but again this is not the explicit intention of such a grounding. Basic human rights typically include the right to life (or the right not to be killed), and the right to liberty (or the right not to be interfered with in living one's own life, provided this does not clash with the similar rights of others). One of the main features of this justification (which some find problematic) is that it tends to rely on whatever values are ascribed to humans *qua* humans. As we noted in Part I, it is not always recognised that 'human' can function both normatively and descriptively. There is a tendency among modern philosophers to regard 'human' as simply 'biologically human'. As a purely descriptive term, it could be argued, 'human' cannot justify moral rights. It is disappointing, however, to find that the otherwise thorough discussion of Sumner simply dismisses the normative use of 'human being': 'It is thus quite inconceivable that we have any rights simply because we are human. If this is what is implied by the rhetoric of human rights then that rhetoric has been used to serve a discriminatory, because speciesist, pro-gramme.'[16] If the term 'human' is being used evaluatively, the values should, of course, be made explicit. There is a similarity here with certain aspects of the discussion of 'persons', when it is not clear what value characteristics are being ascribed to persons.

The idea that rights are owed to rational individuals by virtue of their rationality would exclude some humans (such as babies, idiots and the senile) and would allow some non-humans to have rights, provided that their rationality could be attested. Since 'rationality' is not a precise term, it is not surprising that proponents of this view have also varied in their detailed recommendations. Tooley,[17] for example, emphasised self-consciousness, and argued that an organism must possess the concept of a self as a continuing subject of experiences and other mental states and believe that it is itself such a continuing entity. R. B. Brandt simply says, 'I propose to construe "person" to mean "adult human beings with reasonable intelligence". This is not very precise and if one wants one could spell it out as human beings at least 18 years of age and with an IQ of at least 120 and not temporarily in a psychotic or neurotic, or even a highly emotional, state of mind.'[18] The difficulties with such a justification are similar to the difficulties we have already encountered in interpretations of 'person'. If rationality is pitched very high, the results are counterintuitive in the view of many people (viz. in the resulting exclusions). Moreover, despite certain advantages (it does not, for instance, favour human beings indiscriminately, because it specifies value-grounds other than 'humanity', although rationality is one of the features traditionally associated with human beings), there is no good reason to favour rationality in this way. Some modern interpretations of 'rational persons', as we have seen, simply encourage a form of élitism, which acts as a cover for enhancing the claims of the human species, admittedly in a way that is abhorrent to many other human beings.

In an effort to avoid the unwelcome implications of both these positions, McCloskey, followed by Feinberg, has proposed that to qualify as a being with rights one must have interests. This might exclude some human individuals (e.g. congenital idiots), depending one one's understanding of interests, and include some non-human individuals. Feinberg accepts that 'things' and artefacts, however beautiful or precious, and however much in need of care and protection if they are to be preserved, cannot have rights because they cannot press their own claims or be directly represented by an agent. Following his explication of interests in terms of desire and conation, aims and goals, latent tendencies, direction of growth and natural fulfilment, Feinberg argues that non-human animals can have interests. If it is agreed, further, that animals should be treated well, not simply for the sake of human sensibility or because the law requires it, but for their own benefit, then animals can be said to have rights. At this point, McCloskey parts company from Feinberg, although he is not unsympathetic to animal welfare.

The conclusion that animals can have interests is disputed at some length by Frey in his monograph *Interests and Rights* and his book, *Rights, Killing and Suffering*. He argues against the emphasis often given to sentiency, particularly the experience of pain, by defenders of animal rights. His main criticism, however, is that there has been a failure to analyse the concept of 'interest', and this is crucial to any philosophical attempt to show that animals have interests. Interests, he says, presuppose appropriate desires and beliefs. In response to Regan's suggestion that severely disoriented, retarded but sentient children can desire something to ease the pain of toothache, even though they cannot form beliefs of the requisite kind, Frey asks, in effect, how one knows what links retarded children make between their beliefs and their desires. Since desires normally presuppose beliefs, why should Frey's scepticism about the mental workings of retarded children be allowed to assume such a significant role as a blocking device? (It is hardly an argument.) One might equally question Frey's assumptions about animals and their feelings. But, even if one grants his assumption[19] that desires normally presuppose beliefs, it is not clear why his somewhat restricted interpretation of desires and beliefs should carry the day. Is it not sufficient to point to animal needs expressed in terms of behaviour as indications of genuine interests? There seems little justification for Frey's assimilation of animal needs and wants to the way that a car or tractor may need oil and water. A cow may 'need' water as a car 'needs' water, but the argument tends to imply that animals are just like machines and cannot have interests. It is true, of course, that if the prerequisites for having interests are sufficiently steep and include self-consciousness, or even a minimal language, as Frey and Tooley argue, then the case against animals having interests and rights becomes much stronger. These criteria will also exclude foetuses, congenital idiots and the senile. Non-human animals have interests related to needs, in a way that machines do not; they also can have original purposes, and to that extent beliefs. What cannot be attributed to them is the ability to articulate such beliefs in language used self-reflexively. There is as yet no evidence for a capacity to use language self-reflexively. This is not to say that animals do not communicate with each other or use signs in ways that are similar to certain aspects of human language.

A different justification of rights might try to locate interests within a wider utilitarian justification of morality. Despite the obvious difficulties, rights and utility have been increasingly brought together in recent discussions. Part of the impetus for such a move lies within utilitarianism itself, particularly in Mill's *Utilitarianism*, chapter 5, 'On the Connection between Justice and Utility'. Increasingly uneasy about suggestions that utility alone can cope with issues of moral justification, many utilitarians attempt to relate utility and rights. In the past, rights have been seen as more likely to be opposed to utility (cf. Dworkin). A number of factors have begun to modify such a contrast. The great increase in discussion of human rights, welfare rights, women's rights, children's rights and animal rights has made it more attractive to give them a normative role. Modifications in the understanding of utilitarianism from the classic emphasis on utility, interpreted in terms of measurable pleasure, to an interpretation of utility which not only includes rules, but makes 'rational preferences' central and regards utility as a formal principle, seems much more compatible with 'rights' than the older emphasis on pleasure did. Several philosophers have recently tried to combine utilitarianism and rights more closely. Even Hare has tried to incorporate rights and utility at different levels of moral thinking. Griffin has argued that we should regard 'personhood' as the first and most important ground of human rights, and that it is 'not incompatible with utilitarianism'.[20] His analysis and discussion raise interesting questions about the justification of rights, but ultimately the question has to be asked whether 'utility' retains determinative significance in his conceptual scheme or whether 'utility' is subordinate to 'rights' and 'persons'. The objection, however, that the whole point of human rights is to mark out an area not dependent on utilities, seems fatal to utilitarian justifications. 'Human rights, if they obtain at all, it would seem, must be part of the framework within which utility is calculated, and therefore logically prior to and not grounded in it.'[21]

A rather different basis for human rights is argued for in A. I. Melden's *Rights and Persons*. Melden is impressed by the significance of the human structures and relationships in which rights talk is embedded. Parental rights, for instance, are not simply a result of parents being good at parenting. This view comes close to Adam's view that 'personhood' is an office, but it seems to identify human rights with the moral enterprise *per se*. To argue that one 'qualifies for rights . . . by having the complex structure of powers, experiences and concerns that enables people "to employ the language of morals, to apply the concept of rights along with the conceptual structure in which it is embedded, during the course of their transactions with others"'[22] seems circular, as Melden admits. Having argued that rights are not supervenient qualities or attributes possessed by persons but inherent in personhood, he examines various plausible candidates, such as the intrinsic worth of human beings, or personal autonomy, freedom or equality, only to reject them because they are, in many cases, simply restatements of human rights rather than grounds of human rights. 'It is not, therefore, by reference to some sort of attribute that constitutes the essence of human beings, to their rationality, autonomy, uniqueness or to the actual or potential realisation of value in the experience of individuals . . . that it is possible to comprehend how it is that each person has the moral status as the possessor of human rights.'[23] 'The philosophical understanding of the rights of human beings must come to rest on nothing less, and on nothing else than, this enormously complicated and moral form of human life itself.'[24] Having a right is not like possessing an attribute or quality. The decision to withhold rights from animals, but to grant them to those who are unable to use the language of rights (e.g. psychopaths; those in a terminal coma; the very young), is argued for with sensitivity, but, ultimately, Melden can only compare the basis of human rights with the justification of promises. At some point we reach an end of justification. We either accept the institution of promising or we reject it. For those who accept the moral life, the basis of human rights is part and parcel of what is meant by morality; and for those who do not, any justification is illusory. Much of what Melden says is extremely appropriate to a characterisation of rights. Ultimately, however, having rejected all extrinsic justifications of human rights, he seems to identify his intrinsic justification with his characterisation of what a human right is.

One of the most sustained attempts to develop a consistent basis for human rights is Gewirth's attempt to establish a logical connection between the structure of agency and human rights.[25] From the dialectical principle that 'every agent logically must accept that he ought to act in accord with the generic rights of his recipients as well as of himself', Gewirth argues that every agent has an obligation to act in this way. In short, an essential part of the meaning of agency is purposive action which presupposes freedom and a certain measure of well-being. There is a conceptual connection between agency and such necessary goods. This is the foundation of the rights to freedom and well-being. These are fundamental human rights, grounded in the nature of agency. Gewirth is then able to reinterpret Kant's formulation of morality in terms of human dignity and respect for moral agents. Human dignity is the basis of human rights, not because rational agents belong to a noumenal world in which there is a necessary link between rationality and morality, but because every empirical agent is necessarily committed to the free, purposeful nature of agency. Such free, purposeful agency presupposes the worth of the action of the agent. 'Now, there is a direct route from the worth of the agent's ends to the worth or dignity of the agent himself.' 'Agency is both the metaphysical and the moral basis of human dignity.'[26] Controversy still surrounds Gewirth's formulation. Has he succeeded in bridging the is–ought gap, at least from the agent's point of view (i.e. in first-person terms)? Or has he simply given expression to a normative view? Although it points in the right direction, Gewirth's account of agency, and his attempt to establish a necessary connection between agency and rights, need to be supplemented by a fuller account of agency. 'The internal normative structure of agency would have to be richer than Gewirth allows to warrant the conclusion that such behaviour on the part of others would be a violation of an agent's rights.'[27] Adams claims to find such a normative structure in personhood, understood not simply as the factual autonomy of living one's own life, but as the office or responsibility of defining and living one's own life. 'Human rights . . . are grounded in and governed by the responsibility to define and to live a life of one's own under the guidance of one's knowledge and critical judgement, which is a component of one's constitutive/normative self-image as a person.'[28] Against such a background, thinks Adams, 'the doctrine of natural rights (that there are rights inherent in the nature of human beings as such) becomes intelligible'. His suggestion that 'personhood' is essentially an office, which is then a natural receptacle for normative judgements, has something to commend it. He does not, however, examine the substantive and conflicting normative claims that may legitimately be made about the office. Rather, he simply assumes a humanistic conception which does not go much beyond the 'rational agency' of Gewirth which he finds inadequate. It is difficult to avoid the impression that there is a normative basis to Gewirth's argument. Gewirth defends himself against such criticisms by arguing that the only normative features of his interpretation are built into the concept of action itself. It has been pointed out, however, that Gewirth's concept of agency relies on certain empirical features which are not true of all actual human beings (e.g. infants or the senile), and that, in so far as he implicitly distinguishes 'human' and 'person', he appears to be 'committed to an élitist conception of human rights'.[29]

Several other writers also seek to ground 'rights' in 'personhood' (e.g. McCloskey, Adams, Griffin, Singer and Tooley).[30] It is noticeable that, despite some similarities, there are significant differences between their views of personhood. Some (e.g. McCloskey) do not include non-humans in the category of persons.[31] Whether all humans are persons is also answered differently.[32] Distinctions which we have already noted in concepts of personhood are clearly relevant to the attempt to ground 'rights' in 'personhood'. Several of the above writers refer to persons as 'beings with a life of their own to lead'.[33] Some degree of autonomy, consciousness and time seems to be envisaged, as in Tooley and Warren. It does not follow, of course, that all those who think of persons in this way also attribute rights to them. B. Williams, for instance, sees no need for 'rights' language at all.

Such a rejection of rights language, we have already said, is counter to growing interest in rights and the recognition that, even if not clear, it corresponds to some deep-seated moral convictions and aspirations. It is for this reason, perhaps, that religious and theological justification is being taken more seriously. V. Haksar's[34] unusual and interesting defence of human rights and equal respect in terms of what he calls 'perfectionism' provides a valuable perspective both on 'persons' and religious or theological justifications of human rights. By 'perfectionism' he means the principle that all human beings are to be regarded as having equal worth

(irrespective of empirical differences), not on the grounds of
any social contract theory or Rawlsian interpretation of an
original position of ignorance, but on the ground that egalitarianism presupposes that human beings have more value than
any other form of life, such as non-human animals or rational
Martians. He makes a plausible case for his view that Rawls
and many others do, in fact, underpin their egalitarianism with
an implicit perfectionism of the sort which attributes special
value to human beings. He is particularly critical of Parfit's
theory of complex personal identity, which he regards as 'not
only incompatible with a rights based approach . . . but also
with any kind of humane morality'.[35]

The Christian metaphysic (that God is equally the father of
all) seems to satisfy Haksar's strictures about secular egalitarianism and its implicit perfectionism, but he is not happy with
the Christian metaphysic as such. It does not have the weaknesses of the secular version of the family argument, in which
some members of the human family are, in fact, more closely
related to us than others (which would undermine the egalitarianism), but there are other features of the Christian view that
are 'difficult to accept'.[36] Haksar claims to be 'against the use
of metaphysical arguments that involves going against empirical evidence', but not against appealing to metaphysical
perfectionist considerations that do not flout empirical evidence. He thinks both Rawls and Parfit, in different ways,
appeal to a 'metaphysical theory of the nature of the person'
(p. 22). Rawls appeals to a 'simple' view of persons as persistent
entities, whereas Parfit's 'complex' view appeals to a loose form
of identity marked only by psychological continuity. Although
he regards the Christian metaphysic and view of persons as
ultimately unsatisfactory, the reasons for this are never
adduced.

Our earlier chapters have indicated how a Christian view of
personhood takes into account both the richness of human
personhood (embodied and relational as well as rational) and
the idea that human beings are made in the image of God. We
have argued that there is no value-free interpretation of
'humanity'. We now need to look more closely at what might

be involved in a theological justification of rights in terms of personhood. It is not denied that there may be secular versions of human good which serve to ground rights and personhood. There is no case, however, for simply excluding metaphysical and theological considerations. 'To constitute a morality adequate to guide a human life, we need a scheme of the virtues which depends in part on further beliefs, beliefs about the true nature of man and his end.'[37] The view that all persons have rights by virtue of being created and sustained by God is one of those further beliefs that needs to be examined and explored.

If we start with the witness of the Bible, we do not find any explicit discussion of human rights, although there is a considerable amount of case-law in the Old Testament which is about the rights of slaves and their owners, husbands and wives, children and parents, and other social groups. Some would see in these valuations of men and women in contrast to property a significantly different evaluation from that found in some of the surrounding cultures. Without exaggerating such differences, it seems clear that the emphasis in the Law and Prophets on covenant-law as the basis of Israel's morality points to a conception which is at once relational and developmental, rather than static and purely contractual. The covenant-God is understood in terms of righteousness and mercy. Above all he is thought of as Creator and Redeemer – of Israel and of all mankind. There is, at times, a crude emphasis on the solidarity of the community (cf. Joshua vii), but this is increasingly refined and purged of less personal collectivist notions. The individual is affirmed as having worth in his or her own right as a creature of God. The universalism of Amos and Deutero-Isaiah, the personalism of Hosea and Jeremiah, and the individualism of Jeremiah and Ezekiel are transformed in the teaching of Jesus and Paul into an ethic which is clearly centred on the fundamental worth of each individual in the family of God, from which none are excluded and whose purposes of love will at the end prevail. 'There is no such thing as Jew and Greek, slave and freeman, male and female; you are all one in Christ Jesus' (Galatians iii. 28). From such a starting-point it is possible to argue that the basis of human rights is not the ability to participate actively in the moral club,[38] but God's purposes in creation. The rights of children and psychopaths are not simply the extension of rights due to rational adults, but the rights of weaker members of the human family who share with rational adults creaturely status in God's family. This does not solve all the questions about the definition and basis of rights or classes of rightholders, but it creates a powerful predisposition against the manipulation of the weak, and it may offer a more satisfactory metaphysical basis for human rights than 'equal respect for persons' understood in a purely rational or utilitarian context.

There is, however, at least one objection to this line of thought that may be voiced by both humanist and the Christian. If God is who he is said to be (i.e. all powerful Creator and Redeemer of all mankind), how can a creature have rights against the Creator? Would not human rights compromise the sovereignty of God? What can the clay say to the potter? Admittedly, this nuance is not absent from the Bible, but the more predominant emphasis is on the covenant relationship. All rights emanate from God, but our dependence on God is not normally described in such a way as to take away human rights of self-determination. In fact, human freedom to sin against God, to break God's law and covenant and go one's own way is described at some length. This freedom is dependent on the right to self-determination, which is how God has made us. In the covenant, God promises, not that he will grant all Israel's desires, although some of the promises may seem to come close to that (cf. Isaiah lxi; lxv. 13–25), but that he will bless Israel by his steadfast love. The blessing is not chiefly the material embodiments of blessing, important though these are, but his presence and his loyal love. God's covenant-law also creates rights and obligations between human beings. This is well expressed by J. L. Allen: 'to speak of rights in these relationships . . . is not to compromise God's sovereignty but to express it, because the rights that reflect what it is truly to be a person and therein a child of God are the expression of how God in his sovereign will has bound himself in steadfast love towards his creatures. The Christian understanding of God and man, far from being contradictory to the concept of moral rights belonging to persons, is inseparably connected with it.'[39]

Human rights have not been a frequent topic of theological consideration in the history of the Christian church, and some have argued that Christians should emphasise responsibility and service, not rights, but the numerous claims about human rights in the modern world have begun to be taken up and explored in more recent theological discussion (cf. K. Cronin, *Rights and Christian Ethics* in this series). In the opening chapters of *On Human Dignity*, J. Moltmann summarises some of the historical background to ecumenical dialogue on human rights, and tries to lay bare what he sees as the essential theological basis of human rights. Despite different approaches to human rights among Christians (e.g. Roman Catholic, Lutheran and Reformed), Moltmann finds a real convergence among all shades of Christian opinion about the source of human dignity, namely in man's creation in the image and likeness of God. He does not conceal that real differences exist. The Reformed tradition, by its explicit theological stance and theological justification of human rights, has the drawback that it is 'acceptable only for Christians'. In the Lutheran position outlined by Tödt and Huber, 'a Christian foundation for human rights is rejected', although 'they recognise in human rights similarities and analogies to the Christian faith'.[40] In contrast to the Reformed emphasis on sin and grace, the Roman Catholic stresses a dualism of nature and grace, in which human reason and natural law prefigure the grace of the gospel. Moltmann's own discussion contrasts what he sees as the Western European emphasis on civil and political rights, where the individual is usually the recipient and focus, with socialist and Marxist conceptions of human rights which make economic and social rights primary, and with Third World conceptions which stress rights to national economic self-determination. He regards 'human rights' as the language and framework by means of which, in political and social matters, the church is able to relate to the world. When he discusses the theological basis of human rights and the link which holds the different conceptions of human rights together, he notes two different theological approaches. H. E. Tödt and W. Huber, followed by the Lutheran World Federation,[41] claim to find three basic elements in all human rights: freedom, equality, and participation. 'In this triad Tödt and Huber see the ideal basic contour of human rights. They use this figure as a hermeneutical key to the understanding of the plurality of human rights.'[42] The Roman Catholic and Reformed positions,[43] on the other hand, make the distinction of human rights and human dignity central. The rights may be plural; the dignity is common and prior. 'The dignity of humanity is the one indivisible, inalienable and shared quality of the human being. The different human rights portray a wholeness because the human being in his or her dignity is a totality.'[44]

Once again, as in so many of our earlier discussions, it emerges that one of the central issues is 'what is human'. Even theological documents tend to represent this differently, although the characterisation of what is human is the chief contribution of Christian theology to the debate. The World Council of Churches, through its Commission on International Affairs in 1974, referred to 'the value of all human beings in the sight of God', and to 'the atoning and redeeming work of Christ that has given to man his true dignity'.[45] The Roman Synod of Bishops in 1974 said, 'The dignity of man has its roots in the fact that every human being is an image and reflection of God. As a result of this all men are equal with one another in their essence.'[46] Clearly there are differences in perspective and approach between the various theological traditions, reflecting their historical situation and development. The perspectives are not altogether incompatible, however. All refer to human dignity and creation in God's image.

Moltmann also claims to find a significant unifying factor in the experience of liberation which all the churches affirm. The different traditions start from different aspects of experience – experience of life in the church, for example, or personal experience of the Holy Spirit. There is no simple common denominator. But it is possible to characterise what is essential in these varieties of Christian experience. 'We have learned from liberation theology to begin where we ourselves really

exist in our own people. Experience in the praxis of liberation
from inhumanity is for Christians and churches the concrete
starting point for the commitment to human rights.'[47] Whether
it is the experience of liberation or the *praxis* of liberation
theology that Moltmann is referring to is not clear. There does
seem to be a suggestion that it is the *praxis* of liberation theology
that can provide some unity; but this seems somewhat opti-
mistic, since there is no agreement what that might be. That
Christian community should be emancipatory, however, is an
important characteristic (cf. chapter 12) and, as such, it represents a significant feature of what Christian theology means by
'human'.

There is one element of Moltmann's account that requires
further discussion. The theological task is represented as 'the
grounding of the fundamental human rights upon God's right
to human beings'. In 'Christian Faith and Human Rights' this
is expressed as follows: 'The specific task of Christian theology
in these matters is grounding fundamental human rights in
God's right to – that is, his claim upon – human beings, their
dignity, their fellowship, their rule over the earth and their
future.'[48] He develops the theme of God's claim upon human
beings by reference to the history of Israel and Jesus Christ.
One of the problems with this justification is that it seems more
like a justification of divine rights than human rights. It
explicates creation not so much as a divine gift which creates
rights for humans, but rather as a divine act which secures
rights for the Creator. Human rights would only be preserved if
it were made clear that in creation the Creator established a
human *telos* and established or guaranteed the conditions for
achieving such a *telos*. Moltmann's interpretation of human
rights and their justification reads more like 'duties to the
Creator'. This impression is reinforced by his fuller description
of the Reformed position, which he shares: everything hinges
on man's co-responsiveness to God. This suggests there are no
rights (at least from God) for unbelievers.

It is true that any theological justification will need to take
account of the immeasurably superior power of the Creator.
There may also be some analogy between Creator's rights and

parental rights. But a theological justification of human rights can be more positive about the rights of the creature, particularly in the light of the covenant relationship to which Moltmann refers. The covenant relationship is important in establishing human freedom (including the freedom to rebel and go against God's will and the freedom which, in seeking God's will, nevertheless retains a genuine measure of autonomy and independence) and equality between human beings. By emphasising God's claim upon human beings as the foundation of human rights, Moltmann has turned away from those features which are found in both philosophical and theological justifications of human rights, namely freedom and equality.

The Lutheran account also, despite its reference to freedom and equality, tends to keep human rights at arm's length because of its two kingdoms doctrine. Rights are a valuable secular commodity, but they remain outside the theological camp. Their justification is in terms of this world, not the Kingdom of God. It is perhaps true that, from a theological perspective, rights have to be understood as derivative or delegated rights, rather than owner's rights. The covenant relationship offers a more positive description and justification than Moltmann allows. Creation and covenant can function as a basis of the creature's or recipient's rights as well as the creator's or donor's.

If one of the essential features of the 'image' language in Genesis i. 27f is to convey a 'representative' purpose, God gives into the hands of his agent *'Adam* (humankind) both responsibility and rights. It may perhaps be argued that human beings are given too dominant a role (cf. chapter 15) and that the failure to distinguish between 'humans' and 'persons' has encouraged human exploitation of the rest of creation. This is not the whole story, however. Passmore gives reasons for thinking that it was the subsequent combination of a Jewish–Christian view of human nature with Greek self-sufficiency ('man is the measure of all things') and Roman Stoicism that encouraged later thinkers in the Western European Christian tradition (e.g. Descartes) to downgrade non-human animals (and perhaps humans as well) by drawing on machine analogies and placing human reason on a pedestal.[49] If the account of creation in Genesis is interpreted in terms of stewardship rather than despotism, then, although this may seem to weaken human power, and therefore rights, in the long term stewardship safeguards the moral quality of rights by making it apparent that they relate to standards which the steward upholds and rights which he/she receives by virtue of the office of steward. God's role and power as Creator are not diminished. But he has delegated to human beings (not simply to Christians) the role of stewards of creation. In so far as the steward represents the Creator, it becomes necessary to take account of the character of the Creator.

Reference has already been made to narratives in Old and New Testaments which describe God's character. God is Israel's covenant-God, requiring justice and righteousness from his creatures, not only in relationship to himself, but in their relationship with one another. He has chosen Israel that all nations might be blessed. He has liberated Israel, not because of anything deserved, but because of his love. This liberation of the enslaved and poor represents his pattern of dealing with all his children, not only Israel. This is illustrated best in his Son, Jesus Christ, who was rejected by those to whom he came. God does not embark on any tit-for-tat rejection, but the crucifixion and resurrection of Jesus and the birth of the church are the beginning of a universalisation of God's salvation of Israel. If God's purpose in creation is a salvation freely accepted, this presupposes a world in which human beings exercise free, responsible agency. Such agency presupposes both the possibility and the exercise of moral rights. From this it can be argued that creation can serve as a theological support for human rights.

But it may be objected: what does creation add to free responsible agency? Would it not be simpler to base human rights on free responsible agency alone? It would perhaps be simpler, although it would not be identical. It is, of course, a valid option for the Christian theologian to endorse the 'Lutheran' conception of rights as a secular phenomenon. This view attempts to safeguard the autonomy and freedom of the world and make human rights independent of God, while attempting an overall theological exposition which takes account of rights. On such a view, rights would depend for their justification on criteria worked out independently but potentially in harmony with whatever theological exposition overall was adopted. It might appeal to criteria of freedom and equality, as secular philosophers do. It would, however, present a somewhat negative theological justification of human rights.

If, on the other hand, rights are tied more closely to an understanding of creation, it needs to be explained how this does not undermine the very principle which rights-talk seeks to safeguard. Compared with the rights and power of the Creator, the rights of the creature might turn out to be rather flimsy and insubstantial. One way to counter this would be to develop a view in which substantial rights, the equivalent of what is referred to by human rights to life and self-determination, together with such rights against the Creator as are necessary to make human rights actual (e.g. the capabilities of the planet to support human life and free responsible agency) are bestowed by the Creator. Such a gift of rights would mean that they acquired independent status, almost as in the 'Lutheran' view. The chief difference would lie in the explicit link between rights and creation.

A more satisfactory way, however, is to take account of what we have argued about the character of God and his covenant in creation, and to relate rights and creation by means of the analogy of God's personhood and human personhood. In reply to our earlier question (what does creation add to free responsible agency?) it can be argued that: it expresses a richer conception of persons, agency and rights, particularly with regard to mutual relationships and community; and it also expresses an interpretation of the world as a whole in which rights are not simply invented or plucked out of the air and arbitrarily made into fundamental aspects of human experience, but represent part of a moral view which coheres with, and supports, an overall view of the world and of God. As C. Villa-Vicencio says: 'A theological-ethical study of human rights is ultimately about a vision of what society can become.'[50] His analysis makes it clear that, although human rights have often been interpreted in individualistic terms in Western political thought, a more social understanding has many advantages and is imperative if the world is to become truly one world and not leave Third World countries in economic dependence and poverty. 'The message contained in the biblical vision of society is a message concerning the individual worth and dignity of all people, *realised in community with others*' (his italics).[51]

This emphasis on the communitarian nature of rights discourse agrees with the view of personhood we have put forward, both in terms of social justice and the more general understanding of persons in society. The individualistic interpretation of rights to life, liberty and property is not the only interpretation of such rights. Life, liberty and property may be given a communitarian interpretation. If it is granted that persons are essentially interdependent, living in communities which form networks of mutual support rather than small atomistic, unrelated groups, it is possible to develop a richer and more realistic conception of life than that envisaged in the 'physical life of a solitary individual'. It is important not to overlook the individual, but it is clearly a move in the right direction to give more weight than in eighteenth- and nineteenth-century versions of rights to individuals in relationship and community. The scourge of poverty, which denies to millions the right to decent shelter, food or employment, cannot be dealt with in individualistic terms. The 'Bias to the Poor' programme of many Christian churches in the late twentieth century is a sign that Christians, however belatedly, recognise this and are attempting to do something about it by both education and action.

Where the implementation of human rights is hindered by existing political or economic structures, those who have committed themselves to this ethical vision will find it their duty to work for social change through the democratic processes at their disposal, including possibly legislation which will provide for the redistribution of wealth and property as well as the creation of equal opportunities. The concern of rights for *all* humanity on the basis of God's creation has implications also for the natural world and environmental ethics. 'Because human rights are about what is essential to life, the protection of the earth is such a right.'[52]

It is in this context that attempts to justify animal rights on theological grounds are most naturally considered. The association of rights and personhood gives rise to controversial questions about the moral status of non-human animals: do they form part of the community of persons? and do they possess moral rights? As noted earlier, questions about the moral status of non-human animals have climbed steadily up the agenda of philosophical ethics in recent years. The distinction and contrast between 'person' and 'human being' was accompanied by an attempt to relate 'person' and 'non-human animal' more closely in terms of interests and capabilities common to humans and non-human animals. In an interesting ethical reversal of Darwinian anthropology, human rights were to be extended to non-human animals. As we noted,[53] there were numerous objections to the strong defence mounted by those who supported the extension of moral rights to non-humans. Among the strongest were those of Passmore, who is not opposed to animal welfare, but who objects to the ideas and terminology of animal rights. 'Ecologically, no doubt, man forms a community with plants, animals, soil',[54] but not a moral community, since there are no mutual ethical obligations. If it were ever decided that we 'ought to treat plants, animals, landscapes precisely as if they were *persons*' (i.e. part of a moral community in a strict sense), this would spell the end of human action, according to Passmore. 'The idea of "rights" is simply not applicable to what is non-human.'[55] Passmore's objections, based on secular, ethical humanistic grounds, are shared by a number of theological writers who wish to maintain a strict separation of human and non-human on the ground that humanity has a special and superior position in creation.

It is important, however, not to confuse the attribution of (moral) rights with personhood in the case of non-human animals. That animals have certain legal rights (e.g. the right not to be treated inhumanely or cruelly) is clearly established in the legislation of many countries. On the other hand, it is equally clear that there are important areas where the law allows what many would regard as cruel or inhumane, as for example, in field sports, in the way animals are used for food, and in scientific experiments on live animals, sometimes for medical research, but often in safety tests on cosmetics. Even if non-human animals are not regarded as persons, there may be a case for extending their moral rights, without the corollary that they must also have moral obligations.

If the only criterion for personhood or rights was sentience, there would be a strong case for regarding non-human animals as persons possessing rights. This is not a view that can easily be reconciled with what we have argued about divine or human personhood. Animal welfare is not dependent, however, on extending personhood in this way. The issue of animal rights is somewhat different. In discussing the justification of rights we have already referred to the Reformed theological tradition, which emphasises God's rights as the basis of all rights. Although this seems to confer rights on God rather than on creation, and to emphasize the duties of creatures towards God, consideration should be given to A. Linzey's support for what he calls '*theos*-rights' as a basis for giving the interests of non-human animals a more significant voice in moral debate about animal welfare. It is not claimed that human and non-humans have identical interests or rights. Non-human animals depend on humans to put their case. They cannot speak, nor do they have moral obligations. But they have '*theos*-rights', rights given them by God, says Linzey.

In that rights language has traditionally been about funda-mental *human* claims and liberties, it may be confusing to talk of '*theos*-rights', although theologically it may be true that all rights depend on God's creative moral power. Linzey's points about divine generosity in creation and about human responsi-bility to be considerate towards animals, particularly in terms of their defencelessness and dependence on human power, can be taken account of by stressing the need for humans to treat animals well and to reassess what this means in respect of field sports, scientific experiments and food production. There is little doubt, in our mind, that there has been a great lack of sensitivity in these areas, and that theology has been complacent in assuming that humans have virtually unlimited power to manipulate and use animals for human profit. There is no theological mandate for humans to use or exploit God's creation solely for human benefit, as we shall see in chapter 15. Animals have their own interests, and, although these may sometimes be in conflict with human interests, they should not be ignored. *Theos*-rights may not be the most helpful terminology, however, for pressing the case of defenceless creatures. It may be more positive to strengthen legislation which supports and protects animal welfare, while simultaneously providing better education and information about animal welfare. Public protests about live animal exports from the UK, for example, indicate growing public concern about the failure of present legislation to protect sheep and calves that are transported long distances without adequate lairage, food or water. Industrialised food-production methods that involve cruelty or inhumane treatment (e.g. battery cages that are so small that hens have no room to move around) should be replaced by better animal husbandry, leading veterinarians have argued. On balance, therefore, there seem to be better alternative ways of responding to animal welfare than by introducing *theos*-rights. There is, however, one important respect in which Passmore seems to be mistaken and which would support Linzey's case: the nature of moral community. This need not be limited to community of equals. Passmore grants ecological community, but argues that a strict moral interpretation would require animals to assume moral obligations which they are incapable of. It can, however, be argued that ecological community by itself requires human responsibilities to non-human animals and thus confers something akin to animal rights, even if rights language is not extended because it requires humans to present their case.[56] It should be clear, however, that a Christian view, which is based on convictions about creation and the future transformation and liberation of all creation, is bound to take animal welfare and animal liberation seriously. Bearing in mind that in many cases the process of transformation and liberation will have begun with an act or word of forgiveness, we turn next to the integrity and transformation of creation.

# CHAPTER 15

# *The integrity and transformation of creation*

One of the underlying themes in our discussion of personhood has been its consequence in a communicative ethic which recognises the importance of relationships and difference as well as of universality and reason. Unless relationality can be extended to the whole of creation, however, an ethic which emphasised personhood would do little to alleviate our environmental and ecological problems. The intention of this chapter, therefore, is to illustrate how a Christian communicative ethic holds together the human and the non-human, the origin and the end of creation, suffering and glory, beckoning to a transformation of all things in Christ.

In considering the implications of personhood for a Christian ethic, we have referred to love of neighbour/enemy, forgiveness and rights/responsibilities. There are also ecological consequences. God's relation to the world as creator matters greatly both to God and the world. Human beings are part of a vast eco-system of incredible beauty and great intricacy which includes all living creatures, all plants, flowers and trees, all rocks, soil, water and air. It has become clear, however, that our planet is in deep trouble. The massive impact of modern technology on all forms of life is being experienced in traditional as well as so-called advanced industrial societies. Ecological pollution is perhaps the clearest sign of this impact.

Although there is some disagreement about details and about the policies needed to effect change, the scientific community, along with others, has voiced its concern about the problems of population growth, land, sea and air pollution, the over-rapid use of non-renewable energy resources, the destruction of the rain forests, the irreparable loss of wildlife species, the occurrence of pesticides in the food chain, the safe storage of toxic and nuclear waste, the thinning of the ozone layer and climatic changes triggered by material human developments. Citizens of the industrial world are beginning to recognise that they (and their children) may be faced with the choice of planetary destruction or changing their way of life.

Part of the problem is that nation states and multinationals are not yet persuaded that exploitation of the biosphere for short-term advantage is a form of suicide. Even among those who are aware of the issues, many have persuaded themselves that all that is needed to resolve the problems thrown up by technology and science is more science and technology. The strategic importance of human purpose and control and human values is overlooked. It is still frequently assumed that the biosphere is *a resource for us*.

It is frequently alleged that the Christian tradition, through its understanding of creation, is partly, if not largely, responsible for the present situation, because it has encouraged the development of a science which has tried to dominate nature, first by subjecting it to purely rational and often mechanistic explanation, and secondly by its tendency to exploit that understanding for human profit, without consideration of the wider effects of its interventions.

In 1966, Lynn White drew attention to 'the historical roots of our ecologic crisis'.[1] He pointed out that human beings have often been 'a dynamic element in environmental change'. Even the landscape is not the work of unaided nature. 'Our ecologic crisis is the product of an emerging, entirely novel, democratic culture.'[2] When we examine the presuppositions of our culture, however, we find that the roots of Western science lie in the Middle Ages. 'Man and nature are two things and man is master.' Medieval man was conditioned by 'the victory of Christianity over paganism'. 'Christianity, in absolute contrast to ancient paganism and Asia's religions (except perhaps Zoroastrianism), not only established a dualism of man and nature but also insisted that it is God's will that man exploit nature for his proper ends.'[3] White is careful to point out that it is not easy to disentangle human motives and that 'Christianity is a complex faith', embracing many forms of devotion and religious-ethical practice,[4] but Christianity is clearly implicated in the development of Western science. Although there have been alternative Christian traditions (e.g. the tradition of St Francis of Assissi), they have not received the same attention and consideration.[5] There are signs, however, that this is slowly beginning to change.

Our study has emphasised the significance of the interaction of divine and human personhood for a Christian ethic. The implication of White's view is that the continued influence of the 'dominion' tradition of Genesis i. 27f is a large part of the ecological problem today. It has to be admitted that there is more than a grain of truth in the accusation. Writing in 1992, Paul Santmire argues that theologians who champion responsible stewardship are still reluctant to let go of the dominion tradition because of its scriptural basis. The intrinsic value of nature is either denied or, if affirmed, affirmed simultaneously with the conflicting dominion tradition.[6]

We have already referred to the debate and the literature about Genesis i. 27f.[7] From the point of view of personhood and its ethical implications, what is needed is an indication of how personhood can cope with ecological issues which seem, at first sight, to challenge a Christian understanding of creation and thereby cast doubt on the value of any interactive view of divine and human personhood. In its original context, the 'dominion' tradition emphasises human responsibility to care for God's creation. The relationship of God, humanity and the animal and plant kingdoms is strongly inscribed, but the divine–human relationship remains special. Does this presuppose a hierarchy of relationships? Can it, should it, be given a less hierarchical note, emphasising participation and partnership?

Various responses are possible. One is to argue that, as God and humanity are related, so are humanity and the rest of creation. But, unless the radical distinction of God and humanity is dissolved and the transcendence of God minimised, humanity retains a hierarchical prominence in relation to the rest of creation, and this is alleged to be at the root of the problem. Another, more satisfactory, response, is to argue that, although the original tradition does contain elements of a hierarchical pattern, it was significantly different from the Graeco-Roman view which emphasised 'man as the measure of all things'. Moreover, there were elements of genuine partnership in the tradition: 'it is not good for '*adam* to be alone' (Genesis i.).[8]

The question then becomes one of how best to interpret this tradition for today. Santmire argues that 'what is needed is a new paradigm for Reformation theology, not a completely new theology'.[9] He seeks to elicit such a paradigm from a combination of what he calls the overwhelming mountain experience and tradition with its metaphor of ascent, and the tradition of promised land and fertility with its metaphor of fecundity. He regards the mountain tradition as spiritual–ascetic, the promised land tradition as ecological. 'The "new" ecological paradigm, then, is an itinerary of the mind that begins with the experience of fecundity and moves towards a fulfilling experience of overflowing earthly blessings' (p. 68).

The metaphors are complex. The mountain tradition is much more than a metaphor for spiritual ascent in ancient Israel. It is associated with the giving of the Law; it is also the mythic mountain of Canaanite/Jebusite tradition, which links Jerusalem with the seat of the king of righteousness and the renewal of the Law, and eventually with the presence of God in the new Jerusalem (cf. Revelations xxi. 3) and a renewed earth in which death no longer has dominion (cf. Isaiah xxiv.). In Isaiah ii. 2–4, the prophet pictures the nations of the world streaming to God's holy mountain, Zion, 'that he may teach us his ways'. God will arbitrate in the disputes of the nations (Northern Ireland, Bosnia, Israel, Chechnya, Tibet, Rwanda etc.) 'and they shall beat their swords into ploughshares'. More than spiritual ascent is involved. Social justice and international relations are also part of the equation. Why, then, should spiritual ascent be emphasised? And how does spiritual ascent function as a new paradigm? Something similar might also be said about the blessing of the promised land, which not only is about milk and honey, but is linked with the blessing of countless progeny, and, more importantly, the blessing of God's presence. How does this overcome the problem of the dominion tradition in Genesis i. 27f. and the divine command to be fruitful and multiply? The reference to spiritual ascent and divine blessing is not meant to distract us from the very real practical problems and disputes of principle: what should be the nature and limit of human intervention in the so-called natural world? Some of Santmire's later comments begin to point in the direction of the arguments we have advanced for a communicative ethic. He describes the originating divine covenant as 'God's resolve to communicate God's infinite life to interrelated and interdependent communities of finite beings in fitting ways and to enter into communion appropriately with every community of finite being mediated by the eternal Logos of God and energised by the eternal Spirit of God, in order to manifest the divine glory through a universal history, which God wills to bring to its completion when the time is right.'[10] The emphasis on community and future fulfilment seems to capture the right notes for a Christian ecology based on the integrity and transformation of creation. The 'integrity of creation' is the phrase chosen by the World Council of Churches to redress the balance of previous creation-dominion theology and to give expression to the fact that creation is not simply a resource for humanity. It has its own dignity. There has to be respect for nature as well as respect for persons. Cruelty to animals, for instance, is wrong not simply because it disfigures the human beings who perpetrate it or is counter-productive in utilitarian terms. It is wrong because it damages the integrity of creation and infringes that communion which includes both human and non-human animals, plants and trees, rocks, soil, water and air.

What, then, does the integrity of creation involve? J. Cobb has urged that ecological theology should not accept the restrictions of Kantian anthropocentrism which he finds in Metz's preoccupation with history (at the expense of nature).[11] He has also urged that we should recognise that 'limits' are not simply deficiencies, but may be judgements about what is possible and appropriate, since the juggernaut of industrial 'development' is not the answer to the problems of the 'undeveloped' world. More recently he has written that 'if the church is truly concerned with eco-justice, or with peace, justice and the integrity of creation, it cannot continue to leave unchallenged economic thinking based on assumptions it rejects'.[12] These assumptions are the assumptions of anthropocentrism, dualism and individualism. Anthropocentrism means that 'the non-human world has value only as it is valued by human beings. This value is measured by the price someone will pay.' We might illustrate this by saying that when water is relatively unpolluted and freely available, it is cheap. But when clean water becomes scarce, then those who have money are prepared to pay more for it, although they themselves may be the biggest polluters of the water and a much simpler remedy would be to desist from polluting the water supply! Dualism in this context means that instead of recognising the true nature of scarce resources, human beings regard the biosphere, and particularly land, as nothing more than a commodity to be bought and sold. Capital is regarded as a substitute for natural resources, and, since capital can be artificially extended, there need be no limits to resources or growth. Individualism has similar harmful consequences, since it is made to seem that the goal of the economy is 'to increase the total value of goods consumed with value determined by price', even when the price includes a mobile work-force, which results in the loss of stable communities. In a similar vein, J. Zizioulas has argued that an individualistic approach to creation cannot do justice to the insight that personhood is not opposed to nature but related to it.[13]

We have referred to Cobb's view that concentration on history as the arena of God's self-revelation may perpetuate a Kantian anthropocentrism. In fact, Christian theology at its best holds nature and history, creation and resurrection together. In chapter 12 we noted that the early church communities saw themselves as embodiments of the crucified and risen Christ. They had been baptised into His death and resurrection, and their new life was empowered by the Holy Spirit. It is significant that Paul brings these themes together in a passage of great emotional power in Romans viii. Following the magnificent opening ('There is now, therefore, no condemnation for those who are in Christ Jesus'), Paul considers what such freedom means. It is a life in the Spirit, not in the flesh. Verse 11 sets the seal on a complex discussion of spirit/flesh, life/death. 'If the Spirit of him who raised Jesus from the dead dwells in you, he who raised Christ Jesus from the dead will give life to your mortal bodies also, through his Spirit which dwells in you.'

On this basis Christians are to live a new life: not a life of slavery but as members of God's family. Their relationship with God is to be marked by the same intimate conversation and vocabulary used in prayer by Jesus himself – 'Abba, father' – and taught to the disciples, 'Father, thy kingdom come . . .' It is the Spirit who inspires such deep longing and prayer, confirming them in God's family. Paul's thought becomes ecstatic, without losing coherence or control and without forgetting the Christian's creaturely finitude: 'if children of God, then heirs of God, fellow heirs with Christ – provided we share in his suffering'. This suffering, however, is only the prelude to an even greater glory.

At this point Paul extends his thinking to include the whole of creation, which is waiting with eager longing for the revelation of God's children. Humanity and creation together will be set free. It is a time of bondage and struggle, even for those who have the first-fruits of the Spirit, but when we are finally adopted into God's family and our bodies redeemed, then the rest of creation also will be set free to experience the same. This transformation is still in the future, but Paul is confident that what has already happened is sufficient to guarantee that the time of fulfilment will soon arrive: 'Christ is the first born of many brethren.' For this reason the Christian has nothing to fear. Nothing in the world can ever separate us from the love of God in Christ.

This 'Pauline vision of intimate solidarity between humanity and creation', in Romans viii. 19–22, does not resolve our ecological crisis.[14] It does not answer all the theological and ethical questions and issues which are being raised by ecology. It is a religious vision in which, for a brief moment, we catch a

glimpse of what Paul fervently looks forward to: the transformation of all things in Christ. This solidarity of humanity
and creation may be interpeted as each being necessary for the
salvation of the other. There is a solidarity both in sin and
redemption. This does not mean that nature can be sinful. It
would be a mistake to think of human disobedience making
rivers and mountains sinful, but human sin has prevented
creation from fulfilling its purposes, including that of revealing
the creator to humanity. Against a background of apocalyptic
and the Flood tradition, 'the intrinsic and inseparable unity of
humanity and creation in the redemptive glory of God' stands
out clearly.[15] In the liberation of humanity creation is also
transformed. This transformation is made possible by the
resurrection of Christ, which is the beginning of a new creation.
'For Paul the "bodily" character of the resurrection manifests
the resurrection as an event that not only occurs in time but
also signals the "bodily" ontological transformation of the
created order in the kingdom of God.'[16] Here is further
confirmation that the timeless disembodied deity of Greek
philosophy is not the living Lord revealed in the narratives of
the early church. We are bound to ask, however, whether Paul's
rhetoric can withstand the searching criticism of modern
questioning. How far does Paul's vision take us? Are we still left
with a transcendent God and a hierarchical anthropology, in
which humanity is the priest of creation, which some see as the
root of the problem?[17]

Theological response to the ecological crisis has been extremely varied. There are those (e.g. some New Age cults) who
virtually deify nature; there are others who still regard humankind as the leading shoot of creation with the responsibility to
subdue recalcitrant nature. There are others, but they do not
normally offer any theological justification for their attitude,
who not only wish to build on every wilderness, but feel no
compunction about plundering the planet and polluting land,
air and water, provided it brings temporary material advantage.
The majority of Christians, to judge by a flood of publications
and other media expressions, belong to none of these groups.
They have a deep unease about the scale of human interven-

tion and sustainability of economic policies in the light of information emanating from scientific studies of the environment. They are practically involved in small-scale conservation measures, such as recycling, energy conservation and what might be called matters of lifestyle (including vegetarianism). But they are uncertain about the theological interpretation of inherited tradition. Some regard the biblical text as their primary authority. Others see the issue more widely, involving, not only biblical interpretation, but the whole gamut of human reason and experience expressed in science, philosophy, theology, ethics and politics. Among the predominantly theological responses, much of the discussion has revolved round the transcendence and immanence of God, the significance of *creatio ex nihilo* and what it means to be created, and the possibility of cosmic redemption. Dualisms which favour rationality and immateriality are increasingly rejected; anthropocentrism which privileges only a section of the biosphere, and conceptions of deity which emphasise sovereign transcendence or lack of involvement in the world are more and more likely to be regarded as irrelevant and insensitive. Considerable store has been placed by some on Trinitarian theologies, in which intra-divine relations are hailed as the model for all non-exploitative relationships.

There are growing signs, however, that further reflection is provoking revision and reconsideration of positions rejected in the first flush of heightened ecological awareness.[18] What is 'nature'? Can nature be restored? Is 'nature' inseparable from human 'culture'? Is there a romantic drift in all language about nature? Is it not humanity that is responsible for the awful choices which may have to be made? This is not to say that theological speculation and imagination have dried up. How to (re)conceive God's relationship with creation has only just begun!

Even a rudimentary knowledge of planetary life indicates its complexity. It is easy to overlook obvious truths. 'Humans did not create nature; we remain largely (and dismally) ignorant of nature's constitution and dynamics; we remain powerless to alter many (but not all) of nature's basic processes, and the

attempt to preserve nature may well disturb ecological processes anyway. (Canada was an ice sheet only 15,000 years
ago.)'[19] The Christian has to work within the limits of what is
known, but is constrained by more than considerations of self-
interest and prudence to develop and practise an ethic of
environmental responsibility related to belief in God's creative
goodness and design. There are good reasons, as we have seen,
for thinking that, despite the element of truth in the dominion
tradition, it is its combination with the more humanistic Greek
tradition of 'man as the measure of all things' which is
responsible for its decline into despotism.[20] In the light of all
this, how, if at all, does our reading of personhood (divine and
human) and its ethical implications influence our understanding of the integrity and transformation of creation?

If persons are essentially related to other persons, and
community is important, this will steer the emphasis from the
individualistic aspect towards the community without lessening
individual responsibility.[21] Moreover, persons stand in relationship, not only to other persons, but to all living creatures. For
Christians, the whole biotic community in all its diversity is
created by God. And the process of creation is dynamic and
ongoing. Whatever is, is kept in being by God's creative goodness and power. It is perhaps because of this that many
Christians feel under pressure to go further and not only to
recognise the intrinsic value of everything created, but to move
towards a deep ecology view which presupposes a fundamental
unity (and equality?) of everything included in earth's community of life.[22] This is not a view, however, which Christians can
contemplate lightly, since it conflicts with other basic cosmolo-
gical beliefs and Christian understanding of God as Creator
and Redeemer. It is not necessary to regard non-human
animals as moral agents or persons in order to accept that they
have rights (e.g. not to be tortured or treated with cruelty, and
many would say, not to be killed for food). There is an
overwhelming case for Christians to widen the circle of ethical
concern to include the whole of creation. There is nothing in
scripture that forbids this and a great deal that supports it. The
unhappy ambiguity of Christian tradition on the issue is a

matter for regret, but not something that should prevent us from recognising the fundamental error in thinking of non-human animals as merely a resource for humans. The readings of personhood examined in our study confirm rather than overturn this. In Paul's vision, creation and humanity are so closely related that their ultimate salvation is spoken of in the same breath and understood as interdependent. This must be a further element in moving a Christian environmental ethic towards deep care and concern for the whole of creation and helping to break down the barriers of privilege and unconcern which have resulted in enormous waste, injustice and distress.

Such an ethic will still be faced with hard decisions. The rights and interests of particular groups within the biotic community will continue to lead to areas of dissent and even conflict. How to preserve the planet from further degradation is a practical and ethical task that will increasingly occupy all of us. The responsibility to hand on to future generations a creation that is 'good, very good' will require Christians to extend the love command to a much wider circle than previously thought necessary or possible. 'Rooted and grounded in love' (Ephesians iii. 17), Christians are called to develop their understanding of God's love for all creation and to embody it. Concern for the good of all creation need not become a pious but impractical hope or a counsel of despair. It is significant that once scientists had discovered the hole in the ozone layer, measures to remedy the situation were undertaken and seem to be having some effect. It is not the case that individuals and elected governments can do nothing about global issues. Christians are not alone in their ethical concerns, and some of their convictions are also shared by others. They have much to learn from others who have different experiences and views. A communicative ethic of persons in community will encourage dialogue across our divisions without stifling 'qualified' particular visions of what is good. We have not suggested that the practical steps will be obvious or easy, particularly when we cannot agree where the roots of particular problems lie. But is there any better way?

The understanding of personhood we have advocated does

not imply either a doomsday scenario or paradise of self-fulfilment. The transformation of creation is a costly process rooted in God's self-giving in creation, incarnation and atonement. Human beings are invited to share in that process by responding to God's love and living in accordance with God's will. 'Live simply, that others may simply live' has become a rule of life for many Christians.

But how, it might be asked, can creation be transformed when hundreds of thousands still die from starvation and disease each year? Or when the number of abortions worldwide rises inexorably? And how should a Christian ethic respond to the intellectual problems posed by Parfit and Tooley in terms of the moral standing of future generations and potential persons?

Eschatological hope and longing are not without effect on how we live now. A Christian ethic supports aid and relief (medicine, food, agriculture, education, employment) through government agencies and charities where they are needed most and where there are Christian communities involved. Clearly the Christian church represents only a small part of the total picture, but, for Christians, such considerations find a permanent place in their thinking and giving. It is sometimes objected that the missionary aid enterprise and subsequent partnerships have exacerbated rather than relieved the problem, which is largely political and related to the imbalance of power and trade between First and Third World countries. It is for this reason that liberation political theology has argued for a different approach to economic and social development. From a different quarter (e.g. Garret Hardin and Paul Ehrlich)[23] it has been argued that aid now means ruin later. World resources are limited and population numbers must be limited accordingly to prevent global famine and ruin. A lifeboat ethic is called for. 'Are we justified in doing good when the foreseeable consequences are evil?' Today's neo-Malthusian objections make a number of unjustified assumptions about resources, the future growth of population and the nature of human community. Earth's resources *are* finite, but that does not justify comparing the earth with the much more limited lifeboat. Hardin assumes that population growth is the chief problem and fails to devote sufficient analysis to other relevant issues (e.g. the consumption of resources by developed countries; the slowdown of population growth associated with rising living standards in developing countries; the imbalance of power in world trade). His suggestion that 'mutually agreed coercion' will be needed to curtail population growth fails to address the moral and practical issues with sufficient consideration for all the interests involved, although it has undoubtedly provoked debate.

It would be helpful to separate the issue of demographics and population policy at government level both from family planning and parental choice and from conceptual issues connected with the status of future and potential people and our obligations to future generations. Governments are entitled, and indeed ought, to estimate demographic trends as accurately as they can. They may also legitimately try to influence people's reproductive choices by education, tax incentives and social planning. The sort of eugenic policies tried (and abandoned) in Singapore (1984)[24] would clearly not be acceptable in most democracies and would certainly not find support in a Christian ethic. Sadly Christians are divided about family planning, but there seems no good reason why, in this area, parental choice should be restricted by an interpretation of 'natural law' which ties the reproductive and unitive aspects of sexual intercourse between husband and wife so closely that contraceptive methods other than the 'safe period' are not allowed. It seems likely, however, that if the sort of dialogue envisaged in a communicative ethic were developed, most Christian parents would regard this area of sexual ethics as one where parents should be encouraged to develop their own responsible decisions without too much pressure from church authorities.

Abortion raises more serious and contentious issues. The status of the foetus is crucial. Our discussion of 'personhood', however, has indicated that 'personhood' is not a purely factual question. It has also pointed to the importance of not radically separating 'person' and 'human being'. A Christian ethic which takes account of personhood, we have argued, will do so by its understanding of the values involved in being and becoming human. The foetus is clearly 'human' in a biological sense from conception, and that alone should afford the foetus a considerable measure of protection. Our argument offers little support, however, to anti-abortionists, who stake everything on the personhood of the foetus and insist that this particular value should be conserved above every other value. It is one of the tragedies of present debates about abortion, which cannot be settled by arguments about the ontological status of the foetus, that the values associated with being and becoming human (embodied, responsible, reflective self-determination in community with others) are ignored or flouted. Hauerwas' valuable emphasis on the other-regarding values that Christians brought to the care of infants and family life can and should be brought into closer relationship with women's rights to self-determination.

There are other conceptual issues associated with the status of future people and future generations which go beyond the limits of the present study. Parfit's proposal that the conceptual issues are best clarified impersonally has been strongly challenged.[25] Whether potential people should be included in the moral community (as an impersonal view would favour) or whether all genethical choices should be related only to existing people, as those who favour a person-affecting view tend to argue, is an unresolved issue. D. Heyd's *Genethics*, which makes use of the Genesis narrative of creation to make a philosophical rather than a religious point, suggests that we should in these situations consider ourselves as divine creators *ex nihilo*. Our own discussion of personhood and the *imago dei* theme does not exalt human choice to the same degree as Heyd. In a Christian ethic, the *imago dei* theme acts as a constraint as well as a support. There is no sense in which Christians can be their own gods. To usurp divine powers was, and is, *'adam's* temptation. There will continue to be different explorations of Christian narrative ethics, but our discussion suggests that central to theological cum ethical interpretation of what it means to be a person (human) will be the Christian message of creation and salvation through Jesus Christ.

# Conclusion

The ideas and arguments assembled and analysed throughout our study form part of an attempt to construct a reading of personhood that adequately reflects its past and is also able to respond to the creative changes that are taking place in a variety of disciplines that have an interest in personhood. The inquiry we have pursued suggests that personhood has a depth and complexity that is not always adequately represented even in those definitions and arguments which make personhood central to ethical debate, particularly in relation to the boundaries of the beginning and end of life (cf. abortion and euthanasia) or in relation to the boundaries between human and non-human (cf. animal welfare) where in both cases the status and rights of the (moral) subject are in question. A repositioning of personhood, we argued, is called for in ethical contexts to do justice to the social dimension of personhood. This would take account of what happened in previous centuries in response to social, cultural and religious movements of ideas, and would include reconsideration of the significance of Christian traditions of personhood. Although there may be a certain attraction in the idea that 'person' as a purely moral term could fulfil a useful role in moral argument, our examination of the varied historical usage indicates that contemporary 'moral personhood' reflects a partial usage selected for a limited normative role.

Because personhood is not a concept that we can neatly tie to a particular period or author or consider with total objectivity, and its normative features invade our own self-understanding and discourse about ourselves, there is a natural tendency for each group of specialists, philosophers of mind, ethicists, theologians and social theorists to regard their own contributions as determinative of the main issues. Straying across academic boundaries is always a dangerous exercise, but in the case of personhood it is a risk we have judged necessary. Our particular interest is both ethical and theological. We analysed the tangled roots of personhood and argued that an account of personhood that gives more emphasis to embodied persons in community without disparaging reason is preferable, ethically and theologically, to a view which emphasises chiefly rationality. In an open society characterised by social freedom (not the same as maximum choice for each individual), religious and secular visions will clearly compete. A religiously based interpretation of personhood still has a great deal to offer.

Divine personhood may not resonate very strongly in the post-modern world, and may be regarded as irrelevant by agnostics and non-theists, but the concept brings with it a long and interesting history. For Christians, the concept of personhood has particular significance through its association with Christological and Trinitarian debate. Our analysis underlined the problems encountered in attempts to argue directly from the immanent Trinity to human relationships, but pointed positively to the importance of embodied relationships, for which divine personhood, expressed in the economic Trinity in terms of personhood rather than substance, is both a significant analogy and an experienced reality in Christian history. As long as God is thought of as timeless and incapable of embodiment, however, there are real obstacles to the analogy between divine and human personhood. On the other hand, once it is seen that Greek philosophical categories contributed largely to the way in which God's immutability and impassibility have been traditionally understood and that these categories may be revised, the way is open to a restatement of God's personhood in a way which allows for a significant relationship between divine and human personhood. By inflating human personhood, Enlightenment thinkers in effect transferred some of the distinction and honour associated with divine personhood to human beings. Failure to notice this contributes to the inflated value subsequently attached to whatever attributes are regarded as constitutive of personhood. Sometimes rationality is stressed (as in Kant); at other times relationships assume greater significance (as in Feuerbach). Divine personhood has links with both rationality and relationality, but the roots of the concept appear to lie in discourse and relationships. This suggests that there has been too much emphasis on individuality and rationality in the concept of person often held in modern philosophy.

In seeking to relate this broader view to a Christian ethic, we examined the fruitful role of narrative, but resisted any sharp division between a rational, universal ethic and a 'qualified', Christian ethic. To adopt a transport analogy, a rational, universal ethic is like a transport system, the qualified religious ethic is like a particular vehicle. Good communications require both. A combination of a narrative ethic with a modified version of Habermas' discourse ethic along the lines proposed by Benhabib, we argued, could offer a more useful model, if it can be made compatible with an understanding of revelation and the narrative of Christian scripture. From the New Testament we drew on the teaching about love of neighbour/enemy for such a communicative ethic, and indicated the importance of community for this ethic. This process also demonstrated how, for Christians, the 'ethical' is constantly being stretched by their attachment to Jesus as the embodiment of God.

The application of personhood in a Christian ethic, although it takes its bearings from divine personhood, does not proceed directly from a model of inner divine relationships but via creation and theological anthropology. What it means to be human cannot be decided without reference, in other words, to a theological understanding of relevant disciplines which take account of the physical, mental, social and spiritual aspects of human life. To be human has both genetic and environmental dimensions. Particularly important is the genesis and growth of human sociality and values. The process of becoming more human (not just more civilised or more technically competent) is impossible without the help of others. It requires community of mind, heart and action. 'Not only is community necessary for self-understanding, agency, and the overcoming of way-wardness, but a certain way of acting and interpreting is necessary for community.'[1] To be human is more than an endowment of birth; it is a calling which begins in infancy and develops into the tapestry of a whole life. It cannot be reduced to moral rules or theories, but, because morality is so important and pervasive in 'becoming human', morality forms an important part of personhood. For the Christian the direction and details of the moral life are strongly influenced by an understanding of God's character as creative and redemptive love, and by attachment to Christ and guidance by His Spirit.

That both forgiveness and human rights are significant aspects of such an ethic may confirm that a Christian ethic is right to resist the limitations of a Kantian view of morality and the even greater limitations of utilitarianism. Nevertheless, a Christian ethic which pushes beyond them has to engage with them and recognise that, in so far as they meet the criteria of impartial ethical reflection, they are still forces to be reckoned with.

We drew attention to the effect of this understanding on a Christian's response to the use of personhood in discussions about abortion and animal rights. Despite the mainly theoretical orientation of our study, certain principles are clear. The attempted resolution of the abortion debate by Tooley and Singer, in terms of a precise but restricted understanding of personhood, is clearly inadequate. Equally clearly, attempts to move directly from 'the foetus is a (potential) person created by God', to the exclusion of abortion on principle, are not convincing when they ignore the context or operate with a simplistic understanding of ethical argument. The communicative ethic for which we have argued will be based on Christian narrative and will therefore include the unborn child in God's family. It will also take account of the whole context of the impending birth, including the other lives involved, and seek to arrive in faith at a judgement which is in harmony with what we know about God's creating and redeeming activity in Christ. It will express confidence in God's ability to sustain and direct those who put their trust in Him and His empowering

Spirit. The study offers no support to those who wish to argue that the Christian faith is committed to one particular outcome in every case where abortion is considered as an appropriate response to human suffering (e.g. in the case of a severely damaged foetus).

On the question of animal liberation, the study offers some support to those who argue that animals should be included in the moral community without being regarded as persons. In this instance, Singer's defence of animal welfare is welcomed, but for other reasons than those he gives. The non-human animal creation has value for the Christian both in its own right and as part of God's creation, like humanity. That non-human animals and humanity are together part of God's creation does not, however, make them identical, or give humanity the right to exploit animals. Non-human animals are not simply a resource for humanity (see chapter 15). Created together, we shall be saved together (cf. Romans viii. 21). We considered the very real ethical problems now apparent in the relation of humanity and the natural environment, and noted that a revised view of personhood is also applicable in this debate and compatible with a thoughtful ecological approach.

Lastly, there is a significant normative direction indicated by the study as a whole, and that is the way in which personhood is closely connected with our understanding of community and sociality and issues of social ethics. These words are being written in January 1995 on the fiftieth anniversary of the Russian entry into Auschwitz, where over a million Jews were exterminated because they were Jews by a state which had dissolved and replaced all signs of personhood, including political freedom and equality, with an ideology of racial purity. In 1938, Marcel Mauss spoke of a concept that was still 'imprecise, delicate and fragile'. The effect of Parfit's 'person-phases', however altruistic the intention, would be to acquit those responsible by relaxing the links of moral responsibility. There is still a place for the unitary self – within a community of related persons. Since 1945, there have been countless other abuses of human rights and disfigurations of creation. A Christian ethic must be concerned, both at the meta-ethical and normative levels, with issues that profoundly affect civilisation now and into the future. It is an ethic that takes account of revelation as well as reason. Our hope is that it will contribute to the welfare and emancipation of all those 'groaning in travail together until now' in eager expectation and anticipation of the transformation of creation itself.

# *Notes*

## INTRODUCTION

1 See B. Williams, *Ethics and the Limits of Philosophy*, Fontana/Collins, 1985, p. 114.
2 Kant, *Grundlegung zur Metaphysik der Sitten*, 1785, see 428.
3 H. T. Engelhardt, *The Foundations of Bio-ethics*, Oxford University Press, 1986, p. 104.
4 J. Zizioulas, *Being as Communion*, Darton, Longman & Todd, 1985, pp. 36 and 43. For more details see chapter 1 of *Being as Communion*.


## PART 1 'PERSON' IN CONTEMPORARY ETHICS

### I 'UNE CATÉGORIE DE L'ESPRIT HUMAIN: LA NOTION DE PERSONNE'

1 Cf. H. G. Kippenberg,et al. (eds.), *Concepts of Person in Religion & Thought*, Mouton, New York, 1990, p. 29 'When a philosopher tries to explain what "person" really is, he at the same time uncovers something of the ideological foundations of our society.' It is problematic for Oosten whether a concept of person derived from 'enlightened Christian humanism, liberalism and individualism' (p. 31) can be applied to ideas of self and society found in other cultures. Awareness of ideological context, however, can be used to illuminate some of the philosophical and ethical disputes about 'persons'. One of the arguments of this book is that the Christian faith does make a difference to how one understands 'person', and this affects the use of the concept in ethical contexts.
2 In *Concepts of Person in Religion & Thought*, p. 10f., Hubbeling offers an historical overview similar to that of Mauss, but from a more philosophical standpoint. He selects four systematically recurring features which he regards as key elements in a conceptual map of personhood: self-consciousness (or, better, ego-consciousness,

Notes to pages 13-19

since plants and animals may have a form of consciousness but not ego-consciousness since they cannot use the language of 'I' and 'self'); human will; aesthetic and moral values; relationship to God and others. Since different thinkers make different use of these features, there are many different, partially overlapping concepts of person. Personal identity constitutes a somewhat different issue, but is related to the previous characteristics in so far as it deals with what constitutes a person (e.g. identity may be regarded as being constituted by (i) body; (ii) brain; (iii) memory–consciousness; (iv) ego–will; (v) communications with others). (i)–(v) are, in effect, other ways of referring to the key features of personhood.

3 See *Journal of the Royal Anthropological Institute* 68, 1938, pp. 263–81. A translation into English can be found in M. Mauss, *Sociology and Psychology*, Routledge and Kegan Paul, 1979. For a revised translation see *The Category of the Person*, ed. M. Carrithers et al., Cambridge University Press, 1985.

4 M. Carrithers, ibid., p. 1.

5 Ibid., p. 2.

6 Ibid., p. 14.

7 Ibid., p. 17.

8 Ibid., p. 18.

9 Ibid., p. 19.

10 S. Schlossmann, *Persona und prosopon im Recht und im Christlichen Dogma*, Kiel, 1906.

11 Cf. Cicero, *De Officiis*, 1. 34 ('magistratus gerit personam civitatis').

12 Mauss, *Sociology and Psychology*, p. 20.

13 Ibid., p. 22.

14 The situation may be beginning to change; see the publication of the text referred to in n. 16 below and *Concepts of Person in Religion & Thought*, ed. H. G. Kippenberg et al. C. Taylor's *Sources of the Self* represents the most significant attempt to locate this area of human thought in the context of Western philosophy and social change. See also the following in the bibliography: P. F. Strawson; B. Williams; D. C. Dennett; D. Wiggins; A. Rorty; M. Tooley; D. Parfit.

15 Cf. n. 29 below.

16 M. Carrithers, S. Collins and S. Lukes (eds.), *The Category of the Person*, Cambridge University Press, 1985.

17 See S. Collins, 'Categories, Concepts or Predicaments' in M. Carrithers, ibid., p. 48.

18 Ibid., p. 58, citing Soltau, *French Political Thought in the 18th Century*, p. 307. NB Soltau's equation of consciousness and person.

19 Ibid., p. 60, citing Hamelin, *Le Systeme de Renouvier*, p. 159.
20 Ibid., pp. 60–1, citing Hamelin, p. 160.
21 Ibid., p. 58.
22 Ibid., p. 60.
23 See S. Lukes and J. Lukes, 'Durkheim's "Individualism and the Intellectuals",' in *Political Studies* 17, 1969, p. 26.
24 Ibid., p. 30.
25 M. Carrithers et al. (ed.), *Category of the Person*, p. 76.
26 Ibid., p. 236.
27 Ibid., p. 249.
28 There is a more relativistic, sociologically determined view of person in Mauss' essay of 1929 ('L'âme, le nom et la personne. Intervention à la suite d'une communication de L. Lévi-Bruhl: 'L'âme primitive' in *Œuvres* II, pp. 131–5) in which he emphasises the socially determined role aspect of persons which clearly varies from culture to culture. In the lecture of 1938 there is a much clearer emphasis on self-consciousness as the culmination of social ideas of personhood. There is an equally clear refusal to examine Hegelian and later developments, whether from a belief that these were simply variations on Fichte's bold declaration or, as seems more likely, because Mauss was not concerned primarily with philosophical debate but with anthropology and morality. In this sense, Fichte represented for Mauss a high point of development, which he regarded as endangered by modern society. The specific nature of these dangers is not discussed. In 1798, Fichte argued that 'God could not be thought of as a "person" without inner contradiction' on the ground that personhood required a 'thou' over against the 'I'. God, being All, could not be a person (Cf. Schillebeeckx, *Jesus*, Collins/Fount, 1983, p. 664).
29 Ibid., p. 294 – 'Foucault deconstructs the modern subject by investigating the institutions and norms that have formed it, which include apparatuses of discipline and control, of confinement, treatment, rehabilitation and therapy.' Deconstruction of the self is at the heart of deconstructionism. Fragmentation, loss of temporal continuity and responsibility move outward into all aspects of culture from the fragmented self. Cf. K. J. Gergen, *Saturated Self*, Basic Books, 1991, p. 7. Cf. also Lauritzen, *JRE*, 1994, pp. 189–210, who contrasts Rorty's welcome for the end of any search for a single 'true self', because it encourages a variety of playful selves that can be constructed in response to changing desires and patterns of self-creation, with the very different emphasis of Charles Taylor and Ernest Wallwork, who seek a more continuous, engaged, narrative self, that is capable of making sense of a whole life in relationship with others. Cf. Rorty,

*Essays on Heidegger and others*, Cambridge University Press, 1991; C. Taylor, *The Ethics of Authenticity*, Cambridge University Press, 1991; E. Wallwork, *Psychoanalysis & Ethics*, Yale University Press, 1991.

30 M. Carrithers et al. (ed.), *The Category of the Person*, p. 276; cf. p. 279 'One of the root ideas behind some of these early interpretations [which Mauss uses] may be that one comes to full status as agent-plus by being inducted as interlocutor into some great conversation, which is alone the locus of agents-plus. To have the name, or perhaps the mask, is to be the interlocutor.'

31 Ibid.,p.278. Cf. p. 276 – 'language as the locus of disclosure is not an activity of the individual primarily, but of the language community'. Cf. *Sources of the Self*, p.35f.

32 *Sources of the Self*, pp. 305f describes and interprets these cultural shifts ('large scale transformations in common assumptions and sensibility') more fully. The interiorisation of personhood, which began with the definition of person as 'individual substance of rational nature', is now taken to include rationalism, romanticism and pietism in their various forms. Frequently concomitant and not always separable in the development of Western values have been two other movements: the affirmation of ordinary life, which was one of the motifs of the Protestant reformation and is manifested in a variety of later movements, including the growth of the empirical sciences and technology; and the rise of naturalism which begins to invade all forms of human inquiry and discourse.

33 *Sources of the Self*, p. 337.

## 2 MEANING AND CRITERIA: PERSON/HUMAN BEING

1 R. Liebe, *Zeitschrift für Theologie und Kirche* 7, 1926, p. 122: 'Gewiss das Wort ist schrecklich'. He laments the way the term is misused, but argues that the value of personal purposeful behaviour is the sole meaning of human existence.

2 Cf. *PPA* 4, 1975, pp. 202f, and especially p. 221.

3 Ibid., pp. 210f.

4 P. Foot, 'Moral Beliefs' in P. Foot, (ed.), *Theories of Ethics*, Oxford University Press, 1967; H. Putnam, *Reason, Truth and History*, Cambridge University Press, 1981, chapters 6 and 9; J. McDowell, 'Are moral requirements hypothetical imperatives?', *PAS* Supp. 52, 1978, pp. 13–29; K. Lee, *A New Basis for Moral Philosophy*, Routledge and Kegan Paul, 1985, chapter 1.9.

5 *Freedom and Reason*, Oxford University Press, 1963, p. 221.

6  *Ethics and Belief,* Sheldon, 1977, p. 79–80.

7  'Abortion and the Golden Rule', *PPA* 4, 1975, p. 221–2.

8  Hare's sharp disjunction of critical and intuitive thinking neglects interaction between them and gives the impression that intuitive thinking is really not thinking. This interpretation of Hare is supported by his attempt on p. 172 of *Freedom and Reason* to link fanaticism with intuitionism and the refusal or inability to think critically. He brings no evidence to support this view, but implies that the missing link may be related to faulty or inadequate moral education. The conclusion is assumed rather than argued for.

9  In A. Peacocke and G. Gillet (eds.), *Persons and Personality,* Blackwell, 1987, pp. 56–74.

10  Ibid., p. 73–4.

11  Cf. C. McCall, *Concepts of Person,* Avebury, 1990, pp. 174f.

12  In A. O. Rorty, (ed.), *The Identities of Persons,* University of California Press, 1976.

13  *Sameness and Substance,* Blackwell, 1980 p. 174 n. 29.

14  A. O. Rorty, (ed.), *The Identities of Persons,* p. 177.

15  Ibid., p. 193.

16  Ibid., p. 193.

17  Ibid., p. 159.

18  Ibid., p. 160.

19  'The Person as Object of Science, as Subject of Experience, and as Locus of Value' in Peacocke and Gillett (eds.), *Persons and Personality,* pp. 56–74.

20  E.g. M. Tooley in a variety of articles (see bibliography), and *Abortion and Infanticide* Oxford University Press, 1983; P. Singer, *Practical Ethics* Cambridge University Press, 1979; H. T. Engelhardt, *The Foundations of Bio-ethics,* Oxford University Press, 1986.

21  C. Gill (ed.), *The Person and the Human Mind,* Oxford University Press, 1990, p. 76, 'Still, it is worth preserving conceptual room (if we can) for the thought that there could be persons who are not biologically human.'

22  C. McCall, *Concepts of Person,* p. 178.

3 MORAL PERSONHOOD IN M. TOOLEY AND P. SINGER

1  *The Foundations of Bio-ethics,* Oxford University Press, 1986.

2  Ibid., p. 104.

3  *The Value of Life,* Routledge and Kegan Paul, 1985.

4  Ibid., p. 19. He goes on: 'If this concept of person is not accepted, another concept will be needed:

1 To enable us morally to distinguish between persons and animals, fish, plants and so on.

2 To have an account of the point at which and the reasons why the embryo or any live human tissue becomes valuable.

3 To recognise when and why human beings cease to be valuable or become less valuable than others.

4 To provide a framework that would in principle enable us to answer the question, 'are there other people in the universe?'

5 To give us an account of what it is that's so great about ourselves.'

5 *Practical Ethics*, Cambridge University Press, 1979, pp. 74–6, 97, 117–26.

6 Ibid., p. 74.

7 'Indicators of Humanhood: A Tentative Profile of Man', *The Hastings Center Report*, 2/5, 1972.

8 Singer, *Practical Ethics*, p. 97.

9 In 'The Struggle Against Speciesism', in D. Paterson and R. D. Ryder (eds.), *Animal Rights – A Symposium*, Centaur Press, 1979, p. 4 Ryder notes: 'When I promulgated the awkward word "speciesism" to describe mankind's arrogant prejudice against other species, I was not conscious that anyone else had published on the subject of animals' rights at all – indeed, at that time I felt very much alone.' In n. 8 he refers to a pamphlet, entitled 'Speciesism', which he published in 1970, and to his first public letters on the subject, *Daily Telegraph*, April/May 1969.

10 Singer, *Practical Ethics*, p. 117.

11 Ibid., pp. 117f.

12 Ibid., p. 126. Cf. *Epistle of Barnabas* (*c.* CE 130) section 19; T. Wiedemann, *Adults and Children in the Roman Empire*, Routledge, 1989 p. 36; K. R. Bradley, *Discovering the Roman Family*, Oxford University Press, 1991, p. 140; B. Rawson, (ed.), *Marriage, Divorce and Children in Ancient Rome*, p. 9.

13 R. Hursthouse, *Beginning Lives*, Blackwell, 1987. pp. 131f.

14 Ibid., pp. 157–8. Cf. N. Hoerster, 'Kindstötung und das Lebensrecht von Personen', *Analyse und Kritik* 12, 1990, pp. 226–44. Hoerster takes particular issue with Singer's attempt to blur the distinction between abortion and infanticide. He shows convincingly how Singer's restriction of infanticide to the first month exacerbates rather than alleviates practical problems.

15 J. Feinberg, (ed.), *The Problem of Abortion*, Wadsworth, 1984, pp. 51f.

16 M. Tooley, *Abortion and Infanticide*, Oxford University Press, 1983, p. 52.

17 Ibid., p. 57.

18  Ibid., p. 95.
19  Ibid., p. 95.
20  There is an interesting discussion of a metaphysical approach to the issue of a rational soul in chapter 11.4, pp. 333–47, in the course of which Tooley sets out briefly in fifteen steps an alternative view of persons. This is not followed up, however. He criticises some of the assumptions and conclusions involved in the argument that rationality results from a purely immaterial soul. He does not examine the more plausible interactionist version which envisages compatibility and relationship between mind and body-brain.
21  Ibid., p. 99.
22  L. W. Sumner, *Abortion and Moral Theory*, Princeton University Press, 1987, p. 129.
23  K. E. Goodpaster, 'On Being Morally Considerable', *JP* 75/6, 1978.
24  Sumner, *Abortion and Moral Theory*, p. 143.
25  Ibid., p. 144.
26  Ibid., p. 145.

4 PERSONAL IDENTITY AND RESPONSIBILITY IN D. PARFIT

1  'Personal Identity', *Philosophical Review* 80, 1971; 'Later Selves & Moral Principles' in A. Montefiore, (ed.), *Philosophy and Personal Relations*, Routledge and Kegan Paul, 1973.
2  *Reasons and Persons*, Oxford University Press, 1984, p. 347.
3  Ibid., pp. 443. Cf. pp. 76–7, 511 n. 44.
4  Ibid., p. 80. Cf. J. Glover, *PAS* Supp. 49, 1975.
5  *Reasons and Persons*, p. 444.
6  Ibid., p. 267.
7  *Philosophical Explanations*, Blackwell, 1980, p. 65.
8  G. Madell, *The Identity of the Self*, Edinburgh University Press, 1981, p. 35; cf. J. Habermas, *The Theory of Communicative Action*, vol. 2 Polity, 1987, pp. 103–5 for a discussion of 'I'.
9  *Identity of the Self*, p. 46.
10  Ibid., p. 47.
11  Ibid., p. 47.
12  Parfit, *Reasons and Persons*, p. 517 n. 36.
13  Madell, *The Identity of the Self*, p. 117.
14  Cf. P. Ricoeur, 'Narrative Identity' in D. Wood (ed.), *On Paul Ricoeur*, Routledge, 1991. He takes issue with Parfit's *Reasons and Persons*, in terms of its methodology ('which allows only an impersonal description of the facts whether relating to a psycho-

logical criterion or to a bodily criterion of identity' – p. 192) and its conclusion that personal identity is not what matters. 'But, I would ask, to whom does identity no longer matter? Who is called on to be deprived of self-assertion if not the self that has been put in parentheses in the name of impersonal methodology?' (p. 193). He then contrasts Parfit's use of puzzling cases of science fiction (imaginable but not yet realisable) which admit of no clear answer ('it is impossible to decide whether I survive or not', p. 194) with the very different examples of uncertain character identity which occur frequently in narratives. In Parfit's science-fiction cases the subject suffers alone; 'in fictional narratives, on the other hand, interaction is constitutive of the narrative situation' (p. 197). The most important difference between Parfit's narratives and historical/fictional narratives, however, lies in response to the question *who* is the self. If we say with Parfit, 'Identity is not what matters', 'it is still someone who says this'.

15 Parfit, *Reasons and Persons*, p. 445–6.
16 Ibid., p. 451.
17 Ibid., p. 454.

### 5 HUMAN SUBJECT AND HUMAN WORTH

1 K. Wilkes, *Real People*, Oxford University Press, 1987, pp. 21–6, and 230–4. The following quotation is from p. 22. She discusses the vexed question of multiple personality at length, pp. 109–31.
2 B. E. Rollin, *The Unheeded Cry*, Oxford University Press, 1989, pp. 140f.
3 *Essay Concerning Human Understanding*, 1690, Bk. 2, chapter 27.
4 Cf. J. W. Yolton, *Locke: an Introduction*, Blackwell, 1985, p. 25.
5 Ibid.
6 Section 23.
7 Ibid., p. 30.
8 Ibid., p. 97.
9 Dr South, writing in reply to Dr Sherlock in 1693, put forward a 'new hypothesis' about 'persons' and undertook

to give the world a much better and more satisfactory Explication of this great Mystery (of the Trinity), and that by two new Terms or Notions (purely and solely of his own Invention), called, Self-Consciousness and Mutual Consciousness . . . Now, the Effects of these two (as I noted before) are very different. For Self-Consciousness (according to him) is the Constituent Principle, or formal Reason of Personality. So that Self-Consciousness properly constitutes, or makes, a Person, and so many Self-Consciousnesses make so many distinct Persons. But Mutual

Consciousness, so far as it extends, makes a Unity, not of Persons (for Personality as such imports distinction and something personally Incommunicable) but a Unity of Nature in Persons. So that after Self-Consciousness has made several distinct Persons, in comes Mutual Consciousness and sets them all at one again; and gives them all but one and the same Nature, which they are to take amongst themselves as well as they can.

10 C. C. J. Webb, *God and Personality*, Allen & Unwin, 1918, p. 57–8.
11 *Human Agency and Language*, Cambridge University Press, 1985, p. 98.
12 A clear example of the newness of the appropriation of 'self-consciousness' by Locke and others is the contrast which is to be found between Locke's use and that of Hobbes only a few decades earlier. In *Leviathan*, Hobbes wrote: 'A Person, is he, whose words or actions are considered, either as his own, or as representing the words or actions of an other man, or of any other thing to whom they are attributed, whether Truly or by Fiction. When they are considered as his owne, then is he called a Naturall Person: And when they are considered as representing the words and actions of an other, then is he a Feigned or Artificiall person.' One could say that the moral or forensic use is clearly indicated in Hobbes, but without any reference to self-consciousness. Hobbes then considers who may be personated and how a group may be considered one person. His interest in the composition and representation of groups, and what happens when a group is fairly evenly divided, takes the discussion away from consideration of the person as individual into the realms of social and political philosophy, which is his real concern.
13 Cf. K. I. Parker, 'John Locke and the Enlightenment Metanarrative. A Biblical Corrective to a Reasoned World', *SJT* 1996, pp. 57–73.
14 H. J. Paton's translation, p.88 in *The Moral Law*, Hutchinson's University Library, 1948 – *Grundlegung*, 421/52.
15 Ibid., pp. 95–6 (section 428).
16 B. Aune, *Kant's Theory of Morals*, Princeton University Press, 1979, p. 73.
17 P. Haezrahi, 'The Concept of Man as an End in Himself' in R. P. Wolff (ed.), *Kant*, Macmillan, 1968, pp. 291–313.
18 H. E. Jones, *Kant's Principle of Personality*, University of Wisconsin, 1971, chapter 1.
19 Ibid., p. 24.
20 Paton, trans., pp. 98 and 105.
21 Cf. *Doctrine of Virtue*, p. 99 (= 434).

22 G. Schrader, 'Persons, Roles & Duties' in *Akten des 4ten Internationalen Kant-Kongresses*, 3, 1974, pp. 124–48.

23 Durkheim, 'Individualism and the Intellectuals'; see the translation by S. and J. Lukes in *Political Studies* 17, 1969, pp. 14–30, especially 21. Cf. J. Habermas, *The Theory of Communicative Action*, vol. 2, Polity, 1987, p. 84: 'Finally, in the manifestation of *modern individualism* Durkheim sees signs of a quasi-religious revaluation of the individual, of a "cult of personality or individual dignity", which commands everyone, as it were, "to be more and more of a person"'. Cf. E. Durkheim, *Division of Labour*, Macmillan, 1933, pp. 400 and 405.

24 J. G. Fichte, *Grundlage der gesamten Wissenschaftslehre* (1794), 2nd edn, 1802, Veit, 1845–6, p. 221; T. Rockmore, *Fichte, Marx and the German Philosophical Tradition*, South Illinois University Press, 1980, p. 12.

25 F. Wagner, *Der Gedanke der Persönlichkeit Gottes bei Fichte und Hegel*, Gerd Mohn, 1971, pp. 20–38.

26 Cf. F. Schiller's comment that, for Fichte, the individual is the source of all reality, in T. Rockmore, *Fichte, Marx and the German Philosophical Tradition*, p. 122. Rockmore's main thesis is 'to demonstrate a significant parallel in the positions of Fichte and Marx, arising from their respective conceptions of man as an active being'.

27 Ibid.

28 *Phenomenology of Mind.*

29 Ibid.

30 Ibid., p. 457.

31 Ibid., p. 504.

32 Cf. T. McFarland, *Coleridge and the Pantheist Tradition*, Oxford University Press, 1969, p. 235.

33 Cf. M. W. Wartofsky, *Feuerbach*, Cambridge University Press, 1977.

34 J. Bradley, 'Across the River and Beyond the Trees: Feuerbach's Relevance to Modern Thought', pp. 139–62 in S. W. Sykes and D. Holmes (eds.), *New Studies in Theology*, Duckworth, 1980.

35 *Pace* Buber's brief reference, *Between Man & Man*, p. 182:

> By man whom he considers as the highest subject of philosophy, Feuerbach does not mean man as an individual, but man with man – the connexion of I and Thou. 'The individual man for himself', runs his manifesto, 'does not have man's being in himself, either as a moral being or a thinking being. Man's being is contained only in community, in the unity of man with man – a unity which rests, however, only on the reality of the difference between I and Thou' . . . But in those words Feuerbach,

passing beyond Marx, introduced that discovery of the Thou, which has been called the 'Copernican revolution' of modern thought.

36 *Todesgedanken*, p. 6–7 (J. A. Massey, trans., *Thoughts on Death and Immortality*, University of California Press, 1980, pp. 10–11).

37 Ibid., p. 8: 'Die pure, nackte Persönlichkeit wurde allein als das Wesentliche erfasst' (Massey, p. 11).

38 Ibid., 'Die reine Person ist hier nur eine vorgestellte, eine ideale.'

39 Ibid., 'Die reine Person ist näher die sünden – und makkelose, mit der Tugend selbst identische Person; die Moralität, die tugendvollkommene Persönlichkeit ist daher das Wesen der Personen.'

40 Ibid., p. 20 (section 17) in Massey's translation, *Thoughts on Death and Immortality*.

41 Ibid., p. 18, vol. 1 (W. Bolin and F. Jodl eds. 1903–11):

An und für sich ist der Tod als natürlicher das letzte Versöhnungsopfer, die letzte Bewährung der Liebe. Der Tod hat seinen Mittelpunkt im Geiste selber; bewegt sich um ihn wie ein Planet um seine Sonne. Indem du liebst, erklärst und anerkennst Du die Nichtigkeit Deines blosen Fürsichselberseins, Deines Selbst; Du anerkennst nicht Dich selber sondern deinen geliebten Gegenstand als Dein wahres Ich, als Dein Wesen und Leben an; so lange du nun liebst, lebst Du in der Verneinung Deiner selbst, in der ununterbrochenen Bestätigung der Nichtigkeit Deines Selbst; zugleich in der Bejahung, in dem Genusse, in der Ansschauung des geliebten Gegenstandes.

42 Ibid., p. 25 (= paragraph 23) in Massey's translation.

43 Ibid.

44 Ibid., paragraph 25.

6 RESITUATING PERSONHOOD: EMBODIMENT AND CONTEXTUALITY

1 Cf. D. Robinson, *Royce and Hocking – American Idealists*, Christopher Publishing House, 1968.

2 Cf. L. H. De Wolf, 'Personalism in the History of Western Philosophy', *The Philosophical Forum* 12, 1954, pp. 29–51.

3 B. P. Bowne, *Personalism*, Houghton Mifflin, 1908, p. 88.

4 P. Deats and C. Robb, (eds.), *The Boston Personalist Tradition*, Mercer University Press, 1986, p. 57.

5 B. P. Bowne, *Theism*, American Book Company, 1902, p. 18.

6 Deats and Robb, (eds.), *The Boston Personalist Tradition*, p. 60.

7 Cf. De Wolf, 'Personalism'; Deats and Robb, *The Boston Personalist Tradition*, pp. 5f.

8 His main statements on personalism are to be found in *Manifeste au service du personnalisme* (1936, ET *A Personalist Manifesto*, Longman, Green and Co., 1938), *Traits du caractere* (1946, ET *The*

*Character of Man*, Harpers, 1956), and *Le personalisme* (1949, ET *Personalism*, Routledge and Kegan Paul, 1952) and the journal *Esprit* (1932 onwards).

9 J. Amato, *Mounier and Maritain*, University of Alabama Press, 1975.
10 *Personalism*, p. 3.
11 Ibid., pp. 3–4.
12 Ibid., p. 21.
13 There are good articles and bibliographies in the following anthologies: C. Card, (ed.), *Feminist Ethics*, University of Kansas Press, 1991; A. Jagger and P. T. Rothenberg (eds.), *Feminist Frameworks: Alternative Theoretical Accounts of the Relations Between Men & Women* McGraw-Hill, 1993³; E. F. Kittay and D. T. Meyers (eds.), *Women & Moral Theory*, Rowman and Littlefield, 1987. See also N. Noddings, *Caring*, University of California Press 1984; C. Gilligan, *In A Different Voice*, Harvard University Press, 1982; C. Pateman, *The Sexual Contract*, Polity Press, 1988; D. Hampson, *Theology & Feminism*, Blackwell, 1990; E. Storkey, *What's Right with Feminism*, SPCK, 1985; J. Grimshaw, *Feminist Philosophers*, Harvester Wheatsheaf, 1986.
14 N. Fraser and L. J. Nicholson, 'Social Criticism without Philosophy' in T. Docherty (ed.), *Postmodernism*, Harvester, 1993.
15 Ibid., p. 423.
16 M. Z. Rosaldo, 'Women, Culture & Society: a Theoretical Overview' in M. Z. Rosaldo and L. Lamphere (eds.), *Woman, Culture & Society*, Stanford University Press, 1974.
17 Fraser and Nicholson, 'Social Criticism', p. 424.
18 Cf. the pertinent criticisms in M. Moody-Adams, 'Gender and the Complexity of Moral Voices' in C. Card (ed.), *Feminist Ethics*, University of Kansas Press, 1991. She notes Gilligan's uncritical restriction of examples of women's issues to issues of reproduction and her failure to allow for a plurality of women's voices. Other feminists objected to the lack of a clear feminist methodology.
19 Cf. S. Parsons, 'Feminism and the Logic of Morality' in S. Sayers and P. Osborne (eds.), *Socialism, Feminism & Philosophy*, Routledge, 1990, pp. 69–99.
20 Cf. M. O'Neill, *Women Speaking, Women Listening*, Orbis, 1990 p. 57: 'That Western feminists are often imperialistic was the view expressed by the Islamic feminist Riffat Hassan at a recent interreligious dialogue . . . [She said], I get very tired of Western women who tell me they sympathize with Islamic women without even knowing what Islamic feminists want.' And in the following paragraph, citing Suchocki, O'Neill notes that there is now ample research showing that ideas of womanhood and women's dignity

vary from culture to culture. What appear to be oppressive practices to Western women (e.g. the custom of veiling) may not be seen in the same light by other women, for whom it may be a mark of status rather than submission or oppression.

21 E. Frazer and N. Lacey, *The Politics of Community*, Harvester, 1993, p. 102. This view, they say, 'entails not only that conceptions of selfhood, personhood and agency are socially produced and specific, but also that actual persons are too. There is great variation between communitarian writers as to how radically socially situated their conception of the human self turns out to be, and hence between their different ideas about the human capacity for self-reflection and agency. However, one idea common to all communitarians is that the self is situated and embodied' (p. 108).

22 Cf. in addition to E. Frazer and N. Lacey, *The Politics of Community*, S. Benhabib, *Situating the Self*, Polity, 1992; L. Nicholson (ed.), *Feminism/Postmodernism*, Routledge 1990.

23 Frazer and Lacey, *Politics of Community*, p. 53.

24 *Situating the Self*, p. 3. Cf. p. 8 *et passim*.

25 Ibid., p. 5.

26 Ibid., pp. 5–6.

27 Ibid., p. 8.

28 Ibid., pp. 160 and 162. Cf. Frazer and Lacey, *Politics of Community*, p. 55.

29 *Situating the Self*, p. 190.

30 Frazer and Lacey, *Politics of Community*, pp. 151f.

31 Cf. ibid. p. 152:

Communitarians and many feminists abandon the disembodied, liberal, choosing self as both theoretically flawed and patriarchally constructed. But in doing so, we risk finding ourselves in the arms of the radically embodied communitarian self, a determined product of her or his circumstances, social conditioning and community culture. The situation of a being whose consciousness is determined by structure, communities, and institutions seems to be that of a helpless subscriber to the dominant conception of value. Arguably, the communitarian conception of personhood hardly deserves the name.

32 Benhabib, *Situating the Self*, pp. 186f.

33 Frazer and Lacey, *Politics of Community*, p. 178:

The notion of the relational self, in contrast to both atomistic and inter-subjective selves, nicely captures our empirical and logical inter-dependence and the centrality to our identity of our relations with others and with practices and institutions, whilst retaining an idea of human uniqueness and discreteness as central to our sense of ourselves. It entails the collapse of any self/other or individual/community dichotomy without abandoning the idea of genuine agency and subjectivity.

34 *Situating the Self*, p. 38.

35 'On the Alleged Methodological Infirmity of Ethics', *APQ* 27/3, 1990, pp. 225–35.

36 R. Rorty, 'Postmodernist Bourgeois Liberalism' in T. Docherty (ed.), *Postmodernism*, Harvester, 1993, p. 325; he continues: 'For purposes of moral and political deliberation and conversation, a person just *is* that network.' Cf. Frazer and Lacey *Politics of Community*, p. 156. Cf. Lauritzen, 'The Self and its Discontents', *JRE*, 1994, pp. 189–210 and chapter 1 of the present study, n. 29.

37 Cf. the idea that 'God is the infinite horizon which is implicitly presupposed in every act of human self-transcendence' (C. Schwöbel in D. Ford (ed.), *The Modern Theologians* vol. 1, p. 262.

## PART 2 'PERSON' IN CHRISTIAN PERSPECTIVE

1 In 1894, J. R. Illingworth argued that belief in a personal God was not simply rational inference but 'the outcome of our entire personality acting as a whole' – 'Our reason, our affections, our actions all alike, feel about for contact with some supreme reality; and when the mind, speaking for its companion faculties, names that reality a Person, it is giving voice also to the inarticulate conviction of the heart and will', *Personality Human and Divine*, p. 80. In his Boyle Lectures of 1920, *Studies in Christian Philosophy*, W. R. Matthews devotes a whole lecture to 'Divine Personality' (pp. 158–91). The basis of his discussion is that personality involves 'a centre of consciousness'. Personality 'escapes analysis, not because it is unreal, but because it is the highest manifestation of that which is most genuinely and ultimately real'. Self-consciousness is an absolute pre-requisite, but is not by itself sufficient. 'There are selves such as children who have attained some degree of self-consciousness who yet would be but doubtfully described as persons' (pp. 172). A further pre-requisite of personality is moral responsibility and the capacity to be directed by principles (drawing on J. Royce, *The Conception of God*, pp. 258, 278f). A person is more than a self; it is a 'formed will'. 'We are not fully persons, but we are, we may hope, becoming persons; and in that process of becoming, we may find indications of what full personality would be' (p. 175). Royce's monism fails, said Matthews, because he is unable to recognise that God creates a world that is distinct from God.

2 *World and God*, Nisbet & Co., 1935, p. 49.

3 Cf. Hodgson, *Winds of the Spirit*, pp. 148f. 'My proposal is that God is the one true and perfect person – not *a* person but *the* person, personhood, since the power that God has absolutely is the constitutive power of personhood . . . God is social being.' This is later worked out in terms of God's triune figuration.

## 7 THE RELEVANCE OF HISTORY AND CHRISTOLOGY

1 J. S. Mill, *A System of Logic*, Book IV chapter 4 (p. 449 in 8th edn, 1900).
2 *After Virtue*, Duckworth, 1981, p. 173.
3 Ibid., p. 174.
4 Cf. R. Hirzel, *Die Person: Begriff und Name derselben im Altertum*, Munich, 1914, who shows that *soma* (body) often did duty for 'person' from Homer onwards. Wilkes' statement (*Real People*, Oxford University Press, 1987, p. 129) that *soma* should be translated as 'corpse' does not appear to be justified. Words for parts of the body (e.g. head, eye, face) also stood for 'person'. A similar phenomenon can be observed in other cultures (cf. ancient Israel). The word *psyche* (soul), as in Republic VI, 496 b, can sometimes be translated 'inner person', but it is not what distinguishes one person from another. There is a good discussion of Greek ideas in C. J. de Vogel, 'The Concept of Personality in Greek and Christian Thought', *Studies in Philosophy and the History of Philosophy* 2.
5 'Der theologische Personalismus als dogmatisches Problem', *Kirche und Dogmatik*, 1, 1954–6, pp. 23–41.
6 Cf. R. Sorabji, 'Body and Soul in Aristotle', *Philosophy* 49, 1974, pp. 63–89, reprinted in J. Barnes (ed.), *Articles on Aristotle*, vol. 4, pp. 42–64. There is an extensive bibliography on relevant Aristotelian literature, pp. 179 87. NB nos. 41 and 74. E. Hartman, *Substance, Body & Soul*; and G. E. R. Lloyd and G. E. L. Owen (eds.), *Aristotle on Mind and the Senses*. There is a good discussion in J. L. Ackrill's, 'Aristotle's Definitions of psyche', printed in Barnes, *Articles on Aristotle*, p. 65f., where he examines three related formulae from *De Anima* II 1. For Plato see M. Nussbaum, *The Fragility of Goodness*, Cambridge University Press, 1986; C. Rowe, 'Philosophy, Love and Madness' in C. Gill (ed.), *The Person and the Human Mind*, Oxford University Press, 1990; C. de Vogel, 'The *Soma-Sema* Formula' in H. J. Blumenthal and R. A. Markus (eds.), *Neoplatonism and Early Christian Thought*, Variorum, 1981, p. 79–95.
7 Ackrill regards Wiggins' identification of *psyche* in Aristotle with 'person' (in the sense of 'individual human being') as mistaken.

8  Cf. A. O. Rorty (ed.), *The Identities of Persons*, University of California Press, 1976, pp. 301–23.

9  Cf. K. Rahner, *Encyclopaedia*, Burns & Oates, 1975, p. 1207; A. Guggenberger, article 'Person' in *Handbuch Theologischer Grundbegriffe*, vol. 2, pp. 295–306; W. Pannenberg, article 'Person' in *RGG* (3rd edn), vol. 5, pp. 230–5.

10 In modern psychological literature, 'persona' is sometimes used to refer to the outward manifestation which a person presents to the world. Sociological literature abounds in references to the roles people play. Cf. the excellent *Rules, Roles and Relations* (Macmillan, 1966) by D. Emmet.

11 H. Rheinfelder, *Das Wort, Persona*, Halle, 1928.

12 'Naturae rationabilis individua substantia', *Contra Eutychen et Nestorium*, chapter 3.

13 'The Concept of Personality in Greek and Christian Thought', *Studies in Philosophy and the History of Philosophy*, vol. 2, Washington, 1963. For an account of Stoic understanding of human nature see A. Long, *Hellenistic Philosophy*, Duckworth, 1986 and T. Engberg-Pedersen, 'Stoic Philosophy and the Concept of Person' in C. Gill (ed.), *The Person and the Human Mind*, Oxford University Press, 1990.

14 'Intelligendum etiam est duabus quasi nos a natura indutos esse personis; quarum una communis est ex eo, quod omnes participes sumus rationis praestantiaeque eius, qua excellimus bestiis, a qua omne honestum decorumque trahitur et ex qua ratio inveniendi officii exquiritur, altera autem, quae proprie singulis est tributa, ut enim in corporibus magnae dissimilitudines sunt, alios videmus velocitate ad cursum, alios viribus ad luctandum valere, itemque in formis aliis dignitatem inesse, aliis venustatem, sic in animis existunt maiores etiam varietates.'

15 Cf. also A. H. Armstrong, 'Form, Individual, and Person in Plotinus', *Dionysius* 1, 1977, pp. 49–68.

16 *Adv. Praxean*, chapter 7.11–12. 'Quaecumque ergo substantia sermones (= tou logou) fuit, illam dico personam et illi nomen filii vindico et, dum filium agnosco, secundum a patre defendo.' Cf. E. Evans, 'Tertullian's Theological Terminology', *ChQR* 139, 1945, pp. 56–77, especially 64–8; C. H. Dowdall, 'The Word "Person"', *ChQR* 212, 1928, pp. 229–64.

17 A. von Harnack, *Lehrbuch der Dogmengeschichte*, 1, Tübingen, 1931⁵, p. 576 n. 2; G. Krueger, *Das Dogma von der Dreieinigkeit und Gottmenschheit in seiner geschichtlichen Entwicklung*, Tübingen, 1905, p. 144.

18 *Das Wort, Persona*, p. 148.

19 *De Spectaculis*, section 23.
20 C. C. J. Webb, *God and Personality*, Allen & Unwin, 1918, p. 66, 'I think we should be nearer the truth in seeking our principal clue to the theological meaning of the term in the sense which it had come to bear and still bears in grammar, when we speak of the first, second and third persons in the conjugation of a verb.'
21 C. Gunton, 'Augustine, The Trinity, and the Theological Crisis of the West', *SJT* 43, 1989, pp. 39 and 52–4; ibid., pp. 33–58; R. W. Jenson, *The Triune Identity*, Fortress, 1982, pp. 103–14.
22 Cf. J. N. D. Kelly, *Early Christian Doctrines*, A. & C. Black, 1977⁵, pp. 265f. See also the discussion of Zizioulas at the end of the present chapter.
23 Cf. Letter 38 of Basil of Caesarea.
24 Cf. B. Studer, *Trinity and Incarnation*, T. & T. Clark, 1993, p. 143: 'It is the merit of Gregory of Nyssa, the greatest Christian philosopher among the Eastern Church fathers, to have reinforced . . . the distinction between *ousia* and *hypostaseis*.' Studer admits that Gregory does not say *how* this is possible.
25 Cf. Gunton, *The One, the Three and the Many*, Cambridge University Press, 1993, p. 191: 'What was lost was the force of the Cappadocian desynonymizing of *ousia* and *hypostasis*.'
26 *Being as Communion*, Darton, Longman & Todd, 1985, p. 43; cf. Schwöbel, C. and Gunton, C. (eds.), *Persons Divine and Human*, T. & T. Clark, 1991, p. 43: 'If biological birth gives us a hypostasis dependent ontologically on nature, this indicates that a "new birth" is needed in order to experience an ontology of personhood.'
27 Cf. *Adv. Arium*, i. 20. 3 (PL 8, 1053): 'Faciamus cooperatori dicit, necessario Christo. Et secundum imaginem dicit. Ergo homo non imago dei, sed secundum imaginem. Solus enim Jesus imago dei, homo autem secundum imaginem, hoc est imago imaginis. Sed dicit: secundum imaginem nostram. Ergo et pater et filius imago una . . . Multa cum sit quaestio de quo dixerit: faciamus hominem iuxta imaginem nostram, concedendum nunc quod de anima hominis . . . ipsa enim sola est iuxta imaginem dei et iuxta similitudinem. Imaginem dicimus esse dei, Christum; ipsum autem, logon. Iuxta imaginem ergo dei, animam dicimus, rationalem dicentes; non enim logos anima, sed rationalis.
28 *De Trinitate* v. 9. 9. Tamen cum quaeritur quid tres, magna prorsus inopia humanum laboret eloquium. Dictum est tamen tres personae, non ut illud diceretur, sed ne taceretur.
29 *St Augustine on Personality*, Macmillan, 1960, pp.8–9:
Augustine [in *De Trinitate* v. 3. 4; v. 5. 6; v. 6. 7] is the great innovator. He counters the Arian argument that if God is unbegotten and the Son

unbegotten, then there is no substantial unity, by showing that the fourth Aristotelian category (relation) is neither accident nor substance *per se*, but can be either as the subject matter requires . . . In other words relation transcends the categories and may be somehow called what the Schoolmen later termed a transcendental. The Father is related in his whole substance to the Son and stands in living relation to the Son, not by any accident but by the very depth of his Fatherly substance, if I may express it in this way. And as the Son is related to the Father, so too, is the Holy Spirit related to Father and Son, united in One Divine Substance . . . This leads Augustine to declare that a Divine Person is at one and the same time a. Reality identical with itself, existing *in se*, an Absolute and b. also a Reality *ad alium*, essentially directed toward Another and dynamically directed toward the others. Here we find all the elements for what St. Thomas will call a relatio = *subsistens*, when, following wisely in the steps of Augustine, he gives more systematic expression to Augustine's earlier intuition (*ST* i.29.4). This subsistent relation is one identical with the Divine Nature, or Divine Substance, as Divine Essence. That is to say, the Divine existence or *esse* in God is a relation by identity and there is no other subsistence in God than that of the Three Persons. God alone is really personal, not by his having intellect and will, for that is common to all Three Persons, and, as attributes of the Divine Nature, does not distinguish them, but as being tri-Personal, constituting a network of subsisting relations . . . This means that God is the perfect, in fact the only perfect, prototype of that which all love between persons tends to achieve – absolute unity and yet distinction – to be one with the other not by losing ones identity, but by perfecting it, even at the very source of ones being. That is why Divine existence is the ideal of all personal existence – to be fully oneself, but only in dependence upon, and in adherence to, another in the communion of unity.

30 T. F. Driver, *Christ in a Changing World*, SCM Press, 1981, p. 105.
31 J. P. Mackey, *The Christian Experience of God as Trinity*, SCM Press, 1983, p. 158f; R. W. Jenson, *The Triune Identity*, Fortress, 1982, pp. 114–30.
32 See bibliography.
33 J. Moltmann, *The Trinity and the Kingdom of God*, SCM Press, 1981, p. 174.
34 Ibid., pp. 143 and 169.
35 Ibid., p. 145, following Bantle, 'Person und Personbegriff in der Trinitätslehre Karl Rahners', *Münchener Theologische Zeitschrift* 30, 1979, pp. 11–24, who pinpoints the weakness of Rahner's immanent and modalistic Trinitarian thought in his deficient concept of 'person'. Moltmann argues that Rahner's view of the modern concept of 'person' represents a form of individualism ('everyone is a self-possessing, self-disposing centre of action'), which takes no real account of the personalism of such philosophers as

Hölderlin, Feuerbach, Ebner and Rosenstock. For them, and for Moltmann, 'person' implies a genuine social relation.

36 For Plotinus' view of man and soul see A. H. Armstrong (ed.), *Later Greek and Early Medieval Philosophy*, Cambridge University Press, 1967, pp. 29 and 222f.

37 C. C. J. Webb, *God and Personality*, p. 54.

38 Cf. H. Chadwick, *Boethius*, Oxford University Press, 1981.

39 'La structure du concept latin de personne', in *Etudes d'histoire littéraire et doctrinale*, series 2, 1932, pp. 121–61.

40 V. Schurr, *Die Trinitätslehre des Boethius im Lichte der skythischen Kontroversen*, Paderborn, 1935, p. 51.

41 M. Nédoncelle, 'Les variations de Boèce sur la personne', in *Revue des Sciences Réligieuses* 29, 1955, pp. 201–38.

42 J. Bidez, 'Boèce et Porphyre' in *Revue belge de philologie et d'histoire* 2, 1923, pp. 189–201.

43 S. Otto, *Person und Subsistenz*, Vilhelm Fink Verlag, 1968, pp. 171f.

44 Blackfriars edition, ed. Velecky, Appendix 6 ('Divine Relations'), p. 143.

45 'Et ideo alii dixerunt quod hoc nomen "persona" in divinis significat simul essentiam et relationem.' (*ST* 1 a. 29. 4c).

46 W. J. Hankey, *God in Himself*, Oxford University Press, 1987.

47 C. Morris, *The Discovery of the Individual, 1050–1200*, SPCK, 1972.

48 Cf. V. Lossky, *In the Image and Likeness of God*, Mowbrays, 1975, pp. 116f.; J. D. Zizioulas, 'Human Capacity and Human Incapacity: a Theological Exploration of Personhood', *SJT* 28, 1975, pp. 401–47.

49 Lossky, *In the Image and Likeness of God*, p. 120.

50 Cf. W. Pannenberg, 'Speaking about God in the face of atheist criticism', *Basic Questions in Theology*, vol. 3, SCM Press, 1973, pp. 111–12. Although he begins from the statement that, 'Anyone who says "God" says "person"', Pannenberg bases his understanding of persons on the understanding of freedom. 'A person is the opposite of an existent being.' 'Human beings are persons by the very fact that they are not wholly and completely existent for us in their reality, but are characterised by freedom, and as a result remain concealed and beyond control in the totality of their existence.' Later there is more of an emphasis on the importance of interpersonal relationships: 'man is not a person of himself . . . by the constitution of his ego . . . Thus man achieves his being as a person, as a free subjectivity, only from the encounter with other persons, and in fact basically by turning in love to others.'

51 Lossky, *In the Image of God*, pp. 137–8.

52 Cf. G. A. Jonsson, *The Image of God: Gen. 1. 26–8 in a Century of Old Testament Research*, Almqvist & Wiksell, 1988, pp. 219–25. C. Westermann, *What does the O.T. say about God?*, SPCK, 1979, especially p. 14 and notes.

53 Zizioulas, *SJT* 28, 1975, p. 402.

54 Ibid., p. 445.

55 Ibid., p. 447.

56 Ibid., p. 420 n. 1.

8 DIVINE EMBODIMENT AND TEMPORALITY: IS GOD A PERSON?

1 *Coherence of Theism*, Oxford University Press, 1977, pp. 99–101.

2 P. F. Strawson, *Individuals*, Methuen, 1959, pp. 102f.

3 Cf. H. G. Frankfurt, 'Freedom of the Will and the Concept of a Person', *Journal of Philosophy*, 78, 1971, pp. 5–20.

4 J. Harrison, 'The Embodiment of Mind, or what use is having a Body?', *PAS* 74, 1974, pp. 33–55.

5 Cf. A. Thatcher, 'The Personal God and a God who is a Person', *RS* 21, 1985, pp. 61–73.

6 G. M. Jantzen, *God's World, God's Body*, Darton, Longman & Todd, 1984, p. 80.

7 Ibid., p. 144.

8 In Peacocke and Gillett (eds.), *Persons and Personality*, pp. 191–2. Swinburne makes his modified dualism very clear: 'The only form of dualism which is biblical, and the one which I have wished to defend, is the second – that there are two things, soul and body, and that it is the continuing of the soul which is essential for the continuing of the person . . . The person can continue if the soul continues, but linked with a different body. . . Christian theology does need a substance dualism in this form.'

9 This is not the view of the biblical writers. See H. W. Wolff, *Anthropology of the Old Testament*, SCM Press, 1974, chapter 4.

10 Cf. T. F. Tracy, *God, Action and Embodiment*, Eerdmans, 1984, pp. 74f.

11 W. Kneale, 'Time and Eternity in Theology', *PAS* 1961, pp. 87–108; R. Coburn, 'Professor Malcolm on God', *Australasian Journal of Philosophy*, 1963; N. Pike, *God and Timelessness*, Routledge, and Kegan Paul, 1970; J. R. Lucas, *A Treatise on Time and Space*, Methuen, 1973, chapter 20. A series of articles in *Religious Studies* 14/3, 14/4, 15/1 and 15/3, 1978–9 (by R. B. Edwards, P. Helm, W. L. Craig, R. Paterson and S. T. Davis), and in *IJPR* 17/3, 18/1, 20/2, 1985–6 (by M. Martin, W. P. Alston, W. L. Craig and D. Basinger).

12 N. Wolterstorff, 'God Everlasting' in S. M. Cahn and D. Schatz (eds.), *Contemporary Philosophy of Religion*, Oxford University Press, 1982, p. 77.

13 Ibid., p. 78.

14 Ibid., p. 79.

15 Cf. B. Davies, *An Introduction to the Philosophy of Religion*, Oxford University Press, 1993, chapter 8, for a contemporary defence of this view.

16 J. R. Lucas, *Treatise on Time and Space*, p. 300: For Lucas it is critical that God is able to interact with mankind; prayer would lose its meaning otherwise. That God loves mankind and saves mankind means for Lucas that He cannot be timeless and must, therefore, be in time. No definition of 'person', however, is offered. If one were to piece together the various attributes of God that Lucas indicates to be important, it is clear that his understanding of personhood would underline consciousness and might tend towards the Cartesian. Other writers have subjected 'knowledge' and 'consciousness' to closer examination, and tried to be fairly explicit about their understanding of 'persons' in relation to time and timelessness. R. C. Coburn, for instance, in his article, 'Professor Malcolm on God' (see n. 11 above) thinks there are at least three important ways in which God may be thought of as related to time: he reflects and deliberates (activities which take time); he anticipates and intends (this must have temporal reference); and he remembers (again, temporal reference). 'Knowledge' need not have a temporal reference, however. Some views of omniscience would require these features to be restated in a way that made it clear that God's knowledge could be timeless. On the other hand, certain strong views of omniscience are incompatible with human freedom and for that reason may be less attractive than the view that God is in time.

17 A. N. Prior, 'The Formalities of Omniscience', *Philosophy* 37, 1962, p. 116; see D. Burrell, 'Divine Practical Knowing', in B. Hebblethwaite and E. Henderson (eds.), *Divine Action*, T. & T. Clark, 1990, pp. 93–102, for a defence of God acting in the world without being in time: 'there is simply no way for divinity to be in time, subject to change, unless the relation of God to the world be other than what we have meant by creation'. In response to Burrell, it should be noted that God is the author of change, rather than subject to change, in the view of those who wish to relate God and temporality more closely.

18 Cf. J. J. O'Donnell, *Trinity and Temporality*, Oxford University

Press, 1983, p. 176, referring to Whitehead, *Process & Reality*, Harper Torchbooks, 1960, p. 529.

19 *God, Eternity & the Nature of Time*, St Martin's Press/Macmillan, 1992, pp. 122–6. For a contrary view cf. P. Helm, 'God and Spacelessness', *Philosophy* 55, 1980; he argues that, since parallel objections to God's timelessness and spacelessness can be constructed, either both arguments succeed or both fail. This does not follow, of course. It depends what is meant by being in time and space. God's embodiment in incarnation and narrative, as explained on pp. 150–151 above, is not about occupying space or having spatial parts. Cf. A. Padgett, pp. 136–7; and I. A. Dorner, *Divine Immutability* (trans. R. R. Williams), Fortress Press, 1994, pp. 188–9.

20 Cf. A. Thatcher, *Truly A Person, Truly God*, SPCK, 1990. The main focus of interest is Christological, but it illustrates how a Strawsonian concept of 'person' requiring both M and P predicates can provide the basis for retaining the idea of 'person' in a modern Christology purged of the metaphysical notions of Chalcedon but not unfaithful to what the church was attempting. His fear, however, that any attempt to refer to God as a bodiless person would prove incoherent and indefensible, particularly to nontheists, persuaded him to relinquish talk of God as 'a person', provided that the personal nature of God's dealing with the world is not overlooked or neglected.

21 Cf. P. Scott, *Theology, Ideology and Liberation*, Cambridge University Press, 1994, pp. 100–1. Cf. I. Ellacuria and J. Sobrino (eds.), *Mysterium Liberationis*, Orbis Books, 1993, p. 215: 'For this open progressive moral theory the basic categories are the person and personal autonomy.' Such a moral theory is mistaken, they argue, because it does not take social relations seriously. 'Person' in such theory means 'individual', they assume.

22 H. H. Rowley, *Faith of Israel*, SCM, 1956, p.61.

23 C. C. J. Webb, *God and Personality*, Allen & Unwin, 1918, p. 68 n. 7 – 'illi naturae vere competeret ratio personae' (in Bk. i. ch. 23 qu. 1, section 15).

24 Ibid., pp. 63–5.

25 D. Martin, *The Dilemmas of Contemporary Religion*, Blackwell, 1978, p. 73 refers to the totally subjective new female man who regards himself as a 'pure person . . . freed from all contingent labels. For him there is neither male nor female, Jew nor Greek, Christian nor pagan, public nor private, sacred nor profane. The only distinction is that between those who have recovered wholeness and personal authenticity and those who have not; the bond

and the free. And the old are by definition bond and the young free.'

26 Cf. J. E. Toews, *Hegelianism*, Cambridge University Press, 1980, p. 46, quoting Schlegel's *Dialogue on Poetry*, p. 151: 'the symmetry and organisation of history teaches us that mankind, during its existence and development, genuinely was and became an individual, a person'.

27 *Coherence of Theism*, p. 99.

28 *Encyclopaedia Britannica*, vol. 18, p. 265.

29 Cf. *Systematic Theology*, vol. 1, J. Nisbet & Co., 1968, p. 271: 'Personal God does not mean that God is a person. It means that God is the ground of everything personal, and that he carries within himself the ontological power of personality. He is not a person, but he is not less than personal.'

30 Ibid.

31 *Theology of Culture*, Oxford University Press, 1959, p. 61.

32 *Biblical Religion*, J. Nisbet & Co., 1955, p. 84.

33 H. Küng, *Does God Exist?*, Doubleday & Company, 1980, pp. 631f.

34 W. Pannenberg, 'Speaking about God in the Face of Atheist Criticism', *Basic Questions in Theology*, 3, 1973, p. 111.

35 Ibid., p. 112.

36 *Systematic Theology*, vol. 1, p. 430:

The persons (sc. of the Trinity) are referred to the other persons. They achieve their selfhood ec-statically outside themselves. Only thus do they exist as personal selves. In this respect human personality is similar to the trinitarian persons. Historically, these features of human personality emerge only in the light of the doctrine of the Trinity, as its concept of person, constituted by relations to others, is transferred to anthropology. Each I lives by its relation to the Thou. It is constituted by its relation to a social context. This is an insight which we owe decisively to the trinitarian concept of person. For this reason alone the argument that the trinitarian concept of person has no relation to the modern view is mistaken . . . On the other hand, there are in fact important differences between being a human person and the divine personality of the Father, Son and Spirit.

37 H. Ott, *God*, St Andrew Press, 1974, chapter 4.

38 K. Rahner, *Foundations of Christian Faith*, Darton, Longman & Todd, 1978, p. 26.

39 Ibid., p. 31.

40 Ibid., pp. 71–5.

41 Ibid., p. 74.

42 Ibid., pp. 134–5.

43 1960, reprinted in *Theological Investigations*, vol. 4, Darton, Longman & Todd, 1966, pp. 77–104.

44 *Theological Investigations*, vol. 4, p. 101.

45 J. Moltmann, *The Trinity and the Kingdom of God*, SCM Press, 1981, pp. 144–8.

46 A similar criticism is voiced by W. Kasper, *The God of Jesus Christ*, SCM, 1984, p. 299, arguing that both Barth and Rahner operate with a concept of person that is flawed by unnecessary individualism and subjective reference (e.g. consciousness). They think of God as Absolute Subject rather than Absolute Substance in the manner of the early church. The fact that 'the human person exists only in relations of the I–Thou-We kind' can be related to the Trinitarian understanding of God. Despite the great differences between divine and human persons, there is a core insight that personhood involves reciprocal relationships and dialogue between persons.

47 *Theology of Hope*, SCM Press, 1967, pp. 77f. Bauckham, 'Jürgen Moltmann' in D. Ford (ed.), *The Modern Theologians*, vol. 1, Blackwell, 1989, p. 299:

> Christian eschatology is therefore the hope that the world will be different. It is aroused by a promise whose fulfillment can come only from God's eschatological action transcending all the possibilities of history since it involves the end of all evil, suffering and death in the glory of the divine presence indwelling all things. But it is certainly not therefore without effect in the present. On the contrary, the resurrection set in motion a historical process in which the promise already affects the world and moves it in the direction of its future transformation.

48 J. Moltmann, *The Crucified God*, SCM Press, 1974, p. 243.

## 9 DIVINE AND HUMAN: RELATIONALITY AND PERSONHOOD

1 For a spirited defence of a view of personhood as *nous* (conscience, soul, spirit, mind) see S. R. L. Clark, 'Reason as *Daimon*' in C. Gill (ed.), *The Person and the Human Mind*, Oxford University Press, 1990, pp. 187–206.

2 Cf. W. Alston, 'How to think about Divine Action' in B. Hebblethwaite and E. Henderson (eds.), *Divine Action*, T. & T. Clark, 1990, p. 57 – 'It is but a vulgar prejudice to suppose that decibel level or number of observers is a measure of the divine activity level.' See also chapter 10 below on revelation.

3 Cf. Locke, *Essay Concerning Human Understanding*, 1690, Bk 2, chapter 23, section 2.

4 N. Lash, 'Considering the Trinity', *Modern Theology*; 2:3 1986, p. 183.

5 Cf. D. Nicholls, 'Trinity and Conflict', *Theology* 96, 1993, pp. 19–27: 'In this article I am suggesting that our commonly accepted

judgements about the secular order have influenced and indeed distorted our trinitarian theology, by eliminating totally the idea of conflict from the "internal life" of the Godhead.' C. M. La Cugna, *God for Us*, HarperCollins, 1991, pp. 221–30 is very relevant.

6 S. Coakley, 'Why Three? Some Further Reflections on the Origins of the Doctrine of the Trinity' in D. Pailin and S. Coakley (eds.), *The Making and Re-Making of Christian Theology*, Oxford University Press, 1993, pp. 35–6: 'as a meditation on the trinitarian logic of divine love with its mutuality, non-exclusivity and non-possessiveness, it might well provide some answer to our systematic question and be a formal complement to the experiential response (to Wiles to which I now turn)'.

7 Cf. R. S. Franks, *Doctrine of the Trinity*, Duckworth, 1953.

8 *God in Christian Thought and Experience*, J. Nisbet & Co., 1930, p. 193: 'we can go further and say that the two analogies really converge'.

9 L. Boff, *Trinity and Society*, Burns & Oates, 1988; P. Wilson-Kastner, *Faith, Feminism & the Christ*, Fortress Press, 1983; C. Gunton, *The Promise of Trinitarian Theology* T. & T. Clark, 1991; J. D. Zizioulas, *Being as Communion*, Darton, Longman & Todd, 1985; C. Yannaras, *The Freedom of Morality*, St Vladimir's Seminary Press, 1984; C. M. La Cugna, *God for Us*, HarperCollins, 1991.

10 R. Olson, 'Trinity & Eschatology', *SJT* 36, 1982, pp. 213–27.

11 Cf. *The Trinity and the Kingdom of God*, SCM Press, 1981, p. 161: 'The concept "mutual relationship" does not equate God's relationship to the world with his relationship to himself. But it says that God's relationship to the world has a retroactive effect on his relationship to himself – even though the divine relationship in the world is primarily determined by that inner relationship.' As Olson comments, 'But if the immanent Trinity is conceived as future, and thus not a completed reality at any point in the historical process of the divine life (how could it be if it is really "affected" by the events in the history of this life?), how does it "primarily determine" that process and life?' ('Trinity & Eschatology', p. 221).

12 Cf. The Eleventh Council of Toledo (675) stated that the Son was begotten *de utero Patris* ('from the womb of the Father').

13 *History and the Triune God*, SCM, 1991, p. xvi: 'Feminist theology has made mutuality one of its basic terms. Mutuality can clearly be recognised in the trinitarian perichoresis, in which it takes on a richer significance than in the I–Thou philosophy of Martin Buber, from which it is derived.'

14 Cf. F. J. van Beek, *Christ Proclaimed: Christology as Rhetoric*, p. 169: 'it

is unnecessary and linguistically mistaken to argue that "subsistent relationship" (as predicated of the person of the Word) or "relational being" is what "person" really means, as Galot does ... If Galot means that the word 'person' really means *être relationnel*, he must show that this is what people really mean when they use the word in ordinary language ... which seems a difficult thing to do, no matter how much relationships are part and parcel of "persons".' It is more difficult than that, however. Even if some people (e.g. theologians) do use 'person' to mean 'relational being', that does not mean they are justified by their own usage. 'Usage' is more complicated than that.

15 Cf. C. Schwöbel and C. Gunton (eds.), *Persons, Divine and Human*, T. & T. Clark, 1991, p. 59.

16 See pp. 102 and 117 above.

17 Cf. Pannenberg, *Anthropology in Christian Perspective*, T. & T. Clark, 1985, pp. 23f.

18 Cf. T. Torrance, 'The Goodness and Dignity of Man in the Christian Tradition', *Modern Theology* 4/4, 1988, pp. 320f: 'It cannot be stressed enough that it was this Trinitarian doctrine of God that actually gave rise to the concept of *person* (his italics), which was quite unknown in the world before, and to the realisation that God has created human beings in such a way that their inter-human relations are meant to be inter-personal, and as such are meant to reflect *on the level of the creature* [my italics] the inter-personal relations of God himself.' We have already noted that there *were* concepts of personhood in ancient Israel and ancient Greece. The saving qualification is perhaps 'on the level of the creature'. There is an important caveat in C. Schwöbel and C. Gunton (eds.), *Persons Divine and Human*, T. & T. Clark, 1991, p. 155: 'It is at this point that utmost theological caution is called for.' He notes the problems of *analogia entis* in reference to God's Trinitarian being and says:

'Barth's counter-proposal of understanding the analogy as the *analogia fidei* could be accepted as more adequate, if faith is not only understood epistemologically as the mode in which we perceive the analogy between God's relational being and human relational being, but ontologically as the way in which human relational being is constituted and restored through the relationship of the trinitarian God to humanity. This is, however, only possible if the analogy between the trinitarian persons and the human person is strictly interpreted as an *analogia transcendentalis* both in its ontological and epistemological sense.'

19 *Doctrine of the Trinity*, Scottish Academic Press, 1976, p. 24.

20 Cf. LaCugna, *God For Us*, pp. 252–4: 'Despite his emphasis on the

divine persons as modes of God's being . . . the essence of God is uni-personal . . . In the end, neither Barth nor Rahner was able to break away entirely from the Cartesian starting point.'

21 Cf. LaCugna, *God for Us*, p. 227: 'All of this points to the liabilities of imprecise usage and encourages severe discipline in the use of the terms "economic" and "immanent" Trinity – if indeed theologians continue to use them at all – taking care not to use economic Trinity as a synonym for God as God appears to us, and immanent Trinity as a synonym for God as God really is *in se*.'

22 The idea that the modern emphasis on personal relationships was part of Cappadocian Trinitarian theology seems anachronistic, to say the least. But cf. W. Kasper, *The God of Jesus Christ*, SCM, 1984, p. 290:

> The divine persons are not only in dialogue. They are dialogue . . . J. Ratzinger in particular has made his own these insights. According to him, the concept of person 'by reason of its origin expresses the idea of dialogue and of God as a dialogical being. It points to God as the being who lives in the Word and subsists in the Word as I and Thou and We.' Ratzinger is aware of the revolution which this concept of person as relation represents. Neither the substance of the ancients nor the person of the moderns is ultimate, but rather relation as the primordial category of relation.

But the previous paragraph is a good example of the relationships Kasper has in mind; it is pure immanent Trinity!

23 Cf. LaCugna, *God for Us*, pp. 279–82.

24 *TS*, 1975, pp. 627–46.

25 Ibid., p. 638.

26 Ibid., p. 640. For the following quotations see pp. 642–3.

27 A similar tactic is proposed by C. M. LaCugna in relation to P. Wilson-Kastner's use of perichoresis to describe her 'vision of an egalitarian human community' which reflects the mutuality of relationships between the three members of the divine Trinity. In order to prevent monarchical models, La Cugna seeks to avoid Latin theology's emphasis on God in himself and returns to 'the economy of salvation and the revelation of the concrete forms of human community proclaimed by Jesus as characteristic of the reign of God. Otherwise it seems that feminism, as much as patriarchy, projects its vision of what it wishes would happen in the human sphere on to God, or onto a transeconomic, transexperiential realm of intra-divine relations' (p. 274). Does not the criticism of the immanent Trinity need to be extended to the economic Trinity, so that we can at least indicate that the

economic Trinity has not simply become the reserve receptacle or vehicle of human wishes?

28 LaCugna, *God for Us*, p. 282.

29 There is a similar problem about A. McFadyen's attempt to relate divine and human persons; cf. his article, 'The Trinity and Human Individuality', *Theology* 95, 1992, pp. 10–17. He expressly notes the problems and his disquiet with solutions based on a symbolic immanent Trinity. Only a proper economic Trinity will do. But even that may not be enough, if it remains only a model. '. . . what is needed is not a model, but the communication of the energies of true relation and individuation from the Triune being of God' (p. 13). In the second part of the article, however, which is intended to suggest a more adequate method, we are given what read like brief job descriptions for the members of the Trinity, omitting the Father! In *The Call of Personhood*, McFadyen makes an excellent attempt (cf. p. 27f) to hold together 'relation' and 'individual' by means of the Trinity. But the attempt succeeds only in part, if it does succeed, by using the idea of 'relationship' and construing it as univocal and uppermost in normal usage in respect of both (a) human persons and (b) the divine persons of the Trinity. It would be more accurate to say that an insight about the nature of (a) human persons is being justified in terms of (b) divine persons. Only by extending the distinctive relationships of Father, Son and Holy Spirit to become a model or prototype of relationships in general can (b) become important for (a). This is a move which Christian theology can legitimately make with the necessary care. What is the difference, then, between this procedure and what McFadyen's trinitarian role descriptions do? It may seem to be splitting hairs but it is important not to make it appear that only when we are clear about the intra-divine relations can we be clear about human personhood. Cf. P. Scott, *Theology, Ideology and Liberation*, Cambridge University Press, 1994, pp. 140–2.

30 *Being as Communion*, Darton, Longman & Todd, 1985, pp. 27–49.

31 S. I. Benn, *A Theory of Freedom*, Cambridge University Press, 1988.

32 *Being as Communion*, p. 41.

33 Cf. ibid., p. 49: 'Death for a person means ceasing to love and be loved.' It is the end of communion.

34 *The Trinity and the Kingdom of God*, p. 216.

35 Cf. 'The body tends towards the person but leads finally to the individual', *Being as Communion*, p. 51.

36 Cf. p. 54 'Jesus Christ does not justify the title of Savior because he brings the world a beautiful revelation, a sublime teaching

about the person, but because he realises in history *the very reality of the person* and makes it the basis and "hypostasis" of the person for every man.'

37 *God for Us*, p. 265.
38 Ibid., p. 287.

## 10 RELIGION AND MORALITY: PERSONHOOD, REVELATION AND NARRATIVE

1 *Faith and Ethics*, Gill & Macmillan, 1985, p. 23.
2 Ibid.
3 Art. on 'Imitation' in *A New Dictionary of Christian Ethics*, SCM Press, 1986, p. 293.
4 N. Snaith, *Distinctive Ideas of the Old Testament*, Epworth, 1944, p. 49.
5 M. J. Borg, *Conflict, Holiness and Politics in the Teaching of Jesus*, E. Mellen Press, 1984, pp. 56–87.
6 A. H. Armstrong, 'Form, Individual and Person in Plotinus', *Dionysius* 1, 1977, p. 68.
7 The literature on 'revelation' is extensive. It has attracted both theologians and philosophers. W. Pannenberg, *Systematic Theology*, vol. 1, T. & T. Clark, 1991, pp. 189–257 offers a useful overview of historical developments, including discussion of his own views which emphasise the importance of Jewish and Christian apocalyptic and the resurrection of Jesus for a universalist understanding of history based on revelation, cf. W. Pannenberg (ed.), *Revelation as History*, Sheed and Ward, 1969. In addition see J. Baillie, *The Idea of Revelation in Recent Thought*, Columbia University Press, 1964; G. Moran, *Theology of Revelation*, Burns & Oates, 1967; K. S. Murty, *Revelation and Reason in Advaita Vedanta*, Livingston, 1959; for an interpretation of Islamic views see A. J. Arberry, *Revelation and Reason in Islam*, Allen & Unwin, 1957; O. Leaman, *An Introduction to Medieval Islamic Philosophy*, Cambridge University Press, 1985, chapter 4; Y. Zaki, 'The Qur'an and Revelation' in D. Cohn-Sherbok (ed.), *Islam in a World of Diverse Faiths*, Macmillan, 1991.
8 *Summa Theologica*, 1 q. 1, art. 8.
9 K. R. Trembath, *Divine Revelation*, Oxford University Press, 1991.
10 W. J. Abraham, *Divine Revelation and the Limits of Historical Criticism*, Oxford University Press, 1982; C. F. Henry, *God, Revelation and Authority*, Word Books, 1976; K. Barth, *The Epistle to the Romans*, Oxford University Press, 1933 and *Church Dogmatics*, II. 2, T. & T. Clark, 1957; J. I. Packer, *Knowing God*, Hodder & Stoughton, 1973.
11 K. R. Trembath, *Divine Revelation*, p. 64.

12  J. P. Mackey, *Power & Christian Ethics*, Cambridge University Press, 1994, pp. 209f.

13  K. R. Trembath, *Divine Revelation*, p. 67.

14  W. Temple, *Nature, Man & God*, Macmillan, 1934, p. 306: 'only if God is revealed in the rising of the sun in the sky can He be revealed in the rising of a son of man from the dead'.

15  A. Dulles, *Models of Revelation*, Gill & Macmillan, 1983; J. Macquarrie, *Principles of Christian Theology*, SCM Press, 1977 rev.; G. O'Collins, *Fundamental Theology*, Paulist Press, 1981; I. T. Ramsey, *Religious Language*, SCM Press, 1957; M. Polanyi, *Personal Knowledge* Routledge & Kegan Paul, 1973.

16  K. R. Trembath, *Divine Revelation*, p. 76.

17  Ibid., p. 110.

18  C. J. Berry, *Human Nature*, Macmillan, 1986, p.36. The interpretation of human nature should be linked with recent debates about personhood. Personhood is not necessarily identical with human nature. It is at once broader and more flexible, capable of dealing with debates (e.g. about non-human animals, the environment, and sub-classes of human being) that have arisen and will continue to arise because of man's new knowledge and technology. It functions, however, in a very similar way in terms of its theoretical and practical force in ethical contexts. It has both descriptive and prescriptive significance. Cf. also J. Annas, 'Women & the Quality of Life' in M. Nussbaum and A. Sen (eds.), *The Quality of Life*, Clarendon Press, 1993, p. 290.

19  cf. N. Wolterstorff, *Divine Discourse*, Cambridge University Press, 1995.

20  D. Brown, *Choices*, Blackwell, 1983, p. 25.

21  Ibid., p.44. See also pp. 46 and 48.

22  Gustafson, *Ethics from a Theocentric Perspective*, vol. 2, University of Chicago Press, 1984, chapter 2.

23  The eight features are:

   (1) The attempt to answer the question, 'What constitutes the moral as distinct from the non-moral?' The focus on man (or the human subject) even when man is not the highest value.

   (2) The way in which patterns of interdependence and development within which human life occurs become a basis for ethics. This givenness of the human context is not a matter of religious revelation; if it were, the basis of ethics would be private, not public. This position, however, does not exclude indications of divine ordering.

   (3) Morality is not opposed to the natural but gives it shape.

Social morality is never 'de novo'. This is a position which the natural law tradition tries to safeguard.

(4) Morality is related to attitudes and feelings, not just to reason, and the spiritual life is particularly important in this respect.

(5) An interactional model of ethical discourse, based on H. Richard Niebuhr's views of 'responding selves'.

(6) Morality is concerned with the relation of parts to wholes and a theocentric construal devotes particular attention to larger wholes such as the ecosphere or ecosystem. In fact, theology is concerned with 'the whole', even though no single person or group can claim to see or speak for the Whole. That is God's prerogative.

(7) Moral ambiguity and even tragic choice are inevitable. Not everything can be resolved rationally. Situation ethics and existentialist ethics do not resolve this. They simply read arbitrariness into everything.

(8) Finally, theocentric piety and recognition of God's sovereignty imposes self-restraint, self-denial and even self-sacrifice in the pursuit of our varied projects.

24 V. MacNamara, *Faith and Ethics*, Gill & Macmillan, 1985, pp. 187–8.

    i. God is creator and cause of human being. God is the source of the human being's autonomous moral activity. This may appear contradictory but need not be.

    ii. On the analogy of human creation (e.g. artistic creation) the totality of what exists (especially 'persons' and their flourishing) should be understood as the creative plan or purpose of God.

    iii. There is a problem about the limitation of human reason in the sphere of morality, involving human tragedy at times, but God can be appealed to as the ultimate ground and justification of human rationality. God 'wills whatever is the demand of right reason'.

    iv. 'If the Christian and non-Christian alike recognise the way of morality as that of the recognition of the claim of the human person, the Christian knows that in God is found the perfect love of all human beings.'

    v. Moral growth and union with God is the goal of moral striving and flourishing. Moral response is in a real sense sharing in God's reality which is perfect.

25 From G. Ryle, *Concept of Mind* (Hutchinson, 1949) onwards; cf. C. Taylor, *Sources of the Self*, Cambridge University Press, 1989; *Human Agency & Language*, Cambridge University Press, 1985.

26  Eg. A. Baier, *Postures of the Mind*, Methuen, 1985, chapters 3–5; and references to recent literature on Descartes in n. 14, pp. 91–2.

27  Baier, *Postures of the Mind*.

28  Ibid., p. 84.

29  V. MacNamara, *Faith and Ethics*, p. 115; cf. I. Murdoch, *The Sovereignty of Good*, Routledge & Kegan Paul, 1971, p. 80.

30  *Faith and Ethics*, pp. 117 and 119.

31  Collected essays in *Faith, Authenticity and Morality*, Handsel, 1980; cf. also his *Struggle and Fulfilment*, Collins, 1980, and *The Logic of Self-Involvement*, SCM Press, 1963. 'Onlooks' (e.g. I look on my life as a voyage, a dream, a game etc.) include deeply felt basic attitudes and what is sometimes referred to as 'myth', ideology, parable or world-view.

32  *Faith, Authenticity and Morality*, p. 11.

33  Ibid., p. 245.

34  Ibid., p. 257.

35  Cf. S. Katz, 'Martin Buber's Epistemology: A Critical Appraisal' in his *Post-Holocaust Dialogues*, New York University Press, 1985, especially pp. 21f.

36  Cf. G. Fackre, 'Narrative Theology: an Overview', *Interpretation* 37, 1983; G. Comstock, 'Truth or meaning: Ricoeur versus Frei on Biblical Narrative', *JR*, 66, 1986; H. Frei, *The Eclipse of Biblical Narrative* Yale University Press, 1974; F. McConnell (ed.), *The Bible and Narrative Tradition* Oxford University Press, 1986; G. Green (ed.), *Scriptural Authority & Narrative Interpretation* Fortress Press, 1986; W. C. Spohn, 'Parable & Narrative in Christian Ethics', *TS* 51/1, 1990, pp. 100–114; A. Wilder, 'A Story & Story-World', *Interpretation* 37, 1983, pp. 353–64.

37  Cf. G. Fackre, 'Narrative Theology: an Overview', *Interpretation* 37, 1983, p. 342: 'The reclaiming of imagination in countercultural and other movements of the sixties and seventies is inextricable from the growing interest in story. Disenchantment with things abstract, rationalistic, cerebral, didactic, intellectualist, structured, prosaic, scientist, technocratic and the appeal of the concrete, affective, intuitive, spontaneous, poetic contributed to the story focus.'

38  *Narrative & Morality*, Pennsylvania State University Press, 1987, p. 9.

39  A. V. Campbell and R. Higgs, *In That Case*, Darton, Longman & Todd, 1982, pp. 54–5.

40  R. B. Braithwaite, in B. Mitchell (ed.), *Philosophy of Religion*, Oxford University Press, 1971, pp. 84–5.

41 Ibid., p. 85.
42 For a more favourable assessment see H. Palmer, 'Stories' in *Modern Theology*, 2/2, 1986, pp. 707–24.
43 D. Ford (ed.), *The Modern Theologians*, vol. 1, Blackwell, 1989, p. 117.
44 Ibid., p. 131.
45 *Faith in History and Society*, Seabury Press, 1980, p. 157:

> I give the theories about the present situation of Christianity that have been elaborated in argument and are therefore effective from the theological point of view the rather cursory description of transcendental and idealistic theories. This title therefore includes such different approaches as the universally historical and transcendental approaches. If I am lacking in consideration in my generalized description of these approaches it is because I want to clarify in as few words as possible the intention underlying the post-idealistic narrative and practical-political approach.

46 Ibid., p. 210:

> There can, of course, be no *a priori* proof of the critical and liberating effect of such stories, which have to be encountered, listened to and told again. But surely there are, in our post-narrative age, story-tellers who can demonstrate what stories might be today – not just artificial, private constructions, but narratives with a stimulating effect and aiming at social criticism, dangerous stories in other words. Can we perhaps retell the Jesus stories nowadays in this way?

47 Ibid., p. 211.
48 Ibid., p. 212:

> The same applies to all universally historical approaches, which can only avoid a dangerous totalitarianism of meaning in their attempt to reconcile the histories of salvation and suffering when they keep to a meaning of the end of history that can be narrated in advance. The same can also be said of the recent attempts to connect the history of suffering back to the history of God within the Trinity. These attempts can also only avoid the danger of a speculative gnosis by being deciphered as argumentative narratives. If theology deliberately neglects its narrative character, both the argumentative and the narrative aspects of theology are bound to suffer.

49 A clear, sympathetic discussion of these differences may be found in K. J. Vanhoozer, *Biblical Narrative in the Philosophy of Paul Ricoeur*, Cambridge University Press, 1990, chapter 7; Cf. J. van den Hengel, 'Paul Ricoeur's *Oneself as Another* and Practical Theology', *TS* 55, 1994, pp. 458–80; D. Wood (ed.), *On Paul Ricoeur*, Routledge, 1991.
50 F. Watson, 'Narrative and Reality' in *Text, Church and World*, T. & T. Clark, 1994, p. 26, draws attention to the failure of Frei to relate

textuality and historical reality adequately: 'The failure to speak adequately of the text's relation to the extratextual, historical–theological reality of Jesus is of a piece with the reluctance to allow any contact between the text and any other historical reality. The world must not be allowed to contaminate the text.' H. Frei, 'The "Literal Reading" of Biblical Narrative in the Christian Tradition: Does It Stretch or Will It Break?' in G. Green (ed.), *Scriptural Authority & Narrative Interpretation*, Fortress Press, 1986.

51 Sameness, similarity and difference, like the more puzzling 'permanence', raise questions about what survives through time. Selfhood, however, is about agency, authorship and who is responsible.

52 P. Ricoeur, 'Narrative Identity' in D. Wood (ed.), *On Paul Ricoeur*, p. 197.

53 Ibid., p. 199.

54 van den Hengel, 'Paul Ricoeur's *Oneself as Another*', p. 470.


## PART 3 IMPLICATIONS FOR A CHRISTIAN ETHIC

1 Cf. J. Milbank, *Theology and Social Theory*, Blackwell, 1990, pp. 399f – his discussion of 'counter-ethics and ecclesiology': 'one needs to emphasize more strongly the interruptive character of Christianity and therefore its difference from *both* modernity *and* antiquity'.

2 Cf. Ibid., pp. 411, 423f: 'This counter-ontology speculatively confirms three major components of the counter-ethics: first, the practice of charity and forgiveness as involving the priority of a gratuitous creative giving of existence, and so of difference'.


### II A COMMUNICATIVE ETHIC: HAUERWAS AND HABERMAS

1 Cf. F. J. Tönnies' distinction of *Gemeinschaft* (community) and *Gesellschaft* (society); the former refers to a traditional, tightly knit society based on *Wesenswille* (natural will related to intrinsic value), the latter to a modern society based on *Kürwille* (rational will related to specific objectives).

2 Cf. *After Virtue*, Duckworth, 1981, p. 181: 'it is always within some particular community with its own specific institutional form that we learn or fail to learn to exercise the virtues'.

3 E. R. Winkler and J. R. Coombs, *Applied Ethics: A Reader*, Blackwell, 1993, chapter 19 ('From Kantianism to Contextualism'); cf. B. Hoffmaster, 'Can Ethnography Save the Life of Medical Ethics?' in *Applied Ethics*, chapter 20.

4 Ibid., p. 348.
5 Ibid., p.360.
6 Cf. A. Jonson and S. Toulmin, *The Abuse of Casuistry*, University of California Press, 1988.
7 Cf. K. Barth, *Ethics*, T. & T. Clark, 1981.
8 Cf. J. Annas, 'Women and the Quality of Life: Two Norms or One?' in M. Nussbaum and A. Sen (eds.), *The Quality of Life*, Clarendon Press, 1993, pp. 279–96, especially p. 290:

> What we need then is a notion of human nature . . . on which ethics can build . . . it gives us a basis for our moral judgements but it is not itself a moral notion. This conception of human nature has recently become more respectable in ethics; it is no longer automatically ruled out as a confusion of 'fact' and 'value' . . . Human nature does not impose on us a specific set of things to do and way of living; rather it functions in a more unspecific and negative way, as a constraint on proposed forms of life and ethical rules.

Cf. B. Schüller, *Wholly Human*, Gill & Macmillan, 1986.

9 S. Benhabib, *Situating the Self*, Polity Press, 1992.
10 *The Peaceable Kingdom*, SCM, 1984, p. xxv. Cf. for an excellent critical but sympathetic discussion D. K. Friesen, 'A Critical Analysis of Narrative Ethics' in H. Huebner (ed.), *The Church as Theological Community*, Winnipeg, 1990.
11 *The Peaceable Kingdom*, p. 4.
12 Ibid., p. 5, citing *After Virtue*, p. 2
13 Ibid., p. 20. G. E. M. Anscombe, 'Modern Moral Philosophy', *Philosophy* 33, 1958, pp. 1–19.
14 Ibid., p. 21.
15 Ibid., p. 22.
16 Ibid., p. 25.
17 Ibid., p. 27.
18 Ibid., p. 29.
19 Ibid., p. 31.
20 Ibid., p. 33.
21 Ibid., pp. 50–71.
22 Ibid, p. 55.
23 Ibid., p. 57, quoting J. Fuchs, 'Is there a specifically Christian morality?' in *'Readings in Moral Theology Nr. 2' The Distinctiveness of Christian Ethics* (ed. C. Curran and R. McCormick), pp. 5–6.
24 *The Peaceable Kingdom*, p. 58.
25 Ibid.
26 Ibid, pp. 60–1.
27 Occasionally he points to a more favourable assessment of reason. Cf. *Community of Character*, University of Notre Dame Press, 1981,

p. 26: 'substantive traditions are not at odds with reason but are the bearers of rationality and innovation'; and 'Pacifism: some philosophical considerations' in R. Gill (ed.), *A Textbook of Christian Ethics*, T. & T. Clark, 1995, p.344: 'Such a claim is not peculiar to pacifism, however, but rather denotes how any substantive account of the moral life must work in a world determined by sin. Indeed pacifism in such a world is the very form of moral rationality since it is a pledge that we can come to common agreement on the basis of discussion rather than violence.'

28  *Peaceable Kingdom*, p. 29. Cf. D. K. Friesen, 'A Critical Analysis of Narrative Ethics', pp. 240–1.

29  *Peaceable Kingdom*, p.156 n. 19.

30  Cf. ibid., pp. 26–7.

31  Ibid., p. 70.

32  Ibid., p. 71.

33  Ibid., p. 71. Cf. D. K. Friesen, 'A Critical Analysis of Narrative Ethics', pp. 234–9.

34  *Narrative and Morality*, Pennsylvania State University Press, 1987, pp. 148–9.

35  Cf. 'Pacifism: some philosophical considerations' in R. Gill (ed.), *A Textbook of Christian Ethics*, p. 345: 'Indeed I simply refuse as a pacifist to think I need any account of the state at all.'

36  D. S. Browning and F. S. Fiorenza (eds.), *Habermas, Modernity and Public Theology*, Crossroad, 1992, p. 5.

37  P. Lakeland, *Theology and Critical Theory*, Abingdon, 1990, p. 37: critical theory is interested 'not in intellectual history but in the emancipation of the present for the future'.

38  Ibid., p. 55: 'It is also a project in defense of the human spirit, and as such it has a *prima facie* compatibility with the aims of religion.'

39  S. Benhabib, *Situating the Self*, p. 24: 'The central insight of communicative or discourse ethics derives from modern theories of autonomy and of the social contract, as articulated by John Locke, Jean Jacques Rousseau and in particular by Immanuel Kant. Only those norms and normative institutional arrangements are valid, it is claimed, which individuals can or would freely consent to as a result of engaging in certain argumentative practices.'

40  Ibid., p. 25.

41  Ibid., p. 28.

42  Ibid., p.29.

43  Ibid., p.33.

44  Ibid., p.58 n. 30.

45  Ibid., p. 36.

46 Ibid., p. 38 and pp. 186f.
47 F. R. Dallmayr and S. Benhabib (eds.), *The Communicative Ethics Controversy*, p. 348.
48 S. Benhabib, *Situating the Self*, p. 50.
49 Cf. N. Fraser, 'What's Critical about Critical Theory? The Case of Habermas and Gender', in M. L. Shanley and C. Pateman (eds.), *Feminist Interpretations and Political Theory*, Polity Press, 1991, pp. 253–76; D. S. Browning and F. S. Fiorenza, *Habermas, Modernity and Public Theology*, p. 89 n. 35.
50 S. Benhabib, *Situating the Self*, p. 52.
51 Ibid., p. 52.
52 Ibid., p. 42 and p. 61 n. 48.
53 E.g. A. Giddens, 'Reason without Revolution?' in R. J. Bernstein (ed.), *Habermas and Modernity*, Polity Press, 1985, pp. 95–121.
54 *Situating the Self*, p. 63 n. 51.
55 Ibid., p. 43.
56 Ibid., p. 64 n. 53.
57 *Freedom and Reason*, Oxford University Press, 1963, pp. 159–72.
58 D. S. Browning and F. S. Fiorenza (eds.), *Habermas, Modernity and Public Theology*, p. 79.
59 Cf. A. Thiselton, *New Horizons in Hermeneutics*, Harper & Row, 1992, pp. 612–3.
60 Cf. D. McNaughton, *Moral Vision*, Blackwell, 1988, chapter 10 for an excellent discussion of moral realism and cultural diversity.
61 Ibid., p. 156.
62 J. Cobb, 'Christian Witness in a Pluralistic World', in J. Hick and H. Askari (eds.), *The Experience of Religious Diversity*, Gower, 1985, pp. 158–61.
63 M. Barnes, *Religions in Conversation*, SPCK, 1989, p. 115. Cf. D. K. Friesen, 'A Critical Analysis of Narrative Ethics', p. 246: 'Rather we must enter into dialogue with the descriptions of the world in order to discern how the narrative can be applied in such a way as to intelligibly interpret the world, offering models and creative alternatives to the ruts in which the world is stuck.'
64 A. Thiselton, *New Horizons in Hermeneutics*, p. 613.

12 A COMMUNITY OF ETHICAL DIFFERENCE: INCLUDING THE 'OTHER'

1 C. Burchard, 'The Theme of the Sermon on the Mount' in R. H. Fuller (ed.), *Essays on the Love Commandment*, Fortress, 1978, p. 57.
2 E. P. Sanders, *The Historical Figure of Jesus*, Allen Lane, 1993, p. 7 on T. Jefferson's admiration for the ethic of Jesus and deism!

3  Hosea iv. 2; cf. Isaiah xxiv for a more apocalyptic account.
4  Cf. Horsley, *Sociology and the Jesus Movement*, Crossroad, 1989, rev. 1994; R. A Horsley with J. S. Hanson, *Bandits, Prophets and Messiahs*, Harper & Row, 1985.
5  G. Theissen, *Social Reality and the Early Christians*, T. & T. Clark, 1993, p. 57.
6  Ibid., p. 258.
7  Ibid., p. 259f. Theissen lists six axioms 'shared by the interpretative community of the early Christians' on the phenomenological view: 1.The personal charismatic axiom: that is, the conviction that God can be experienced personally by human beings, through Jesus Christ and His Spirit; 2. The eschatological axiom, that Jesus is the beginning of a new world. The old world is passing away; 3. The conversion axiom: human behaviour is not fixed once and for all. It is open to radical reorientation. Christians are born again through baptism into the death and resurrection of Jesus to a new life of faithfulness and obedience to God. 4. The axiom about the kerygma of suffering: Christians are called to suffer with Christ. Liberation from sin and death may involve martyrdom. 5. The integration axiom: old distinctions disappear in the body of Christ, the new community, into which sinners and the lost are welcomed. The insider/outsider distinction is relativised for those who are converted and incorporated into the body of Christ. 6. The change of position axiom: the first should be ready to assume the position of the last. Within the new community old hierarchies are also relativised in a setting of mutual service.
8  Ibid., p. 270.
9  Ibid.
10  Ibid., p. 277.
11  Ibid., p. 280.
12  *The Moral World of the First Christians*, SPCK, 1987, p. 103.
13  Ibid., pp. 119–20.
14  Cf. ibid., p. 128.
15  S. Fowl, *The Story of Christ in the Ethics of Paul*, Sheffield Academic Press, 1990, p. 199.
16  W. D. Davies, *The Sermon on the Mount*, Cambridge University Press, 1966, p. 149. Cf. W. Schrage, *The Ethics of the New Testament*, T. & T. Clark, 1988, p. 87.
17  Cf. M. J. Borg, *Conflict, Holiness and Politics in the Teaching of Jesus*, E. Mellen Press, 1984, pp. 234–6; cf. W. Schrage, *Ethics of the New Testament*, pp. 68–79.
18  'The Golden Rule: Exegetical and Theological Perplexities', *NTS* 36, 1990, pp. 392–7.

19 A good example of a drama which clearly uses the contrasting logics of equivalence and superabundance, in an ethical context, to explore the nature of justice and women's oppression is Shakespeare's *Measure for Measure*. Isabella pleads for her brother's life and is at first refused by Lord Angelo, the Duke's deputy, who has acquired a reputation for being meticulous in executing justice in what is clearly a very uncivil and permissive society. Lord Angelo, although at first inclined to dismiss her request, is tempted by her purity and agrees to release her brother if she will submit her body to him. Shocked and outraged by this use of power and injustice, Isabella threatens to expose him. Lord Angelo tells her, in words reminiscent of many modern rape cases, that no one will believe her. It is her word against his. His reputation carries more weight (and power). She visits her brother in prison and explains what has happened. At first he supports her, but then reflects that she will be sinned against rather than the sinner if she submits to Lord Angelo. He wants to live, not die. Isabella feels surrounded by male perfidy. At this point a friar, who is really the absent Duke in disguise, suggests a way to confront Lord Angelo with his deception and obtain justice for Isabella and another wronged women, Mariana, the rejected betrothed of Angelo. This brief summary cannot capture the irony and deep pathos of the dialogue, the exploration of justice and mercy, the insights into the nature of social and sexual mores of the time and the moral issues raised. Despite its sixteenth-century setting, it has a modern ring. The dilemmas have not disappeared. Although certain moral boundaries are clear (we cannot – morally – practice what we ourselves condemn) there can be no justice, forgiveness and reconciliation except in a lawfully ordered society. The play depends for its happy outcome on the return of a generous Duke, who knows everything and has the power to command justice and mercy, a solution not normally available in real life, although closely akin to some Christian views of what should, can and will be.

20 Ricoeur, 'The Golden Rule', p. 395.

21 Ibid.

22 Ibid., p. 396.

23 The importance of the reference to Kierkegaard should not be ignored. Kierkegaard clearly draws attention to weaknesses in the conventional Christianity of his day – and ours, when he pillories the dry, irrelevant nature of conventional Christian faith and practice.

24 Published lecture, 'Theology for Tomorrow's World', given by

Professor A. Thatcher at Cheltenham & Gloucester College of
Higher Education in June 1993.

25  'Non-violence and the Love of one's Enemies', pp. 9–39 in R. H.
Fuller (ed.), *Essays on the Love Commandment* (ET 1978).

26  Ibid., p. 12.

27  Ibid.

28  Ibid., p. 23.

29  H. O. J. Brown, 'The New Testament Against Itself: 1 Tim.2.9–15
and the 'Breakthrough' of Gal.3, 28' in A. J. Köstenberger, T. T.
Schreiner and H. S. Baldwin (eds.), *Women in the Church*, Baker
Books, 1995, p. 202.

30  Cf. F. Martin, *The Feminist Question*, T. & T. Clark, 1994, p. 357.

31  Cf. L. R. Donelson, *Pseudepigraphy and Ethical Argument in the Pastoral
Epistles*, C. B. Mohr, 1986, pp. 176f and the literature cited in
n. 158. Donelson accepts the view of D. L. Balch, *Let Wives be
Submissive* (Scholar's Press, 1981), that the codes have a partly
apologetic purpose (i.e. to reassure the political authorities that
Christians will not disturb the civil order). Cf. also F. F. Bruce, *The
Epistles to the Colossians, Philemon & Ephesians*, Eerdmans, 1984,
p. 162 n. 168; D. Schroeder, 'Once You Were No People . . .' in
H. Huebner (ed.), *The Church as Theological Community*, Canadian
Mennonite Bible College Publications, Winnipeg, 1990; D. C.
Verner, *The Household of God*, Society of Biblical Literature, 1983.

32  Bruce, *The Epistles to the Colossians, Philemon & Ephesians*,
pp. 398–9; cf. Schrage, *Ethics of the New Testament*, p. 252: 'The
purpose of the *Haustafel* is therefore to subject the life of Christians
to the lordship of Christ within the institutions of the secular
world.'

33  *Bread not stones*, Beacon Press, 1984, p. 76.

34  Ibid., p. 78.

35  Ibid., p. 83.

36  Ibid., pp. 90–1.

37  D. Lührmann, 'Neutestamentliche Haustafeln und antike Öko-
nomie', *NTS* 27/1, 1980, pp. 83–97. He examines the household
codes of the New Testament in relation to other writings on the
economy in the ancient world and establishes they belong to the
same genre. The household was the unit of production and
consumption (p. 89). Whether this household economy could
provide a model for the state was answered differently by Xeno-
phon and Plato, on the one hand, and by Aristotle on the other.
Early Christianity did not set out to instigate or organise a social
revolution, in his view, but its message had social and economic
consequences (p. 91). He divides the codes into three chrono-

logical groups (Pauline; Colossians–Ephesians; Pastorals) in which he detects shifting concerns (for example, in the first phase, the relation of Jews and Christians in the same household was an important issue, since it affected social integration). 'Kennzeichnend für diese Gemeinden des paulinischen Typs ist eine hohe soziale Integrationsfähigkeit, denn Gal. 3.28 ist nicht ein idealer Grundsatz geblieben, sondern spiegelt, wie G. Theissen für Korinth verifiziert, durchaus die Realität' (p. 93). In the second phase, continuity between generations became a more important issue and, in the third phase, he detects a shift of concern to caring for those in social need. In all three phases the question of the relationship of Christians to the state had an important influence. The Roman state could brook no rival state within a state. But the Christian message made universal ethical and religious claims.

38 Schroeder, 'Once You Were No People . . .', p. 63.
39 Cf. Schrage, *Ethics of the New Testament*, p. 256.
40 Fiorenza, *Bread not Stones*, p. 91.

13 THE LOGIC OF SUPERABUNDANCE: AN ETHIC OF FORGIVING LOVE

1 A. Minas, 'God and Forgiveness', *PQ* 25, 1975, pp. 138f.
2 Ibid., p. 142.
3 M. Lewis, 'On Forgiveness', *PQ* 30, 1980, pp. 236–45.
4 Ibid., p. 239.
5 Ibid., p. 244.
6 Ibid., p. 245.
7 E. Moberley, *Suffering, Innocent and Guilty*, SPCK, 1978, p. 136.
8 Ibid., p. 136.
9 Cf. M. Scheler, *Formalism in Ethics and Non-formal Ethics of Values*, Northwestern University Press, 1973, p. 369 n. 156: '"Forgiving" is not to be understood as the mere abandonment of punitive evil or punishment itself, but as the factual cancellation of evil as a non-formal value, though not, of course, of its bearers, which are factual actions that cannot be undone. Only God can "forgive" in this sense.'
10 Cf. *Dictionary of the Bible*, vol. 2, ed. J. Hastings, T. & T. Clark, 1900, p. 56: 'Forgiveness is a free act on the part of God or man; it restores the offender to the state in which there is no obstacle to his communion with him from whom he has been alienated; it gives peace of mind; removes fear of punishment and quickens love.'

382 *Notes to pages 281–289*

11 *Pauline Christianity*, Oxford University Press, 1983, p. 84.
12 Ibid., p. 87.
13 Ibid., p. 98.
14 Cf. R. Niebuhr, *An Interpretation of Christian Ethics*, Harper & Brothers, 1935, p. 223: 'The crown of Christian ethics is the doctrine of forgiveness.' E. Brunner, *The Mediator*, Lutterworth, 1934, pp. 446–7:

> The divine law – the world-order – requires that sin should receive its corresponding penalty from God. God cannot approach man as though there were no obstacle, as though no block of stone had made the way impassable between us and Him. Indeed, it is the divine righteousness and holiness which gives this obstacle its weight, its objective reality, which is the reason why we cannot push it out of the way. . . Forgiveness, however, would mean the removal of this obstacle, thus it would mean the contravention of the logical result of the world law; therefore, it would mean a process more vast and profound than we could even imagine, a change far more vast than the suspension of the laws of nature. For the laws of nature are laws of the Divine Creation, external laws. But the law of penalty is the expression of the personal Will of God, of the Divine Holiness itself. Forgiveness, therefore, would be the declaration of the non-validity of the unconditioned order of righteousness which requires penalty.

Cf. J. Milbank, *Theology and Social Theory*, Blackwell, 1990, pp. 409, 416.
15 Matthew vi. 12; Colossians iii. 13. Cf. S. Hauerwas, *The Peaceable Kingdom*, SCM, 1984, p. 90: 'As I learn to locate my life within the kingdom of forgiveness found in Jesus' life, death and resurrection, I acquire those virtues of humility and courage that are necessary to make my life my own.'
16 *An Interpretation of Christian Ethics*, pp. 39, 233.
17 Ibid., p. 47.
18 J. A. Hutchison (ed.), *Christian Faith & Social Action*, C. Scribner & Sons, 1953, p. 241.
19 D. W. Shriver, *An Ethic for Enemies*, Oxford University Press, p. 7.
20 *Reasons and Persons*, Oxford University Press, 1984, pp. 323–6.
21 F. Dostoevsky's protest in *The Brothers Karamazov* registers the problems involved here: 'let her forgive the torturer for the immeasurable suffering of her mother's heart. But the suffering of her tortured child she has no right to forgive'.
22 *When Theology Listens to the Poor*, Harper & Row, 1988, p. 48.
23 M. J. Borg, *Conflict, Holiness and Politics in the Teachings of Jesus*, E. Mellen Press, 1984, p. 247.
24 C. R. Bråkenhielm, *Forgiveness*, Fortress, 1993, p. 52.

25 H. Willmer, 'The Politics of Forgiveness – A New Dynamic', *The Furrow,* 30, 1979, p. 212.
26 Bråkenhielm, *Forgiveness,* p. 53, quoting Willmer, ibid.
27 Bråkenhielm, ibid., p. 53.
28 Shriver, *An Ethic for Enemies,* p. 173.
29 Ibid., p. 45–62, and 245 n. 77, commenting on Allen W. Wood's, *Kant's Moral Religion,* Cornell University Press, 1970, p. 239–43 ('Forgiveness as a process in which human social relations are mutually repaired gets little attention here').

14 RIGHTS AND PERSONS: THE RELIGIOUS GROUND OF HUMAN RIGHTS

1 R. Tuck, *Natural Rights Theories,* Cambridge University Press, 1979, pp. 13f. 'It is among the men who rediscovered the Digest and created the medieval science of Roman law in the twelfth century that we must look to find the first modern rights theory, one built round the notion of a passive right.'
2 Ibid., p. 25:

But it was d'Ailly's successor as Chancellor of the university of Paris, Jean Gerson, who really created the theory. He did so in a work entitled *De Vita Spirituali Animae* . . . It contains the following remarkable analysis of the concept of a *ius. Ius* is a dispositional *facultas* or power, appropriate to someone and in accordance with the dictates of right reason . . . I want to say that an entity has *iura,* defined in this way, equivalent to those positive qualities which constitute its identity and therefore its goodness. In this way the sky has the right to rain, the sun to shine, fire to burn, a swallow to build its nest, and every creature to do what is naturally good for it. The reason for this is obvious: all these things are appropriate to these beings following the dictate of the divine reason, otherwise none of them would survive. So man, even though a sinner, has a *ius* to many things, like other creatures left to their own nature . . . This analysis of *ius* is modified by political theorists, who use the term only of what suits rational creatures using their reason.

3 *Creeds, Society and Human Rights,* Eerdmans, 1984, pp. 6–9. Cf. the works cited by R. Martin and J. W. Nickel, 'Recent Work on the Concept of Rights', *APQ* 17/3, 1980, pp. 165–80. To these should be added E. F. Paul et al. (eds.), *Human Rights,* Blackwell, 1984; R. G. Frey (ed.), *Utility and Rights,* Blackwell, 1985; T. Regan, *The Case for Animal Rights,* Routledge & Kegan Paul, 1984.
4 *PPA* 4, 1975, pp. 203–4.
5 'Dispensing with Moral Rights', *Political Theory* 6, 1978, pp. 63–74. Reference to K. Cronin's *Rights and Christian Ethics* allows us to move rapidly over a number of the arguments which support the

need to supply reasons why rights are important for a Christian ethic.

6 See R. Martin and J. W. Nickel, 'Recent Work on the Concept of Rights', pp. 178–80; in addition, J. Feinberg, *Rights, Justice and the Bounds of Liberty*, Princeton University Press, 1980; J. Finnis, *Natural Law and Natural Rights* Clarendon, 1980; A. Gewirth, 'The Epistemology of Human Rights', in E. F. Paul et al. (eds.), *Human Rights*.

7 B. Bandman, 'Do children have rights?', *Philosophy of Education*, 1973, p. 236.

8 Finnis, *Natural Law and Natural Rights*, pp. 199f. J. Finnis summarises and explains these categories as follows:
    (a) A has a claim-right that B should Ø, if and only if B has a duty to A to Ø (where Ø stands for the description of an act).
    (b) B has a liberty (relative to A) to Ø, if and only if A has no claim right (a 'no-right') that B should not Ø.
    (b1) as b., but with A and B reversed.
    (c) A has a power (relative to B) to Ø if and only if B has a liability to have his legal position changed by A's Øing.
    (d) B has an immunity (relative to A's Øing) if and only if A has no power (i.e. a disability) to change B's legal position by Øing.
    Cf. also L. W. Sumner, *The Moral Foundation of Rights*, Oxford University Press, 1987, for a different development of Hohfeld; Sumner wishes to defend a consequentialist theory of rights related to agent choice.

9 Ibid., p. 203.
10 E.g. J. Feinberg, 'The Nature and Value of Rights', in *Rights, Justice and the Bounds of Liberty*, p. 152; T. Regan, *Animal Rights*, pp. 272, 281.
11 H. J. McCloskey, 'Rights', *PQ* 15, 1965; 'Moral Rights and Animals', *Inquiry* 22, 1979; 'Respect for Human Moral Rights' in Frey (ed.), *Utility and Rights*, pp. 124f.
12 E.g. S. I. Benn and R. S. Peters, *Social Principles and the Democratic State*, Allen & Unwin, 1959, p. 8.
13 R. B. Brandt, *Ethical Theory*, Prentice Hall, 1959, p. 441.
14 'Duties, Rights and Claims' in Feinberg, *Rights, Justice and the Bounds of Liberty*, p. 140.
15 Ibid., p. 140.
16 Sumner, *The Moral Foundation of Rights*, p. 206.
17 'A defence of Abortion and Infanticide', *PPA* 1, 1972, pp. 37–65.
18 'The Morality of Abortion' in M. Bayles (ed.), *Ethics and Population*, Schenkman Publishing Co., 1976, pp. 164–81.
19 R. G. Frey, *Interests and Rights*, Clarendon, 1980, pp. 82–3.

20 'Towards a Substantive Theory of Rights', in Frey (ed.), *Utility and Rights*, pp. 137–60. On p. 146 he wishes to argue that if utility is not so much an overarching value, 'in fact, not a substantive value at all, but . . . a formal analysis of what it is for something to be prudentially valuable', then personhood and other apparently non-utilitarian grounds can be perfectly reconciled with overall utility.

21 E. M. Adams, 'The Ground of Human Rights', *APQ* 19/2, 1982, p. 191.

22 Ibid., p. 192, citing A. Melden, *Rights and Persons*, p. 199.

23 Melden, ibid., p. 192.

24 Ibid., p. 199.

25 A. Gewirth, 'Reason and Morality'; and many other articles, e.g. 'The Epistemology of Human Rights', 'The Basis and Content of Human Rights'.

26 'The Epistemology of Human Rights', pp. 23f.

27 Adams, 'The Ground of Human Rights', p. 195. Cf. A. Danto, 'Constructing an Epistemology of Human Rights: a Pseudo-Problem', in Paul and Miller (eds.), *Human Rights*, pp. 25–30.

28 Ibid., p. 195.

29 A. A. Morris, 'A Differential Theory of Human Rights', in J. R. Pennock and J. W. Chapman (eds.), *Human Rights*, Nomos 23., New York University Press, 1981, pp. 161f.

30 On Tooley see chapter 3. Griffin treats utility not as a value but as 'a formal analysis of what it is for something to be prudentially valuable'.

31 T. Regan, *Animal Rights*, avoids the term 'person' and prefers to speak of 'individuals, moral agents or patients, who are "the subject of a life"' (pp. 243f). His criteria for being the subject of a life, however, are very similar to those adduced by Tooley and others as criteria for personhood. Since he argues strongly for animal rights it is possible that he did not wish to weaken or confuse his case by referring to non-human animals as persons.

32 M. A. Warren, 'On the Moral and Legal Status of Abortion', *Monist* 57, 1973.

33 Cf. Lomassky who grounds rights in 'having a personal project' in Paul and Miller (eds.), *Human Rights*, pp. 35–55.

34 V. Haksar, *Equality, Liberty and Perfectionism*, Clarendon, 1979.

35 Ibid., p. 111.

36 'And even if you give idiots full membership of the egalitarian club because you believe in the Christian version of the family argument, or because you believe, as many Christians do, that they have souls, it is worth stressing that you are appealing to

metaphysical-cum-perfectionist considerations. For as we saw earlier the Christian version of the family argument does presuppose such consideration' (p. 79). In its context, this comment appears to regard such considerations as an objection, whereas earlier, on p. 45, it appears that all forms of egalitarianism presuppose considerations of this sort.

37 A. MacIntyre, 'How Virtues Became Vices: Values, Medicine and Social Context' in Engelhardt and Spicker (eds.), *Evaluation and Explanation in the Biomedical Sciences*, pp. 104–5, cited in S. Hauerwas, *Truthfulness and Tragedy*, University of Notre Dame Press, 1977, p. 245 n. 31. Cf. B. Mitchell, *Morality, Religious and Secular*, Oxford University Press, 1980, p. 78.

38 Cf. J. Rawls, *A Theory of Justice*, Oxford University Press, 1972, section 77, 'Only those who can give justice are owed justice'.

39 J. L. Allen, 'A Theological Approach to Moral Rights', *JRE* 2, 1974, p. 132.

40 J. Moltmann, *On Human Dignity*, SCM, 1984, p. 12.

41 'Theological Perspectives on Human Rights', Lutheran World Federation, 1977.

42 Moltmann, *On Human Dignity*, p. 8.

43 Ibid., pp. 8–9.

44 Ibid., p. 9.

45 Ibid., p. 10.

46 Ibid., p. 11.

47 Ibid., p. 15.

48 Ibid., p. 20.

49 J. Passmore, *Man's Responsibility for Nature*, Duckworth, 1974, chapters 1–2.

50 C. Villa-Vicencio, *A Theology of Reconstruction*, p. 164, Cambridge University Press, 1992.

51 Ibid., p. 165. Cf. T. Benton, *Natural Relations* Verso, 1993. For a staunch defence of the primary individual reference of human rights in modern societies linked with a thoughtful critique of communitarianism see R. E. Howard, *Human Rights and the Search for Community*.

52 Villa-Vicencio, *A Theology*, p. 178: 'A theological vision of the fullness of life lived in harmony with the natural order further includes the right of access to water, land and an unpolluted environment, without which the future of life on this planet can only become less complete and less conforming to the harmony with which it was once endowed'.

53 Cf. pp. 313–14 and n. 49 above.

54 Passmore, *Man's Responsibility for Nature*, p. 116. Cf. 'Bacteria and

men do not recognise mutual obligations, nor do they have common interests. In the only sense in which belonging to a community generates ethical obligations, they do not belong to the same community.' There are assumptions here about the nature of both bacteria and community. Bacteria may be beneficial as well as harmful to human interests. The crucial question is whether this prevents a moral community (inclusive of bacteria) in which the obligations rest on humans but not on bacteria. P. Carruthers, *The Animals Issue*, Cambridge University Press, 1992, offers a sustained contractualist argument why rational agents should count more than animals. Although he regards himself as an animal-lover, he concludes: 'there are no good moral grounds for forbidding hunting, factory farming or laboratory testing on animals' (p. 196). Animals do not possess moral standing, because they are not rational agents.

55 Ibid., pp. 116 and 126.
56 Animal rights would require detailed discussion in the same way that human rights do. They would not be identical with human rights and would inevitably be more controversial. They would not be based on claims to personhood but on ecology or a theological view of creation which protects animal interests and welfare. Cf. K. Tanner, 'Creation, Environmental Crisis, and Ecological Justice' in R. S. Chopp and M. L. Taylor, *Reconstructing Theology*, Fortress, 1994, pp. 99–123. Tanner argues that most models of Christian environmentalism are too anthropocentric, despite good intentions. Emphasis on common creaturehood would be better. 'Putting human and nonhuman beings together in this way within a single community of moral concern helps resolve certain issues for human decision making' (p. 120). Experiments on animals, for instance, would, where possible, be replaced by the use of culture tissues in laboratories. Ecological and social justice would be complementary. See chapter 15 below and M. Barnes (ed.), *An Ecology of the Spirit*, University Press of America, 1994, for a good collection of essays illustrating similar developments in Roman Catholic thinking.

15 THE INTEGRITY AND TRANSFORMATION OF CREATION

1 L. White, 'The Historical Roots of Our Ecologic Crisis', 26 December 1966, lecture at Washington meeting of AAAS (reprinted as Appendix 1 in F. Schaeffer, *Pollution and the Death of Man*, Hodder & Stoughton, 1970, p. 70–85).
2 Ibid., p. 73.

3 Ibid., p. 79. S. R. L. Clark, *How To Think About The Earth*, Mowbrays, 1993, p. 18 disputes White's view that Christianity bears major responsibility for the crisis. 'By my account the crisis is the unintended outcome of a general wish to live a little better.'

4 White, 'Historical Roots', p. 80, cf. 'The Greek saint contemplates; the Western saint acts.'

5 Ibid., pp. 82f.

6 'Healing the Protestant Mind: Beyond the Theology of Human Dominion', in D. T. Hessel, (ed.), *After Nature's Revolt*, Fortress Press, 1992, pp. 65f.; cf. J McCarthy, *Theology in Green* 4/1, 1994, p. 24.

7 Pp. 141, 313 above. Cf. G. Wenham, *Genesis 1–15*, p. 26 and the literature cited there.

8 Wenham says, 'This formula sets man and woman on an equal footing as regards their humanity.' Earlier he notes, 'In ecstasy man bursts into poetry on meeting his perfect helpmeet' and observes that 'Hebrew spoke of relatives as one's "flesh and bone"'. The phrase may also be understood theologically as a reference to genuine partnership rather than subordination, which Wenham infers from the fact that man names woman.

9 Hessel, (ed.), *After Nature's Revolt*, p. 66.

10 Ibid., p. 70.

11 J. Cobb, *Process Theology as Political Theology*, Manchester University Press, 1982, pp. 114f.

12 J. Cobb, 'Postmodern Christianity in Quest of Eco-Justice' in Hessel (ed.), *After Nature's Revolt*, p. 36.

13 J. Zizioulas, 'Preserving God's Creation' (Part 3, *Theology in Green* 7, 1993, pp. 20–31.

14 J. McCarthy, 'The Expectant Groaning of Creation: Cosmic Redemption in Romans 8. 19–22', *Theology in Green* 4/1, 1994, p. 24–34.

15 Ibid., p. 31.

16 Ibid., p. 33.

17 Ibid., p. 31 'we, like Christ, act as priests of creation'. Cf. also J. Habgood, 'A Sacramental Approach to Environmental Issues' in C. Birch et al. (eds.), *Liberating Life*, p. 53, 'The priestly role of all human beings toward the whole of nature entails a similar offering through prayer and through the recognition that it belongs to God already.'

18 Cf., for instance, *Theology in Green* (4/2, 1994), especially the articles by P. Scott and J. N. Norris in Issue 4/2, 1994.

19 C. A. Hooker, 'Responsibility, Ethics and Nature' in D. E. Cooper and T. A. Palmer (eds.), *The Environment in Question*, Routledge, 1992, p. 150.

20 Cf. J. Passmore, *Man's Responsibility for Nature*, Duckworth, 1974, chapter 2.
21 Hooker, 'Responsibility, Ethics and Nature', p. 156: 'So while Marxism has no special regard for the environment – humans remain central – it emphasises obligations to the community rather than to individuals. Similarly, the Christian stewardship and creator traditions belong to a communalist trend of Christian thought and underwrite a shift towards primary communal obligations, with humans still the focus of ethical concern.'
22 For a good exposition of an environmental ethic of 'respect for nature' incorporating aspects of deep ecology see P. W. Taylor, *Respect for Nature*, Princeton University Press, 1986. Cf. also A. Carter, 'Deep Ecology or Social Ecology?' in *Heythrop Journal*, 36, 1995, pp. 328–50; T. Hayward, *Ecological Thought*, Polity, 1995, especially pp. 40–52, argues convincingly that the Enlightenment emphasis on reason as criticism rather than domination can be reconciled with emancipatory ecological value; W. French, 'Catholicism and the Common Good of the Biosphere' in M. Barnes, (ed.), *An Ecology of the Spirit*, University Press of America, 1994, pp. 177–94, seeks to retrieve an ecological ethic from traditional natural law concerns for the common good by reference to the Noachic covenant with all creation (not just humanity), Stoic traditions of cosmopolis (not just the city-state) and Aquinas' view that, although only angels and humanity are created in the image of God, other creatures bear 'a likeness of a trace' of their Creator.
23 G. Hardin, 'Lifeboat Ethics: The Case Against Helping the Poor' in W. Aiken and H. La Follette (eds.), *World Hunger and Moral Obligation*, Prentice Hall, 1977; P. Ehrlich, *The Population Bomb*, Pan Books, 1971. Cf. J. Feinberg, *Rights, Justice and the Bounds of Liberty*, Princeton University Press; M. D. Bayles, *Morality and Population Policy*, University of Alabama Press, 1980; S. Hauerwas, 'Moral Limits of Population Control', in *Truthfulness and Tragedy*, University of Notre Dame Press, 1977.
24 C. K. Chun, 'Eugenics on the Rise: A Report from Singapore' in R. Chadwick (ed.), *Ethics, Reproduction and Genetic Control*, Routledge, 1990.
25 Cf. D. Heyd's excellent discussion in *Genethics*, University of California Press, 1992, in which issues relating to the existence, numbers and identity of future persons are examined in detail. Conceptual puzzles (e.g. about claims for wrongful birth) remain, but his adoption of a consistent person-affecting standpoint is worked out with ingenuity and realism.

CONCLUSION

1 R. Eldridge, *On Moral Personhood*, University of Chicago Press, 1989, p. 121.

# Select bibliography

Adams E. M., 'The Ground of Human Rights', *APQ* 19/2, 1982, pp. 191–6.

Allen J. L., 'A Theological Approach to Moral Rights', *JRE* 2, 1974, pp. 132f.

Andresen C., 'Zur Entstehung und Geschichte des trinitarischen Personbegriffes', *ZNW* 52, 1961, pp. 1–39.

Aquinas T., *Summa Theologiae*, ed. T. Gilby, McGraw-Hill, 1964–71.

Arendt H., *The Life of the Mind: Thinking and Willing*, vols. 1–2, Secker & Warburg, 1978.

Armstrong A. H., 'Form, Individual and Person in Plotinus', *Dionysius* 1, 1977, pp. 49–68.

Armstrong D., *A Materialist Theory of Mind*, Cambridge University Press, 1968.

Augustine, *De Trinitate*.

Ayer A. J., *Concept of a Person and other Essays*, Macmillan, 1964.

Baelz P., *Ethics and Belief*, Sheldon, 1977.

Baier A., *Postures of the Mind*, Methuen, 1985.

Bantle F. X., 'Person und Personbegriff in der Trinitatslehre Karl Rahners', *Münchener Theologische Zeitschrift* 30, 1979, pp. 11–24.

Barbour R. S. (ed.), *The Kingdom of God & Human Society*, T. & T. Clark, 1993.

Barnes M., *Religions in Conversation*, SPCK, 1989.

Barnes M. (ed.), *An Ecology of the Spirit*, University Press of America, 1994.

Bayles M. D., *Morality and Population Policy*, Alabama University Press, 1980.

Beck L. W., *Early German Philosophy*, Harvard University Press, 1969.

Becker L. C., 'Human Being: the Boundaries of the Concept', *PPA* 4, 1974, pp. 334–59.

Benhabib S., *Situating the Self*, Polity Press, 1992.

Benn S. I., *A Theory of Freedom*, Cambridge University Press, 1988.

'Freedom, Autonomy and the Concept of a Person', *PAS* 1975–6, pp. 109–31.

Benthall J. (ed.), *Limits to Human Nature*, A. Lane, 1973.

Benton T., *Natural Relations*, Verso, 1993.

Benz E., *Marius Victorinus und die Entwicklung der abendländischen Willensmetaphysik*, W. Kohlhammer, Stuttgart, 1932.

'Der Mensch als Imago Dei', *Eranos Jahrbuch* 38, 1971, pp. 297–33.

Berenson F. M., *Understanding Persons*, Harvester, 1981.

Bergeron Fr., 'La structure du concept latin de personne', *Etudes d'histoire littéraire et doctrinale*, série 2, 1932, pp. 121–61.

Berman M., *The Politics of Authenticity*, Allen & Unwin, 1970.

Berry C. J., *Human Nature*, Macmillan, 1986.

Bertocci P., *Person and Reality*, Ronald Press, 1958.

*The Person God Is*, Allen & Unwin, 1970.

Birch C. et al (eds.), *Liberating Life*, Orbis, 1990.

Blumenthal H. J. and Markus R.A. (eds.), *Neoplatonism & Early Christian Thought*, Variorum, 1981.

Boff L., *When Theology Listens to the Poor* Harper & Row, 1988.

Borg M. J., *Conflict, Holiness and Politics in the Teaching of Jesus*, E. Mellen Press, 1984.

Bråkenhielm C. R., *Forgiveness*, Fortress, 1993.

Browning D. S. and Fiorenza F. S. (eds.), *Habermas, Modernity and Public Theology*, Crossroad, 1992.

Buber M., *I and Thou*, T. & T. Clark, 1937.

*Between Man & Man*, Collins, 1961.

Burchard C., 'The Theme of the Sermon on the Mount' in R. H. Fuller (ed.), *Essays on the Love Commandment*, Fortress, 1978.

Cairns D., *The Image of God in Man*, Collins, 1973.

Campbell A.V. and Higgs R., *In That Case*, Darton, Longman & Todd, 1982.

Card C. (ed.), *Feminist Ethics*, University of Kansas Press, 1991.

Carrithers M., Collins S. and Lukes S., *The Category of the Person*, Cambridge University Press, 1985.

Carruthers P., *Introducing Persons*, Croom Helm, 1986.

*The Animals Issue*, Cambridge University Press, 1992.

Carter A., 'Deep Ecology or Social Ecology?', *Heythrop Journal* 36, 1995, pp. 328–50.

Centore F. F., *Persons*, Greenwood Press, 1979.

Chadwick H., *Boethius*, Oxford University Press, 1981.

Chadwick R. (ed.), *Ethics, Reproduction and Genetic Control*, Routledge, 1990.

Clark G., *Women in Late Antiquity*, Oxford University Press, 1993.

Clark S. R. L., *The Moral Status of Animals*, Oxford, 1977.

*A Parliament of Souls*, Oxford University Press, 1990.

*God's World & the Great Awakening*, Oxford University Press, 1991.

*How To Think About The Earth*, Mowbrays, 1993.

Coakley S., 'Why Three? Some Further Reflections on the Origins of the Doctrine of the Trinity' in D. Pailin and S. Coakley (eds.), *The Making and Re-making of Christian Theology*, pp. 29–56, Oxford University Press, 1993.

Coburn R. C., 'Professor Malcolm on God', *Australasian Journal of Philosophy*, Aug. 1963, pp. 155f.

Cockburn D., *Other Human Beings*, Macmillan, 1990.

Collins S., *Selfless Persons*, Cambridge University Press, 1982.

Comstock G., 'Truth or Meaning: Ricoeur versus Frei on Biblical Narrative', *JR* 66, 1986, pp. 117–40.

Cooper D. E. and Palmer J. A. (ed.), *The Environment in Question*, Routledge, 1992.

Cottingham J., 'Neo-Naturalism and its Pitfalls', *Philosophy* 58/4, 1983, pp. 455–70.

Craig W. L., 'God, Time & Eternity', *RS* 14, 1978, pp. 497–503.

Cranor C., 'Towards a Theory of Respect for Persons', *APQ* 12, 1975, pp. 309–19.

Cronin K., *Rights & Christian Ethics*, Cambridge University Press, 1992.

Cunningham G. W., *Thought and Reality in Hegel's System*, Longmans, 1910.

Cupitt D., *The New Christian Ethics*, SCM, 1988.

Danielou J., 'La Notion de Personne chez les Peres Grecs' in Meyerson, 1973, pp. 113–21.

Daniels N., 'Moral Theory & the Plasticity of Persons', *Monist*, 1979, pp. 265–87.

Davies B., *An Introduction to the Philosophy of Religion*, Oxford University Press, 1993 (revised).

Deats P. and Robb C., *The Boston Personalist Tradition*, Mercer University Press, 1986.

Delattie E., 'Rights, Responsibilities and Future Persons', *Ethics* 82, 1972, pp. 254f.

Dennett D. C., 'Conditions of Personhood' in A. O. Rorty (ed.), *The Identities of Persons*, University of California Press, 1976.

Docherty T. (ed.), *Postmodernism*, Harvester, London, 1993.

Donagan A., *The Theory of Morality*, University of Chicago Press, 1977.

Donelson L. R., *Pseudepigraphy and Ethical Argument in the Pastoral Epistles*, J. C. B. Mohr, Tübingen, 1986.

Dorner I. A., *Divine Immutability* (trans. R. R. Williams), Fortress Press, 1994.

Downie R. S. and Telfer E., *Respect for Persons*, Allen & Unwin, 1969.

Drobner H. R., *Person-Exegese und Christologie bei Augustinus*, Brill, 1986.

Dworkin R., *Taking Rights Seriously*, Duckworth, 1978.

Eldridge R., *On Moral Personhood*, University of Chicago Press, 1989.

Emmet D., *Rules, Roles and Relations*, London, 1966.

Engelhardt H. T., *The Foundations of Bio-ethics*, Oxford University Press, 1986.

Evans C. S., *Preserving the Person*, Inter-Varsity Press, 1977.

Evans D. D., *Struggle and fulfilment*, Collins, 1980.

*Faith, Authenticity and Morality*, Handsel, 1980.

Evans E., 'Tertullian's Theological Terminology', *ChQR* 139, 1945, pp. 56–77.

Fackre G., 'Narrative Theology: an Overview', *Interpretation* 37, 1983, pp. 340–52.

Farley M., 'New Patterns of Relationship: Beginnings of a Moral Revolution', *Theological Studies*, 1975, pp. 627–46.

'Feminism and Universal Morality', in Outka and Reeder (eds.), 1993.

Feinberg J., *Rights, Justice and the Bounds of Liberty*, Princeton University Press, 1980.

Feinberg J. (ed.), *The Problem of Abortion*, Wadsworth, 1984.

Feuerbach L., *Thoughts on Death & Immortality*, University of California Press, 1980.

Finnis J., *Natural Law and Natural Rights*, Clarendon, 1980.

Fiorenza E. S., *Bread Not Stones*, Beacon Press, 1984.

Fletcher J., 'Indicators of Humanhood: A Tentative Profile of Man', *Hastings Center Report*, 2/5, 1972, pp. 1–4.

'Four Indicators of Humanhood – The Enquiry Matures', *Hastings Center Report*, 4/6, 1974, pp. 4–7.

Flew A., *A Rational Animal*, Oxford University Press, 1978.

Fourez G., *Liberation Ethics*, Temple University Press, 1982.

Fowl S., 'The Ethics of Interpretation or What's Left Over After the Elimination of Meaning' in D. Cline et al. (eds.), *The Bible in Three Dimensions*, Sheffield Academic Press, 1993.

*The Story of Christ in the Ethics of Paul*, Sheffield Academic Press, 1990.

Frankfurt H. G., 'Freedom of the Will and the Concept of a Person', *JP* 68, 1971, pp. 5–20.

Fraser N. and Nicholson L., 'Social Criticism without Philosophy' in T. Docherty (ed.), *Postmodernism*, pp. 415–32.

Frazer E. and Lacey N., *The Politics of Community*, Harvester, 1993.

Frei H., *The Eclipse of Biblical Narrative*, Yale University Press, 1974.

French W., 'Catholicism and the Common Good of the Biosphere' in M. Barnes (ed.), *An Ecology of the Spirit,* pp. 177–94.

Frey R. G., *Interests and Rights,* Clarendon, 1980.

Frey R. G. (ed.), *Utility and Rights,* Blackwell, 1984.

Freyne S (ed.), *Ethics & the Christian,* The Columba Press, 1991.

Friesen D. K., 'A Critical Analysis of Narrative Ethics', in H. Huebner, (ed.), *The Church as Theological Community,* Winnipeg, 1990.

Frings M. S., 'Towards the Constitution of the Unity of the Person', in W. Mays and S. C. Brown (eds.), *Linguistic Analysis & Phenomenology,* Macmillan, 1972.

Fuhrmann M., 'Persona, ein römischer Rollenbegriff', *Poetik und Hermeneutik* 7, 1979, pp. 83–106.

Gauthier D., *Practical Reasoning,* Oxford University Press, 1963.

Geach P., *God and the Soul,* Routledge & Kegan Paul, 1969.

*The Virtues,* Cambridge University Press, 1977.

Gewirth A., *Reason and Morality,* Oxford University Press, 1978.

'Are There Any Absolute Rights?' *PQ* 31/122, 1981, pp. 1–16.

'There Are Absolute Rights', *PQ* 32/1, 1982, pp. 348–53.

Gill C. (ed.), *The Person & the Human Mind,* Oxford University Press, 1990.

Gill R. (ed.), *A Textbook of Christian Ethics,* T. & T. Clark, 1995 (rev.).

Gilligan C., *In a Different Voice,* Harvard University Press, 1982.

Gilligan C., Ward J. V. and Taylor J. M. (eds.), *Mapping the Moral Domain,* Harvard University Press, 1988.

Gloege G., 'Person und Personalismus' in *Evangelisches Kirchenlexicon,* 1959.

Glover J., *Causing Death and Saving Lives,* Penguin, 1977.

Glover, J. (ed.), *The Philosophy of Mind,* Oxford University Press, 1976.

Goodman M. F. (ed.), *What is a Person?* Humana Press, 1988.

'Rorty, Personhood, Relativism', *Praxis International* 6/4, 1987, pp. 427–41.

Green G. (ed.), *Scriptural Authority & Narrative Interpretation,* Fortress Press, 1986.

Griffin J., *Well-Being: its Meaning, Measurement & Moral Importance,* Oxford University Press, 1986.

Gunton C., *The One, The Three & The Many,* Cambridge University Press, 1993.

*The Promise of Trinitarian Theology,* T. & T. Clark, 1991.

'Augustine, The Trinity, and the Theological Crisis of the West', *SJT* 43, 1989, pp. 33–58.

Gunton C. and Hardy D. (ed.), *On Being the Church,* T. & T. Clark, 1989.

Guroian V., *Ethics after Christendom,* Eerdmans, 1994.

Gustafson J. M., *Can Ethics be Christian?* University of Chicago Press, 1975.
*Theology and Ethics*, vols. 1–2, Blackwell, 1981–3.
Habermas J., *The Theory of Communicative Action*, vol. 2, Polity, 1987.
Hadot P., 'L'image de la Trinité dans l'âme chez Victorinus et chez saint Augustin', *St Patr* 6, Berlin, 1962, pp. 409–42.
'De Tertullien à Boèce. Le Développement de la Notion de Personne dans les Controverses Théologiques' in Meyerson, 1973, pp. 123–33.
Haksar V., *Equality, Liberty and Perfectionism*, Clarendon, 1979.
Halleux A. de, '"Hypostase" et "Personne" dans la formation du dogme trinitaire', *Revue d'Histoire Ecclesiastique* 79, 1984, pp. 313–69, 625–70.
Hampshire S., *Freedom of the Individual*, Chatto & Windus, 1975.
*Innocence and Experience*, Penguin, 1989.
Hanink J. G., *Persons, Rights and the Problem of Abortion*, Michigan, 1975.
Hankey W. J., *God in Himself*, Oxford University Press, 1987.
Hanley K. R., 'Ideology & the Person', *Communio* 8, 1981, pp. 292–304.
Hannay A., *Kierkegaard*, Routledge & Kegan Paul, 1982.
Hardin G., 'Lifeboat Ethics: The Case against Helping the Poor' in W. Aiken and H. La Follette (eds.), *World Hunger and Moral Obligation*, Prentice Hall, 1977.
Hare R. M., *Freedom and Reason*, Oxford University Press, 1963.
*Moral Thinking*, Oxford University Press, 1981.
'Abortion and the Golden Rule', *PPA* 4, 1975, pp. 201–22.
Harris J., *The Value of Life*, Routledge & Kegan Paul, 1985.
Harrison B. W., *Our Right to Choose*, Beacon, 1983.
*Making the Connections*, Beacon, 1985.
Harrison V., 'Yannaras on Person & Nature', *St Vladimir Theological Quarterly*, 33, 1989, pp. 287–98.
Hartman E., *Substance, Body and Soul*, Princeton University Press, 1977.
Hauerwas S., *Truthfulness and Tragedy*, Univ.of Notre Dame,1977.
*A Community of Character*, University of Notre Dame Press, 1981.
*The Peaceable Kingdom*, SCM Press, 1984.
*Suffering Presence*, University of Notre Dame, 1986.
Hauerwas S. and Jones L. G. (eds.), *Why Narrative?* Eerdmans, 1989.
Hayward T., *Ecological Thought*, Polity, 1995.
Hebblethwaite B. and Henderson E. (eds.), *Divine Action*, T. & T. Clark, 1990.
Heinrichs J., 'Sinn und Intersubjectivität', *Theologie und Philosophie* 45, 1970, pp. 161–91.

Helm P. (ed.), *Divine Commands and Morality*, Oxford University Press, 1981.

Hengel van den J., 'Paul Ricoeur's *Oneself as Another* and Practical Theology' *TS* 55, 1994, pp. 458–80.

Henley J., 'Theology and the Basis of Human Rights', *SJT* 39, 1986, pp. 361–78.

Hessel D. T. (ed.), *After Nature's Revolt*, Fortress Press, 1992.

Henry P., *Saint Augustine on Personality*, Macmillan, 1960.

Heyd D., *Genethics*, University of California Press, 1992.

Hick J. and Askari H. (eds.), *The Experience of Religious Diversity*, Gower, 1985.

Hinchcliff P. and Young D., *The Human Potential*, Darton, Longman & Todd, 1981.

Hirsch E., *Concept of Identity*, Oxford University Press, 1980.

Hirzel R., *Die Person: Begriff und Name derselben im Altertum*, Verlag der Königlich Bayerischen Akademie der Wissenschaften, Munich, 1914.

Hodgson P., *Winds of the Spirit*, SCM Press, 1994.

Hoerster N., 'Kindstötung und das Lebensrecht von Personen', *Analyse und Kritik* 12, 1990, pp. 226–44.

Hollenbach D., *Claims in Conflict*, Paulist Press, 1979.

Holley R., *Religious Education and Religious Understanding*, Routledge & Kegan Paul, 1978.

Hollis M., *Models of Man*, Cambridge University Press, 1977.

Horsley R. A., *Sociology and the Jesus Movement*, Continuum Publishing Co., 1994 (rev.).

*Jesus and the Spiral of Violence*, Harper & Row, 1987.

'Ethics and Exegesis: "Love your Enemies" and the Doctrine of Non-Violence', *Journal of the American Academy of Religion* 54, 1986, pp. 3–31.

Howard R. E., *Human Rights and the Search for Community*, Westview Press, 1995.

Hudson S. D., *Human Character and Morality*, Routledge & Kegan Paul, 1986.

Huebner H. (ed.), *The Church as Theological Community*, Canadian Mennonite Bible College Publications, Winnipeg, 1990.

Hursthouse R., *Beginning Lives*, Blackwell, 1987.

Ishiguro H., 'A Person's Future and the Mind–Body Problem', in W. Mays and S. C. Brown (eds.), *Linguistic Analysis*, Macmillan, 1972.

Jantzen G. M., *God's World, God's Body*, Darton, Longman & Todd, 1984.

Jeanrond W. G. and Rike J. L. (eds.), *Radical Pluralism & Truth*, Crossroad, 1991.

Jenson R. W., *The Triune Identity*, Fortress, 1982.
Johnson L. E., *A Morally Deep World*, Cambridge University Press, 1991.
Jones H. E., *Kant's Principle of Personality*, University of Wisconsin, 1971.
Jones L. G., 'Alasdair MacIntyre on Narrative, Community & the Moral Life', *Modern Theology* 4/1, 1987, pp. 53–69.
*Transformed Judgement*, University of Notre Dame Press, 1990.
Jonson A. and Toulmin S., *The Abuse of Casuistry*, University of California Press, 1988.
Jung P. B., 'A Roman Catholic Perspective on the Distinctiveness of Christian Ethics', *JRE*, 1984, pp. 123–41.
Kant I., *Religion within the Limits of Reason Alone*, Harper & Row, 1960.
*Groundwork of Metaphysics*, trans. H. J. Paton, *The Moral Law*, Hutchinson's University Library, 1948.
Kasper W., *The God of Jesus Christ*, SCM Press, 1984.
Katz S., 'Martin Buber's Epistemology: A Critical Appraisal', *Post-Holocaust Dialogues*, New York University Press, 1985.
Kenny A. J. P., Loguet Higgins C. H., Lucas J. R. and Waddington C.H., *The Development of Mind*, Edinburgh University Press, 1973.
Kingdom E., *What's Wrong with Rights?* Edinburgh, 1991.
Kippenberg H. G., Kuiper Y. B. and Sanders A. F. (eds.), *Concepts of Person in Religion & Thought*, Mouton, New York, 1990.
Kneale W., *On having a mind*, Cambridge University Press, 1962.
'Time and Eternity in Theology', *PAS* 1961, pp. 87–108.
Knight M., *Morals without Religion*, Dennis Dobson, 1955.
Kupperman J., *Character*, Oxford University Press, 1991.
LaCugna C. M., *God for Us*, HarperCollins, 1991.
Lakeland P., *Theology and Critical Theory*, Abingdon, 1990.
Lash N., 'Considering the Trinity', *Modern Theology* 2:3, 1986, pp. 183–96.
Lauritzen P., 'The Self and Its Discontents', *JRE* 1994, pp. 189–210.
Lee K., *A New Basis for Moral Philosophy*, Routledge & Kegan Paul, 1985.
Lewis D. K., 'Counterparts of persons and their bodies', *JP* 68, 1971, pp. 203–11.
Lewis H. D., *The Self & Immortality*, Macmillan, 1973.
*Persons and Life after Death*, Macmillan, 1978.
Lewis M., 'On Forgiveness', *PQ*, 30, 1980, pp. 236–45.
Linzey A., *Animal Theology*, SCM Press, 1994.
Locke J., *Essay Concerning Human Understanding*, 1690.
Lockwood M. (ed.), *Moral Dilemmas in Modern Medicine*, Oxford University Press, 1985.
'Singer on Killing and the Preference for Life', *Inquiry* 22, 1979, pp. 157–70.

Lossky V., *In the Image and Likeness of God*, Mowbrays, 1975.

Lucas J. R., *Freedom of the Will*, Oxford University Press, 1972.

*A Treatise on Time and Space*, Methuen, 1973.

Lührmann D., 'Neutestamentliche Haustafeln und antike Öko-nomie', *NTS* 27/1, 1980, pp. 83–97.

Lukes S., *Individualism*, Blackwell, 1973.

*Moral Conflicts & Politics*, Oxford, 1991.

Lukes S. and Lukes J., 'Individualism and the Intellectuals', *Political Studies*, 17, 1969, pp. 14–30.

Lyons D., *Rights, Welfare & Mill's Moral Theory*, Oxford University Press, 1994.

McCall C., *Concepts of Person*, Avebury, 1990.

McCarthy J., 'The Expectant Groaning of Creation: Cosmic Redemption in Romans 8.19–22', *Theology in Green* 4/1, 1994, pp. 24–34.

McConnell F. (ed.), *The Bible & Narrative Tradition*, Oxford University Press, 1986.

McCool G. A., 'The Ambrosian Origin of St. Augustine's Theology of the Image of God in Man', *TS* 1959, pp. 62–81.

McDowell J., 'Are Moral Requirements Hypothetical Imperatives?', *PAS* Supp. 52, 1978, pp. 13–29.

McFadyen A. L., *The Call to Personhood*, Cambridge University Press, 1990.

'The Trinity and Human Individuality', *Theology* 95, 1992, pp. 10–18.

Mackie J. L., *Problems from Locke*, Oxford University Press, 1976.

*Ethics*, Penguin, 1977.

Mackey J. P., *Power & Christian Ethics*, Cambridge University Press, 1994.

*The Christian Experience of God as Trinity*, SCM Press, 1983.

MacIntyre A., *After Virtue*, Duckworth, 1981.

Mackinnon D. M, 'Death' in A. Flew (ed.), *Essays in Philosophical Theology*, SCM Press, 1955.

Macmurray J., *The Self as Agent*, Faber., 1957.

*Persons in Relation*, Faber, 1961.

MacNamara V., *Faith and Ethics*, Gill & Macmillan, 1985.

McNaughton D., *Moral Vision*, Blackwell, 1988.

Madell G., *The Identity of the Self*, Edinburgh University Press, 1981.

Margolis J., *Persons and Minds*, D. Reidel, 1979.

*Negativities*, C. E. Merrill, 1975.

Markham I., *Plurality & Christian Ethics*, Cambridge University Press, 1994.

Martin F., *The Feminist Question*, T. & T. Clark, 1994.

Martin R. and Nickel J. W., 'Recent Work on the Concept of Rights', *APQ* 17/3, 1980, pp. 165–81.

Mauss M., *Sociology and Psychology*, Routledge & Kegan Paul, 1979 (including his essay of 1938, 'Une Catégorie de l'Esprit Humaine').

Meeks W., *The Moral World of the First Christians*, SPCK, 1987.

Melden A. I., *Rights and Persons*, Blackwell, 1977.

Meredith A., 'Orthodoxy, Heresy & Philosophy: the Latter Half of the Fourth Century', *Heythrop Journal* 16, 1975, pp. 5–21.

Metz J. B., *Faith in History and Society*, Seabury Press, 1980.

Meyerson I. (ed.), *Problèmes de Personne*, Colloques du Centre de Recherches de Psychologie Comparative, XIII, Paris, 1973.

Midgley M., *Animals and Why they Matter*, Penguin, 1983.

'Persons and non-persons' in P. Singer (ed.), *In Defence of Animals*, Blackwell, 1985.

'The Absence of a Gap between Fact and Values', *PAS* 54, 1980, pp. 207–23.

Milbank J., *Theology and Social Theory*, Blackwell, 1990.

Minas A. C., 'God and Forgiveness', *PQ* 25, 1975, pp. 138–50.

Minkus P. A., *Philosophy of the Person*, Blackwell, 1960.

Mischel T. (ed.), *Understanding other Persons*, Rowan & Littlefield, 1974.

*The Self: Psychological and Philosophical Issues*, Blackwell, 1977.

Mitchell B., *Morality, Religious and Secular*, Oxford University Press, 1980.

Moberly E., *Suffering, Innocent and Guilty*, SPCK, 1978.

Moltmann J., *On Human Dignity*, SCM Press, 1984.

*The Trinity and the Kingdom of God*, SCM Press, 1981.

*History and the Triune God*, SCM Press, 1991.

Montefiore A. (ed.), *Philosophy and Personal Relations*, Routledge & Kegan Paul, 1973.

Moody-Adams M., 'On the Alleged Methodological Infirmity of Ethics', *APQ* 27/3, 1990, pp. 125–35.

'Gender and the Complexity of Moral Voices' in Card (ed.), *Feminist Ethics*, 1991.

Mounier E., *Personalism*, Routledge & Kegan Paul, 1952.

Muhlen H., *Der Heilige Geist als Person*, Munster, 1967.

Murdoch I., *The Sovereignty of Good*, Routledge & Kegan Paul, 1971.

Navickas J., *Consciousness and Reality: Hegel's Philosophy of Subjectivity*, Nijhoff, 1976.

Neblett W. R., 'Forgiveness & Ideals', *Mind* 83, 1974, pp. 269–75.

Nédoncelle M., 'Les variations de Boèce sur la personne' in *Revue des Sciences Réligieuses* 29, 1955, pp. 201–38.

Nelson P., *Narrative and Morality*, Pennsylvania State University Press, 1987.

Nicholson L. (ed.), *Feminism/Postmodernism*, Routledge, 1990.

Nino C. S., *The Ethics of Human Rights*, Oxford University Press, 1993.

Noddings N., *Caring*, California University Press, 1984.

Noonan J. T., *The Morality of Abortion*, Harvard University Press, 1970.

Nozick R. A., *Anarchy, State and Utopia*, Blackwell, 1974.
*Philosophical Explanations*, Blackwell, 1980.

Olafson F. A., *Principles and Persons*, Johns Hopkins, 1967.

Olson R., 'Trinity & Eschatology: the Historical Being of God in Jürgen Moltmann and Wolfhart Pannenberg', *SJT* 36, 1982, pp. 213–27.

Onians R. B., *The Origins of European Thought*, Cambridge University Press, 1954.

O'Donnell J. J. *Trinity and Temporality*, Oxford University Press, 1983.

O'Donovan J., 'Man in the Image of God: the Disagreement between Barth and Brunner Reconsidered', *SJT* 39, 1986, pp. 433–59.

O'Donovan O., *Resurrection and the Moral Order*, Paternoster, 1984.

O'Neill M., *Women Speaking, Women Listening*, Orbis, 1990.

Otto S., *Person und Subsistenz*, Munich, 1968.

Outka G. and Reeder J. P. (eds.), *Prospects for a Common Morality*, Princeton University Press, 1993.

Padgett A., *God, Eternity & the Nature of Time*, St Martin's Press/Macmillan, 1992.

Pannenberg W., *Anthropology in Theological Perspective*, T. & T. Clark, 1985.
*Systematic Theology*, vol. 1, T. & T. Clark, 1991.

Parfit D., *Reasons and Persons*, Oxford University Press, 1984.

Parsons S., 'Feminism & the Logic of Morality', in S. Sayers and P. Osborne (eds.), *Socialism, Feminism & Philosophy*, Routledge, 1990.

Passmore J., *Man's Responsibility for Nature*, Duckworth, 1974.

Pateman C., *The Sexual Contract*, Polity, 1988.

Paterson D. and Ryder R. (eds.), *Animal Rights – A Symposium*, Centaur Press, 1979.

Paul E. F., Miller F. D., and Paul J. (eds.), *Human Rights*, Blackwell, 1984.

Peacocke A. and Gillett G. (eds.), *Persons and Personality*, Blackwell, 1987.

Perry J., *Personal Identity*, University of California Press, 1975.

Peters T., 'Pannenberg's Eschatological Ethics' in Braaten and Clayton (eds.), *The Theology of Wolfhart Pannenberg*, Fortress Press, 1988.

*God as Trinity*, Westminster/J. Knox Press, 1993.

Peukert H., *Science, Action and Fundamental Theology*, MIT Press, 1984.

Pike N., *God and Timelessness*, Routledge & Kegan Paul, 1970.

Pinkard T., 'Models of the Person', *CJP* 10/4, 1980, pp. 623–37.

Plant K., 'The Two Worlds of Martin Buber', *Theology* 88, 1985, pp. 281–7.

Plant R., *Social & Moral Theory in Casework*, Routledge & Kegan Paul, 1970.

Plantinga A., 'Things and Persons', *Review of Metaphysics*, 1960–1, pp. 493–519.

Plotinus, *The Enneads* (ed. S. MacKenna), Faber, 1969⁴.

Porter J., *Moral Action & Christian Ethics*, Cambridge University Press, 1995.

Pucetti R., *Persons*, Macmillan, 1968.

Putnam H., *Reason, Truth and History*, Cambridge University Press, 1981.

Quinton A., *The Nature of Things*, Routledge & Kegan Paul, 1973.

Rachels J., *The End of Life*, Oxford University Press, 1986.

Rahner K., *The Trinity*, Burns & Oates, 1970.

*Foundations of Christian Faith*, Darton, Longman & Todd, 1978.

Ramsey P., *Ethics at the Edges of Life*, Yale University Press, 1978.

Rawls J., *A Theory of Justice*, Oxford University Press, 1972.

Rawson B. (ed.), *Marriage, Divorce and Children in ancient Rome*, Oxford University Press, 1991.

Regis E., *Gewirth's Ethical Rationalism*, University of Chicago Press, 1984.

Rheinfelder H., *Das Wort, Persona*, Halle, 1928.

Ricoeur P., 'The Golden Rule: Exegetical and Theological Perplexities', *NTS* 36, 1990, pp. 392–7.

'Narrative Identity' in D. Wood (ed.), *On Paul Ricoeur*, Routledge, 1991.

*Essays on Biblical Interpretation* (ed. L. Mudge), Fortress Press, 1980.

*Oneself As Another*, University of Chicago Press, 1992.

Robbins P., *The British Hegelians, 1875–1925*, Garland Publishing House, 1982.

Robinson D., *Royce and Hocking – American Idealists*, Christopher Publishing House, 1968.

Rockmore T., *Fichte, Marx and the German Philosophical Tradition*, Carbondale, South Illinois University Press, 1980.

Rockmore, T. and Breazeale D. (eds.), *Fichte: Historical Contexts/Contemporary Controversies*, Humanities Press, 1994.

Rorty A. O. (ed.), *The Identities of Persons*, California University Press, 1976.

Rorty R., 'Postmodernist Bourgeois Liberalism' in T. Docherty (ed.), *Postmodernism*, pp. 323–8.

Rosaldo M. Z., 'Woman, Culture and Society: a Theoretical Overview' in Rosaldo and L. Lamphere (eds.), *Woman, Culture & Society*, Stanford University Press, 1974.

Rosenbaum A. S., *The Philosophy of Human Rights*, Greenwod Press, 1980.

Rowley H. H., *The Faith of Israel*, SCM Press, 1956.

Ruddock J. (ed.), *Six Approaches to the Person*, Routledge & Kegan Paul, 1972.

Ryle G., *The Concept of Mind*, Hutchinson, 1949.

Sapontzis S., 'A Critique of Personhood', *Ethics* 1981, pp. 607–18.

Sayers S. and Osborne P. (eds.), *Socialism, Feminism & Philosophy*, Routledge, 1990.

Scheler M., *Formalism in Ethics and Non-Formal Ethics of Values*, 1916 (ET Northwestern University Press, 1973).

Schlossmann S., *Persona und prosopon im Recht und im Christlichen Dogma*, Kiel, 1906.

Schneewind J. B., *Sidgwick's Ethics and Victorian Moral Philosophy*, Oxford University Press, 1977.

Schottroff L., 'Non-violence and the Love of one's Enemies' in R. H. Fuller (ed.), *Essays on the Love Commandment*, Fortress, 1978.

Schrage W., *The Ethics of the New Testament*, T. & T. Clark, 1988.

Schroeder D., 'Once You Were No People . . .' in H. Huebner (ed.), *The Church as Theological Community*, pp. 37–65.

Schurr V., *Die Trinitätslehre des Boethius im Lichte der skythischen Kontroversen*, Paderborn, 1935.

Schwöbel C., 'God's Goodness and Human Morality', *Nederlands Theologisch Tigdschrift* 43, 1989, pp. 122–38.

Schwöbel, C. (ed.), *Trinitarian Theology Today*, T. & T. Clark, 1995.

Schwöbel C. and Gunton C. (eds.), *Persons divine and human*, T. & T. Clark, 1991.

Scott P., *Theology, Ideology, and Liberation*, Cambridge University Press, 1994.

'The Resurrection of Nature?' *Theology in Green* 4/2, 1994, pp. 23–35.

Seidler V. J., *Recovering the Self*, Routledge, 1994.

Shaw M. W. and Doudera A. E., *Defining Human Life: Medical, Legal & Ethical Implications*, Ann Arbor, 1983.

Shimizu M., *Das Selbst im Mahayana-Buddhismus in Japanischer Sicht und die Person im Christentum im Licht des Neuen Testaments*, Leiden, 1981.

Shriver D. W., *An Ethic for Enemies*, Oxford University Press, 1995.

Singer P., *Practical Ethics*, Cambridge University Press, 1979.

*How Are We To Live*, Mandarin, 1993.

*Rethinking Life and Death*, Oxford University Press, 1995.

Singer P. (ed.), *Applied Ethics*, Oxford University Press, 1986.

Slusser M., 'The Exegetical Roots of Trinitarian Theology', *TS*, 49, 1988, pp. 461–76.

Spohn W. C., 'Parable & Narrative in Christian Ethics', *Theological Studies*, 51/1, 1990, pp. 100–14.

Stackhouse M. L., *Creeds, Society and Human Rights*, Eerdmans, 1984.

Storkey E., *What's Right With Feminism*, SPCK, 1985.

Strawson P. F., *Individuals*, Methuen, 1959.

Studer B., 'Der Person-begriff in der frühen kirchenamtlichen Trinitätslehre', *TP* 57, 1982, pp. 161–77.

Zur Entwicklung der patristischen Trinitätslehre, *TG* 74, 1984, pp. 81–93.

*Trinity and Incarnation*, T. & T. Clark, 1993.

Sumner L. W., *The Moral Foundation of Rights*, Oxford University Press, 1987.

*Abortion and Moral Theory*, Princeton University Press, 1981.

Swinburne R., *The Coherence of Theism*, Oxford University Press, 1977.

Tanner K., 'Creation, Environmental Crisis, and Ecological Justice' in R. S. Chopp and M. L. Taylor (eds.), *Reconstructing Theology*, Fortress, 1994, pp. 99–123.

Taylor C., *Human Agency and Language*, Cambridge University Press, 1985.

*Sources of the Self*, Cambridge University Press, 1989.

*The Ethics of Authenticity*, Cambridge University Press, 1991.

Teichman J., 'The Definition of Person', *Philosophy* 60, 1985, pp. 175–85.

Temple W., *The Nature of Personality*, Macmillan, 1911.

Thatcher A., 'The Personal God and a God who is a Person', *RS* 21, 1985, pp. 61–73.

*Truly Person, Truly God*, SPCK, 1990.

Theissen G., *Social Reality and the Early Christians*, T. & T. Clark, 1993.

Thiemann R., *Revelation and Theology*, University of Notre Dame Press, 1985.

Thiselton A., *New Horizons in Hermeneutics*, Harper & Row, 1992.

Tooley M., *Abortion and Infanticide*, Oxford University Press, 1983.

'Abortion and Infanticide', *PPA* 2/1, 1972, pp. 37–65.

'A Defense of Abortion and Infanticide' in J. Feinberg (ed.), *The Problem of Abortion*, Wadsworth, 1973.

'Decisions to Terminate Life and the Concept of Person' in J. Ladd (ed.), *Ethical Issues Relating to Life and Death*, Oxford University Press, 1979, pp. 62–93.

Tournier P., *The Meaning of Persons*, SCM Press, 1957.
Tracy T. F., *God, Action and Embodiment*, Eerdmans, 1984.
Trembath K. R., *Divine Revelation*, Oxford University Press, 1991.
Trendelenburg A., Zur Geschichte des Wortes Person, *Kantstudien* 13, 1908.
Tuck R ., *Natural Rights Theories*, Cambridge University Press, 1979.
Vanhoozer K. J., *Biblical Narrative in the Philosophy of Paul Ricoeur*, Cambridge University Press, 1990.
Veatch R. M., *Death, Dying and the Biological Revolution*, Yale University Press, 1976.
Verner D. C., *The Household of God*, Society of Biblical Literature, 1983.
Villa-Vicencio C. A., *A Theology of Reconstruction*, Cambridge University Press, 1992.
Vogel C. de, 'The Concept of Personality in Greek and Christian Thought', *Studies in Philosophy and the History of Philosophy*, vol. 2, Washington, 1963, pp. 20–60.
Wagner F., *Der Gedanke der Persönlichkeit Gottes bei Fichte und Hegel*, Gütersloh, 1971.
Watson F., *Text, Church & World*, T. & T. Clark, 1994.
Webb C. C. J., *God and Personality*, Allen & Unwin, 1918.
*Divine Personality and Human Life*, Allen & Unwin, 1920.
Wendebourg D., 'Person und Hypostase' in J. Rohls and G. Wenz (eds.), *Vernunft des Glaubens*, Göttingen, 1988, pp. 502–22.
White S. K., *Political Theory and Postmodernism*, Cambridge University Press, 1991.
Whitmore Todd, 'Beyond Liberalism & Communitarianism' in *The Annual of the Society of Christian Ethics*, 1989, pp. 207–25.
Wiedemann T., *Adults and Children in the Roman Empire*, Routledge, 1989.
Wiggins D., 'Truth, Invention and the Meaning of Life', *Proceedings of the British Academy*, 1976, vol. 62, pp. 331–78.
'The Person as Object of Science, as Subject of Experience, and as Locus of Value' in Peacocke & Gillett (eds.), *Persons and Personality*, 1987.
*Sameness and Substance*, Blackwell, 1980.
Wikler D., 'Concepts of Personhood: a Philosophical Perspective' in Shaw and Doudera (eds.), *Defining Human Life*, 1983.
Wilkerson T. E., *Minds, Brains and People*, Oxford University Press, 1974.
Wilkes K., *Real People*, Oxford University Press, 1987.
Williams B., *Problems of the Self*, Cambridge University Press, 1973.
*Ethics and the Limits of Philosophy*, Fontana, 1985.

Williams R. D., 'The Philosophical Structures of Palamism', *Eastern Churches Review*, 9/1–2, 1977, pp. 27–44.

'The Theology of Personhood. A Study of the Thought of Christos Yannaras', *Sobornost* 6/6, 1972, pp. 415–30.

Wilson D. C., 'Functionalism & Moral Personhood', *Philosophy & Phenomenological Research* 44/4, 1984, pp. 521–30.

Winkler E. R and Coombs J. R., *Applied Ethics: A Reader*, Blackwell, 1993.

Wood D. (ed.), *On Paul Ricoeur*, Routledge, 1991.

Yannaras C., *The Freedom of Morality*, St Vladimir's Seminary Press, 1984.

Young I. M., 'Impartiality and the Civic Public: Some Implications of Feminist Critiques of Moral & Political Theory', *Praxis International* 5/4, 1986, pp. 389–401.

Young R., *Freedom, Responsibility and God*, Macmillan, 1975.

'Professor Penelhum on the Resurrection of the Body', *RS* 9, 1973, pp. 181–7.

The Resurrection of the Body, *Sophia* 9/2, 1970, pp. 1–15.

'Dispensing with Moral Rights', *Political Theory* 6, 1978, pp. 63–74.

Zizioulas J. D., 'Human Capacity and Human Incapacity: a Theological Exploration of Personhood', *SJT* 28, 1975, pp. 401–47.

*Being as Communion*, Darton, Longman & Todd, 1985.

'Preserving God's Creation (Part 3)', *Theology in Green* 7, 1993, pp. 20–31.

# Index of subjects

# Index of names

Adams E. M. 305–6, 385 nn. 21 & 27
Andresen C. 127, 133
Aquinas 137–9, 204
Aristotle 124–5
Augustine 130–3, 134, 292, 357–8 nn. 27–32

Bantle F. X. 358 n. 35
Barth K. 156, 167, 178, 198
Benhabib S. 112–16, 243–9
Berry C. J. 202
Boethius 134–7, 153
Boff L. 287
Bowne B. P. 105–6
Braithwaite R. B. 213–15
Bråkenhielm C. R. 289
Browning D. S. 376 n. 36
Buber M. 106
Bultmann R. 216

Cappadocians 6, 128–30
Carrithers M. 21
Carruthers P. 387 n. 54
Carter A. 389 n. 22
Clark S. R. L. 364 n. 1, 388 n. 3
Cobb J. 253, 325–6
Collins S. 19
Coakley S. 175
Comstock G. 372 n. 36
Cronin K. 301, 383 n. 5

Dennett D. C. 33–7, 77
Drobner H. R. 127–8
Durkheim E. 19–21

Engelhardt H. T. 43–4

Farley M. 179–82
Feinberg J. 297–301

Feuerbach L. 95–102
Fichte J. G. 17, 21, 91–2
Fiorenza E. S. 271, 273
Fowl S. 264
Fraser N. 110–11
Frazer E. 115
Frei H. 217–19
Friesen D. K. 375 n. 10

Gewirth A. 304–6
Gill C. 364 n. 1
Gilligan C. 111–12
Gloege G. 124
Gunton C. 128, 177, 357 nn. 21 & 25, 366 n. 15
Gustafson J. M.

Habermas J. 112, 241–7
Haksar V. 306–7
Hankey W. J. 139
Hare R. M. 27–32, 295
Hauerwas S. 233–41
Hayward T. 389 n. 22
Hegel G. F. 92–5, 99–101
Helm P. 362 n. 19
Hessel D. T. 388 nn. 6 & 9
Hoerster N. 346 n. 14
Horsley R. A. 378 n. 4
Hursthouse R. 48

Jantzen G. 148

Kant I. 84–90
Kasper W. 364 n. 46, 367 n. 22
Kippenberg H. G. 341 nn. 1–2
Kneale W. 151–2

LaCugna M. 178–82

408